THE METHODIST CONFERENCE IN AMERICA

THE METHODIST CONFERENCE IN AMERICA

A HISTORY

Russell E. Richey

 KINGSWOOD BOOKS
An Imprint of Abingdon Press
Nashville, Tennessee

THE METHODIST CONFERENCE IN AMERICA: A HISTORY

Copyright © 1996 by Abingdon Press

All Rights Reserved.

Library of Congress Cataloging-in-Publication Data

Richey, Russell E.
    The Methodist Conference in America : a history / Russell E. Richey
        p.   cm.
    Includes bibliographical references and index.
    ISBN 0-687-02187-1 (alk. paper)
    1. Methodist conferences–United States–History. 2. Methodist Church–United States–Government–History.   I. Title.
BX8235.R53   1996
362'.07–dc20   96-8133
                                                                          CIP

Unless otherwise noted, all Scripture quotations are from the New Revised Standard Version Bible, Copyright © 1989 by the Division of Christian Education of the National Council of the Churches of Christ in the USA. Used by permission.

This book is printed on acid-free, recycled paper.

96 97 98 99 00 01 02 03 04 05 — 10 9 8 7 6 5 4 3 2 1

MANUFACTURED IN THE UNITED STATES OF AMERICA

To Elizabeth and William

Contents

CONTENTS

Preface

This essay on "Conference" in Methodism has been a long time in the making, longer than I want to remember. Along the way I have acquired a number of debts. The first is to my family, Merle, William and Elizabeth, who have borne with my prolonged fascination with the topic. A second is to Henry Bowden, who initiated this exploration by asking me along with then Drew colleagues, Kenneth E. Rowe and James E. Kirby, to undertake a new history of Methodism for Greenwood Press. This volume started out to be a part of that history. In a revised and greatly reduced version it will indeed assume that role, but it grew into a book in its own right. It did so through the careful attention of these two colleagues and Bowden who have read, criticized, suggested and encouraged this venture. I owe them both an expression of deep gratitude.

Ken Rowe has now joined me in another project, along with Jean Miller Schmidt; his role as Methodism's bibliographer *par excellence*, and hers as premier interpreter of Methodist women, have steered me away from some of the worst of my errors. Duke colleagues and former colleagues have also read and commented helpfully on my efforts. I am especially appreciate of careful readings from Dennis Campbell, George Marsden, Ted Campbell, and Richard Heitzenrater. My parents, McMurry and Erika Richey, have also read and commented on the volume. Dad's eagle eye caught many errors that spell-checkers don't. More distant colleagues, Michael Cartwright and Randy Maddox, have heard and/or seen and commented on parts of the volume.

I have undertaken most of the research for this volume either at Drew or at Duke and express appreciation again to Ken Rowe at Drew for the care that he bestows on users of that collection, as also to Charles Yrigoyen of the General Commission on Archives and History. I thank Chuck and his colleague Susan Warrick for permission to publish here sections that appeared in different form as essays in *Methodist History*. Roger Loyd and Roberta Schaafsma of the Divinity Library, William King, the University Archivist, and the staff of Duke's Special Collections, were all very helpful. Edwin Schell of the Balti-

more Conference's Lovely Lane Museum, made several days of research there immensely profitable. I also would acknowledge the
patience of my associates in administration, particularly Mary Collins,
who has seen more versions of this project than either of us want to
admit. I thank Sean C. Turner for a very thorough and efficiernt job
of indexing.

Much of the research and a great deal of the writing on Conference occurred with the sponsorship of the Lilly Endowment and as
part of the Duke-based project on "United Methodism and American
Culture" which Dennis Campbell, William Lawrence, and I directed.
The grant made possible a semester's leave, travel to collections,
postage and photocopying. I am deeply grateful to Craig Dykstra of
the Lilly Endowment and James Lewis of the Louisville Institute for
such support.

Russell E. Richey
The Divinity School
Duke University

Chapter 1

The Conference in Methodism

American Methodism ordered and structured itself through conferences. In the Methodist lexicon, 'conference' refers to a body of preachers (and later, of laity as well) that exercises legislative, judicial and (to some extent) executive functions for the church or some portion thereof. Established by John Wesley, the conference remained his creature during his lifetime but on his death inherited much of his decision-making and policy-setting authority. It became a central feature, perhaps the central feature, of Methodist polity. Its political dimensions have been often noted and measured. Indeed, the drama in Methodist histories typically derives from conference, its struggle to political competence and the on-going struggles between conference and episcopacy for authority and power.[1] When analyzed or indexed, 'conference' has that polity meaning. Unfortunately, it frequently bears that meaning alone.[2] But 'conference' possessed a richer significance in Methodist life and discourse than the lexicon admits. This volume explores the American conference both in its narrow political or constitutional roles and in its larger dimension. A hint of the latter is in order.

Conference defined the Methodist movement in other ways than political. On conference hinged religious time, religious space, religious belonging, religious structure, even religiosity itself.[3] Religious time lasted from one conference to the next. That was the duration of appointments of preacher to circuit or church. Appropriately, then, Methodist histories, particularly early ventures, structured time from conference to conference. Periodization was but one of conference's several uses. Conference delineated Methodist space as well. Gradually specific boundaries were drawn and conference came to have geographical meaning. Then preachers belonged to one conference; congregations related to specific conferences. In part because everything, in a sense, belonged to conference, early Methodists built on conference, employing it as foundation for other structures, tying missions, education, publication and financial efforts to that basis. Conference, as least in its early years, gathered in the entire Methodist system. Even spirituality revolved around it. Although largely ob-

13

scured from historical attention, casual notations in letters and journals suggest the importance of conference as a preaching and sacramental occasion. Revivals and conversions often occurred at conference and conferences functioned to sustain and cultivate the religious life.

As American Methodism grew in numbers and national scope, both temporal and spatial dimensions increased. Methodism structured itself in terms of a tier of successively more inclusive conferences. For much of American Methodism, the three basic conferences came to be (1) the quarterly conference which gathered in the leadership and often membership of a single Methodist circuit, (2) the annual conference which brought together the preachers in a geographically defined region, and (3) the general conference whose meetings every four years functioned as legislature and judiciary for the church and typically also set executive policy, defined doctrine and elaborated the structures for the entire church. At every level conference possessed such important power and authority as to make it inevitably and intensely political. Politics did, at times and over time, eviscerate conference, gutting its other functions. But as we shall see, well into the 19th century conference retained the meanings outlined above. Hence one way to understand Methodism is to view the emergence and changes in its basic structure—conference. Methodist histories uniformly recognize, typically even feature, conference's centrality but render that in constitutional, political and polity terms. Such treatments do effectively chart the way in which the conference event developed into a governmental form. Here conference will be viewed as possessing a far more complex identity. It will be the purpose of this volume to present conference as a/the distinctive [American] Methodist manner of being the church, a multifaceted, not simply political, mode of spirituality, unity, mission, governance, and fraternity that American Methodists lived and operated better than they interpreted.

The Wesleyan Conference

Like so much else in Methodism, the conference both reflects older impulses toward Christian organization *and* bears the personal stamp of the Wesleys.[4] In its immediate background lay Protestant efforts to re-order church and world according to New Testament precept, impulses expressed in complex ways in the home of Susanna and Samuel Wesley, a home that refracted both Puritan and Anglican spirituality.

Also influential for Susanna and her sons was the witness of Pietism. Traditionally associated with the efforts of Philipp Jakob

Spener, who gave shape in *Pia Desideria* (1675) to a religion of the heart drawing on ideas and practices then reverberating throughout Europe,[5] Pietism prospered by creating new gatherings. It did so less preoccupied than Puritanism and the larger Reformed tradition with finding biblical warrant for every detail of Christian life and less intent upon having every ecclesial structure conceptually and organizationally coherent with 'Church'. Pietism sought a recovery of the spirit/ Spirit with a variety of practices, including especially small groups for prayer, Bible reading, testimony and Christian conversation. That spirit affected both Susanna's gatherings in the Wesley home and Samuel's society. The Moravians served as another mediator of Pietist practice of Christian gathering.

Precedents abounded. The Quakers, for instance, employed weekly, quarterly and yearly meetings for both governance and the spiritual life. Within the larger Methodist movement, Howell Harris and the Welsh evangelical Calvinists preceded Wesley in establishing a conference. And behind the experiment with conference lay Wesley's own success with smaller and more local gatherings—the bands, classes, and societies. Conference belonged to this web of precedented practice, within and without the Wesleyan movement.

Nevertheless, John Wesley, as Richard Heitzenrater has shown, had a penchant for putting his own distinctive stamp on and establishing claim over widespread practices and established precedent.[6] So he presented conference as an extension of his own deliberative processes.

> In June, 1744, I desired my brother and a few other Clergymen to meet me in London, to consider how we should proceed to save our own souls and those that heard us. After some time, I invited the lay Preachers that were in the house to meet with us. We conferred together for several days, and were much comforted and strengthened thereby.
>
> The next year I not only invited most of the Travelling Preachers, but several others, to confer with me in Bristol. And from that time for some years, though I invited only a part of the Travelling Preachers, yet I permitted any that desired it, to be present. . . .
>
> This I did for many years, and all that time the term *Conference* meant not so much the conversations we had together, as the persons that conferred; namely, those whom I invited to confer with me from time to time. So that all this time it depended on me alone, not only what persons should constitute the Conference,—but whether there should be any Conference at all: This lay wholly in my own breast; neither the Preachers nor the people having any part or lot in the matter.[7]

The name given to the record of these endeavors, "Minutes of

Some Late Conversations Between The Rev. Mr. Wesleys and Others,"
suggests accurately the dominant role played by John Wesley. A
complaint made in 1774, "Mr. Wesley seemed to do all the business
himself."—epitomized the procedure.[8] Wesley posed questions, discussion followed, Wesley framed the conclusion, and he then re-
worked the raw minutes into publishable form.

Both the structure and importance of this engagement can be seen
in what that first, June of 1744 gathering, took as agenda:

> 1. What to teach;
> 2. How to teach; and,
> 3. What to do; that is, how to regulate our doctrine, discipline,
> and practice.[9]

Following a question and answer, catechetical style,[10] initial conferences addressed themselves to points (1) and (2). The first conference,
for instance, hammered away at justification, sanctification and ecclesiology. After the first few conferences, subsequent conferences assumed those doctrinal formulations and largely confined themselves
to (3). To these annual affairs, Wesley and his preachers brought the
fundamental issues generated by the movement. Over the years, these
concerns took permanent form as a series of questions which, by 1770,
defined the order of business and then as Minutes which gathered
and ordered the questions and answers into a legislative record.[11]
Conference, along with the United Societies, gave structural expression of the movement and gradually emerged as basic to and characteristic of Methodist governance.

Conference's Constitutional Function

That centrality eventually assumed quasi-constitutional character.
Essential to this development was the authority deftly conferred on
its Minutes at Wesley's hand. As early as 1749, Wesley gathered the
results of the early conferences into two publications which shared the
title of *Minutes of Some Late Conversations* but which came to be known
as the 'Doctrinal Minutes' and the 'Disciplinary Minutes'. These
Minutes underwent revisions, incorporating the major polity and
doctrinal judgments of subsequent conferences, and appeared in ever
'larger' form in 1753, 1763, 1770, 1772, 1780, 1789, and after Wesley's
death in 1797.[12] Known as the *Large Minutes*, they became quasi-constitutional for Methodism, its book of discipline.

By 1784 despairing of naming an individual as successor, John
Wesley lodged in these *Large Minutes* and in conference his hope for
Methodism after his death and his plan for an orderly transference of

authority. In 1769, Wesley had formulated the problem in this fashion to his assembled preachers:

> You are at present one body. You act in concert with each other, and by unified counsels. And now is the time to consider what can be done, in order to continue this union. Indeed, as long as I live, there will be no great difficulty. I am, under God, a center of union to all our traveling, as well as local preachers. . . . But by what means may this connection be preserved, when God removes me from you?[13]

Wesley's solution was to recognize the Conference as the heir to his authority, to identify its membership in terms of signed adherence to "the *old Methodist doctrines* . . . contained in the minutes of the Conferences" and "the whole *Methodist discipline*, laid down in the said minutes," and to constitute it as a legal entity, initially by planning for election of an executive committee and moderator. Similar compacts were signed and minuted in 1773, 1774 and 1775. Finally in 1784 Wesley sought more precise legal identity of conference by entering a deed poll in the Chancery, spelling out the powers and duties of the Conference and enumerating one hundred individuals who constituted the Conference.[14] This endowed Conference, according to Neely, "with the supreme power which had been centered in Mr. Wesley."[15]

Multivalence

The political function of conference, vital though it was, was only one of its several dimensions. Indeed, assent to conference's normative and constitutional prerogatives probably derived from conference's other competencies, especially the way it picked up and internalized practices associated with the smaller units of Methodism, the bands and classes particularly. It became a family of preachers headed and governed by John Wesley; it was a monastic-like order held together by affection, by common rules, by a shared mission and by watchfulness of each member over one another; it functioned as a brotherhood of religious aspiration and song; it served as a quasi-professional society which concerned itself with the reception, training, credentialing, monitoring and deployment of Wesley's lay preachers; it became a community of preachers whose commitment to the cause and one another competed with all other relationships; it was a body which pooled its resources to provide for the wants and needs of its members. When one of its members died, it constituted the agency of memorial and memory. It served as the spiritual center of Methodism; it was multivalent.[16]

Of all those traits, perhaps the spiritual, nurturing and familial ones most require illustration. A query put in 1747 clearly conveys the spiritual dimensions of conference:

> Q. How may the time of this Conference be made more emi-
> nently a time of prayer, watching, and self-denial?
> A. 1. While we are in Conference, let us have an especial care to
> set God always before us. 2. In the intermediate hours, let us visit
> none but the sick, and spend all our time that remains in retirement.
> 3. Let us then give ourselves unto prayer for one another, and for
> the blessing of God on this our labour.[17]

During its meetings, then, conference concerned itself both with the religious development of its members and with the spiritual well-being of the immediate community. Often that involved services aimed at the Methodist people who would gather where conference met.

Another query of the same year illustrates not only the familial dimension of conference but also the paternal character of that familiarity:

> Q. Are our Assistants exemplary in their lives? Do we enquire
> enough into this?
> A. Perhaps not. We should consider each of them who is with us
> a pupil at the University, into whose behaviour and studies we
> should therefore make a particular inquiry every day. Might we not
> particularly inquire,—Do you rise at 4? Do you study in the method
> laid down at the last Conference? Do you read the books we advise
> and no other? Do you see the necessity of regularity in study? What
> are the chief temptations to irregularity? Do you punctually observe
> the evening hour of retirement? Are you exact in writing your
> journal? Do you fast on Friday? Do you converse seriously, usefully,
> and closely? Do you pray before, and have you a determinate end
> in, every conversation?[18]

In time, such questions would become routinized and ritualized. Initially, they brought the preachers into deep engagement with Wesley and one another. From that intimacy derived the bond of preacher to preacher. Wesley caught the familial, fraternal expecta-tions of conference in 1748:

> Q. What can be done in order to a closer union of our Assistants
> with each other?
> A. 1. Let them be deeply convinced of the want there is of it at
> present, and of the absolute necessity of it. 2. Let them pray that God
> would give them earnestly to desire it; and then that He would fulfil
> the desire He has given them.[19]

To recognize the multivalence of conference is really only to recall conference's place within the entire Methodist impulse. And that, as John Lawson so aptly indicated, was means to a definite end, "a way of life," "that a new awareness of God in Christ, and a new equipment of moral power through the operation of the Holy Spirit, should come into the lives of the people, to the renewal of Church and State."[20] That point is suggested in "The Large Minutes." There Wesley recognized Christian 'conference' as one of five "instituted" means of grace. That designation and the character of the other four—prayer, searching the Scriptures, the Lord's Supper and fasting—suggest how very central to the Christian life and the Methodist movement Wesley placed 'conference'.[21] The reference here was not specifically to the annual or to the quarterly Methodist meetings or conferences but rather to the mode of engagement, discipline, purpose and structure that they shared with all serious Christian encounter. Conference was the way Wesley sought to conduct his affairs with his people. Although Mr. Wesley would find those of the late 20th century very strange affairs, they bear the marks and carry on the functions that he, and perhaps even his mother, intended as Christian conference. And even to this day they remain something of a family affair.[22]

The conference in British and American Methodism—quarterly conference, annual conference, general conference—was the spatial *and* temporal outworking of a set of religious impulses, never fully integrated into theory, but nevertheless characteristic of a peculiar Wesleyan style of organization, unity, mission, reform, spirituality. Constituting the Wesleyan economy, these structural features bore the Wesleyan spiritual and religious impulses, the accent on the priesthood of all believers and the insistence on the mutual interdependence of all parts of the body of Christ. The several structurings of the Wesleyan spirit had emerged in stages and in relation to entities named as the occasion suggested—societies, bands, classes, stewards, trustees, circuits, connexion, conference, quarterly meeting. They cohered because Methodism cohered, because they belonged together in the religious experience and administrative style of John Wesley, because they possessed a center in him, because Wesley envisioned Methodism as an integrated connection.

In the American colonies the shadow of the Wesleys and particularly John's loomed large. Yet, wanting his physical presence as center, the American movement required its own center or epicenter. No place could suffice as spiritual center though Baltimore came closest. No educational institution could be made to stand. No publication posed itself as a possible center until *The Methodist Magazine* and *The Christian Advocate* emerged in 1818 and 1826 respectively. *The Discipline* might be accorded status of center were it not for conference's power to change it. Some have, to be sure, seen the superintending power, bishop or bishops as center. The power of the superintendency was great, but from the start, Wesley's appointee or independently elected bishop contended with a body that aspired to centrality. The conference claimed that place. It did so for a variety of reasons: because Wesley himself intended to confer centrality on the conference; because Wesley's appointees remained accountable to him and recallable; because of the way that the American movement emerged; because of the democratic style in American society; because of the deep, powerful impulses that flowed through conference; because of the great loyalties that it claimed. For all these reasons, conference emerged as the center of American Methodism.

Chapter 2

The American Conference

When the American Methodist movement began, John Wesley had stabilized the annual conference as the decision-making body for the movement. The smaller unit of Methodist work, the circuit, governed itself through the quarterly conference. Other structural features of the Methodist system—bands, classes and societies—and the many concerns of the Methodist movement had been integrated into the rhythm of conferences. Wesley was already worrying about how best to define and constitute the connection so as to preserve the power, rights and prerogatives that were vested in him and transfer them to a legitimate successor. Though he entertained alternatives, Wesley increasingly gravitated toward conference as the obvious heir to his authority. Its political future was assured. But conference was and would certainly continue to be more than a political affair. That complex of aspirations and expectations was carried by Methodists to America.

The first preachers appointed by Wesley arrived on American shores in 1769 to find that local (and lay) initiatives in New York and Maryland had spread the work sufficiently to make plausible the oversight and organization developed in the British conference system. The structures of governance and common life grew as Methodist numbers and Methodist territory demanded: first through quarterly meetings (1769–73), then through a single annual conference (1773–79), next through multiple sessions of a theoretically single annual conference (1779–92) and finally (1792 and after) through a general conference meeting every four years, overarching geographically conceived annual conferences, which in turn overarched circuit-based quarterly conferences.[1] In the midst of that development, occurred the irregular Christmas Conference of 1784 by which American Methodism achieved its independence and stature as a church. All throughout this organizational period, Americans followed English blueprints but found that the resultant structures and practices took on an American aspect. The sheer size of American society made it difficult, from the very start, to replicate British order; the distance from final authority necessitated local decisions; the

21

relative equality of all the preachers militated against the concentration of all authority in a Wesley appointee or Wesley-like figure (though Francis Asbury would certainly contend for such centrality). These factors invigorated traits already observed in the British conference. For convenience we will term these 'conference as polity,' 'conference as fraternity,' 'conference as revival'. We will observe the emergence of these traits in the colonial Methodist movement, examine each in some detail, note the tensions and interplay between them, and then chart their transformations.

The First Conferences: Polity, Fraternity, and Revival

The first quarterly conference for which records exist, that of 1772, was chaired by Francis Asbury, newly appointed as Wesley's Assistant, succeeding Richard Boardman and to be quickly succeeded by Thomas Rankin. The six questions which defined its business disclose an American conference already searching for its own way. After questions like "What are our collections?" and "How are the preachers stationed?" the conference asked "Will the people be contented without our administering the sacrament?" The question posed issues of unity and authority for the little movement and specifically whether Robert Strawbridge, the planter of American Methodism, should set policy by conniving at sacramental authority. Asbury's minuted answer indicated a divided house and divergent policy: "I told them I would not agree to it at that time, and insisted on our abiding by our rules. But Mr. Boardman had given them their way at the quarterly meeting held here before, and I was obliged to connive at some things for the sake of peace." From the start, Asbury (and others) put a high premium on the inner bonds within the conference, on the relationship between and among the preachers, on how a particular conference gave expression to the unity of the preachers, on the religious quality of the gathering. He (and others) captured the fraternal and religious aspects of conference with a summary remark. Asbury's entry for that first meeting suggests the former and perhaps hints at the latter: "Great love subsisted among us in this meeting, and we parted in peace."[2] As Asbury's earlier judgment indicated, however, fraternity often contended against conference's responsibility for discipline, order and the Wesleyan standards. Fraternity could be quite restive with authority. And yet, we must note that Asbury as the superintending presence found that he must exercise power in a fashion different from that of Wesley. He might pose the questions but the answer as well as the discussion came from the entire fraternity.

The tensions in this arrangement can be readily seen in the relations that pertained under Wesley's next assistant. That summer Wesley sent out Thomas Rankin with a new title, 'general assistant'. The title suggested not just supervision of a circuit and authority in a quarterly meeting but authority over the entire American effort.[3] Appropriately, he gathered the preachers in July for what has been reckoned the first annual conference in North America. It was his charge and his purpose to safeguard Methodist discipline. Asbury had greeted the arrival of his replacement with the notation, "He will not be admired as a preacher. But as a disciplinarian, he will fill his place."[4] When, during conference, he took his reading of the American situation, Rankin judged that "[O]ur discipline was not properly attended to, except at Philadelphia and New York; and even in those places it was upon the decline."[5] The first three questions of that meeting disclose Rankin's effort to bring the American conference fully into conformity with British practice and fully subordinate to its authority and that of Wesley:

> Ought not the authority of Mr. Wesley and that conference to extend to the preachers and people in America . . . ?
> Ought not the doctrine and discipline of the Methodists, as contained in the minutes, to be the sole rule of our conduct . . . ?
> If so, does it not follow, that if any preachers deviate from the minutes, we can have no fellowship with them till they change their conduct?[6]

With equal clarity, the conference brought these general principles to bear on the matter that had already proved divisive (and would continue to do so), the sacraments. "Every preacher who acts in connection with Mr. Wesley and the brethren who labor in America, is strictly to avoid administering the ordinances of baptism and the Lord's Supper."[7] This decision took on a different character in Asbury's version of the minutes. "No preacher in our connection shall be permitted to administer the ordinances at this time; except Mr. Strawbridge, and he under the particular direction of the assistant."[8] Asbury's version of the legislation at least opens to question the traditional interpretation of these actions,[9] that the conference did not have the power to act to the contrary. In legislating on what might have been presumed to be beyond its legislative competence, conference set important precedents for itself. In fact, conference faced inertial factors in the American situation which might have forced alternative judgments and which clearly demanded attention. The sacraments to which English Methodists had fairly ready access were quite inaccessible to most colonists. The scarcity of Anglican churches and the infrequent availability of the eucharist in those few made the pretense of conformity much less plausible and the tendencies towards Methodist ecclesial self-sufficiency much more persuasive than in England. Conference found a way of asserting its loyalty to the Wesleyan standard, in principle, while making allowance for a certain measure of variance in practice. So conference stumbled towards political competence in some independence of Wesley's or the British conference's will. It did so initially by reaffirming British practice and making appropriate exceptions. Later it would act more decisively.

Its willfulness was revealed in the second conference when Asbury squared off against the general assistant, Rankin, with apparent support of his brethren. Asbury complained of "the overbearing spirit of a certain person," and of the latter's opposition to his (Asbury's) judgment.[10] There is surprising presumption in Asbury's remark. Actually Asbury infringed Rankin's authority. Just as Strawbridge assumed the right to celebrate the sacraments on something like the ecclesial equivalent of squatter's rights, so Asbury acted out of a sense of his own authority.[11] Both got away with it because they could count on the backing of their 'brethren'. Conference connived a competence that it had no right to. It did so on the strength of emerging bonds of fraternity.

Reinforcing the inertial pressures towards political competence, then, were empowering bonds developing among the preachers. Those feelings are anticipated in Asbury's notation for the annual conference of 1775: "From *Wednesday* till *Friday* we spent in conference with great harmony and sweetness of temper."[12] Freeborn Garrettson, admitted on trial at this conference, spoke of the company of preachers as "this happy family." He fainted and awoke in an upper room surrounded by preachers. They "appeared more like angels to me than men." Recalling the event some fifteen years later, he claimed to have "blessed my dear Lord ever since, that I was ever united to this happy family."[13] Asbury epitomized a quarterly conference early the next year in this fashion: "With mutual affection and brotherly freedom we discoursed on the things of God, and were well agreed."[14] William Watters put a similar construction on the annual conference of the following year:

> We were of one heart and mind, and took sweet counsel together, not how we should get riches or honors, or anything that this poor world could afford us; but how we should make the surest work for heaven, and be the instruments of saving others.[15]

In the intensity of these gatherings, as such statements indicate, powerful currents of spirituality interplayed with the deepening affections among the preachers and the common obedience they accepted to the Methodist cause and its authority.

Methodist purpose and authority functioned in America, as it did in Britain, to set definite boundaries to fraternity. Beginning with the 1774 conference, the Minutes pose the questions that marked those initiated into probationary status, those being received into full connection with Mr. Wesley, and those to serve as his assistants. By these commitments, the preachers bound themselves to the rules spelled out in the (British) Minutes, rules that defined both order and mission. In that year and every subsequent conference, a further question was put which obliged the conference to the scrutiny of each member. It read, "Are there any objections to any of the Preachers?" And answered, "They were examined one by one."[16] This careful attention to one another's religious development, this requirement of personal testimony, permitted conference to function like class, band or love feast. Examination of character would continue to be, well into the next century, a powerful bonding experience; it would heighten the spiritual character of conference proceedings; it would mark the fraternity off as a traveling fraternity.

Tensions Among the Functions

Ideally then, the religious, fraternal and polity aspects of conference reinforced one another. That is evident in perhaps the most dramatic expression of the fraternal affection in 1777 when under pressure of the Revolution and the suspicions that haunted the Methodist movement, a number of the English preachers said their farewells in anticipation of a return home. Among them was Wesley's 'general assistant,' Rankin. Asbury reported:

> Our conference ended with a love feast and watch night. But when the time of parting came, many wept as if they had lost their first-born sons. They appeared to be in the deepest distress, thinking, as I suppose, they should not see the faces of the English preachers any more. This was such a parting as I never saw before. Our conference has been a great time—a season of uncommon affection.[17]

But an earlier phase of that same conference had evidenced the tensions between the claims of conference. Asbury and several other preachers gathered a week prior. They debated "whether we could give our consent that Mr. Rankin should baptize, as there appeared to be a present necessity," "drew a rough draught for stationing the preachers the ensuing year," and decided on "a committee . . . to superintend the whole."[18] While both the extra-ordinary preparatory session and these actions can be understood as emergency measures, necessitated by the Revolution, they were nevertheless instances of fraternity usurping polity, of the conference as a fraternity of preachers claiming authority that belonged to Wesley or his assistant.

American Methodist independence rode as much on the authority which this fraternity of preachers had connived, this spiritual declaration of independence, as it did on the prerogatives conferred on it later by Mr. Wesley. Indeed, a single line in Asbury's journal captures the dynamics of American Methodist independence. After this preparatory session, Asbury reported, "And on *Monday* we rode together to attend the conference at Deer Creek."[19] Conference was to be a cavalry that rode together.

That conference had to wrestle with the future of American Methodism without its deputized leader, Rankin. It found an interim solution in fraternal authority, namely the supervising committee on which the preparatory session had settled. Question 11 of that 1777 meeting asked:

> Can any thing be done in order to lay a foundation for a future union, supposing the old preachers should be, by the times, constrained to return to Great Britain? Would it not be well for all who are willing, to sign some articles of agreement, and strictly adhere to the same, till other preachers are sent by Mr. Wesley, and the brethren in conference?
>
> Accordingly, the following paper was wrote and signed. "We, whose names are underwritten, being thoroughly convinced of the necessity of a close union between those whom God hath need as instruments in his glorious work, in order to preseve this union, are resolved, God being our helper,
>
> 1. To devote ourselves to God. . . . 2. To preach the old Methodist doctrine, and no other, as contained in the Minutes. 3. To observe and enforce the whole Methodist Discipline, as laid down in the said Minutes. 4. To choose a committee of assistants to transact the business that is now done by the general assistants, and the old preachers who came from Britain."[20]

The implications of such fraternal authority were not so evident in the next conference as in the one following. At the very next conference, in 1778, the chair of this new committee, William Watters presided. Asbury as leader appointed by Wesley, former 'assistant,' and second in rank to the departed Rankin would have logically taken leadership, but he had gone into hiding.[21] In that conference the matter of the sacraments again surfaced and was again, but with great difficulty, deferred.[22]

Chapter 3

From 1778 to 1784

The following year American Methodism fought its first schism. Two conferences were held. The first was an illegal, or at best 'irregular,' gathering around Asbury in Delaware. The second represented the regular called conference at Fluvanna, Virginia. The continuity of leadership and the historiographical tradition of Methodism run through the first, that specially convened by Asbury. Despite its irregularity, it has been treated as that year's link in the sequence of Methodist conferences. However, far more of the thematic agenda of Methodism flows though the second, that at Fluvanna, than Methodism's historians have been willing to concede.[1]

The first, ostensibly "considered . . . as preparatory to the conference in Virginia," was held for "the convenience of the preachers in the northern stations." It clearly acted to pre-empt and forestall decisions pending in Virginia. It re-asserted Wesley's and Methodism's commitment to avoid "a separation from the church, directly or indirectly"; proclaimed Asbury the General Assistant for America, largely because he had been appointed by Wesley; and lodged a Wesley-like authority in that position. "How far," it asked, shall the power of the General Assistant extend? "Ans. On hearing every preacher for and against what is in debate, the right of determination shall rest with him according to the Minutes."[2]

The Fluvanna Conference proceeded, in quite contrary directions, towards the establishment of an American Methodist church. It did so by making the fraternity of conference the fount of its religiosity and authority. In particular, Fluvanna lodged authority in conference, in a committee with apparent administrative and appointive powers elected by conference and in a presbytery also elected by conference. The latter was empowered to ordain and those ordained empowered to administer the sacraments in a simple, Scriptural mode.[3] Without a doubt a venture theologically problematic even on congregational or presbyterial principles (since the ordaining presbytery was itself un-ordained and had therefore to ordain itself), Fluvanna nevertheless gave apt expression to conference's sense of its own authority. Clear lines extend from this act to the church constructed in 1784, to

African American assertions of similar rights, and to later schisms that would more dramatically champion the competence of conference over against episcopacy—those of James O'Kelly, of the Methodist Protestants, of the Wesleyan Methodists and of the Free Methodists.[4]

The two conferences went their separate ways. Each reconvened the next year, though only the northern conference was to be represented in the (subsequently) printed Minutes. That body's privileged posture, seemingly calculated to establish rights over the Minutes, was asserted in a series of queries posed by Asbury. They functioned to establish Asbury's leadership and that conference's sole legitimacy. Notably the northern conference answered yes to the questions

> Quest. 20. Does this whole conference disapprove the step our brethren have taken in Virginia?
> Quest. 21. Do we look upon them no longer as Methodists in connexion with Mr. Wesley and us till they come back?[5]

The conference also prescribed conditions and procedure for unity, namely suspension of the sacraments and meeting together in Baltimore.[6]

Though acting contrary to and endeavoring to brake tendencies which enhanced the competences of conference, this meeting nevertheless took several actions that in the long run worked on behalf of those tendencies. One was a seemingly straightforward administrative decision to make the smaller conference unit, the quarterly conference, a two-day event, "to be held on Saturdays and Sundays when convenient." As we shall see, this created possibilities for the spiritual or revivalistic use of conference that were to be of immense importance.

Second, it legislated against slavery, declaring the institution "contrary to the laws of God, man, and nature, and hurtful to society" and urged the preachers to convey "our disapprobation." It also required the "travelling Preachers who hold slaves, to give promises, to set them free." The social and ethical import of this decision and its implications for the complexion of Methodism will concern us in other places. Here we would underscore the significance of conference's claiming of this legislative function. Also of importance was its addition of non-slaveholding to the many, Wesley-given expectations of a preacher. Of members of the fraternity, much could be expected. Thereafter, slavery and race were to function in complex, highly ambiguous ways throughout Methodist history in setting and maintaining the boundaries of conference, in determining what it meant to be a part of that fraternity, in identifying those who belonged and those who did not, and finally in tearing the Methodist fraternity asunder.

Third, in all these actions, in its style of procedure under Asbury's guidance, and in minuting its adherence to that document that both exemplified and specified Wesley's leadership, the British *Minutes*[7], conference made clear its will to function in the Wesleyan manner under strong superintendence. This action was solidified by the capitulation of the Virginia preachers to the northern conditions, a capitulation that included an appeal to Wesley.[8]

Fourth, in both the northern (Baltimore) and Manakintown (Virginia) gatherings, the search for directions reasserted the spiritual and fraternal aspects of conference. They did so both in spite of and in recognition of the authority of superintendency. According to Freeborn Garrettson, the Baltimore conference convened "much united in love." The next day, he reported,

> We set at six o'clock, what brotherly love was among us, ourselves was exceeding happy. In the evening we was to consult what was best to be done with our dissenting brothers in Virginia. We made it a matter of solemn prayer and fasting. When we came together much of the power of God was among us; we all with one (mind) concluded it was best to disown them if they would not return. Oh! it was a cutting thought; to think of losing so many of our dear brother laborers, there was many sorrowful hearts, many sympathetic tears was shed.

The following day,

> was a heavy sorrowful day to me; but Glory be to God we joined in prayer together and it seemed as if the power of God in a wonderful manner came down. Oh, the goodness of God after prayer with one consent we all agreed to have a union conference next spring in Virginia. Oh what union of spirit was among us. We had the love feast at 12 o'clock, it was a love feast indeed to our souls, preachers and people prayed and wept like little children. We had a blessed watch night together and so parted praising and blessing God. Oh Lord go with my dear brothers.

As one of the delegates from the first to the second gathering, Garrettson reported "there seemed to be nothing but love" in beginning when agreement seemed close; then distress as the southern 'brethren' reaffirmed their directions; then again agreement:

> We all met, and Glory be to God to the comfort of all the brethern we came upon a union, had a blessed love feast and parted praising God.[9]

So the schism was healed and the two branches rejoined. In this accord, the preachers established, or we should say re-established, the foundations of American Methodism—a con-fraternity of preachers whose shared affections, mutual support and unity (under superintendence), gave the movement both its political and its religious coherence. Conference's revival, fraternity and order partook of and re-enforced the revival, fraternity and order that characterized Methodism as a whole.

Space, Time, and Gravity

It took a decade or so for Methodists to build much on these foundations. War, persecution, the tardiness of Mr. Wesley in responding to the Americans' plea for a solution to their ecclesial dilemma prevented them from construction. And yet the shape of the American church was already emerging. Separation and reunion, legislation and experimentation, experience and growth had detailed blueprints whose structural lines would become ever more prominent on the American horizon. In reflecting on this period of building, later Methodists have tended to minimize what had been achieved, what was already in place by 1784. They have read these early plans as perhaps guidelines for foundations but have then looked to the Christmas Conference of 1784 for the definitive drawings of Methodism as church. By accepting the 1784 blueprints, this interpretation construes Methodism as a conventional architectural endeavor, some church-like organization similar to the Anglican Church from which these Methodists separated. The standard reading, then, is that the Methodism went into the Christmas Conference of 1784 a 'society' and emerged from it a 'church.' It was transformed by the decisions made, the authority transferred from Wesley and the provisions sent/adopted for doctrine and discipline. So 1784, it is thought, made Methodism a church.[10]

There is much to be said for such an understanding of change. The Methodist aspirations for ecclesial self-sufficiency and integrity which we have just examined suggested such a view. The actors of 1784 concur. By the events of 1784, Methodists moved from one church type to another.[11] Yet, much in early Methodism supports an alternative interpretation (1) that 1784 represented less of a break from earlier American Methodism than was supposed; (2) that 1784 represented less independence from British Methodism than American Methodists have wanted to believe; and (3) that Methodism's intentions for itself and for America were far less conventional, less church-like, more dramatic than subsequent readings have suggested. Methodists sought nothing so conventional as another church on the denominational landscape. They intended to effect a whole new creation. Such construction was, of course, quite beyond human

capacities. But that was precisely the point. Methodism and its conferences were part of God's plans; the blueprints were not even
earthly, human; conference struggled to work with God on plans they
only faintly glimpsed.

One can discern from what Methodists did and said something of
what they thought those blueprints to say. They envisioned a new
creation. And specifically within those plans, conference provided
new conceptions of space, time and gravity. To read and follow these
plans, to labor on this new creation, one had to be something of a new
Newton. Space, time and gravity would assume, did assume a new
character. Each of these (space, time, gravity) will loom larger in our
treatment as we proceed. Here only a glimpse of their beginnings is
appropriate.

Conference would increasingly serve to define space, God's space,
Methodist space. The principle had already been established by
Wesley as a way of relating people (societies, classes, bands) to preachers. Each quarter, the preachers of a specific area and Methodist work,
a circuit, gathered to care for discipline, business, the religious needs
of the movement. American Methodists adhered to the quarterly
meeting design, thereby dividing Methodist land into quarterly conferences. As Methodism expanded, it added to itself by such quarterly
units, the circuits. Lee charted Methodist expansion by the circuits
taken in. For instance in 1781, he noted the adherence of six new
circuits.[12]

That same year, Methodism gave the annual conference a geographical meaning as well. In their brief schism over the ordinances,
Methodist preachers had come to recognize the value of a division of
the land by annual conference. While meeting in two conferences, the
preachers apparently found the "convenience" of this arrangement
to their liking. So in 1781 the now re-united body chose to meet in
two sessions. They had not solved the conceptual problem of how two
sessions could be politically and legislatively one. Consequently, they
sought to explain the division to themselves.[13] They construed the two
meetings as one conference. This style of governance, leaving the final
determination of legislation to the meeting of the Baltimore session,
permitted the elaboration of other conferences. It continued through
and beyond the organizing 1784 Christmas Conference to 1787. Thus
began the process by which conferences would be identified with
specific terrain and conference (annual as well as quarterly) would
become place. Eventually preachers as well as people would become
affiliated with a specific conference.[14] Conference then would become
a polity of place.

Conference had been and would always be a fraternity of time. In the conference of that same year, question 13 asked, "How are the Preachers stationed this year?" The answer began: "West Jersey—Caleb B. Pedicord, Joseph Cromwell" and then followed with twenty-four other circuit places and the preacher(s) appointed to them.[15] From the earliest Minutes down to those of today, conference has, at each gathering, so connected preacher to place. And at quarterly meetings, and in between them on the circuits, adjustment would be made and the actual appointments of each preacher laid out. Quarterly meeting also regulated the rhythms of the lower echelons of Methodist leadership—local preachers, exhorters, stewards. Quarterly meetings were the minute hand, conference served as the hour hand on the Methodist clock. At conference, preacher was connected to place. That appointment stood until the next conference. Appointments lasted from conference to conference. Or until discipline, the pull of other responsibilities, ill health or death claimed a preacher from his traveling.[16] Such claims were experienced as genuine losses to the fraternity, for preachers existed—they remained in time—only while active in the fraternity. When a preacher could not accept an appointment, he 'located,' thereby dropping out of conference time. Death, of course, registered the most telling blow to conference's time. As the early preachers began to die, Conference addressed itself to time's finitude. It did so explicitly for the first time in the regular (not the Christmas) conference of 1784. In that year, the fraternity asked a new question: "What Preachers have died this year?"[17] That question became an important and regular feature of conference sessions and minutes. Conference marked time as well as space.

Gravity and the Relativity of Space and Time

At each conference, space and time would be re-shaped, re-conceived, re-administered so that God's space and time could make use of ordinary space and time. While in conference, while in that process of re-creation, Methodist time stood still and its space went through a similar dissociation. Later Methodism would speak of itself as a machine; and to utilize that metaphor, while in conference, Methodism was quite truly out-of-gear. The machinery of Methodism went into a kind of neutral while conference met. The time and space of Methodism's meeting gradually assumed a very special quality which we might call gravity. By it we refer to the sacral character of conference itself, its spiritual weightiness, the powerful revivifying pull it made on those within its orbit. This quality characterized both the annual and quarterly conference (meeting).[18] In the case of the quarterly meeting the quality of spiritual gravity owed much to its

nature and length made possible by the 1780 decision, already mentioned, to stretch the quarterly meeting into a two-day event. That
permitted it some of the intensity that the longer conference already
possessed. But the dynamics that provided the 'gravity' to both
quarterly and annual conferences were apparently more spontaneous
than deliberate. They can be discerned in a report Asbury rendered
for a quarterly meeting of 1780 at Barratt's Chapel, one blessed with
the presence of a member of the clergy:

> While tarrying after dinner, Dr. Magaw came in. I went home
> with the Doctor, and was kindly received. The Doctor's intentions
> were not to go to the quarterly meeting; but having this opportunity,
> I went and took him along. It was one o'clock before we arrived;
> about three hundred people had been waiting for us. Mr. Magaw
> preached an excellent sermon on "Who shall ascend the hill of the
> Lord?" Brothers Hartley and Glendenning exhorted. We all stayed
> at Mr. Barratt's; Mr. Magaw prayed with much affection: we parted
> in great love.
> *Sunday, 5.* We had between one and two thousand people; our
> house forty-two by forty-eight, was crowded above and below, and
> numbers remained outside: our love feast lasted about two hours;
> some spoke of the sanctifying grace of God. I preached on John iii,
> 16–18; a heavy house to preach in: brother Pedicord and Cromwell
> exhorted.
> *Monday, 6.* I preached to about four hundred people on 2 Chron.
> viii, 18, and had liberty: I spoke of the necessity of getting and
> keeping the power of religion: William Glendenning exhorted af-
> terward; then we parted.[19]

The religious gravity of this particular occasion, though striking, was
slight in comparison with that to be seen after the cessation of the war.
Still the ingredients for the later quarterly and annual conference
revivals were all here—a full array of Methodist leadership, the
Methodist people of the circuit, a sizeable public, several days in which
to stage and present the Methodist gospel, a variety of services to
minister to the needs of people at different stages on the path to
salvation. Under these conditions, the organization itself yielded
revival—a special gravitational force exercised its pull, drew the
faithful closer and dragged in new adherents, some of whom had
come quite unprepared for conversion.

In conference, through conference, Methodists offered themselves as a new opportunity for this new continent, a new creation, a
new blueprint for ecclesial existence. That blueprint expressed itself
in everything Methodism did and said. It expressed itself clearly in
conference. As a new creation, conference sought to imprint Methodist design on the American continent (place), reordering it accord-

ing to conference rhythms (time), so as to achieve spiritual gravity. Accordingly, when in 1784 Methodists took it upon themselves to state their purposes, they spoke ambitiously:

> Q. 4. What may we reasonably believe to be God's design in raising up the Preachers called *Methodists?*
> A. To reform the Continent, and to spread scriptural Holiness over these Lands.[20]

These ambitions Methodists captured in a Biblical word that they (like other denominations) increasingly thereafter applied to their efforts and so also conveyed their sense of conference as blueprint for new ecclesial existence. They employed the word "Zion" when speaking of Methodist endeavors. Asbury noted in 1789, "The number of candidates for the ministry are many; from which circumstance I am led to think the Lord is about greatly to enlarge the borders of Zion." In a letter of 1792 he affirmed, "I feel myself uncommonly moved to believe the Lord will give peace to his church, and great prosperity to his Zion this year."[21] James Haw reported on a Kentucky revival of 1789, "Good news from Zion—The Work of GOD is going on rapidly in the new Western world."[22] The term recurs through early Methodist rhetoric as an ecclesial self-reference seemingly preferred over the more prosaic but also self-limiting "church." "Zion" served to expand rather than limit, to place Methodism central in God's redemptive activities, to claim for it connection with God's people Israel and the whole of redemptive history, to position Methodists as (among) the elect who would march into the New Jerusalem, to warrant the claim on the land, the continent, to put mission and purpose in specifically territorial terms.

Geographic (spatial), historical and eschatological (temporal), redemptive and missional (gravitational), "Zion" expressed Methodist ambitions to conference the continent. "Zion" reconceived space, time and gravity as reforming the continent and spreading scriptural holiness over these lands. With such ambitions a new church would be launched.

Chapter 4

1784 and Beyond

In late 1784, Thomas Coke, Richard Whatcoat and Thomas Vasey arrived from England bearing on their respective persons the clerical orders of superintendent (bishop) and elder, conferred at the hands of Mr. Wesley, and bearing in their hands the provisions he had made for an independent episcopal church. Mr. Coke had been directed to raise Asbury also to the status of superintendent. Asbury laid down his own directive. "My answer then was, if the preachers unanimously choose me, I shall not act in the capacity I have hitherto done by Mr. Wesley's appointment."[1] A richly symbolic act, this gesture had important ramifications for Asbury's relations with both Coke and Wesley then and thereafter. Here we would only note that it served also to clarify and to reassert Asbury's relation to conference. He had emerged as the president of the American conference. That status had been initially conferred by Wesley and reclaimed after Rankin's departure. It had been decisively re-asserted in the resolution of the Fluvanna schism. It had been formally defined in 1782 by a question which asked:

> Do the brethren in conference unanimously choose brother Asbury
> to act according to Mr. Wesley's original appointment, and preside
> over the American conferences and the whole work?[2]

Asbury's insistence on election to the episcopacy as well and that subsequent event established a constitutional principle. On conference's assent (and on Wesley's) rested his episcopacy as well as his presidency.

In the same gathering in which Asbury made this significant declaration—a quarterly meeting at Barratt's Chapel—a second act of similar symbolic proportions was taken.[3] "[I]t was agreed," reported Asbury, "to call a general conference, to meet at Baltimore the ensuing Christmas. . . ."[4] Several points about this call deserve remark: (1) that a conference seemed requisite for establishing this independent episcopal church; (2) that no such conference had been intended; (3) that the call for it was effected by another conference, specifically a quarterly conference.[5] As for Asbury the bishop, so also for The Methodist

Episcopal Church as a whole, power and authority derived both from Wesley and from the existing American conference.[6]

Christmas Conference

No minutes apparently survive from the conference that met at Christmas 1784.[7] Nor a full roster of those in attendance, though a general call was issued through Garrettson. German Reformed Pietism was symbolically present in the person of Philip Otterbein who participated in Asbury's ordination to the episcopacy and tradition places one or more of the Black Methodist preachers there.[8] The journal entries and memoirs of key participants were surprisingly spare, but clearly indicate that conference acted to constitute the church. Asbury noted:

> We then rode to Baltimore, where we met a few preachers: it was agreed to form ourselves into an Episcopal Church, and to have superintendents, elders, and deacons. When the conference was seated, Dr. Coke and myself were unanimously elected to the superintendency of the Church, and my ordination followed, after being previously ordained deacon and elder, as by the following certificate may be seen. [Reproduced]
>
> Twelve elders were elected, and solemnly set apart to serve our societies in the United States, one for Antigua, and two for Nova Scotia. We spent the whole week in conference, debating freely, and determining all things by a majority of votes. The Doctor preached every day at noon, and some one of the other preachers morning and evening. We were in great haste, and did much business in a little time.[9]

In "determining all things by a majority of votes," conference claimed supremacy for itself. It proclaimed its supremacy also by its production of the *Discipline*—by editing of *The Large Minutes* which Wesley had so single-handedly and guardedly constructed, so exercising its authority to establish a governing manual for the church.[10] Those were the real minutes, the legislative record of that gathering.[11]

The Governing Conference[12]

Conference granted to itself supreme electoral, disciplinary and legislative power.[13] It did so by convening itself; it did so by presuming that it had power to act; it did so by acting through majority rule. It did so also formally in the act of and through the letter of legislation, in the *Discipline*. For instance, it reserved to itself the power already exercised of electing the bishops or superintendents (Q. 26). It made the bishop "amenable for his Conduct" to "the Conference" (Q. 27).[14] It did not, however, define its own powers. Nor did it limit its powers, save (1) in recognizing the authority of the bishops elected and (2) in prescribing a continuing oversight to Wesley.[15] Conference symbolized its sense of political self-confidence by publishing its own minutes, which as Lee noted it had not previously done but did thereafter.[16]

The Baltimore Conference System[17]

Its political competence was tested in the years after 1785 as conference strove to exercise authority over a rapidly growing and far-flung work; to clarify its relation to the superintendency and particularly that of Bishop Coke who moved back and forth across the Atlantic; and to find the appropriate way of honoring the debt to and immense influence of Wesley without jeopardizing what seemed to be essential 'American' jurisdiction and authority. Such pressures accentuated the already political character of conference, doubtless reinforcing Methodist sensitivity to and reception of the democratic and republican ideals so powerful in American society.

The premium on conference as polity, on its political function, increased the tension with conference's other values—fraternity and revival. An immediate issue pitted polity against fraternity. How could a conference which had already divided itself into three sessions so that all the brothers could conveniently attend act in unity? How could it legislate as one body when it was—as in 1785—a conference at Green Hill's (NC), in Virginia and at Baltimore, in successive months, April, May and June. Lee noted that in earlier years conference had simply adjourned from one site to another but "Now there were three, and no adjournment." The resolution was awkward:

> The business of the three conferences was all arranged in the minutes as if it had all been done at one time and place.[18]

Unity was achieved by granting preeminence to the last conference held, that in Baltimore. Baltimore enjoyed the final say on legislation, rules and the *Discipline*. That resolution had preceded the Christmas conference, dated from 1780, and reflected the victory in the Fluvanna division of the northern preachers.[19] The arrangement Tigert termed "the Baltimore Conference system of government in American Methodism."[20] It lasted only until 1787.

In that year Wesley exercised the authority over the American movement that he regarded as his. He wrote Bishop Coke:

> I desire that you appoint a General Conference of all our preachers in the United States, to meet at Baltimore on May 1st, 1787, and that

Mr. Whatcoat may be appointed superintendent with Mr. Francis Asbury.[21]

Wesley also nominated Freeborn Garrettson as superintendent for Nova Scotia. The first conference that met, that in South Carolina, apparently acceded to Wesley's wishes and elected Whatcoat. In Virginia, however, James O'Kelly objected strenuously to this exercise of British authority, an objection that he spelled out later in a rambling letter to Asbury:

> 1. Does he look upon our country preachers to be men of so low breeding as not fit to govern?
> 2. Or does he think that we are a class of novices, fond of popularity, and so out of love to us, aims to keep us out of the snare of the devil?
> 3. Or does our dear Father conclude that we are prone to revolt or what he may call rebellion?
> 4. Of is there any political scheme in it?
> . . . Let Conference chuse and if dear brother Whatcoat is their choice well.[22]

O'Kelly's challenge raised a variety of acute problems for the young movement. The most obvious and most frequently commented upon had to do with Wesley's relation to and authority over the American bishops and American Methodism. More abstractly, the power of superintendency—whether that of Wesley or of Coke and Asbury—vis-à-vis conference was at stake. Would conference permit the sort of superintendency exercised by Wesley of proposing and disposing? Or would conference connive to transform its elective power from a proposing into a disposing prerogative? O'Kelly tested the limits of conference power; he also tested the political integrity and unity of this brotherhood, the conference as fraternity. Could the fraternity, when in fact divided into more than one conference, act sufficiently in unity to exercise the authority it had claimed in *The Discipline*? The Virginia crisis was Baltimore's to resolve.

The Baltimore Conference rejected Wesley's proposal of Whatcoat as bishop, despite Coke's appeal to the rubric of the *Discipline* pledging the fraternity to be his (Wesley's) "Sons in the Gospel, ready in Matters belonging to Church-Government, to obey his Commands;"[23] it put conditions on Garrettson's nomination that led him to reject the office; it stripped the above binding rubric from the *Discipline*; and it exacted from Coke a signed affidavit pledging not to exercise his superintendency while absent from the United States and limiting that office while in America to ordaining, presiding and traveling. It also unceremoniously dropped the name of John Wesley from the designated superintendents.[24] These actions vindicated Asbury as well as the conference and were partially motivated by apprehension that the election of Whatcoat might permit Wesley to recall Asbury.[25] Yet, they did indeed, and in the face of formidable exercises of authority by both Wesley and Coke, re-assert conference's political competence. These acts did not resolve the 'how' question—how an expanding Methodism could sustain political cohesion and integrity. And conference actually exacerbated the problem by appointing six conferences for 1788. Seven were held according to Lee, the last of which was in Philadelphia not Baltimore. And for 1789, eleven conferences met, Baltimore falling near the middle of the schedule. The Baltimore system was the first of many casualties of Methodist growth.

Multiple Conferences—Fraternity and Revival

Before proceeding to examination of a proposed solution to this political crisis, the council, it is worth noting that the division of conference, though undermining the unity of the fraternity, had preserved the size and intensity of conference that made fraternity possible, that made conference's many specified functions possible. A large conference could simply not devote the careful attention to the religious state and progress of both probationer and member that the *Discipline* and *Minutes* prescribed. The divided conference permitted that scrutiny. Conference continued to be a time in which each preacher's gifts and graces were carefully sifted and weighed in the ore-detecting system devised by Wesley. The *Minutes* record the decisive question and answer:

> Quest. 9. Are all the preachers blameless in life and conversation?
> Ans. They were all strictly tried, one by one, before the conference.[26]

The *Minutes* do not reveal what journals and diaries disclose, namely that this exercise of discipline by the fraternity over itself was an exacting affair. So the ministerium shed its ineffective members, so it rejected those not fit, physically as well as spiritually, for the rigors of itinerancy, so it dealt with theological heterodoxy. Discipline defined fraternity. It did so judicially by recognizing who was to be elder, who deacon, who in full connection, who on trial, who desist from travelling, who died.[27] Thereby the contours of the fraternity were delineated.

Less noted but perhaps far more powerful was the way in which this exercise of discipline operated psychologically and socially to define and maintain boundaries of the Methodist fraternity. The process which dealt some out worked on psychological, spiritual, affective levels to heighten the commitment of those within to one another. The fact of submitting to and going through these annual trials bound brother to brother. The hearing of one another's spiritual pilgrimage, the recounting of spiritual struggles, the probing of each other's souls, the description of conversion and narrative of perfection functioned to establish familial bonds, to mark the brother and mark off the brotherhood. On this spiritual level, as well, discipline delineated the contours of fraternity.[28]

It should not be surprising that conference continued to nourish revival, that the spirituality within the fraternity would spill outwards, that the political controversy within conference did not totally dissipate its revivalistic potential. In 1787, for instance, Lee did not report actual revivals in connection with the 'annual' conferences. He did, however, connect a considerable revival in southern Virginia with the smaller conferences, the quarterly meeting.

> At one quarterly meeting held at Mabry's chapel in Brunswick circuit, on the 25th and 26th of July, the power of God was among the people in an extraordinary manner: some hundreds were awakened; . . . one hundred souls were converted. . . . Some thousands of people attended. . . .
>
> The next quarterly-meeting was held at *Jones's* chapel in *Sussex* country, on Saturday and Sunday the 27th and 28th of July. This meeting was favoured with more of the divine presence than any other that had been known before. . . .
>
> Soon after this, some of the same preachers who had been at the quarterly-meetings mentioned above, held a meeting at Mr. F. Bonners, ten miles from *Petersburg*, were a large concourse of people assembled; and the Lord wrought wonders among them on that day. As many as fifty persons professed to get converted. . . .
>
> They had another meeting at *Jones-Hole* church; about twelve miles from *Petersburg*, and many people assembled . . . On that day many souls were brought into the liberty of God's children.[29]

The following year, Lee reported more general and extensive revivals, particularly in Virginia, North Carolina and Maryland. That in Maryland culminated at the conference held in Baltimore, at which time Lee noted, "we were highly favoured of the Lord, and souls were awakened, and converted."[30] Methodists expected conference, both the annual gatherings and the quarterly meetings, to deepen the spirituality of the movement, to revive. And their way of doing business made provision for this expectation. In particular, they allowed the probationary, disciplinary, judicial trying of one another's spiritual state its natural spiritual force. The unity of spirituality and business, actually of all three ideals—polity (business), spirituality (revival) and unity (fraternity)—is tersely captured by Asbury's entries for (1791) conference meetings:

> We opened conference in great peace. Many of the preachers related their experience, and it was a blessed season of grace.
> . . . Several of our brethren expressed something like the perfect love of God. . . .

> The business of our conference was brought on in peace; and there was a blessing attended our speaking on our experiences, and in prayer.

> Our conference began, and was conducted in much peace and harmony amongst preachers and people. Our meetings in public were attended with great power.

> We had a tender, melting account of the dealings of God with many souls; and settled our business in much peace.
> . . . We had a fast day; and in the afternoon a feast of love. It was a time to be remembered: some precious souls were converted.

> We attended to the business of the conference with a good spirit. In the course of our sitting we had some pleasing and some painful circumstances to excite our feelings.

> Our conference came together in great peace and love. Our ordinary business was enlivened by the relation of experiences, and by profitable observations on the work of God.[31]

Conference's spiritual intensity, exercise of discipline, and tightening of fraternal bonds proved favorable to revival. Fraternity's bonds and boundaries had a less favorable and pleasant aspect as well. To this traveling brotherhood, some who felt called were not elected. Over the years, various categories of the excluded would raise objections—local preachers, the laity, women. The first who offered themselves only to be repudiated were African American Methodists. The requests by black preachers and societies for conference membership lay ahead. However, already in 1787 the color line around conference had been faintly etched by Richard Allen and black Methodists of Philadelphia who had by that time taken as much racial affront as they could stand. Their separation prefigured a later delineation of conference's boundaries. This fraternity would observe the color line.[32] Black Methodists would have to form their own conference to achieve what all American Methodists had sought in the years leading up to the 1784 Christmas Conference and to which, ironically, Allen may have been a witness.[33]

Methodist fraternity was not achieved, then, without costs. The personal costs have always been noted—the terrible toll on the preachers that itinerancy exacted. Its social costs—the lines drawn and the classes excluded thereby—were no less severe. Methodism's successes, then, had their price. Methodist growth depended upon the energies channeled by this fraternity, a monastic-like male-bonding, that wore out the traveling preachers but gave that role a very special status. Itinerancy would continue to be the badge of membership years and years after real travel had been discontinued.

The Council

The eleven conferences of 1789—through all of which legislation had to pass—established the unwieldiness of Methodism's political apparatus and prompted a short-lived and unpopular solution, a council. Laid before the 1789 conferences by the Bishops who "had made it a matter of prayer" and presented it as "the best that they could think of," the council was, according to the enabling legislation, to "be formed of chosen men out of the several districts as representatives of the whole connection." The representatives designated by the following rubric were "Our bishops and presiding elders. . . ." Lee, who reproduced the entirety of this legislation, complained that this was no representation at all:

> This plan for having a council, was entirely new, and exceedingly dangerous. A majority of the preachers voted in favour of it, but they were soon sensible, that the plan would not answer the purpose for which it was intended. The council was to be composed of the bishops, and the presiding elders: the presiding elders were appointed, changed, and put out of office by the bishop, and just when he pleased; of course, the whole of the council were to consist of the bishops, and a few other men of their own choice or appointing.[34]

The council possessed two other features well devised to doom it. One was the provision that all legislation required unanimity.[35] The other was that legislation would be binding as concurred in by each conference: "Provided, nevertheless, that . . . nothing so assented to by the council, shall be binding in any district, till it has been agreed upon by a majority of the conference which is held for that district." Lee thought that a "dangerous clause," prone to divide the connection.[36]

In its first meeting, the council addressed itself to and adopted a constitution that remedied these three glaring defects. It provided for election of "the most experienced elders in the connection . . . by ballot in every conference," a two-thirds majority rather than unanimity as requisite for legislation (plus however "the consent of the bishop"), and only the concurrence of "a majority of the several conferences."[37]

It is worth remarking that this political experiment—and one that raised the political anxieties of the conferences—nevertheless sustained the revivalistic and fraternal characteristics of conference. Asbury reported that "During our sitting we had preaching every night; some few souls were stirred up, and others converted." Fraternity benefitted as well.

> We spent one day in speaking our own experiences, and giving an account of the progress and state of the work of God in our several districts; a spirit of union pervades the whole body, producing blessed effects and fruits.[38]

Even in this revised form and despite such efforts to clothe it in traditional conference garb, the council was experienced as what Neely terms "a dangerous centralization of power."[39]

Outspoken on this issue and leading the charge against the council was James O'Kelly. Asbury reported:

> I received a letter from the presiding elder of this district [South Virginia], James O'Kelly; he makes heavy complaints of my power, and bids me stop for one year, or he must use his influence against me. Power! Power![40]

Others shared O'Kelly's concern. The conference at Charleston sought to constrict the council's power to "advice only" and to make the "consent of the conference decisive"[41] At Petersburg Asbury reported, "Our conference began; all was peace until the council was mentioned. The young men appeared to be entirely under the influence of the elders, and turned it out of doors."[42] Asbury is reported to have said: "Ye have all spoken out of one mouth. Henceforth you are all out of the union."[43] Following the Leesburg conference where similar agitation prevailed, Asbury made a further concession:

> To conciliate the minds of our brethren in the south district of Virginia, who are restless about the council, I wrote their leader a letter, informing him, "that I would take my seat in council as another member"; and, in that point, at least, waive the claims of episcopacy. . . .[44]

The Southern Virginia preachers met under O'Kelly's leadership at Mecklenburg and resolved "to send no member to Council."[45]

The second meeting of the council did not stem the tide of opposition. O'Kelly had, in fact, rallied Coke to that side. Lee also played an important oppositional role. Nevertheless as its minutes attest, the council did show a capacity to act, to initiate, to address itself to the connection's needs, a political capacity that had been missing.[46] It proceeded in traditional Wesleyan fashion through thirty-one policy queries and action answers. Methodism had, in recent years, wanted for that administrative and legislative ability, for a body to frame policy.

Chapter 5

General Conference

1791 proved a momentous year for American Methodism. John Wesley died March 2. The news reached Asbury (and Coke) in very late April. Subsequent conferences that year took observance of Wesley's passing. The council also died that year. The two events were not related. Yet both deaths resolved important questions about the nature and exercise of authority in American Methodism.

Bishop Coke returned to the U.S. and met Asbury in late February 1791. At their meeting, Asbury jotted the following in his journal:

> I found the Doctor's sentiments, with regard to the council, quite changed. James O'Kelly's letters had reached London. I felt perfectly calm, and acceded to a general conference, for the sake of peace.[1]

A general conference had been mooted but dismissed when the plan for a council was initially introduced.[2] Both Lee and O'Kelly had pressed for a conference rather than a council. Lee reiterated that proposal on July 7, 1791, submitting the matter in writing. "This day," recorded Asbury, "brother Lee put a paper into my hand, proposing the election of not less than two, nor more than four preachers from each conference, to form a general conference in Baltimore, in December, 1792, to be continued annually."[3] Lee's notion of an annual meeting did not prevail—general conferences came to be quadrennial rather than annual affairs, adding a very distinctive rhythm to the Methodist sense of time. Neither Lee's proposed date nor his plan for a delegated general conference found acceptance. But he, O'Kelly and Coke had their way. The first general conference was called for November 1792. When it gathered, the council proposal was given a very unceremonious burial. "For soon after we met together," Lee reported, "the *bishops* and the preachers in general, shewed a disposition to drop the *council*, and all things belonging there. And the bishops requested that the name of the *council* might not be mentioned in the conference again."[4]

No minutes of this first general conference survive; it left its record in the *Discipline* which it revised.[5] Several of its actions had long-term consequences for the nature of conference in Methodism. Perhaps most importantly, it decided to convene again in four years in a conference "to which, all the preachers in full connection were at liberty to come."[6] That plenary definition of itself, its claim to a future and its assumption of the authority to legislate, specifically to revise the *Discipline*—two-thirds majority being required for new actions or total rescission of existing legislation but only a majority to amend—provided what Asbury had sought through the council, namely a politically competent and sovereign center to the movement.[7] General conference also claimed the right to elect and try bishops.[8] Thus, said Tigert, "this body became the permanent organ of connectional government in American Methodism."[9]

The general conference also gave further impetus towards what would in the future be termed annual conferences by authorizing the uniting of two or more of the districts (the purview of the presiding elders) and between three and twelve circuits (the assignment of the travelling preachers).[10] Here, as in the case of general conference, annual conference is defined, in the *Discipline*, by its membership—the traveling preachers in full connection. Its leadership was also given formal definition. Presiding elders with supervisory responsibility for a district of circuits and the various levels of preachers attached to them had already emerged. General conference moved towards the stabilzation of this important annual conference office by recognizing presiding elders and assenting to the bishops' authority to select, station and change them.[11] It also limited the term of presiding elders in one place to four years. In this action, the fraternity of preachers expressed its apprehension over the growing power and independence of this potentially aristocratic office. So Tigert suggested. It was a worry dramatized in the style of a specific presiding elder, James O'Kelly, an individual with a penchant for autonomy.[12]

The Shattered Fraternity

That worry had already proved itself well placed. The second day of General Conference O'Kelly had placed a motion giving preachers who thought themselves "injured" by the bishop's appointment the "liberty to appeal to the conference" and the right, if the appeal was sustained, to another appointment.[13] It is unfortunate that the following "long" debate was not minuted. Lee indicated that "the arguments for and against the proposal were weighty, and handled in a masterly manner." He continued:

There never had been a subject before us that so fully called forth
all the strength of the preachers. A large majority of them appeared
at first to be in favour of the motion.[14]

The motion, and doubtless much of the affirmative argument, made
appeal to what we would now term the language or ideology of
republicanism. O'Kelly had invoked the rhetoric of the Revolution
and the American republic—that powerful strain of radical Whiggery
that bifurcated social reality into a people with real but fragile rights
and authority whose natural tendency was to tyranny and usurpation
of rights. The liberties of the people demanded collective resolve on
the part of the people, a unity founded in virtue, watchful monitoring
of authority, forceful response against authority's inducements, and
resistance to luxury. Liberty and virtue were easily corrupted and the
people's resolve dissipated; authority was ever encroaching; freedom's hope demanded vigilance; unless liberty were defended, the
people would be reduced to slavery. So taught the history of repub-
lics.[15]

This imagery had tremendous appeal at that point in American
history. It had brought a new republic into being. Methodists too had
pressed for and achieved their independence, in large part out of a
sense of the demands and constraints of their new political location,
but in some measure also in expression of American liberties. Should
not the church now conduct its life in accord with the principles which
had, in some measure, brought into being? Should not an American
church conduct itself along American principles? The republican
appeal was then more than societal and extrinsic. Further, republicanism gave forceful and meaningful expression to those powerful
but inchoate tendencies which we have termed 'fraternity', those
bonds that bound preacher to preacher, member to member. And
there was much in the preachers' experience that found resonance in
O'Kelly's republican motion. Had they not been injured by appointments? did not Coke and Asbury connive to increase their power? had
they not had to check episcopal tyranny already? was not the preachers' liberty in danger? would it not be better safeguarded in conference rather than episcopal hands?[16] The rhetoric had appeal. Thomas
Ware concurred in Lee's judgment that the motion initially seemed
destined for passage but for the spirit with which the campaign was
led and the radical character of the argument.

Some of them said that it was a shame for a man to *accept* of such a
lordship, much more to *claim* it; and that they who would submit to
this absolute dominion must forfeit all claims to freedom, and ought
to have their ears bored through with an awl, and to be fastened to

their master's door and become slaves for life. One said that to be denied such an appeal was an insult to his understanding, and a species of tyranny. . . .[17]

The motion failed.[18] O'Kelly walked out with a party of supporters to form a rival movement that took the republican banner into its name.[19] O'Kelly's was not the first Methodist fracturing of fraternity. The controversy over the sacraments and ordination had earlier more completely divided the young movement. Black Methodists under Richard Allen had initiated a break in Philadelphia that would be imitated across the church by the creation of separate African congregations and would lead in the decades ahead to full-fledged separate denominations.[20] That racial flaw in fraternity would prove to be the most tragic. And at roughly the same time that O'Kelly rallied opposition in Virginia and North Carolina, William Hammett took a course towards independence in Charleston. There, too, the authority of Asbury was challenged. However, O'Kelly was at this juncture perceived to be the greatest threat, in part because he mounted a republican cause.

Republicanism and Fraternity

Controversy, conflict, competition for adherents and a pamphlet war ensued. That controversy has largely shaped later Methodist assessment of O'Kelly and the Republicans. The Republican cause is portrayed as schismatic, heretical (particularly on the doctrine of the Trinity), driven by O'Kelly's own megalomania, excessive in its portrayal of Asbury.[21] Methodists have wanted to minimize the effect of the Republican departure and discount its size and importance. Here several different points deserve mention.

First, the republican or Whiggish language, though in some ways alien to the Wesleyan tradition and John Wesley's Toryism, nevertheless proved capable of expressing the powerful egalitarian and fraternal currents that were quite central to Wesleyanism. O'Kelly and the Republicans indeed found that language to be entirely apt for powerful egalitarian sentiments of the fraternity of preachers. Equality among the preachers was their maxim.[22] The Republicans voiced that egalitarianism by hoisting the anti-slavery banner. They did so at a point when the Methodist Episcopal Church was already finding anti-slavery problematic. The Republican schism, then, drained off anti-slavery sentiment from the church. In so doing, it may well have opened a less egalitarian door for the larger Methodist body. Certainly, it damaged the ideal of fraternity. Fraternal sentiments were marred. So also the Republican Methodist departure represented the loss to the connection—at least to that generation in the connection—of this very significant intellectual expression to and interpretation of fraternity.

Second, the fraternity of conference was doubtless also damaged by having its ideals lifted and encapsuled in what was to be regarded as a schismatic movement. The appropriation of the republican banner by a cause that divided and then fizzled stamped republicanism. Both the republican version of fraternity and the actuality of fraternity were hurt.

Third, the human losses to the fraternity, to conference, were quite real. O'Kelly meant something to the 'brothers.' James Meachem, who served under O'Kelly, represented many hurt by O'Kelly's departure. After a committee charged with waiting on O'Kelly to dissuade him from his announced walk failed in its mission, Meachem made this entry in his journal:

> He has taken his fare well of conference. I think my poor heart scarcely ever felt the like before, I could not refrain from weeping deeply I hope God will still direct aright, & give us our dear old bro. & yokefellow back again—if he comes not back, I fear bad consequences will accrue.[23]

For the rest of the century, the small Methodist movement had to contend with O'Kelly and his "fraternity."[24] Some returned to the old brotherhood; others did not; the brothers had begun the process of what would be a sequence of fallings out.

Fourth, republican ideas and ideals would grow in importance in American Methodism, notwithstanding the opprobrium they earned from this controversy. Almost immediately the African (African American) Methodists would make appeal to republican ideals in quest of rights of self-government, rights to representation, and rights to conference membership and ordination. A generation later, the Methodist Protestants would hoist the same banner to mount another but different attack on episcopacy. The Wesleyan, Free Methodist and other holiness movements also made use of republican sentiments. And though Methodist Episcopacy resisted application of republicanism to the episcopal office it too would eventually find republican ideals important to conception of the church's role in American society.

Chapter 6

Living out the New Order

With the two creations of 1792—annual and general conferences—Methodism could now be thought of as a movement fully ordered through conference—general conferences every four years for the entire connection; annual conferences for each region; quarterly conferences for the circuits; and then weekly conference-like structures in society and class in communities across the new nation. The three explicitly named conference structures, quarterly, annual and general, each had a turn in the overall governance of the movement. The succession of these efforts, the search for political stability and the untidy evolution of governance had distributed certain functions at one level, others at another. It would be tempting to conclude that the three ideals of conference had lodged themselves successfully in the three conference levels: polity in general conference, fraternity in annual conference, revival in quarterly (conference) meeting. That distribution, which will be reviewed in the following sections, sufficiently approximates Methodist realities to give shape to Methodist historical analyses. Political and constitutional accounts follow the early quarterly and annual conference governance but then lose interest in those levels when General Conference assumes legislative supremacy. Though fraternity has not been given much explicit historical attention, conference histories do it most justice, often serving in one way or another to remember the fraternity and its members.[1] Studies of revival have typically looked at quarterly meetings and their more expressive counterpart, camp meetings.[2] However, that sorting of conference ideals was not immediately operative or obvious and remained/remains approximate. In fact, each level of conference sought to preserve all three ideals, each continued important aspects of the conference structure that had previously guided American Methodism, and each found it difficult to resist polity's tendency to encroach on fraternity and revival.

It would be easy—it certainly has been the Methodist habit—to ascribe the ascendency of the polity and the political to some failure of the Methodist spirit. That jeremiadic accounting, satisfying to those looking for something to blame, does little justice to the perplexities

Methodists faced as they struggled to live out their ideals in a new and rapidly expanding society. Their struggles were gargantuan: the testing of limits and possibilities under the emerging rules of voluntarism and toleration; the pressures of religious competition; the demands put on religious structure for social/political/legal services, especially under frontier conditions; the opportunities and burdens presented groups willing to assume responsibility for order in American society as a whole; growth itself. Growth alone proved more than Methodists could handle. In coping with growth, Methodists struggled to make General Conference more politically accountable, finally following civil precedent to a delegated or representative model; they put boundaries on annual conferences thereby stabilizing their membership; and they found a new vehicle for the revivalistic force of quarterly meetings. In the first decade of the new century, growth wrought subtle changes in polity, fraternity and revival; it wrought subtle changes in all three levels of conference. The perils of growth do not suffice as an explanation for the changes that conference underwent. But growth provides a neutral way into what would be important and vexing change. Its effects on the annual conference level were most immediate and obvious.

Boundaries and Belonging

The number of annual conferences had continued to expand—seventeen in 1792 according to Lee,[3] and nineteen in 1793. They went year round, throwing the Methodist sense of both time and place into chaos. Two perceptions of the chaos and its resolution are striking. Methodism's first two major historians came to quite different judgments of what was a fundamental change, the reduction of conferences from that large number of seventeen (1792) to seven (in 1795). Both assessed the issue in terms of the Methodist temporal/spatial order.

With the benefit of hindsight, Nathan Bangs saw the fewer conferences and the consequently larger territory they represented as an inconvenience to the preachers in distant appointments and disruptive to the societies they served.[4] He construed the motivation for this change as political:

> This diminution in the number of the conferences was made in consequence of the general opposition of the preachers to having so many, by which they thought the powers of the conferences were abridged, and those of the bishop proportionably augmented. . . .[5]

For Bangs, polity and fraternity conspired against conference's larger religious (revivalistic) mandates.

In his closer retrospective, Lee made no reference to power, though one can surmise that at the time he would have been quite concerned with conference's power. Instead, Lee spoke of the brotherhood. He viewed the multiplication of conferences and length of the conference season as damaging to the fraternity's rhythms. He had in mind the way the number of conferences fragmented the once unified brotherhood into bodies out of touch with one another and the way that the length of the conference season actually frustrated their efforts to stay in touch.

> It was upwards of eleven months from the time of holding the first of these conferences, until the close of the last: of course there was no opportunity of getting the annual minutes printed and circulated before the conferences began for the following year, and many of the preachers had taken their stations for the next year; by which means, a correspondence with the old preachers was greatly obstructed. For we could not tell where the preachers were stationed until we saw the minutes; and by that time the stations or appointments were altered.[6]

The multiple conferences seemed to Lee to frustrate the communication of the brothers. A strange, seemingly maudlin complaint. Yet, it makes sense when viewed in terms of what the brothers affirmed about being together and what they wrote one another. The evidence suggests that these men who quite often rode together, who called each other yoke-fellows, who shared the adversities of the itinerancy, who coached each other on ministry—did indeed cherish their time together[7] and when apart cherished whatever communication was possible. James Meachem made this entry in his journal:

> May 26, 1792 rode to Hanover Town to meet with my Elder bro J.E. who brought in several Letters from Sundry Brothers, we had sweet union while Together, my soul thinks it a great blessing to be with the Elder Brethren & Preachers.[8]

Two rather remarkable collections of letters attest the general character of Meachem's sentiments and the legitimacy of Lee's concern—The Dromgoole papers at The Southern Historical Collection and Hitt letters at Ohio Wesleyan University. A typical concluding note and salutation from the Hitt letters illustrates the structure and value of this communication network to which Lee alluded:

> I expect God willing, to set out for Pee Dee, in South Carolina, in about two or three weeks, near to where brother Martin & Benny

are; so if you have a mind to send out any letter, you may have them ready; I expect to call fore on my way out.

From your Loving Brother,

S. G. Roszel

I take this opportunity to salute you, Dear Bro. though we are parted in body, yet [ink spot] we are one in Spirit, for my part the distance which separates us, seems to increase the ties of friendship, which makes me, that I seldom bow before the throne of Grace without makeing mention of you, that we may be co-workers together here, & co-heirs of the Kingdom of Glory. . . .

E. Scholfield[9]

A later retrospective caught well the fraternal feeling that conference bred and that held this collegium together. William Burke described preachers' gathering

with warn and tattered garments, but happy and united like a band of brothers. The quarterly meetings and annual conferences were high times. When the pilgrims met they never met without embracing each other, and never parted at those season without weeping. Those were days that tried men's souls.[10]

Sentiments like these lend some plausibility to Lee's construction. The fraternity had become genuinely perplexed by its own fragmentation. So in 1796, the General Conference legislated both the number and the boundaries of the conferences, establishing on the North American landscape six geographically defined conferences. The fraternity sought the reduction in number and increase in conference size.[11] However, it was the specification of boundaries that, in time, would both give new life to fraternity and most alter its character, perhaps under Lee's motivation but with the effect that Bangs specified. A conference with specific boundaries could be a more politically cohesive entity for it was possible and would be increasingly the pattern for preachers to belong to one conference. That notion, that a preacher actually belonged to one conference, previously quite foreign to a collegium which had been deployed across the entire seaboard and inland as far as the population stretched, came into Methodist thought in 1804.[12]

Henceforth, Methodism's fraternity would be divided into relatively cohesive regional bodies. Movement between conferences would continue, though lessening as the years passed, but even that movement underscored the new walls that had been established within, for thereafter redeployment of preachers amounted to more than just a new episcopal appointment; it involved the changing of membership. Methodism's fraternity had acquired internal boundaries. Determining the boundaries of conferences would be the work of successive General Conferences; in 1816, the task deserved the creation of a Committee on Temporal Economy; and by 1820, a General Conference structuring itself with standing committees established a Committee on Boundaries.[13]

Another item of legislation in 1796 also increased the cohesion of annual conferences. That was a social boundary for conference. In answer to a question posed in the Wesleyan manner, "Who shall attend the yearly conferences?" General Conference decreed:

> Those who are in full connexion, and who are to be received into full connexion.
>   N.B. This regulation is made that our societies and congregations may be supplied with preaching during the conferences.[14]

Though ostensibly motivated by the concern to keep those on trial and local preachers back on the circuits, the effect was to return conference to the more closed affair established by Wesley. This decision too would strengthen the fraternity—of traveling preachers—by delineating its social boundaries, reinforcing those drawn by region.

By strengthening conference's fraternal character, these decisions made conference, each annual conference and the collectivity of annual conferences, politically more competent as well, a point that will emerge in later sections. But the more sharply defined annual conferences had thereafter more difficulty in serving the Methodist faithful who had heretofore assembled on such occasions. The revivalistic dimension of conference gradually diminished. Limitation of conference to those in full connection was a decision on behalf of the fraternity and its poltical competence but at the expense of revival. Or perhaps it would be more accurate to say that reinforcing the fraternity and stabilizing it as a political unit worked to the larger religious and revivalistic effectiveness of Methodism even as it made conference sessions themselves less revivalistic occasions. For not only did the legislation assure that local preachers remained to preach to the societies during conference but more importantly the repair to the conference structure made it possible for Methodism to continue its expansion nationally not with a chaotic, ever changing, patchwork of geographically overlapping, episcopally called conferences, with indeterminate membership but with the self-contained, stable regionally configured units, each with a definite membership and increasingly internal cohesion and esprit de corps. The enabling legislation explicitly anticipated expansion and implicitly enunciated the new principle of cellular growth by permitting the calling of new conferences in the Western and New England Conferences.[15]

What made Methodism open, expansive and inclusive in one respect closed it in others. Whether so intended or not, this 1796 legislation would have served to make conference an all white affair.[16] Three years later Richard Allen was ordained a deacon. Though under the supervision of the Philadelphia Conference, he as a deacon would not be a member of it. The next year, in 1800, General Conference gave formal authorization to such 'African' ordinations but set the ceiling for African leadership to deacon only and chose not to print the legislation, in deference, Lee reported, to the preachers from the southern states. "This rule is at present," (in 1810) when Lee wrote, "but little known among the Methodist preachers themselves, owing to it's having never been printed; yet it is a regular rule which has been standing for nine years."[17]

By the time that Lee wrote, annual conferences symbolized and exercised the boundary-keeping function by establishing an office— that of door-keeper.[18] The door-keeper did not, in fact, watch to keep out African Americans or to discourage German attendance, but the office stood for the exclusive character of the fraternity.

A more decisive door-keeping, as we noted earlier, constituted the main business of conference—assessing those who presented themselves to be admitted on trial, reviewing the character and process of those on trial, and determining who would be admitted into full connection, i.e. as full members of conference, who ordained deacon and who ordained elder. These actions followed the order of questions in the *Discipline* and often were minuted in short hand as the first, second, etc. disciplinary question. Over the years Methodist theologians have sometimes complained about the movement's idiosyncratic, two ladder route to full ministerial standing—through the traditional three fold pattern of orders (deacon, elder and bishop) and via conference membership (probationer to full member). Whatever its theological problems, Methodists would, following Wesley, exercise ministry fraternally in conference and conference membership. And so, year-in-year-out the work of staffing and thereby defining them would go on.

The boundary-maintenance work of the conference becomes more visible after 1800 when General Conference mandated that each annual conference to appoint a secretary to keep its records.[19] A few entries from the New England Conference indicate how seriously this work was taken and how deeply invested in it the entire conference became:

Daniel Nicker, He was recommended to this Conference as a proper candidate for the traveling ministry—but was rejected. He being obliged, by his promise, to marry a certain person, at some future tho' uncertain period—and it being uncertain how long should his life be protracted, he would continue in the traveling order. It was argued, that should he be received, and travel but a short time, he then desisting, woud wound the cause—but may be useful as a Local Preacher.

Joshua Soule, A man of great tallents, so called, he being absent was examined, and tho' brother Taylor, who spoke concerning him tho't him in great danger of highmindness, Yet he with others judged that if brother Soule continued humble and faithful, he would become a useful Minister in our Church, and Connection. He, sustaining a good moral character, is continued on trial.

Truman Bishop, He, sustaining a good character, after due examination, was admitted into our Connection, and elected to the office of a Deacon, in our Church—but he was not willing to take a station, unless, it could be in Pittsfield District for as much as he is under age, and his father, would be unwilling that he should go a great distance from home. He is appointed to a station, there, at Granville.[20]

In such reviews, the conference did not mince words or spare feelings, as this entry from 1801 indicates:

Examinations, John Merrick, was examined, having travelled two years, and after a long debate, in which many things were said for, and against, him. Levity of conversation, neglect of meeting the Classes, and the want of Gifts, and Grace adequate to the work of the Ministry, together, with the want of zeal, and vigilance, were alledged against him. It was voted that he should be continued on trial provided the Bishop would give him a reprimand; which was given, and after considering thereupon—he consented to fill an appointment.[21]

Conference's close attention to its members could lead it to find unproclaimed strengths as well as fault. Consider, for instance, its response to one preacher's request to desist from traveling, leave the conference and locate:

Timothy Merritt, requested a location alledging for his principal reason that he thought himself deficient as a Disciplinarian. His brethren believed it to be a temptation & so they were unwilling to lose him from the travelling connection, he consented to take an appointment again at Bath Ct, which was granted him.[22]

In determining its membership, conferences showed a decided preference for the single estate. In 1806, New England reviewed twenty-one candidates for admission on trial, accepting only two married men, rejecting three candidates, two of them married, the only single person rejected being of "doubtful; or singular character." Its actions on the two married men bear citation:

> Joseph Peck, m. age 40, recom'd from New Grantham Cir't. three years a local preacher, godly, large family—rejected.

> Cyrus Story, m. age 34, recom'd from Hanover Cir't. a local preacher 3½ years, travelled about 2 months, has four children, devout, useful. On the question shall he be rec'd? An equal division of the Conf.[23]

Asbury certainly shared the conference's preference for single preachers. He viewed marriage as inimical to Methodist ministry. At the Virginia Conference in 1809, he found only three married men, apparently of the eighty-four present, noted that marriage to a Methodist preacher was socially disdained and celebrated the single-ness that disdain produced.[24] So Methodism drew boundaries around its ministry; so it found boundaries drawn; so groups of largely young, white males, in each region of the country shared their intense religious experiences, committed themselves to go where sent and bound themselves into a fraternity they called conference.

They still desired that conference serve the revivalistic purposes that it had previously. So they found places within conference's rhythms to make space for public events.

> On Saturday Conference closed by singing and prayer, after which the ordination of the Deacons took place & on Sabbath, a Lovefeast was held, five sermons were preached, the Eucharist administered to about 230 communicants, & Epaphras Kibby, Comfort C. Smith, Asa Heath, Daniel Webb, & Reuben Hubbard, were ordained Elders, in the presence of nearly 3000 people, as it was judged.[25]

Reports of this sort would continue for several decades. Even at General Conference, where the political function was paramount, the preachers sought to sustain the revivalistic ideal of conference by preaching on the side. Indeed, the General Conference of 1800 produced something of a revivalist wildfire that spread out from Baltimore, where conference sat, to the Delmarva Peninsula.[26] Yet the primary revivalistic function of conference took another form, through quarterly meeting and increasingly through camp meeting.

Quarterly and Camp Meetings

Just at the point at which the new boundaries and the attention to prerogatives made conference less accessible to the Methodist people and less conducive to revival, Methodists discovered the camp meeting. When it was first held, who deserves ownership, where it began—the whole debate over origins—need not concern us here.[27] When and where the first tents were pitched is less important to us than the fact that at the turn of the century the camp meeting captured the Methodist imagination. It did so because, despite its novelty, it looked familiar. American Methodism had, as we have seen, an established tradition of revivalistic quarterly meetings and annual conferences. As soon as they saw them, Methodists recognized the camp meetings as an institution appropriately their own and a very serviceable one at that.[28] The camp meeting proved to be deliberately structured for the revivals that had been, in a sense, incidental to the business of the quarterly or annual conference and was unencumbered with the obligations to do church (conference) business.

Methodist fascination with and discovery of the camp meeting showed itself in a curious place. Lacking its own paper or magazine, American Methodists reported on the camp meeting via correspondence with the British periodical, *The Methodist Magazine.*[29] Beginning with a letter from Asbury to Coke, the Americans described "the revival of Religion in America," dramatically manifested in awakenings in Kentucky and Tennessee, but also as Asbury noted on "Every Circuit upon the Eastern and Western shores," [Md.] with even a stir in New Jersey.[30] The sequence of letters over the next several years put on the record what must have blazed across the informal communication networks—the news of revival and the increasingly vital place therein of camp meetings.[31] Asbury's surviving correspondence and journal notations show him to have been intentional and effective in establishing and sustaining that camp meeting blaze.

Ezekiel Cooper called the outpouring on the Delmarva Peninsula "a pentecost indeed"; Stith Mead wrote Coke from Georgia, "Glory be to God, *primitive Methodism* shines in this Country, and thro' America."[32] The letters that followed reinforced those points. Methodism recognized itself in the camp meetings. Here was *primitive Methodism,* the pentecost for which Methodism labored. Camp meeting results impressed Methodists; but so did the form, the groves that had served from the 1760s whenever the crowd exceeded the modest spaces in which Methodists preached and the sequence of religious services that around conferences that had produced such crowds. Very quickly, the Methodist connection took up the institution and began to promote it zealously. By late 1802, Asbury had taken the step that made manifest Methodism's recognition of itself in the camp meeting. He wrote the preachers directing that they establish camp meetings in connection with annual conference. George Roberts of the Baltimore Conference was informed:

> The campmeetings have been blessed in North and South Carolina, and Georgia. Hundreds have fallen and have felt the power of God. I wish most sincerely that we could have a campmeeting at Duck Creek out in the plain south of the town, and let the people come with their tents, wagons, provision and so on. Let them keep at it night and day, during the conference; that ought to sit in the meeting.[33]

Camp meetings did not find their way into the formal structure of the movement or gain a place in the *Discipline*.[34] They did become standard practice, and in just the way that Asbury specified. It became customary for Methodists to hold camp meetings in connection with conference.[35] As the Illinois Conference proceeded to business in its very first meeting:

> Brother Samuel H. T[h]ompson and John Dew were then nominated and elected to superintend the appointments for Divine service to be performed at the Camp Ground during the Conference.[36]

Bishop McKendree distinguished such a "camp-meeting Conference" from other conferences.[37] Camp meetings became most affixed to the quarterly conference and especially to the quarterly meeting held typically in late summer.[38] The conjunction extended what had long been a great two-day Methodist festivals and put a premium on the planning, preparation, attention to grounds and lay-out, provision for order and liturgical staging that guaranteed success. Camp meetings stylized the conference revival, established revival and conversions as an expectation and made what would otherwise have been an intra-Methodist and perhaps even intra-leadership occasion into a great annual public display.[39] Their promotion became a Methodist business and a central preoccupation of the person essential to any quarterly meeting, the presiding elder. So Asbury instructed Jacob Gruber, presiding elder in 1811 in the Baltimore Conference:

> Mr dear wrestling Jacob:
> Oh what manner of men we ought to be in labor, in patience, in courage, 6000 miles a year to ride, we to meet 8 conferences, you to hold camp-meetings, quartermeetings, give me the number, and nomination, number of people upon probability that attended, preachers present; and guess at the number connected. I rejoice that

campmeetings still prevail more or less, in all the states, provinces of Upper Canada, Tennessee, New York, Jersey, and Pennsylvania . . .

Doubtless, if the state and provinces hold 12 million, we congregate annually 3 if not 4 million in campmeetings! Campmeetings! The battle ax and weapon of war, it will break down walls of wickedness, part of hell, superstition, false doctrine, persecution ceased without but will rise within, of our selves. Will men arise to change and cripple the administration, men that want to be great without labor, and martyrdom in the glorious cause.[40]

Indeed, the quarterly camp meeting became, particularly in the summer, the work of that official. Of a presiding elder, 1808–12 on Muskingum district, Ohio, John F. Wright later observed:

The labors of the presiding elder were usually greater than any other preacher, because he had to be nearly all the time employed at camp meetings through the whole of the warm season. For months together, he almost literally lived in the woods in attending the numerous camp meetings on his district.[41]

The camp meeting then institutionalized conference as revival. And in the short run it preserved the revivalistic dimension of conference itself, because camp meetings so frequently were held in conjunction with conference and particularly quarterly meetings. In the long run, this institutionalization *and externalization* of conference's revivalistic dimension permitted conferences themselves to become less revivalistic. The changes that altered conference's revivalistic substance came slowly and piecemeal and in what seemed like Methodist interest. For instance, in 1804 General Conference legislated that quarterly conferences keep minutes,[42] an appropriate step toward responsible governance. By such legislation and by the imposition of procedures, offices and structures the informality, festivity and intensity of quarterly meeting would wane. And its disciplinary and political functions, always important, would increase. These, though, were future developments that turn of the century Methodists cannot be expected to have foreseen. It is curious nevertheless that they took the camp meeting so much to heart and saw no need to incorporate it into the body. It remained outside the polity and outside the *Discipline*.

Chapter 7

Safeguarding Methodist Polity

General Conference suffered no such exclusion. In sessions of 1800, 1804 and 1808, it acted to define itself and the church. Its political supremacy, as we have seen, was immediate and plenary. And as we have also seen, General Conference assumed care of the polity of the church. Illustrative of its exactitude in this was a motion placed in 1804:

> Brother G. Roberts moved, that this conference revise the Discipline of our Church, and that in revising it, it shall be read chapter by chapter, section by section, and paragraph by paragraph. Carried.[1]

Gone were the days in which Asbury and Coke could huddle with a hand-picked few to re-write Methodist polity. Polity and therefore politics would be now the business of General Conference. But it like the other levels of conference yielded other ideals—revival and fraternity in this case—unwillingly and gradually. We have already noted the revival associated with the General Conference of 1800. Preaching for the larger community and its revivification would continue to be a custom whenever and wherever Methodist preachers gathered. So General Conferences would feature such preaching. For 1808, Henry Boehm reported "much eloquent and powerful preaching," several conversions, but "no such scenes as occurred during the General Conference of 1800."[2] For 1812, Boehm confined himself entirely to the preaching, especially that of Asbury, excusing that focus with the remark, "I need not give an account of the doings of the General Conference, which the reader can find in the printed journals."[3] Methodists struggled also to sustain General Conference's fraternal character. The early secretaries (up through 1808) did their part by minuting actions by brother this or that. For instance, the 1808 *Journal* reads:

Thursday, May 12, 1808
   Brother M'Claskey and brother Cooper asked leave to withdraw the motion for seven additional bishops; which was refused.
   Brother George Pickering moved, and was seconded by brother

Joshua Soule, that the conference decide on the motion now before them, whether there shall be seven additional bishops or not. Carried.

    Brother Ostrander's motion for two additional bishops, being put to vote, was lost.

    Brother Roszel's motion, for one additional bishop, to be elected or ordained at this conference, being put to vote, was carried.[4]

Actions of this sort divided the fraternity. Fraternal feeling could not be sustained by salutations or minutes. Politically difficult questions, ones that raised emotions more than the above, proved as erosive of fraternity as of revival.

A Delegated General Conference

One such question vexing these early General Conferences was the matter of membership. "All in full connection" was a principle quickly threatened by expanding territory and an expanding ministry. It also put little premium on experience, wisdom, political savvy— the 'gifts' sometimes guaranteed by seniority or office.[5] In 1800, General Conference imposed a modest restriction, to those who "have travelled four years," cutting size and guaranteeing some maturity. That did not address an equally serious matter, the misrepresentation of the several conferences. In the next conference, for instance, the 112 present came primarily from those conferences close to Baltimore, the 'central conferences' one interpreter termed them:[6]

Philadelphia	41
Baltimore	29
Virginia	17
New York	12
South Carolina	5
New England	4
Western	4 [7]

As Lee conceded in 1810, "we had not a proportionable part of preachers, from each part of the connection."[8] A proposal in 1804 for a delegated general conference, an idea advanced some ten years earlier by Lee, received some attention but was decisively defeated.[9]

    In 1806, the New York Conference initiated legislation calling for a delegated annual conference, though in this instance a special called session, to deal specifically with a crisis in leadership occasioned by the death of Bishop Whatcoat and the loss of Coke to the European conferences.[10] Carried from annual conference to annual conference and pressed by Asbury, the measure passed also in the New England, South Carolina and Western conferences, but was blocked in Virginia, largely and ironically on the opposition of Lee as "pointedly in opposition to all the rules of our church," and "dangerous" though perhaps well-intentioned.[11]

Not to be deterred, New York passed a similar memorial with respect to the regular General Conference of 1808, calling for

> a representative or delegated General Conference, composed of a specific number on principles of equal representation from the several Annual Conferences . . . [as] much more conducive to the prosperity and general unity of the whole body, than the present indefinite and numerous body of ministers, collected together unequally from the various Conferences, to the great inconvenience of the ministry and injury of the work of God.[12]

The central conferences—Baltimore, Philadelphia and Virginia—apparently chose not to act on this memorial, but the other four concurred.[13] When General Conference convened, the conditions and inequities that prompted New York's memorial were manifest. The delegate list was again heavily imbalanced:

Philadelphia	32
Baltimore	31
Virginia	18
New York	19
South Carolina	11
New England	7
Western	11 [14]

When General Conference convened and despite the hesitance of the larger (and more fully represented annual conferences), it proceeded to take up the matter of delegation, empowered by a skillful maneuver on Asbury's part to establish a committee of two persons from each conference.[15] Out of this group, Joshua Soule, Ezekiel Cooper and Philip Bruce were commissioned to draft plans for a delegated general conference. Both Soule and Cooper produced legislation; Soule's was reported out, a multi-faceted proposal the initial points of which provided for delegation through elections; but Cooper continued to press for an agenda that might best be termed "fraternal," or decentralized. He wanted (in committee) one bishop for each conference and when that failed, moved in conference that presiding elders be made elective. Soule's plan for a delegated conference not only preserved the pattern of an itinerant general superintendency but provided for explicit limitations on General Conference's legislative power in several crucial areas, among them any alteration of the plan of an "itinerant general superintendency." Soule's draft, with this set of "Restrictive Rules" at its heart, came eventually to be regarded as the constitution of the church. From its introduction it was recognized as a critical turn in the denomination's history.

However, debate proceeded on the matter for several days. Cooper's motion functioned as a diversionary tactic. Jesse Lee attacking Soule's scheme from another angle, defending conference rights by insisting on representation through seniority rather than by election.[16] This formidable opposition initially held and a motion to adopt the first provision, that General Conference be composed of delegates, went down to defeat. All but one of the New England contingent and several from the Western Conference made plans to depart.[17] Asbury and his newly ordained episcopal colleague, William McKendree importuned the delegates to remain. The body also recognized the crisis and passed a reformulation, one delegate for every five annual conference members.[18] Yet another stratagem by Soule fully caved the opposition. Lee had earlier advocated delegation and Soule put a motion that by combining Lee's principles neutralized his opposition:

> Moved by Joshua Soule, and seconded by George Pickering, that each annual conference shall have the power of sending their proportionate number of members to the General Conference, either by seniority or choice, as they shall think best.[19]

The logjam broke and conference then proceeded by seriatim motion to enact the constitutional legislation for a delegated General Conference.

> Moved by Jesse Lee, and seconded by William Burke, that the next General Conference shall not change or alter any part or rule of our government, so as to do away episcopacy, or to destroy the plan of our itinerant general superintendency. Carried.
>
> Moved by Stephen G. Roszel, and seconded by George Pickering, that one of the superintendents preside in the General Conference; but in case of the absence of a superintendent, the Conference shall elect a president *pro tem*. Carried.
>
> Moved by Stephen G. Roszel, and seconded by Nelson Reed, that the General Conference shall have full powers to make rules and regulations for our Church, under the following restrictions, viz:—
>
> 1. The General Conference shall not revoke, alter, or change our articles of religion, nor establish any new standards or rules of doctrine, contrary to our present existing and established standards of doctrine. Carried.
>
> 2. They shall not allow of more than one representative for every five members of the annual conference, nor allow of a less number than one for every seven. Carried.
>
> 3. They shall not revoke or change the "General Rules of the United Societies." Carried.

4. They shall not do away the privileges of our ministers or preachers of trial by a committee, and of an appeal; neither shall they do away the privileges of our members of trial before the society, or by a committee, and of an appeal. Carried.

5. They shall not appropriate the produce of the Book Concern or of the Charter Fund to any purpose other than for the benefit of the travelling, supernumerary, superannuated, and worn-out preachers, their wives, widows, and children. Carried.

6. *Provided*, nevertheless, that upon the joint recommendations of all the annual conferences, then a majority of two-thirds of the General Conference succeeding shall suffice to alter any of the above restrictions. Carried.[20]

This legislation[21] gave episcopal Methodism its political form and it stamped General Conference as thereafter essentially political, as the forum within which the church would care for public and polity matters.[22] Its relation to revival and fraternity would henceforth be mediated. It would oversee Methodism's revival and it would do so on behalf of the fraternity of preachers. But it would do so as polity, as a delegated conference. Revival and fraternity would be located elsewhere in Methodism's conference structure. This future, an ironic one, was not what the preachers willed. They had acted—really both proponents and opponents had acted—on behalf of "fraternity." Advocates pressed for delegation and for definition of general conference's powers so that the preachers and conferences at a great distance from the site of a general conference would not have their fraternal and political rights diluted by their underrepresentation and the overrepresentation of the more central conferences. Opponents had worried that delegation would undercut the authority of the fraternity as a whole. Both hope and fear were well placed. Delegation circumscribed the plenary authority of the once (theoretically) plenary body. Tigert put his finger on the transformation. He said of the subsequent "delegated" conferences:

> This word indicates, not only that the members of these later bodies are elected representatives, or delegates, but that the Conference itself exercises delegated powers. It is an agent, not a principal. It is a dependent body, with derived powers. These powers are defined in a Constitution issuing from the body that ordained the Delegated Conference. Historically the fountain of authority in Episcopal Methodism is the body of traveling elders. They created the existing General Conference, ordained its Constitution, and finally admitted laymen to their seats in the body.[23]

Delegation made General Conference *the* political forum, the arena within which differences and disputes would be settled, and also the political prize. Thereafter, Methodism sent its leadership to General Conference. Election proved to be a highly significant and sought-after recognition. And, in addition, the delegates to General Conference would elect, typically from among their ranks, the bishops. The church has not been especially eager to recognize the political character of its life and the politicizing of General Conference. That oversight has served to obscure also the subtle but important changes that the politicizing of General Conference worked in the other levels of conference, but that is to anticipate the story.

Drawing Conference Color and Language Lines

The same General Conference cast the "fraternity" of annual conferences 'free' to deal separately with the matter of slavery.

> Moved by Stephen G. Roszel, and seconded by Thomas Ware, that the first two paragraphs of the section on slavery be retained in our Discipline; and that the General Conference authorize each annual conference to form their own regulations relative to buying and selling slaves. Carried.[24]

The action was but one step in the church's gradual retreat from its forthright Wesleyan anti-slavery stance[25] and from a racially open movement towards racially defined conference, society and class fellowships. It permitted southern conferences to embrace within their ranks the slave-holding preacher. It suggested little hope for inclusion of African Americans preachers within northern conferences.

On local levels, the color line was being sharply drawn, particularly in the North.[26] Black local deacons, among them Richard Allen and Daniel Coker, took charge of the African classes and congregations. Functioning restively under white elders, the African American leaders and congregations pressed for the prerogatives that would give them ecclesial legitimacy and standing.[27] Included in this agenda were full ordination as elders and conference membership. Initiatives already taken were later to be seen as the steps toward the formation of separate African Methodist denominations, but in 1808 the bonds had not been broken. The African deacons remained in the appointive system. Would the conferences concerned—Baltimore, Philadelphia and New York—and the bishop stabilize that membership by embracing as members and ordaining African Americans as elders? Within the decade the answer became clear to the congregations in Baltimore, Philadelphia, Wilmington and New York. They, then, took the necessary step of establishing their own conferences.

One such in 1816, brought together delegates from Philadelphia, Salem (NJ), Baltimore, and Attleborough (PA), an effort to unite African churches. The convention called itself the African Methodist Episcopal Church,[28] ordained Richard Allen as bishop, created two conferences, and structured itself along Methodist lines.[29] A similar break of fraternity was occurring in Wilmington (DE). The leader of the "African chapel" there, Peter Spencer, though apparently present at the AME conference threw his efforts into making his African Union Church an alternative denomination.[30] So also in New York, though a few years later, Black Methodists gravitated hesitatingly towards independence, their situation complicated by involvement with William Stillwell, an elder who led both blacks and whites out of the MEC. Eventually the black New York based movement stabilized as the African Methodist Episcopal Zion Church.[31]

So Methodism segregated by conference, indeed by totally separate denominational conference structures.[32] By these actions—black overtures for membership, white conference refusal, black initiative to establish separate conferences (churches)—conference fraternity drew the color line. This boundary, once drawn, would prove very difficult to erase. Slavery, anti-slavery and race would however continue to be conference issues.

Conferences drew other ethnic boundaries at this time, most notably that between German and English-speaking 'Methodists.'[33] Here, too, prejudice, disdain for other peoples, unwillingness to accommodate difference nullified initial efforts at unity and comity. Among the German Americans, William Otterbein and Martin Boehm exercised leadership for the scattered Reformed and Mennonite peoples. The early developments were quite distinct from the Methodists, roughly contemporaneous but stylistically similar, owing to shared Pietist principles. Otterbein convened other traveling preachers just prior to the Revolution, in a series of semiannual meetings held in and around Frederick (MD) and Baltimore. Again after the war—in 1789 and 1791—larger groups including Boehm and other Mennonites met. Both sets of gatherings concerned themselves with the order and discipline of German-speaking classes and congregations, tied together primarily by the bonds among their leadership. These bonds remained, however, highly informal; formal conference structures were not established.

During this period Otterbein, Boehm and others became familiar with the Methodists and the two groups recognized each other as kindred, a relationship symbolized by Otterbein's role in Asbury's ordination and Boehm's son's later extensive traveling with Asbury. In 1800, Otterbein and Boehm were elected bishops (or superintendents) in another conference in Frederick. Calling themselves the United Brethren in Christ, these thirteen or fourteen preachers, apparently at Asbury's urging, moved toward discipline along Methodist lines. They agreed, on a motion put by Otterbein, to have the Methodist *Discipline* translated into German. That translation came too late to be followed precisely; they had established patterns of structure and belief by 1808 when it appeared; Methodist influences operated more informally. Still, on both sides, efforts were made to bring the movements closer. Christian Newcomer, one of several, to assume leadership from Otterbein and Boehm, then in their 70s, indicated as early as 1803 eagerness for closer ties. The Baltimore Methodist Conference reciprocated, conveying through him a proposal for closer union and pressing for adoption of a Discipline to make that possible.

Fourteen letters exploring that possibility went between Baltimore (and Philadelphia) Conferences and the United Brethren. Methodists insisted on a Discipline as the basis for unity. Newcomer drafted one and had it printed in 1813, ironically just as the Methodists were giving up on negotiations. In his eagerness, Newcomer and the Eastern Annual Conference over which he presided had apparently not achieved assent to the new Discipline by the Miami Annual Conference.[34] The latter's opposition resulted in the calling of the first General Conference, thus giving this branch of the German Pietists a 'Methodist-like' conference structure.

Newcomer intended his Discipline to serve as a basis for union not only with the Methodists but also with the other Methodist-like German denomination, the Evangelical Association. The latter, a movement among Lutherans led by Jacob Albright, had perhaps even closer Methodists ties. In its first formal conference in 1807, it had called itself the "Newly-Formed Methodist Conference"[35] and charged Albright to draft articles of faith and a discipline. Like Otterbein and Boehm, Albright came to appreciate Methodist structure and discipline through German Pietist religious experience. Soon after his conversion, Albright was drawn by a neighbor and Methodist class-leader into active leadership among Methodists. As a class leader and then a licensed exhorter, Albright began itinerant preaching among German-speaking communities in Pennsylvania, Maryland and Virginia in the late 1790s. He apparently never broke formally with the Methodists but found it necessary to create structures to sustain himself and others who joined him in caring for the newly formed German classes and societies, an initiative necessitated by Asbury's distinterest in sustaining German-language work. At a conference in 1803, Albright was ordained and recognized as leader.[36] Unable after the 1807 conference (by age and health) to carry through on the mandate to prepare a discipline, Albright left that task to his associate George Miller. Miller took advantage of the translation into German of the Methodist *Discipline* (of 1804) and "compiled Articles of Faith and Discipline, partly out of the Word of God, and partly according to the Episcopal form of church government."[37]

The Discipline was adopted by the annual conference of 1809 by which time the movement was terming itself, "Those Designated as Albright's People."[38] Both Methodists and United Brethren made overtures for unity, some formal, some informal. Each wanted accord on its own terms. For instance, in 1810 John Dreisbach encountered Asbury and Martin Boehm's son Henry. Asbury entreated him to withdraw from Albright, "go with them to Baltimore to attend their Conference; there to join them, and to travel a year with Jacob Gruber, who was then presiding elder, for the purpose of better acquainting myself with the English language . . . that I might be able to preach, . . . both in German and English." Dreisbach counteroffered unity:

> "If you will give us German circuits, districts and conferences, we are willing to make your Church *ours*, be *one* people with you, and have one and the same Church government." "That cannot be—it would be inexpedient," was the bishop's reply.[39]

In 1813, the two German groups explored unity but disagreed on standards for conference membership.[40]

In 1816, a general conference met, and selected the name 'The Evangelical Association,' both acts symbolizing that this fraternity would go its own way. That conference also received an overture from the United Brethren, not the first nor the last efforts on the part of the two to seek unity. Delegations from the two denominations met the following year but failed on the same issues. Gestures toward unity would be made over the years but the conference fraternities proved difficult to unite.

Language, race, ethnicity, ecclesial ancestry, polity differences, creedal matters, separate episcopal leadership—proved to be 'good' reasons for separate organization. Conference as polity served to give ecclesial integrity to divisions within the Methodist fraternity, indeed to establish separate fraternities. Though separate, the several bodies shared the conference way of structuring the church. Quarterly, annual and general conferences defined space and time; deployed and changed itinerant's circuits; committed each movement to revivalistic expansion; and provided the structural grammar in terms of which new territory would be conquered. Each of these denominations saw their mission in continental terms.

Chapter 8

Conferencing the Continent

Beginning in 1796 when it established specific annual conference boundaries, General Conference appended the following proviso, initially to its demarcation of the Western Conference:

> *Provided*, That the bishops shall have authority to appoint other yearly conferences in the interval of the General Conference, if a sufficiency of new circuits be anywhere formed for that purpose.[1]

General Conference reiterated that proviso up to 1832.[2] By that point the pattern had been established; conferences would march west with overall American settlement; religious territories would emerge on the landscape much as political ones, indeed in advance of the latter. Evangelization, revival, was Methodism's business; the fraternity of preachers (conference) the primary agent; and therefore new conferences (polity) needed where revival had worked its wiles. So after reducing the number of conferences in the interest of communication, efficiency, fraternal authority, the preachers authorized their increase as the church exploded west, north and south. Six in 1796, seven in 1800, nine in 1812, eleven in 1816, twelve in 1820 along with three provisos, seventeen in 1824, twenty-two in 1832, twenty-nine in 1836.[3]

Conferences West

This was Methodism offering itself as a new opportunity for the continent, imprinting the Methodist design on the land, reordering time and space according to Methodist rhythms, re-creating the country.[4] Much of the drama occurred on the circuit level, as local preachers and itinerants blazed a Methodist path to isolated cabins and settlements. Asbury remarked on that drama when speaking to a western audience in the woods:

> "We followed you to the wilderness," said he, "when the earth was our only resting place, and the sky our canopy; when your own subsistence depended on the precarious success of the chase, and

73

consequently you had little to bestow on us. We sought not *yours* but *you*. And now show us the people who have no preacher, and whose language we understand, and we will send them one; yet, we will *send* them one: for the Methodist preachers are not militia, who will not cross the lines; they are regulars, and they must go."[5]

That penetration began a pattern that culminated with the formation of conference—settlement and lay witness, local preacher initiatives, formation of class(es), extension of existing circuits to incorporate them, visitation by the presiding elder or even the bishop, the division of the new area into a new circuit, quarterly meetings and annual conferences in the region, the establishment of a regional annual conference.[6] Knitting frontier folk into both church and society were the classes, quarterly meetings and camp meetings, continuing their function (in the movement west) of consolidating those gained into the Methodist orbit.[7] The Methodist economy and the conference system—with its balanced ideals of revival, fraternity and polity—functioned effectively to carry the Methodist message and mission west.[8] Methodist expansion is a familiar story and one touched on elsewhere in this volume.[9] Here we would simply underscore what the multiplication of conferences implies, namely that the church, having now given conferences specific geographical meaning, cared for expansion by cellular addition—new conferences—each of which would be a fraternity in its own right.

Conferences provided the structure and the grammar of the Methodist evangelical message. Conferences tied the classes, circuits, itinerants, local preachers, exhorters, presiding elders—the human resources of the Methodist missionary machine—into a coherent whole. So it was highly material whether the new conferences would be replicas of the old, would be tied together into the larger fraternity, would be part of a fraternal whole. In Methodist understanding, the fraternity enveloped the totality of conferences—so they had viewed the successive conferences in the Baltimore system as one, so they had experimented with a Council, so they created a General Conference, so they had pressed for reduction in the number of annual conferences, so they had struggled into formulation of a delegated General Conference. Methodism understood itself to be connectional. Connection sustained itself, of course, by the bishop or bishops, the itinerating general superintendents, as we note elsewhere. Connection was also maintained by General Conference, its power and authority then being stabilized. But connection also had depended on the sinews and bonds within the fraternity of preachers. How, as the church expanded, would the cohesion of the larger body be sustained? Would each conference go its own way? How would the fraternity stay one? Growth and multiplication posed important problems of cohesion, connection and communication.

The issue clearly concerned the conferences; so their minutes show. One way they cared for unity was through direct contact, either by sending emissaries or through missives. In 1805, for instance, the Western Conference took correspondence on as its first act of business:

> Resolved, that two Committees be appointed, the 1st a Committee of Address, consisting of three members. 2nd, A Committee of Appropriations, consisting of four members.

That conference then put the Committee of Address to heavy work, sending letters off in every direction: "to the several Quarterly Conferences," "to the several Annual Conferences," "to the Trustees of the Chartered Fund," "to the Brethren at Ebenezer," "to the absent members of the Conference," "to the General Book Stewards." The minutes also note the reception of addresses from Virginia, Baltimore, Philadelphia, New York and New England Conferences "which gave a summary statement of their temporal and spiritual concerns."[10]

The New England Conference met later than the Western, actually in 1806. It also gave correspondence serious attention.

> Dan'l Webb read letters from the Western, and South Carolina Conferences. Voted that Friday, the first of August next, be recommended to be observed as a day of fasting and prayer by the several societies within this Conf. Martin Ruter read a letter from Bishop Coke. Daniel Webb read a letter from the Baltimore, Philadel'a and New York Conferences to Bishop Coke. Voted that this Conf. approve of the alterations in the minutes propos'd by the Western Conf. Voted that the committee of address draught an answer to bishop Coke's circular letter.[11]

Here, the conferences wrestled with the offer by Thomas Coke, made through a multi-page circular letter, to commit himself to the American church.[12] The overture required the conferences to respond, in concert, and to do so between general conferences. By letter, courier and the good offices of the other bishops they did so, reaching consensus to reject his offer. In the next several years, conferences corresponded over the matter of delegation to General Conference, correspondence, as we have seen, that eventuated in its transformation into a delegated body. Such conference absorption with polity matters has been well observed.

These letters expressed concern over much more than polity, as the above should suggest. They touched the range of conference concerns—the various dimensions that we have summarized as revival, polity and fraternity. Conferences cared for the spiritual health of each other and the whole. The Western Conference's 1805 overtures to the other conferences called for collective fasting and prayer. They sent them in that spirit/Spirit. To that end, on the fifth day of their sitting, they resolved: "We have this day covenanted to pray for our brethren in the succeeding Conferences; especially in the time of their sitting."[13] The spirituality of each conference belonged to the whole fraternity and made the polity whole.

Of course, conferences nurtured the spiritual potential of their own gatherings. Conferences continued the practices that produced their revivalistic or spiritual quality. They provided for public preaching during their sitting. They met, at times, in conjunction with a camp meeting, a custom even more common for the quarterly meeting. Most importantly, they attended to the religious character and journey of one another, the probing and frankness protected by the closed conference doors.[14] Conferences continued to evoke spiritual narratives in less judicial personal fashion as well. The Western Conference in 1805 minuted that: "The Conference spent a few hours, this evening, in speaking of the work of God in their souls and Circuits."[15] In the 1807 New England Conference, "Mr. Asbury read several letters he had rec'd from the preachers, giving an account of the work of God." Later in the same conference, "Mr. Asbury read a letter from br. Chandler giving an acc't of the great revival in Delaware District—also a letter from br. Stith Mead giving an acc't of the work of God in Richmond District, Virginia." That conference then devoted time and attention to their own spiritual estate: "To close the present sitting an hour or two was spent in conversing on the state of the Lord's work among the people under our charge, and in our own souls."[16] These were the spontaneous spiritual exercises for preachers who believed "God's design in raising up the Preachers called *Methodists*," was "To reform the Continent, and to spread scriptural Holiness over these Lands."

This expansive mission, this spirituality, required order. Indeed, spirituality and order, the freedom Methodists found through conversion and the discipline to which they subjected themselves and others, represent two sides of the evangelical impulse, a point made suggestively by Daniel Walker Howe.[17] So conferences began to devote more exacting attention to their own political structure, to polity. Until the first decade of the 19th century, conferences depended on the questions of the Discipline for structure and procedure to their sessions. So in 1808, conferences attended closely to the following queries, minuted actions and reported the results:[18]

1. Who are admitted on trial?
2. Who remain on trial?
3. Who are admitted into full connexion?
4. Who are the deacons?
5. Who have been elected and ordained Elders this year?
6. Who are the Bishops and Superintendents?[19]
7. Who have located this year?
8. Who are the Supernumerary Preachers?
9. Who are the superannuated and worn-out Preachers?
10. Who have been expelled from the connexion this year?
11. Who have withdrawn from the connexion this year?
12. Were all the Preachers characters examined before the Conferences?
13. Who have died this year?
14. What numbers are in society?
15. Where are the preachers stationed this year?
16. When and where shall our next conferences be held?[20]

These questions continued, indeed continue to this day, to shape conference workings. So queried, conferences gave account of themselves by tables, lists, charts and graphs—a spiritual calculus for which Methodists have aptitude by heredity.

Committees and Rules

By the first decade of the century, conferences wanted more structure and procedure. Committees were established, charged typically with handling preacher's financial claims, business or communication.[21] Gradually the practice developed of constituting those in the organization of the conference. Around 1810 formal rules came in. This formalization took place on the populist edge of the movement, in the west, as early as it did in the east. For instance, by 1810 the Western Conference in organizing itself "proceeded to elect by Ballott a Committee of Appropriations" and "a Committee to adjust the book accounts.[22] On the second morning of the Western Conference's sitting:

> John Sale from the Committee of Appropriations haveing progressed in forming Rules for the Government of the Sittings of the Annual Conference Reported. The Conference Proceeded to receive the report Rule by Rule, on the final Reading the Conference Received the whole of the rules. . . .

Then followed 19 rules, governing parliamentary order and procedure, mandating the election of a secretary on organization, and covering the keeping, safeguarding and reporting of proceedings. The next year,

> The Chair called for the reading of the rules adopted for the Government of Conference while sitting.—The Secretary proceeded to read them. The Conference adopted sd. Rules without amendment.[23]

Other conferences moved to formalize their working, though not all did so in 1810. New England took this step only later in the decade.[24] The 1810 Western Conference also created a much more elaborate committee structure. In organizing, "A Committee of Appropriations," also charged as we have just seen to deal with rules, then "a Commitee to adjust the book accounts," later a special committee for person on trial accused of immorality, "a Committee of Review" (nominated by Asbury), another committee "in a case of delicacy," then two more such committees (the two identical in composition).[25]

By rules, committees and routinized behavior, conferences undertook the business of ministry. New roles emerged, leadership requirements changed, assignments increasingly went to expertise. The secretary, for instance, came to be an important and powerful position. He kept the memory, fashioned into coherent sentence and paragraph the torrent that flowed from these men of the word, sustained the agenda, gave mood and texture to the occasion—and did that one day so that it could be approved the next. The role has that potentiality in any organization. The special power in the Methodist conference secretary derived from two peculiarities of the system—the presiding officer, the bishop, was absentee and as the century wore on, was frequently rotated;[26] the secretary stayed in the conference, and more strikingly, stayed in the role and stayed in the role and stayed in the role. For instance, seven secretaries served the New England Conference for most of the 19th century—Ralph Williston 1800–03; Thomas Branch 1806–10; Daniel Fillmore from 1813–37, interrupted by a two-year interim for Martin Ruter and a year for Timothy Merritt; C. Adams 1842–52; W. R. Bagnall 1853–59; E. A. Manning 1860–89; and thereafter James Mudge 1889–1918. It was the secretary, Mudge himself noted, who knew the political complexion of the conference, who was who, how the body operated. The bishop depended upon the secretary.[27]

The business of conference had begun, but only begun, to take business form. As the century progressed, a complaint voiced by Bishop James O. Andrew in remarks to the Ohio Annual Conference would become more common: "Once an Annual Conference was a season of joy; a jubilee; but now they are a toil and burden. . . ."[28] Such commentary would increase toward the end of the century. Earlier Methodism was just the explosive, popular movement so well described by Nathan O. Hatch, Jon Butler and others. The spread of circuits, march of conferences west evidenced that.[29] But it is important to take note of the trends that would yield later bureaucratic structure and procedure. The trends begin early and are begun in the effort to carry out the church's evangelical mission. A history of Methodism makes the point in its title, *Organizing to Beat the Devil*.[30] The organizational and the spiritual impulse went hand-in-hand. Polity served revival; revival required polity; the conference fraternity kept the two together.

Chapter 9

Fraternity Versus Polity

Ideally, we have argued, Methodist principles cohered. Ideally the principled impulses that pulled in different directions remained in dynamic tension. Ideally authority (connection, superintendency, centrism, discipline, polity, conference, clergy) and freedom (Arminianism, populism, localism, initiative, pragmatism, fraternity, lay prerogatives) worked together for revival (conversion, holiness, testimony, education, concern for the neighbor). For the most part they did, both in the church's early decades and its movement west. However, from the first conference gatherings some have recognized one principle as controlling, preferred, most important.

Certainly from Rankin's superintendency, the fraternity of preachers and sometimes the people have stirred restively under the exercise of authority. Often that disquiet focussed on the bishop or bishops. We have already seen that in O'Kelly's democratic movement. The authority-freedom issue could also focus on conference, as it did in the African American quest for membership.

As the church grew, demographically and geographically, authority expanded naturally, inevitably, incrementally. It also became more diffuse, particularly after the death of Asbury in 1816. While he lived, Asbury was the bishop, no matter whether Coke or Whatcoat or McKendree also served. Asbury understood matters that way; the conferences knew that to be the case; the other bishops lived with it. He personalized authority, both in the sense of having it focussed upon his person and in the sense of exercising it in personal fashion. Not everyone remained happy under Asbury, but, with exceptions and crises we have noted, the church found his energetic, sacrificial, personal, exemplary episcopacy acceptable. He was the father of the church; he modeled what he expected of offspring; and the sons, for the most part, respected his paternity and example.[1]

At Asbury's death, McKendree, the first American-born to hold the office, a son of the west,[2] entered a new day of relations between authority and freedom and with him, so did the church. McKendree would lead by method, by rule, by law, a style symbolized by his proposing to Asbury to station preachers with the advice of a council

81

of presiding elders and his initiating, to the surprise and consternation of Asbury, an episcopal address to the General Conference of 1812,[3] an act of agenda-setting followed to this day. McKendree appropriately took such initiatives because under him and his successors, others would strive to put items on the church's agenda. Some matters focussed on episcopal prerogative, others on conference. Election of presiding elder's, inclusion of local preachers, lay representation, Canadian independence, abolition, anti-masonry—the issues were fought out in conference; would increasingly politicize conference, enhancing polity at the expense of both fraternity and revival; would divide conferences; would eventuate in new conferences (denominations).

The Election of Presiding Elders?

In the 1820s, controversy over the first three matters and particularly over the election of presiding elders divided the church. The office, which intruded into Methodist community at its most basic levels, proved an ideal lightning rod for tension between episcopacy and the fraternity, for built-up static over authority and its exercise. The presiding elder, Tigert argued, was "coeval with the Church itself." Already in the 1786 *Discipline* the elder's duties included

> To exercise within his own district, during the absence of the superintendents, all the powers invested in them for the government of our church.[4]

From legislation, which applied generically to elders, the church gradually elaborated two distinct offices, the traveling elder and the presiding elder, the latter first formally defined by rubric in the *Discipline*, in 1792.[5] Prior *Disciplines* (covering "elder" generically) provided for the constitution of an elder by election and laying on of hands. The 1792 *Discipline* created a distinct section, the first question of which read:

> *Quest.* 1. By whom are the presiding elders to be chosen?
> *Ans.* By the bishop.[6]

Thus the office became an extension of the episcopacy, indeed the extension of episcopacy into the affairs of every preacher and member. Great power was concentrated in a position that was simply appointive and into which there was no formal, elective or ceremonial passage.[7] The presiding elders were simply read out with all the other appointments and the individuals concerned would be subsequently appointed elsewhere. They never left the fraternity. But for the interim of their tenure in that office, they functioned within and as part of the episcopacy.

The ambiguity of the office made it controversial, perhaps from the start. Suspicions deepened and sensitivities heightened as the church internalized the republican or democratic ethos of the country, a process slowed but not stopped by the departure of and controversy with the Republican Methodists and invigorated by the war of 1812. Further, the preachers and conferences came to experience the presiding eldership differently as the church gradually formalized the office and gave geographical definition to conference boundaries, processes occurring simultaneously. Formalization, a part of that larger processes of routinization already explored, clarified the 'episcopal' authority to be exercised. But whereas the bishops were elected (initially) by conference and accountable to it, the presiding elders were neither elective nor accountable, reporting only to the bishop(s). The latter development did not alter the presiding eldership so much as it defined and confined the (conference) population within which these elders 'presided.' Preachers came to have membership in a specific annual conference; presiding elders would be appointed from that population; they would exercise authority over their 'brethren'; issues of power and authority, previously diffused by movement of preachers or whole circuits from conference to conference, were now bottled up within the conference. The presiding eldership became very much a conference issue.

Those who raised it, for instance Ezekiel Cooper and Jesse Lee in 1808, like William McKendree earlier, were leaders of the church. Proponents at the General Conference of 1812 included Lee and Nicholas Snethen, both of whom had traveled with Asbury and had exercised the office of presiding elder. In 1816, Nathan Bangs, whose star was then only rising but who would be every bit as luminous in the middle decades of the 19th century as Lee had been in the church's morn, offered a motion for election of presiding elders.[8] With Asbury though recently deceased very much there in spirit, the conference soundly defeated Bang's motion and a later motion interpreting election of presiding elders as not contrary to the constitution. It also rejected a petition by local preachers for representation, a matter to which we will return below.[9]

By 1820 when General Conference again assembled, the church had established Tract and Missionary societies, launched *The Methodist Magazine* and was showing greater seriousness about higher education—structural indications of engagement with the larger Protestant community on behalf of a Christian America. These alone did not earn

Methodists a place in the Protestant establishment. Entry required a fight and that also had begun, notably against the church's genteel critics, Calvinists and Episcopalians. Bangs led there as in the structural revolution with *The Errors of Hopkinsianism Detected and Refuted*, *The Reformer Reformed: or, A Second Part of the Errors of Hopkinsianism, Detected and Refuted*, *An Examination of the Doctrine of Predestination* and *A Vindication of Methodist Episcopacy*.[10] Further accommodation with slavery, adherence by middling and even upper class persons, flourishing women's organizations, improved church properties—the signs of respectability—increased. Deeper engagement with American society meant, of course, communication in its language. Dominant then in the American idiom were strains of republicanism. Republicanism heightened suspicion of authority and intensified democratic aspirations.[11]

In the episcopal address, McKendree both celebrated and worried over such 'progress.' In the same sentence, he acknowledged the "desirable intimacy which subsists among different denominations" but warned of "the danger of being injured by the influence of men—especially of men of the world professing religion. . . ." He called for more rigorous nurture so "the rising generation may be made early to see the danger and vanity of the wealth and splendor of the world, and to appreciate the dignity and happiness of true godliness and intellectual worth." And doubtless concerned that some of that worldliness might be present and voting, he reminded the conference that the 1808 conference had settled the constitutional issues. "It is presumed that no radical change can be made for the better at present."[12]

Undeterred by this admonition, Timothy Merritt of New England and Beverly Waugh of Maryland put the issue of an elective presiding eldership again before General Conference.[13] The proposal divided the bishops (William McKendree, ill but staying nearby the conference, Enoch George and Robert R. Roberts) as well as the body. George may have authored the proposal itself, as also a measure to reach compromise, a committee of six, three from each side of the issue.[14] While the committee conferred, General Conference elected Joshua Soule to the episcopacy. John Emory drafted a consensus document for the committee providing for episcopal nomination and conference election of presiding elders. General Conference passed the compromise (61 to 25). Soule, elected but not yet consecrated as bishop and the author of the 1808 'constitution,' then tendered his resignation in a stinging challenge to the constitutionality of the measure just passed. The letter, read by McKendree, in a rare appearance before the body, said:

> I was elected under the *constitution and government of the Methodist Episcopal Church UNIMPAIRED.* . . .
> *I solemnly declare, and could appeal to the Searcher of hearts for the sincerity of my intention, that I cannot act as Superintendent under the rules this day made and established by the General Conference.*[15]

McKendree submitted another letter, also pronouncing the legislation unconstitutional and himself "under no obligation to enforce or to enjoin it on others to do so."[16] These dramatic acts won the day and the conference subsequently accepted Soule's resignation and suspended the legislation until the next General Conference.[17]

To the subsequent round of annual conferences, McKendree submitted a letter setting forth his position on the unconstitutionality of elective presiding elders and asking that the annual conferences concur in that judgment.[18] Seven did, but the five northern and eastern conferences did not.[19] Other hands also conveyed the issue to wider audiences, notably the connection of 'reformers' who now created their own medium of expression, the *Wesleyan Repository and Religious Intelligencer*. Appearing first in April 1821 and edited by William Stockton, a New Jersey printer and lay member, the semi-monthly spoke on behalf of election of presiding elders, but also a constellation of reform measures. Included were rights of local preachers, lay representation, procedures in church trials, check on episcopal tyranny—in short, the reform of the church. Such advocacy involved risk, for the preachers under appointment; in consequence, articles appeared under pseudonyms.[20]

Nicholas Snethen, one of several spokespersons—former traveling companion of Asbury's, secretary of the 1800 General Conference, anti-slavery advocate, chaplain to the House of Representatives, and unsuccessful candidate for Congress—framed the reform cause in republican terms. In one early piece he identified himself as "one of those theorists, who conceives that the love of power is so general among men, that in any order of society, civil or religious, those who yield the principle of liberty will never want a master . . . "[21] An essay entitled "On Church Freedom," argued that "The very essence of church freedom, consists in having a voice personally, or by our representatives, in and over the laws by which we are to be governed, and in being judged by our peers."[22] So Snethen defended the liberties of the fraternity of preachers against encroachments by episcopacy, encroachments most effectively made through appointment of presiding elders and the 'constitution' of 1808.

> To conclude, the bishops of the Methodist Episcopal Church have unlimited executive power. In the choice and appointment of pre-

siding elders, and the formation of the districts, they possess the power of making the means and instruments of despotism. By the agency of presiding elders, they can manage and control the legislative and judicial departments. By the construction given to the enactments of the General Conference of 1808, the power of the bishops is not only put beyond the General Conference, but of eleven-twelfths of the annual conferences.[23]

Enlarging the Fraternity?

Snethen spoke not only on behalf of the fraternity of preachers but also for preachers outside the fraternity, the local preachers of which he had been one. Local preachers constituted a diverse but large population. Outnumbering the traveling preachers three to one, they, with class leaders, constituted, at this period, the mainstay of Methodist congregational or local ministry. The office itself derived from Wesley. It was exercised under the authority of the traveling preacher and quarterly conference. By 1796 the *Discipline* devoted a distinct paragraph to it. Ordination to deacon's orders had been legislated in 1789 and to elder's orders in 1812.[24] The office served as the entry into itinerancy for some, a permanent status for others, and the station to which traveling preachers resorted for family, health or financial reasons. The *Minutes* annually asked, "Who have located this year?" and then identified by name those who had left the 'traveling' fraternity.[25] Lee and Bangs cited the number each year, again sounding a somber note.[26] The General Conference Committee of Ways and Means reported in 1816 on loss to church through locations, of its experienced, trained and pious "ornaments."[27] Included among the ranks of this population, quite literally left out of the fraternity, were some of its brightest stars, persons who had exercised conference and national leadership. Many continued active ministries but were excluded from the associations, activities and authority of annual conference. Snethen was but one among this rank of the disenfranchised, of the fraternity outcasts.[28]

What was the church, what was the conference, to do with the gifted persons who remained in ministry, but did so outside the traveling ranks? The 1820 General Conference made a stab at the problem, providing district conferences for local preachers, transferring to it authority previously vested in the quarterly conference and giving it some of the character of an annual conference.[29] Separate and very unequal, this experiment was doomed, though lasting as disciplinary provision until 1836, when its functions and authority were restored to quarterly conference.

Snethen and the reformers wanted real incorporation into the political life of the denomination. He affirmed in 1823:

> When the power of the Methodist Episcopal Church was lodged exclusively in the hands of travelling preachers by themselves, their minds approached towards the state of those who believe themselves to be infallible. They did not, they could not look forward to consequences. . . . Was it foreseen that in process of time, there would arise in the Methodist church, a body of local preachers, numerically greater than the actual number of travelling ones? If so, was it anticipated that they should be deprived of all the honors and emoluments of office, and be wholly excluded from the legislative and executive departments? Be it so. And was it likewise foreseen that by this privation of all their rights and privileges, they would be *ipso facto*, ministerially degraded? . . . The power of an itinerant ministry has been the idol of the system. It is the end, not the means.[30]

The same political principles that pointed toward the rights of local preachers could be invoked on behalf of the laity. Ought they also to be included in annual conference? General Conference? Ought they to be involved in the body(ies) that acted legislatively on, for and over them? Snethen thought so.

> In several particulars it has been asserted by competent judges that our system is nearly allied to, if not identical with, Popery. Amongst these, the following deserve a particular notice:—1st. The popish clergy make laws for the laity without their consent.—So do the travelling preachers for the Methodist Episcopal Church. 2. The pastoral functions are all derived from the bishops, without whose authority or consent no flock can have a pastor.—So our travelling preachers and congregations depend upon our bishops, who have the sole power of all appointments. 3dly, The right of presentation to livings, which is sometimes in the bishops, or the governments, or the lay patrons, is wholly in our bishops. 4th. The generals or heads of the orders of friars or travelling monks, can send them where they please—so our bishops can send travelling preachers.[31]

So the agenda was expanded; so the ring fixed for yet another round, the General Conference of 1824. The larger political agenda that Snethen had set was not taken up. The issue of presiding elders could not be avoided. The last General Conference had suspended legislation and the annual conferences had dealt with its constitutionality.

Debate over the prerogatives and boundaries of the fraternity had divided the fraternity. Acrimony operated as Gresham's Law, politicizing conferences and pressing out fraternity and revival. One special quality of conference gatherings—at whatever level—had been their gravity, the spiritual weightiness of these constellations of preachers, brought together for a time away from time, for a time to be together.[32] Now the gravity pulled with political rather than spiritual force. There were to be no revivals associated with the General Conference of 1824. Indeed in the heat of controversy, the delegates may well have failed to observe Aldersgate Day.[33] Nor could fraternal relations be genuinely nourished. Bangs noted the suspicions that each side held for the other, observing that "it was this which sometimes gave an irritating poignancy to some of the remarks and arguments, and led to momentary interruptions of brotherly affection."[34] The General Conference of 1824 evidenced that process. It was a heated gathering and particularly heated over the suspended legislation. The decisive resolution interpreted the votes taken in the conferences:

> Whereas a majority of the Annual Conferences have judged the resolutions making presiding elders elective, and which were passed and then suspended at the last General Conference, unconstitutional; therefore
> Resolved, That the said resolutions are not of authority and shall not be carried into effect.[35]

The measure passed sixty-three to sixty-one. Similar split votes came on elections to the episcopacy, the constitutionalists putting in Soule and the reformers Elijah Hedding. Presiding elders would not be elected. Nor, at this stage, would laity or local preachers be brought into the assembly.[36]

The debate had exposed and reinforced significantly different Methodist self-understandings. The issue had been joined at a constitutional level and those that invoked the 1808 General Conference legislation in defense of an appointive presiding eldership repudiated appeals to democratic practice and the language of rights. The reformers made that appeal, explicitly and repeatedly, later renaming their journal *Mutual Rights* and proclaiming, "what scripture authority can you produce to authorise you to govern Americans otherwise than as free men?"[37] It was not the case, however, that one side used political appeals and the other did not. The notion of 'constitution' itself had unmistakable political overtones, particularly in a new nation then working out the meaning of its new constitution. The two sides functioned with different sets of political analogies, yielding quite different views of church and of conference. One spoke for responsibilities invoking Tory, court or Federalist principles on behalf of the connection (the fraternity as a whole) and episcopacy. The other appealed to rights and liberties invoking whiggish, country or Republican principles on behalf of a decentralized political structure in which power devolved from below and authority was vested in the 'fraternity' of annual conference.[38] Bangs grasped the difference as "two opposite views" of "the doctrine of responsibility."

> The former traced responsibility from the General Conference, who made the regulations and judged of episcopal acts, to the episcopacy, and thence down through the several grades of Church officers: the latter traced it up through the societies, to quarterly and annual conferences, to the General Conference. . . .[39]

The latter, it is generally recognized, had sanctioned (sanctified) American political principles for conference and church. The former did as well, but perhaps in less overt fashion. Both appeals, and the exchange between the two sides, made conference gatherings, both annual and general, very political affairs. And by politicizing conference, the contestants changed dramatically what both had wished only to preserve. Acculturation came as much by act as it did by advocacy.

The Methodist Protestants and Other Divisions

While General Conference met, a number of reformers, including seventeen members of General Conference, convened to constitute the Baltimore Union Society.[40] The new society acted to found a new periodical, *The Mutual Rights of Ministers and Members of the Methodist Episcopal Church*[41], the first issue of which appeared in August; to encourage the formation of other such societies "whose duty it shall be to disseminate the principles of a well balanced church government, and to correspond with each other"; and to draft and disseminate a circular setting forth these principles.[42] Snethen, Asa Shinn, Alexander McCaine and others voiced the reform cause, other union societies emerged, the agitation spread, the church plunged into confusion. The Baltimore annual conference, rent with the controversy, sought to suppress the movement. In 1827, it denied (by vote of conference) a member, Dennis B. Dorsey, an appointment for refusal to address questions about his involvement. Broadcasting that gesture, it then passed a motion of censure against members who circulate or support "any works defamatory of our Christian, and ministerial character, or in opposition to our Discipline and Church Government."[43]

At this juncture, Alexander McCaine fanned the flames with a blast on episcopacy, *History and Mystery of Methodist Episcopacy*, arguing that the present form of government was surreptitiously introduced; and that it was imposed upon the societies, under the sanction of Mr. Wesley's name."[44] Immediate responses came from John Emory,

Defence of "Our Fathers" and Thomas Bond, "An Appeal to the Methodists, in Opposition to the Changes Proposed in Their Church Government."[45]

Much of the debate to this point had been framed in terms of "rights"—rights of conference, rights of the preachers, rights of local preachers, rights of the laity—republican language implying that fraternity drew its rationale from democratic practice. That would continue, but McCaine reoriented the discussion to the nature, essence and origin of Methodism, specifically to church government as received from Wesley and found in the New Testament. This, too, was a republican ploy, a primitivist appeal to Anglo-Saxon liberties prior to the imposition of Norman tyranny. And McCaine prefaced his exposition with the warning to Methodists that their continued acquiescence in monarchy imperiled state as well as church:

> It is believed that a community living under the influence of such a form of government as that of the Methodist Episcopal Church, where the members are not permitted to participate in legislation, will sooner or later prefer a monarchical form of civil government to the pure republican institutions of our happy country. And it is desirable that the government should be revised and placed on such a foundation, that the rights of all our ministers and members shall be secured, and that posterity may be able to look back with veneration at the institutions of the church, as they shall have received them from their fathers.[46]

Here, McCaine got into view a more complex relation between the church and the social order, an interactive one, in which the church affected as well as was affected by society and in which the church's polity functioned to shape that of the state. That element of the argument alone made democratic church government more than capitulation to civil precedent.[47]

The appeal to the fathers also reoriented the question back onto ecclesial grounds. In fact, McCaine provided the warrant for a new ecclesiology. In the above citation, McCaine framed the matter as the responsibility of the church fathers, including himself and his compatriots, to their posterity. The volume as a whole impugned the responsibility and fidelity of their fathers, specifically Coke and Asbury, both now dead for only a little over a decade, the latter especially viewed as 'father.' And he challenged the faithfulness of Coke and Asbury to the unquestioned father of the faith, Wesley. Did Wesley intend and act to set up episcopal government? "Did Mr. Wesley, by appointing Dr. Coke a superintendent over the Methodist societies in America, intend to constitute him a bishop, and institute for those societies an episcopal form of government?" Was there, in fact, explicit Wesleyan counsel as the 1785 *Minutes* state, recommending *"the episcopal mode of church government?"*[48] McCaine argued not. The father in the faith had willed a fraternal not a monarchical church.

Emory thought differently. He undertook *A Defence of "Our Fathers,"* reviewed the early documents, events and conferences, and reached the opposite conclusion. Episcopacy was the original design. Throughout he impugned McCaine and his fraternity for the disrespect that they as sons had showed the father, Mr. Asbury, and concluded by observing that the rebellion of the sons had occurred literally over the father's grave:

> Have the Union Society of Baltimore forgotten that the remains of Bishop Asbury were disinterred, and removed from Virginia, and deposited in their city, as a place peculiarly dear to him? Have they forgotten the solemn rites with which, by the joint act of the General Conference, and of the Baltimore Society, they were placed under the pulpit of the Eutaw church, as in a sacred and chosen asylum, where his ashes might rest in honoured peace, under their affectionate and generous protection? With what feelings they could such of our brethren as may have sanctioned the publication of Mr. M'Caine's book stand in that very pulpit, over those ashes, to preach to those whom they know to hold the name of that venerable man in so much filial love and reverence?[49]

Bond shifted the defense to the character and quality of fraternity. His response to the reformers probed the effect the proposed changes, notably the inclusion of local preachers and laity, would have on the fraternity, on conference. He thought the reformers struck the very genius of Methodism, itinerancy itself and the principle of sacrifice inherent in it.

> This great and wonderful success, must then have been owing to the MISSIONARY character of our ministry,—a body of evangelical preachers, itinerating over the continent under the direction of a general superintendent, with power to distribute the labour as circumstances may require. To submit to such absolute direction, required on the part of the preachers great sacrifices of feeling, and incalculable privations of personal comfort. . . . He must rely implicitly on Providence and the bounty of his brethren, for his maintenance. The people on their part, in order to support this itinerant plan of ministerial labour, have consented to surrender the right of choosing their pastor, and permit these missionaries to make the regulations by which the whole Church, preachers and people, are to be governed in spiritual things—which, after all, amounts to no more than authority to enforce the moral discipline of the Bible. The whole system, in fact, is a system of sacrifices, made for the purpose of promoting the great interests of the Redeemer's kingdom. . . .[50]

Bond also objected to the localization of ministry implicit in the reformers' scheme. He appealed, as had McKendree and others, to changes which would damage a national fraternity and national itinerancy.[51] According to Bond,

> The regulations by which the whole Church is now governed, are made by those who have no local or fixed residence; they may be in Maine one year, and in Alabama or Missouri the next. They can therefore have no local preferences or partialities. Circulating through the whole connexion, they not only have a common interest and a common feeling with the members on each and every part of their pastoral charge, but they necessarily acquire a knowledge of the local circumstances and particular necessities of our member-ship, in the different sections of the United States.[52]

So Bond defended a national itinerancy—"the different conferences contribute to the supply of each other's necessities"[53]—, an ideal even then suffering erosion through the politicizing of conference, the church's growth and sectionalism.

He endeavored to show "that the attempt to introduce into our economy a lay and local representation will endanger the peace and harmony of the Church, and tend to loosen the bonds which have heretofore held us together and enabled us to do so much good in the world."[54] Bond only alluded to the spiritual gravity and intense interaction between and among the brothers while in conference. He dealt explicitly with the damage that might affect it. He pointed out difficulties in the representative principle among laity and local preachers.[55] And he feared the consequences of changes and agitation for changes on conference. Among the 'brothers,' "parties and cau-cuses will be formed, which will necessarily alienate their affections from each other; brotherly love no longer continuing, strife, and envy, and malice, evil-speaking, misrepresentation, and slander, will take the place of those fruits of the Spirit. . . ." He saw and foresaw the politicizing of conference, citing as evidence the positions, slander and misrepresentation in *Wesleyan Repository* and *Mutual Rights*.[56]

Damage to conference, politicizing of conference, came as much from Bond's side. Presiding elders in the Baltimore Conference levied charges and initiated trial proceedings against twenty-five laity and eleven local preachers, expelling the former and suspending the latter, Alexander McCaine included. The charges were

> 1st. Becoming a member of the Union Society. 2d. Directly or indirectly supporting the *Mutual Rights* . . . 3d. Approving the 'His-tory and Mystery' written by Alexander McCaine . . . [57]

In that climate, the union societies, now some twenty-four in number, met in a general convention (November of 1827).[58] The convention elected officers, established a committee of vigilance and correspondence, and drafted a memorial to General Conference. Early the next year, a quarterly conference confirmed the expulsions and suspensions. The Baltimore Conference followed suit, expelling two elders, Dennis Dorsey and William C. Poole and reproving James Sewell. The procedures were initiated as the character of each came up for review, juridical procedures intended to test the spiritual fitness and gift for ministry now turned to political use. Fraternity and revival were subsumed under polity.

The General Conference of 1828 declared the (suspended) presiding elder legislation void, dismissed the memorials from the reformers' convention (rejecting lay representation), confirmed the suspensions, and offered relief from these decisions only if the union societies were dissolved and *Mutual Rights* suspended.[59] Having faced this challenge to its polity and constitution, the conference also initiated the first amendment of the constitution, namely that of refining the procedure for amendment of the Restrictive Rules, substituting a majority of three-fourths of the members of annual conferences rather than all the conferences, and excepting the first, doctrinal restrictive rule. By this action, General Conference restored to the entire fraternity of preachers the decisive political and constitutional prerogative. To the entire connection, and not to the several annual conferences as constituted bodies, would future constitutional appeals be made. By the action, Tigert noted, "The Annual Conference rightfully ceased to be in any sense a constitutional unit."[60]

With expulsions continuing and new congregations forming, the second General Convention of Methodist Reformers met in Baltimore and laid plans for new conference, the formation of a new denomination. Articles of Association were adopted (to be worked into a *Discipline* two years later) which provided for equal lay and clergy representation in annual and general conferences and an elective presidency, but retained the "Articles of Religion, General Rules, Means of Grace, Moral Discipline, and Rites and Ceremonies in the main of the Methodist Episcopal Church."[61] The convention deputized agents, including Nicholas Snethen and Alexander McCaine, to travel on behalf of the cause. By the 1830 General Convention, they had organized twelve annual conferences. That convention, also in Baltimore, where the movement had its greatest strength,[62] ratified the new *Constitution and Discipline*,[63] elected as president Francis Waters (ordained but functioning as an educator), at his prompting chose the name The Methodist Protestant Church, appointed a book committee, and authorized the transformation of *Mutual Rights* into an official church weekly.[64] The new entity accomplished two of the three major Reformers' aims, an elective superintendency and lay representation; local preachers were not granted conference membership. The president would station preachers, though subject to revision by an annual conference committee.

In Methodist Protestantism, conference fraternity was enlarged. Its political authority vis-à-vis superintendency was defined and strengthened. Indeed, in Methodist Episcopal view, superintendency was destroyed.[65] But revival? In their several gatherings, the Reformers had taken care to provide amply for services, including nightly preaching (featuring Snethen). However, temperatures ran too high at these conventions, they were too devoted to polity, for revival to take place. No, revival would be the future test, the measure of the religious integrity, the scriptural character, the fidelity to Wesley of the systems, the polity of Methodist Protestants and Methodist Episcopals. Both sides would look at the numbers, at conversion, at revival to assess their own and the other side's faithfulness.[66] An appeal to the Spirit amid the contentions, fights over property and mutual recriminations that thereafter divided the once united fraternity.

Similar 'conference' breeches and similar recriminations had occurred in Charleston and environs with William Hammett's Primitive Methodist Church (the 1790s); the Reformed Methodist Church led by Pliny Brett, in the northern U.S. and Canada (the mid-1810s); the New York based movement led by William Stillwell (the early 1820s); and the English 'Primitive Methodists' a movement precipitated by the American Lorenzo Dow and then exported to the U.S (in 1829).[67] A less acrimonious but every bit as political a line was drawn between U.S. and Canadian Methodism. The 1828 General Conference acknowledged the desire on the part of "the brethren" in "the province of Upper Canada" to "organize themselves into a distinct Methodist Episcopal Church in friendly relations with the Methodist Episcopal Church in the United States" and established the procedures for amicable separation.[68] Less friendly would be another division of Methodism within the U.S.

Chapter 10

Zion Divided Again

The Methodist Protestant Church, though committed to liberty, took exception when it came to "colored members," denying them vote and membership in General Conference and permitting each annual conference to form its own rules "for the admission and government of coloured members within its district; and to make for them such terms of suffrage as the conferences respectively may deem proper."[1] The Church expressed its ambivalence in its Constitution with this qualification:

> But neither the General Conference nor any Annual Conference shall assume powers to interfere with the constitutional powers of the civil government or with the operations of the civil laws; yet nothing herein contained shall be so construed as to authorize or sanction anything inconsistent with the morality of the holy scriptures.[2]

Methodist ambivalence on slavery betokened its growing 'respectability,' the adherence to it in north and south of the propertied (and slaveholding) class, the church's coming to terms with culture, its concern for and investment in the social order.[3] Methodist Protestants, strong in what would become border states, evidenced the 'doubleness' of Methodist acculturation—adjustment to society's values, symbolized in acceptance of the slaveholder into communion and efforts to transform society, manifested in educational endeavor, particularly the founding of colleges.[4] The Methodist Episcopal Church showed the same pattern, finding other vehicles than anti-slavery for the gospel of social transformation and adopting with respect to slavery what Mathews terms strategies of 'compromise,' namely the mission to the slave and commitment to the American Colonization Society.

Sectional Crisis

Methodists participated in the revived antislavery of the 1830s, other dimensions of which we treat elsewhere. Here we would note how that controversy animated conference life. Two changes in Methodism made conferences particularly susceptible or hostile to the antislavery gospel. Of great importance were the media then available, newspapers and magazine, which we have already seen proved important in the spread of the Reformers' cause. In the Methodist Episcopal Church, one national paper, *Christian Advocate and Journal* (New York), competed with six regionals for Methodist Episcopal attention, the *Western Christian Advocate* (Cincinnati), *Zion's Herald* (Boston), the *Pittsburgh Christian Advocate*, and three southern papers—the *Southwestern Christian Advocate* (Nashville), the *Richmond Christian Advocate* and the *Southern Christian Advocate* (Charleston). The *Methodist Magazine* reached the ministers.[5] A second factor was the increased sectional character of the church, reflected in the clergy's deployment of themselves on a regional basis—the bishops' sectional itineration but also the transformation of the fraternity from a national to a conference affair.[6] Preachers, as we have seen, increasingly lived out their careers in a single conference; the *Minutes*, beginning in 1824, were structured on a conference by conference rather than unified basis;[7] the reward structure, including election to General Conference presupposed close annual conference ties and support; and General Conference came to structure itself in accordance with such regional patterns. The latter established committees "one from each annual conference."[8] As the church gave itself more sophisticated structure, it did so honoring region and representation, a formula for political activism. That would be ominously indicated in the provision in 1840 for ten standing committees, four to be representative: episcopacy, boundaries, itinerancy and *slavery*.[9]

Sectional media, sectional ministry and sectional episcopacy reinforced the powerful sectional currents at work among the people. The MEC divided along regional lines, in various ways, on various issues, including (already) the knotty constitutional problems posed by the Reformers.[10] Subsequent historiography has divided, essentially along sectional lines as well, as to whether the issues that would eventually divide the church were at bottom constitutional, ecclesial and theological *or* political, sectional, and ethical (over slavery and race).[11] In my judgment, race and slavery underlie the controversy and divisions, as well as the subsequent polemics/historiography. However, those who masked fundamental issues with constitutional, ecclesial and theological rhetoric believed what they said. And since those who spoke with such language sought thereafter to live within the ideational world they had built, we cannot afford simply to dismiss that rhetoric. The church divided over slavery. But in dividing and once divided, the church(es) lived out, in the several parts, the polemical positions taken. Ideology became important, even if, in the first instance, it served to mask racism and social self-interest.

The battles embroiled the papers and the conferences. In the New England Conference (MEC), converts to the abolitionist cause, notably La Roy Sunderland and Orange Scott used existing structures—camp meetings, quarterly conferences, rallies, letters, petitions and elections—to attack colonization, the church's acquiescence in slavery, and editors' suppression of antislavery.[12] A particular target was Nathan Bangs, editor of the *Christian Advocate* (New York) after 1834, who denied abolitionists access but in articles and editorials defended the status quo. In late 1834 Orange Scott, Shipley Wilson and others circulated "An Appeal on the Subject of Slavery Addressed to the Members of the New England and New Hampshire Conferences." The appeal charged that Bangs did "apologize for the crimes of the enslavers of the human species and attempt to justify the system;" positively it set forth the Methodist case against slavery, including a reprinting of Wesley's condemnation.[13] Orange Scott followed up the attack of the "Appeal" with a weekly column on "Slavery" that ran from January to April. Responses, criticisms and a counter-column prompted Scott *et al.* to publish the "Appeal" along with a "Defence of the 'Appeal'" as a *Zion's Herald . . . Extra.*[14] In May, a New England Wesleyan Anti-Slavery Society was established. In June, abolitionists gained six of the seven delegates to the following General Conference. They failed to pass antislavery resolutions, the questions not being put by the presiding bishop, Elijah Hedding, but did beat back motions of censure.

Hedding had a hand in a "Counter-Appeal" signed also by key members of the church's intelligentsia, including D. D. Whedon, professor and Wilbur Fisk, president of Wesleyan University and Abel Stevens. Hedding joined with Bishop John Emory in a pastoral letter to that conference (and also New Hampshire), published in the *Christian Advocate* further reprimanding the abolitionists.[15] Other conferences adhered more to the bishops' position and the subsequent General Conference, acted to muffle the antislavery cause.[16] Indeed, the conference censured two delegates for abolitionist activity. It issued a "Pastoral Address" which dealt with "abolitionism" at some length and exhorted the members and friends of the church "to abstain from all abolition movements and associations, and to refrain from patronizing any of their publications. . . ." The Address continued:

> From the most calm and dispassionate survey of the whole ground, we have come to the solemn conviction, that the only safe, Scriptural, and prudent way for us, both as ministers and as people, to take, is wholly to refrain from this agitating subject, which is now convulsing the country, and consequently the Church. . . .[17]

The bishops endeavored to see that the following annual conferences take this "safe, Scriptural, and prudent way," and suppressed abolition. The New York Conference welcomed this posture and condemned *Zion's Watchman*, launched the prior year by La Roy Sunderland, to "defend the discipline of the Methodist Episcopal Church against the SIN OF HOLDING AND TREATING THE HUMAN SPECIES AS PROPERTY."[18] The 1836 New England Conference followed suit, at least to the extent of charging Sunderland with slandering Nathan Bangs. However, it also created a committee on slavery and abolition. Hedding, who presided, using tactics of delay 'failed' to bring that committee's report up for action; in addition, he stripped Orange Scott of his presiding eldership and reassigned him to a church. In the next session, Hedding brought charges against both Sunderland and Scott; the bishop also denied that abolitionists had the right to introduce memorials or the committee to publish its report. Analogous to the suppression of petition and debate in the Congress, this episcopal stance gave to abolition a second cause, "conference rights." Thereafter Scott and another reformer, George Storrs, went from conference to conference (in the north) preaching abolition and raising the conference rights banner.[19] The bishops attempted to inhibit this abolitionizing and employed the annual review of the character of the preachers to press charges against those who 'agitated' the issue.

The church's papers generally followed the bishops' practice of muzzling the controversy, led in that cause by Nathan Bangs and the New York-based *Christian Advocate*. Abolitionist ferment, however, drew active response in Southern papers and conferences, where tacit acceptance of slavery turned into an explicit pro-slavery rationale.[20] In his prospectus (1837) for the *Southern Christian Advocate*, William Capers, the editor, noted that service to Methodists and Methodist adherents alone would be sufficient rationale,

> But considered in connexion with the feeling which is known to pervade all classes of men on the subject of our domestic institutions, it not only justifies our undertaking as one that is expedient, but strongly urges it as necessary to the Church.[21]

Conferences issued resolutions condemning abolition, denying that slavery was sin, and insisting that the institution ought, as a civil matter, to be beyond the church's attention. "It is the sense of the Georgia Annual Conference that slavery, as it exists in the United States, *is not a moral evil*."[22] The South Carolina Conference resolved to similar effect. Much of the church, including some of its strongest conferences, like Baltimore, found themselves torn between the two poles, fighting both explicit pro-slavery sentiment and abolition.[23]

Bishops saw fit not to muzzle these Southern defenses of slavery and attacks on abolition as their episcopal counterparts had muzzled the abolitionists. The problem was not slavery but abolition. In their address to the next (1840) General Conference, the bishops called to mind the Pastoral Address of 1836 and its counsel "to abstain from all abolition movements," but regretted "that we are compelled to say, that in some of the northern and eastern conferences, in contravention of your Christian and pastoral counsel, and of your best efforts to carry it into effect, the subject has been agitated in such forms, and in such a spirit as to disturb the peace of the Church."[24] That finding would hold for the next thirty years (at least), and for south as well as north, during which Methodist media and Methodist conferences found themselves politically animated by the moral crisis of slavery. We must not lose sight of the larger moral and social dimensions of this crisis. It divided the church—indeed, four divisions can be traced directly to it, those represented by the Wesleyan Methodist Church, the Methodist Episcopal Church , South, the Free Methodists and the Colored Methodist Episcopal Church. (To some extent other holiness movements also trace their concerns with the church back to this politicizing of it.)[25] And the church divisions prefigured, if they did not directly effect, the division of the nation.[26]

Without losing sight, then, of the larger contours of this crisis, we ought nevertheless to underscore its politicizing effect on conference. Proslavery and antislavery agitation and efforts to keep both out and struggles to maintain the unity of the church each increased the political aspect of conferences,[27] minimizing or eliminating those dimensions we have termed fraternity and revival. It did so in several ways, in both north and south, accelerating trends that the 1830s had set.

(1) Memorials, resolutions and legislation on slavery, elections of 'slates' to General Conference, trials and other 'political' use of the annual reviews made conferences into political forums and political forums seemingly persuaded and possessed of their own sovereignty. The bishops in their 1840 address identified the trajectory in characterizing their opposition:

> They maintain that all questions of law arising out of the business of our annual or quarterly conferences are to be, of right, settled by the decision of those bodies, either primarily by resolution, or finally by an appeal from the decision of the president: "that it is the prerogative of an annual conference to decide *what* business they will do and *when* they will do it:" that they have a constitutional right "to

discuss, in their official capacity, all moral subjects:" to investigate the official acts of other annual conferences—of the General Conference, and of the general superintendents, so far as to pass resolutions of disapprobation or approval on those acts.

The bishops argued that "The General Conference is the only legislative body recognized in our ecclesiastical system," the general superintendents elected by and responsible to it, annual conferences also its creature—whatever their number, "are all organized on the same plan, are all governed by the same laws and all have identically the same *rights, powers,* and *privileges.*" "These powers, and rights, and privileges," the bishops continued, "are not derived from themselves, but from the body which originated them."[28] It followed, then, that conferences could and should tend only to the business set for it by the *Discipline.* The bishops criticized northern abolition conferences and boasted of "the utmost harmony, and confidence, and affection" that had existed between superintendents and the majority of the conferences. However, their strictures, in fact, might as readily be applied generically to all the conferences which became politically consumed. "We are," the General Conference said in its 1840 Pastoral Address, "a voluntary association, organized, as we believe, according to the will of our Lord Jesus Christ, for purposes of a *purely spiritual* nature."[29] The business of conference was spirituality, some thought, and politics consumed it.[30]

(2) The bishops touched on a second dimension of the politicizing of conference, namely the way in which 'moral' passion or righteous indignation led conferences to judgments on other parts of the church and particularly on other annual conferences. That pattern was anticipated in the report of the Committee on Itinerancy at the 1840 General Conference. By resolution and amendment, it voiced what the conferences were saying about each other:

> The action of the Georgia conference, in declaring that slavery, as it now exists in these United States, is not a moral evil, contradicts the sense of the General Rule and the 10th section of the Discipline on that subject, and is, therefore, irregular.

> The New England conference, as has appeared to the Committee, have been, during the last four years, disorganizing in their proceedings; indeed, to have pursued a course destructive to the peace, harmony, and unity of the Church, in that,
> (1) They have gone beyond the proper jurisdiction of an annual conference; and, in doing so, have pronounced upon the characters of those brethren who were not at all responsible to them . . .[31]

In the face of such mutual animosity, those who cried 'unity and fraternity,' may have been most concerned to defend the status quo and slavery, as thought the abolitionists, but they did nevertheless point to a legitimate concern. The church was politically divided, politically partisan. Conferences had once sought fraternity within and through the connection. Fraternity had genuinely mattered and perhaps no more so than to Bangs, who closed his four volume history in 1840 and closed it with a listing of the entire Methodist fraternity, alphabetically arrayed, but grouped under each letter by the year they entered the connection.[32] Politics consumed fraternity as well.

(3) Tension between conferences and superintendents did not begin with, nor would it end after, the sectional crisis. However, the sectional crisis exposed another political division, that of (certain) conference(s) over against bishop(s), a division most acutely expressed, as we have seen, between Hedding and the New England Conference. The tension in Methodist ideals, the tension particularly between authority and freedom, intensified and in places the bond broke.

(4) Not new but intensified was a fourth dimension of politicization also criticized by the bishops, namely the heightened interest in the political or constitutional prerogatives of conference. Always a concern of General Conferences and intensified by the disputes that led to Methodist Protestantism, such political self-preoccupation was generalized to all the annual conferences and made acute by slavery and war. Methodist gravity pulled constitutionally.

(5) The preceding points suggest how the sectional crisis swept the church itself into political activity, turned internal church structures and processes to partisan use, developed the political dimensions of conference. The crisis also and obviously tuned the church into the political affairs of American society. This acculturation made less obvious and persuasive the bishops' plea that church government was "peculiarly constructed" and "widely different from our civil organization."[33] Again, each of the parties contributed to this embrace of society and culture—abolitionists by their involvement in and importation of anti-slavery tactic and gospel; conservatives, including the bishops, by their employment of the 'proven' strategy of compromise and concession to the south and suppression of northern activism; southerners by proposing exceptions to church precept against slavery thus permitting slave-holders to be ordained and preventing blacks from testifying in church trials where civil law proscribed manumission and 'colored' testimony.[34] In a richly symbolic gesture, the bishops refused to bring into General Conference a petition by Baltimore African American Methodists protesting this latter action.[35] Conference thus made its concession to culture, specifically the slave

culture. The distinction between Methodist space and time and that of the culture gradually collapsed.

(6) By riveting conference attention on the nation (U.S. and eventually Confederacy), the crisis brought Methodism to internalize a public or civil theology, the belief in a Christian America, a peculiarly Calvinist conception of the state as itself the bearer of redemptive and ecclesial purpose. The southern version of that differed markedly from the northern, but constituted no less a civil religion.[36] About both, and this new creation into which Methodists plunged, more later.

In the 1840 General Conference, southerners won the key battles. Conservative hands were placed at the helm of the northern papers, Thomas Bond over the *Christian Advocate*, Abel Stevens over *Zion's Herald*, and Charles Elliott over the *Western Christian Advocate*.[37] Conceding defeat and its message, "The M. E. Church, is not only a slaveholding, but a slavery defending, Church," Orange Scott and Jotham Horton withdrew, the first stage in the formation of yet another Methodist body, the Wesleyan Methodist Connection.[38] The movement viewed itself as it titled its paper, *True Wesleyan*; it pledged in its organizing convention at Utica in 1843 to uphold Wesleyan principles on slavery; and it committed itself specifically to holiness.[39]

These "come-outers" continued to appeal to and recruit among northern Methodists with sympathies for the slave, solicitations that ironically had more transforming effect on the Methodist Episcopal conferences from outside than it had had from inside. Northern conferences increasingly claimed their antislavery heritage, passing resolutions to that effect in preparation for the 1844 General Conference. "Whole conferences," reported Abel Stevens, "which once rejected antislavery resolutions now sustain them with scarce a dissent, and it cannot be doubted that soon, very soon, all our northern conferences will be of one mind on the subject."[40] Southern conferences and papers intensified their defenses, proclaimed slavery to be no moral evil, insisted that the institution itself lay beyond the church's purview, proposed the election of a slaveholding bishop, and prepared for division, should that be necessary.[41] The General Conference of 1844 would be war.

Is Conference "The Sun in Our Orderly & Beautiful System"?[42]

Each division had yielded fresh nuances in Methodism's understanding of itself and of conference, nuances institutionalized in movements each of which claimed fidelity to the Wesleyan standard.

Certainly, 1844 would prove no exception.[43] The questions posed by
slavery were quite fundamental: the nature of sin, the relation of the
church to the social and political orders, the 'real' meaning of church
membership, constraints to be placed on office holding for classes of
people (African Americans),[44] the nature and unity of the ministerial
fraternity, the relation of episcopacy and conference, the location of
sovereignty, the exercise of authority. The church put the questions
to itself, in memorials and petitions which poured in to General
Conference from conference and quarterly meeting. The presentation of them went on for two weeks, as day after day, the roll call of
annual conferences dramatized the concern of the church (north):

> [May 4, New Hampshire] C. D. Cahoon presented . . . memori-
> als, on the subject of slavery, from Claremont and Athens, which
> were referred to the Committee on Slavery. Also a memorial of the
> New Hampshire Conference on slavery, which document he asked
> to have read. A. B. Longstreet moved to dispense with the reading.
> This motion was lost; and the document was then read, and referred
> to the Committee on Slavery. Also certain resolutions of the New-
> Hampshire Conference, on the appointment of slaveholders to the
> office of Missionary Secretary, or missionaries, under the direction
> of the Parent Board, which were read and referred to the Committee
> on Slavery. Also resolutions on the subject of coloured testimony:
> read and referred to the same committee.[45]

Particularly striking were the concurrences in resolutions which had
gone, annual conference to annual conference, testing for common
conference resolve:

> [May 4] Black River Conference.—G. Baker presented six reso-
> lutions of this Conference: 1. On the Genesee Conference resolution
> on slavery; 2. On the New-York Conference resolution on temper-
> ance; 3. On the New-York Conference resolution on slavery; 4. On
> the New-Jersey Conference resolution on the trial of local preachers;
> 5. Asking the General Conference to rescind the resolution upon
> coloured testimony; 6. Asking the General Conference to define the
> "evil of slavery."[46]

The fraternity in annual conferences acted in concert, albeit on a
regional basis. The new fraternal consensus showed itself in tactics
and leadership. At this General Conference, the conservative middle
and particularly the Baltimore Conference, not the abolitionists and
New Englanders, would tackle slavery, the result apparently of a deal
struck between the parties just prior to conference.[47] The gathered
representatives showed immediately a dramatic shift.

Indeed, the first slavery resolution prompted a motion to establish
a committee "to be constituted by one member from each Annual

Conference," a proposal that Capers and the south met by attempting "to lay this on the table," hoping that "the motion would not be entertained."[48] The south suffered the first of a series of defeats.[49] Another came over an appeal from the Baltimore Conference by Francis A. Harding, who "had been suspended from his ministerial standing for refusing to manumit certain slaves which came into his possession by his marriage."[50] That action foreshadowed the decision that would be made in the case of Bishop James O. Andrew, whom the Conference knew to be in the same situation and whose entanglement in slavery compromised the church's symbol of itself, its principle, and its unity—a superintendency, genuinely itinerant, really general.[51]

Both south and north looked forward, some with dread, to the test: a bishop elected when not entangled with slavery, now by marriage and bequest a slaveholder, and prohibited by Georgia law from manumission.[52] To forestall impending division, Capers moved and Stephen Olin, president of Wesleyan University, seconded the establishment of a committee to draft a plan "for the permanent pacification of the church." Olin, a centrist who had served and enjoyed following in both south and north, urged unity and conciliation and asked the conference to suspend "our duties for one day, and devote it to fasting and prayer, that God might help us if he would, that if we have not union we might have peace."[53] With others, he wanted to preserve the fraternity and was later reported to have whispered: "Brother A., I would gladly lay my head upon the block this very day to save the union of the Methodist Episcopal Church."[54] Olin represented a dying species, a member of the fraternity who had itinerated nationally, in both north and south. The question at hand was, Could Andrew do so as well? Would he be accepted in northern conferences? Neither pacification nor prayers proved able to stave off the problems posed by a slaveholding bishop.

Andrew had come to General Conference prepared to resign, had so indicated to southern delegates, but had been formally overtured to desist.[55] The Committee on Episcopacy, to which the matter had been referred, reported out the facts of the situation, prompting a motion requesting his resignation.[56] After heated exchanges, Ohio delegates proposed a substitute:

> Whereas, the Discipline of our Church forbids the doing anything calculated to destroy our itinerant general superintendency, and whereas Bishop Andrew has become connected with slavery by marriage and otherwise, and this act having drawn after it circumstances which in the estimation of the General Conference will greatly embarrass the exercise of the office as an itinerant General

Superintendent, if not in some places entirely prevent it; therefore,

> *Resolved*, That it is the sense of this General Conference that he desist from the exercise of this office so long as this impediment remains.[57]

This framing of the issue permitted constitutional questions to subsume moral and political ones. James Finley, one of the movers, put the constitutional question baldly:

> This General Conference is restricted against doing anything which will destroy our itinerant general superintendency. This principle must be conceded. That Bishop Andrew has become connected with the great evil of slavery, he himself has declared on this floor. . . . This fact will not be denied; and that this connection with slavery has drawn after it circumstances that will embarrass his exercising the office of an itinerant general superintendent, if not in some places entirely prevent it. . . . Hence, the question follows, Will this General Conference permit one of its vital and constitutional principles to be broken down and trampled under foot, because one of her general officers has seen fit to involve himself in circumstances which will trammel that office in more than half of all the field of his labour?[58]

"There ought," argued L. L. Hamline, "to be two questions before us. First. *Has the General Conference constitutional authority to pass this resolution? Second. Is it proper or fitting that we should do it?*"[59] Addressing himself to the first, Hamline insisted that conference indeed possessed the authority to remove a bishop "for anything unfitting that office, or that renders its exercise unwholesome to the Church."

> This conference is the sun in our orderly and beautify system. Look into the Discipline. First you have our "articles of religion," in which God appears. What is next in order? The General Conference, which, like the orb of day, rises to shed light on the surrounding scene. It is first shaped or fashioned, and then, like Adam by his Maker, is endowed with dominion, and made imperial in its relations; and saving the slight reservations of the constitution, is all-controlling in its influence. Let it never be lost sight of, that the General Conference is "the *sun of our system.*"[60]

Others vehemently disagreed. William Winans argued:

> Properly speaking, the General Conference, as such, possesses not a particle of original administrative power. All the administrative power it does possess is conferred upon it by its own action in another capacity. It is purely a creature having delegated attributes, and none others. What are these delegated powers? They are few, and exceedingly simple. Where are they found? Where every Methodist ought to look, in the book of Discipline. . . . God forbid that the

majority of this conference should be invested with plenary power
to be used at will! [Amen, Amen.][61]

Concurring, Bishop Soule focused the constitutional issue on his
office and his person:

> I wish to say, explicitly, that if the superintendents are only to be
> regarded as the officers of the General Conference of the Methodist
> Episcopal Church, and consequently as officers of the Methodist
> Episcopal Church liable to be deposed at will by a simple majority
> of this body without a form of trial, no obligation existing growing
> out of the constitution and laws of the Church, even to assign cause
> wherefore—I say, if this doctrine be a correct one, everything I have
> to say hereafter is powerless and falls to the ground. . . . I desire to
> understand my landmarks as a bishop of the Methodist Episcopal
> Church—not the bishop of the General Conference, not the bishop
> of any annual conference. I thought that the constitution of the
> Church—I thought that its laws and regulations—I thought that the
> many solemn vows of ordination the parchment which I hold under
> the signatures of the departed dead—I thought that these had
> defined my landmarks—I thought that these had prescribed my
> duties—I thought that these had marked out my course.[62]

The constitutional framing of the issue[63] would prove to have
long-term significance in both regions (churches), serving to resolve
into political philosophy the host of issues posed by racism and slavery.
That was, however, the way the fraternity experienced the issue, when
so gathered, as a fraternal crisis of principle, unity and authority.[64]
This had not been the first time nor would it be the last when having
the fraternity of preachers constitute the government of the church
would permit ecclesial matters to be resolved into fraternal ones and
pose thereby problems for the church.[65]

Division

After over a week of intense debate, the other four bishops
submitted a letter proposing that the matter concerning Andrew be
held over till the next General Conference, arguing that a decision
"whether affirmatively or negatively, will most extensively disturb the
peace and harmony of that widely-extended brotherhood which has
so effectively operated for good in the United States of America and
elsewhere during the last sixty years, in the development of a system
of active energy, of which union has always been a main element."[66]
The New Englanders thought fraternity need no longer be bought at
the price of slavery, gathered the delegates of those conferences,
agreed to "secede in a body, and invite Bishop Hedding to preside

over them,"[67] and conveyed that resolve to Hedding. Hedding then withdrew his signature from the bishops' initiative,[68] effectively collapsing what Tigert concluded was the only "hope of harmonizing the difficulties of the Conference."[69] The motion "to desist" then passed.

On the next business day Capers offered resolutions to divide the church,[70] which were referred to a committee of nine. Two days later, the south offered an interpretive resolution:

> A. B. Longstreet, in behalf of the delegations from the Southern and South-western Conferences, presented the following declaration, which was read:
> The delegates of the Conferences in the slaveholding states take leave to *declare* to the General Conference of the Methodist Episcopal Church, that the continued agitation on the subject of slavery and abolition in a portion of the church; the frequent action on that subject in the General Conference; and especially the extra-judicial proceedings against Bishop Andrew, which resulted, on Saturday last, in the virtual suspension of him from his office as Superintendent must produce a state of things in the South which renders a continuance of the jurisdiction of this General Conference over these Conferences inconsistent with the success of the ministry in the slaveholding states.[71]

That was followed by the submission of a carefully worded "Protest" that reiterated and refined the position that the southern delegates had moved towards in their debate.[72] It set forth understandings of the impending division, of the nature of the church, of slavery, of episcopacy, and of conference that would define and characterize the southern church. Among those points was the insistence that "the episcopacy is a co-ordinate branch, the executive department proper of the church."[73]

As if timed so as to accent the emerging northern understanding of general conference supremacy, the following day, the Committee on Slavery reported resolutions rescinding the proscription in church trials of testimony by "persons of colour," stipulating that no slaveholding bishop be elected, urging that Conference take measure "entirely to separate slavery from the church," but proposing no change in the General Rules on slavery.[74] The fuller and also carefully honed northern understanding of conference and episcopacy came in "The Reply to the Protest."[75]

The Committee of Nine on the Division of the Church followed the design outlined by Capers and reported plans for an amicable division of the church. It provided for measures to assure peaceful delineation of a boundary between the church and to divide property. A key provision, an enabling constitutional revision of one of the

restrictive articles, required three-fourths majorities in annual conferences—assured that the debates and concerns of General Conference
would become those of the following annual conferences.[76]

> Dr. Bond . . . understood the intention of the committee to be to
> provide for peace, and love, and harmony still to be perpetuated in
> the great Methodist family. . . . Why then . . . if the object is to
> procure peace and to prevent conflicts—why, then, does it provide
> for a border warfare from Delaware to the Ohio River?[77]

The resolutions nevertheless passed. After adjournment, the delegates from the slaveholding states met,[78] called a Convention to be
held in Louisville, May 1, 1845, for the annual conferences "within
the slaveholding States," and issued an explanatory Address "To the
Ministers and Members of the Methodist Episcopal Church, in the
Slaveholding States and Territories."[79] Methodist conference would
now define a new relationship to the American landscape, a new vision
of itself as new creation. Conference would take regional form, a
fraternity of place (and race), its boundaries drawn by slavery and
attitudes held thereunto.

Chapter 11

Fratricide and Business

The separation proposed is *not* schism, it is *not* secession. It is a State or family, separating into two different States of families, by mutual consent. As the 'Methodist Episcopal Church' will be found North of the dividing line, so the 'Methodist Episcopal Church' will be found South of the same line.[1]

The annual conferences, north and south, which followed confirmed the predictions of Bond and Cartwright. They set off the first volleys in what would be a war, section against section, conference against conference, church against church. 'Family' Methodism may have been; family disputes can be bitter; this one would sunder "our beloved Zion."[2] Indeed, some conferences already saw "Zion" as sectionally delimited. So spoke Mississippi of "the injury . . . inflicted upon our beloved Zion by the intemperate and unjust denunciation of the *whole North*."[3] A Methodism that once would conference the continent now divided the people of God into a northern and southern kingdom. A Methodism that once had viewed its purposes in eschatological and biblical terms now reduced Zion to its own tribal ends and contested borders. Judah and Israel looked each to its own interest.

The 'tribal' squabble also continued the transformation of conference, heightening its political and legislative potentialities and making conference 'fraternity' and 'revival' difficult. Further, the division north and south both accentuated and revealed the organizational revolution within Methodism, the drift of conference at all levels away from revival, the shattering of fraternity, the increased preoccupation with matters of politics, polity, prerogative.

The Political Conference

The Kentucky Conference, the first in the south to meet after separation, set the pattern by establishing a committee of division, condemning the actions of General Conference[4] and approving the holding of the Louisville Convention. So the conference structured and choreographed itself for politics.[5] North Carolina meeting with

Bishop Soule as president, took action to make itself politically expressive. It amended the rules so that "any members of the church who may be invited by the members shall be permitted to be present as spectators during our sessions" and then drafted a pastoral address which it adopted, ordered published in the *Richmond Christian Advocate*; and required to be read by the pastors "at every appointment."[6] Other conferences in the slaveholding states followed suit with formal expressions of disapproval over the 1844 General Conference, the establishment of committees on separation or division, approval of the convention, passage of the amendment to the sixth Restrictive rule that would permit the division of property, and provision for dissemination of actions. Such initiatives were taken without dissent, according to Bishop Soule.[7] Dissent nevertheless flowed from their actions.

The southern conferences gave expression to their resentments against the 1844 General Conference in resolutions, pastoral letters and especially in a torrent of editorial remark, portraying the (northern) majority as repressive, acting illegally, motivated by abolitionism.[8] The editors of the northern papers (*Zion's Herald*, the (New York) *Christian Advocate and Journal*, the *Western Christian Advocate*, the *Pittsburgh Christian Advocate* and the *Northern Advocate* entered counter-criticisms.[9] The first MEC conferences to meet voted before this *Advocate* warfare was felt and acted favorably on the key constitutional issue in the division of the church, the amendment of the sixth Restrictive Rule, so as to permit proportional division of the Book Concern and the Chartered Fund. New York, which met June 12th, passed the constitutional amendment 143 to 38. Providence, which met next in early July, did so unanimously.

By August when North Ohio met, MEC resentment was building and that conference defeated the amendment, as did most of the following conferences. Ohio voted 132 to 1 against the change. These conferences also put their judgments before the public. North Ohio affirmed:

> The Methodist Episcopal Church in these United States, having always been considered a unit, can not, it is believed, be divided into separate and distinct organizations, unless it be by a secession of one party, in which case the portion seceding would thereby disfranchise itself of the rights and privileges of the Methodist Episcopal Church.[10]

Illinois resolved:

> (1) That we do not concur in the resolution of the late General conference to alter the sixth Restrictive Rule. . . .

(2) That we do not concur in, but strongly deprecate and oppose, any sectional division of, or separation from, the Methodist Episcopal Church,. . . .

(4) That a copy of these resolutions be forwarded to the *Western Christian Advocate*, by the secretary, for publication, with a request that all the General conference papers copy.

(5) That each of the bishops be furnished with a copy of the foregoing resolutions, and be requested to lay them before the several annual conferences at their next sessions.[11]

Ohio expressed pain over "the *politico-religious* aspect which the question of division has assumed at the south."[12] In truth, MEC (northern) conferences assumed an equal, if not more intense, *politico-religious* aspect. Ohio, in fact, found itself initially chaired by Bishop Joshua Soule, on an invitation tendered by Bishop L. L. Hamline, to the very Soule who with James O. Andrew had already pledged allegiance to the southern conferences. Such presidency Ohio voted "inexpedient and highly improper"[13] and forced Soule from the chair.

Conferences, north and south, roiled with politics. And each controversial act seemed to stimulate others. The property issue alone, defeated by the votes of the northern conferences festered for years, drawing attention from conferences as well as *Advocates*. Even its resolution ten years later, by the Supreme Court, did not end the comment.

And the boundary issue excited conferences, particularly the border conferences, from 1844 to the Civil War and beyond. The Louisville Convention had proceeded with calm deliberation to carry out the will of the several southern conferences, voting

> That it is right, expedient, and necessary to erect the Annual Conferences represented in this Convention, into a distinct ecclesiastical connexion, separate from the jurisdiction of the General Conference of the Methodist Episcopal Church, as at present constituted. . . .[14]

The Convention then took action to implement the Plan of Separation, action calculated to insure further politicization of conference:

> Resolved, That this Convention request the Bishops, presiding at the ensuing session of the border Conferences of the Methodist Episcopal Church, *South*, to incorporate into the aforesaid Conferences any societies or stations adjoining the line of division, provided such societies or stations, by a majority of the members, according to the provisions of separation adopted by the late General Conference, request such an arrangement.[15]

Existing conference boundaries and the line drawn thereby between the MEC and MECS did not circumscribe sentiments and loyalties. The boundaries crossed state lines; the northern conferences encompassed slave-holding areas; some anti-slavery sentiment existed in southern conferences, notably in Kentucky; itinerants and presiding elders enjoyed close relations with circuits and congregations cut off by the new lines. Who counted and who got counted when elections were held? If no vote had been taken, to which church could adherence be presumed? How long did such voting go on? Could small segments of a circuit go their own way? And was the boundary to be construed as the line as originally set or the line as redrawn by subsequent acts of re-alignment?[16] Conference lines which had been drawn and redrawn many times now took on great significance. Border conferences especially developed a territorial imperative. And for land, conferences squared off against one another. Especially affected were the Delmarva Peninsula, western Virginia, Kentucky, Ohio and Missouri.

In the border skirmishes that ensued, each side attempted to claim and consolidate within its borders the congregations and circuits that, in its judgment, it should have by right, by prior possession, by family relation, by convictions. Each side saw the other's comparable actions as illicit. Each side accused the other of deceit, intrigue and misconduct. Philadelphia (MEC) believed itself not a border conference, thought having land (the Baltimore Conference, MEC) and water (the Chesapeake) between it and the MECS would save it from incursions, but found boundaries with the MECS on the Delmarva difficult to hold. On the peninsula, Virginia (MECS) preachers excited congregations with the information that the MEC were abolitionists and gained adherents. In response, the Philadelphia Conference devoted much effort and a "Pastoral Address . . . to the Societies . . . of the Northampton and Accomac Circuits."[17] The Baltimore Conference viewed Virginia (MECS) efforts in Westmoreland, King George, Lancaster and Warrenton in similar fashion.[18] Ohio thought illegal the MECS efforts in Cincinnati and especially on the Kanawha district, actually in Virginia, but some 75 miles from the border and separated by five circuits from the MECS territory.[19] A few areas in Kentucky toyed with adherence to the MEC but stayed with the MECS. Intense conflict ensued in Missouri.[20] Such warfare turned conference membership—for ministers and people—from fraternal and missional into political and 'military' purposes.

Perhaps fittingly the 1848 MEC General Conference, after having received fraternal delegations from the British and Canadian Methodists and returned their fraternal expressions, pointedly rebuffed a similar expression from the MECS. Lovick Pierce had presented its

"Christian salutations," seeking "warm, confiding, and brotherly, fraternal relation" and expecting acceptance "in the same spirit of brotherly love and kindness." Instead, the MEC noting the "serious questions and difficulties existing between the two bodies" did not "consider it proper, at present, to enter into fraternal relations with the Methodist Episcopal Church, South." Pierce responded that his communication was "final on the part of the M.E. Church, South."

> She can never renew the offer of fraternal relations between the two great bodies of Wesleyan Methodists in the United States. But the proposition can be renewed at any time, either now or hereafter by the M.E. Church. [21]

The General Conference also undid the work of 1844. It declared that the constitutional amendment had failed. Under the guidance of a Committee on the State of the Church, the conference repudiated, declared "null and void," the Plan of Separation, judging that the General Conference (1844) could not legally divide the church.[22] And General Conference authorized the formation of a Western Virginia Conference, a stake on territory also claimed by the MEC or so asserted the MECS bishops in their address to the following MECS General Conference (1850).[23] In response, the southern church also organized a West Virginia Conference.[24] Conference 'fraternity' indeed took on a sectional, political aspect.

On the eve of secession and during the Civil War, conference politicization intensified. In the late 1850s, the Genesee Conference found itself embroiled in controversy over slavery, holiness, choirs, pew rent, secret societies—all touchstones for accommodation to the social order.[25] The conference divided itself politically between "Nazarites" who called for return to the fraternal, revivalistic old standards and those they characterized as "New School Methodists" or the "Buffalo Regency." Forced from editorships and from pulpits, the critics founded their own paper, *The Northern Independent*, held laymen's conventions, garnered support for ousted ministers and in 1860 founded the Free Methodist Church.

To stem defections, the MEC General Conference passed in 1860 a "new chapter" on slavery explicitly declaring that "the buying, selling, or holding of human beings, to be used as chattels, is contrary to the laws of God and nature."[26] Border conferences meeting thereafter were deluged with petitions and resolutions calling for its repeal. Some, like Philadelphia acted to demand repeal and then directed "the printing in tract form of 5,000 copies of the report of the Committee on the State of the Church"; and its publication in the

Christian Advocate and Journal, the *Methodist*, and the *Baltimore Christian Advocate*.[27] Others, like Baltimore, experienced actual formal division (see further discussion on the Baltimore action below) or the breaking away of preachers and congregations. Politics hovered over conference activities and conferences ordered themselves (or disordered themselves) for politics.[28]

Secession and war brought similar political disruption in the MECS. And during the war, conferences passed patriotic resolutions, administered oaths to themselves and their probationers,[29] brought the flag into their sessions, encouraged the war effort and Methodist participation therein, supported chaplains, demanded stronger national action on slavery and denounced the secessionists.[30] Southern conferences, perhaps somewhat more circumspect in their declarations, were no less politicized by the events, particularly after Bishop Edward Ames secured from Secretary of War Stanton a directive ordering officers to turn over to the MEC churches belonging to the MECS "in which a loyal minister, who has been appointed by a loyal Bishop of said Church does not officiate."[31] Would the MECS simply cave in to a northern take-over? Ministers and laity in the Missouri conference gathered in 1865 and issued a declaration of independence.

> *Resolved*, That we consider the maintenance of our separate and distinct ecclesiastical organization as of paramount importance and our imperative duty.

This Palmyra Manifesto went on to ground continuation of the MECS on "our Church doctrines and discipline" and on opposition to "the prostitution of the pulpit to political purposes."[32] So was sounded an anti-political political creed, a refrain that would politicize the MECS and its conferences under the guise of eliminating politics from the church, a refrain that established purity (southern) by contrast to prostitution (northern).[33]

> Preach Christ and him crucified. Do not preach politics. You have no commission to preach politics. . . .[34]

And the politically fervid atmosphere of southern conferences continued into Reconstruction sustaining (or criticizing) MEC efforts on behalf of the freed slaves. In this new warfare between the churches for souls to save and organize, the fights to establish borders and claim constituency gradually extended from the border states proper to the entire nation. Northern conferences in southern territory and southern in northern made for a continuous state of warfare.

"End of the Spiritual Part"?

In the 1830s and 1840s, before politicization had 'possessed' conference, the Disciplines of Methodism had set forth conference boundaries, detailed the work of its societies and set forth policies in a major section entitled "The Temporal Economy." For several decades a single line floated by itself, considerably down the page from the very end of the prior section. It said simply "End of the Spiritual Part." Fittingly, the line disappeared after the 1844 Discipline.[35]

Easily lost sight of, amid the sectional strife, nation-wide controversy over slavery, warfare and reconstruction were the dramatic changes, slow but gradual, affecting Methodism from below. Gradual shifts in practice, as well as sectionalism and politicization, fundamentally altered conference 'fraternity and revival.' Illustrating those shifts best perhaps was quarterly conference.

Some appreciated the change that had affected quarterly meetings (conferences). The Orange Scott, who bedeviled Bishop Hedding with resolutions and lectured the church on slavery[36] through *Zion's Herald*, alongside those very political columns, took note of atrophy of quarterly meeting:

> The fame of our Quarterly meetings in former times, has come down to us from the fathers,—some of whom still remain with us, though many have fallen asleep. These meetings make a part of our economy; and they used to excite a great interest among the people.
>
> Twenty-five or thirty years ago, it was not uncommon for our brethren to go *thirty* and even *forty* miles to attend a Quarterly Meeting. But now, since our circuits are made so small that they are held in almost every neighborhood, there are many not disposed to attend them.[37]

The bishops touched on the same point in 1844. They complained as well that the emergence of the station and erosion of the circuit gave quarterly meeting conferences "scarcely . . . an existence except in name . . . " and sought the recovery of the institution, so that

> Members of the Church, as in former days of Methodism, would come together from the different appointments to improve their spiritual state, and strengthen their Christian fellowship, by mutual attendance on the means of grace, and by religious intercourse in conversation and prayer.[38]

Why the loss of this means of 'revival'? The same address complained of that engine that slowly changed quarterly meeting as it changed Methodism, the 'stationing' of the itinerant. The bishops averred that

> There is a strong and increasing tendency to locality in our traveling ministry. Preachers with local views, and habits, and interests, have greatly multiplied on our hands; and in some of the Conferences little or nothing remains of the itinerant system, but the removal of the preachers once in two years from one station to another. . . ."[39]

Both itinerancy and quarterly conferences yielded to "locality," to the settling of the itinerant into stations and to the reduction of circuit gatherings into station oversight.

Ironically, as quarterly meeting waned as a dramatic circuit event in the Methodist calendar, it acquired more definite *Disciplinary* salience and status. At the next (1846, 1848) General Conferences, the MEC and MECS brought the several duties of the quarterly meeting together and gave the institution its own section in the *Discipline*.[40] By such recasting of the *Discipline*, General Conferences did not and probably could not define away the non-administrative, revivalistic and fraternal dimensions. But nor could they sustain those dimensions. Increasingly, administration had simply displaced fraternity and revival. Or to put it differently, fraternity and revival found other expressions and other vehicles than conference. In particular, Sunday schools increasingly took over purposes of nurturing piety that class meeting, love feast and quarterly meetings had exercised[41] and in their own way Sunday schools knit local Methodists into larger networks. So also the missionary, Bible and benevolence societies served fraternity and revival in the locale and connected Methodists in common cause. And camp meetings, once the setting for quarterly meetings underwent a gradual metamorphosis into summer vacation assemblies, a trend that would culminate in the Chautauquas. Protracted meetings and the annual revival within a station or charge compensated for the change in camp and quarterly meetings. However, such changes dissociated 'fraternity and revival' from conference and, until the church found a place for the initiatives within the polity, made them extra, without clear organizational standing. And quarterly conference was left with 'business.' The Free Methodists quite correctly noted that Methodism had changed. In giving quarterly conferences more business to do, assigning more responsibilities and reports and oversight to it, dedicating a separate Disciplinary section to quarterly conference, the MEC also appropriately recognized the trend.

The extrusion of revival from conference had a tribal aspect to it as well and one not unrelated to the transformation of circuits into respectable congregations. Who could and should share a pew? Conferences, quarterly conferences and congregations increasingly would not extend grace indiscriminately but embrace only their own.

The 1844 General Conference established the Indian Mission Conference, capitalizing on several decades of efforts with Native Americans.[42] The bishops that year also proposed the creation of a "German Missionary Conference,"[43] recognizing the fruits of a decade of effective mission work with the German Americans and conference did make provision for presiding elders' districts.[44] The 1856 General Conference (MEC) set aside separate German districts and the 1864 General Conference established German annual conferences (a conference that also segregated African Americans into separate annual conferences).

Racial segregation and the exclusion of African Americans from leadership were old patterns. The sectional crisis just gave racism fresh structural expression. The MECS in its first general conference (1846) dealt with African Americans through its Committee on Missions. The committee proposed and conference adopted a ten point plan for the mission to the slave, endorsing missionary efforts where circuits did not embrace the Black population but prescribing separate sittings when African Americans remained in a congregation, galleries for buildings, accommodations "at the back of the stand, or pulpit" in camp meetings, distinct class meetings for *oral* catechetical instruction—with all efforts to be reported to quarterly conference.[45]

And the MEC, with the end of the Civil War and the abolition of slavery in sight, acted to segment African Americans into separate districts. The 1864 Philadelphia Conference passed such a resolution calling for the bishops and presiding elders to organize "our colored people into district Circuits . . . with a view of furnishing them with ministerial service by preachers of their own color." General Conference authorized the bishops

> to organize among our colored ministers, for the benefit of our colored members and population, Mission Conferences—one or more—where in their godly judgment the exigencies of the work may demand it. . . .[46]

As a result, Delaware and Washington Conferences were established.

The next year the Philadelphia Conference acknowledged, with little sign that fraternity had been broken, that such separation had been achieved. It would become far more exercised about the division of the white churches and preachers into two conferences.[47] The southern church proceeded in the same direction, though motivated by northern and AME/AMEZ missions among the 'freedmen,' and participated in the release of congregations and properties and the ordinations that would set up the Colored Methodist Episcopal Church.[48]

Quarterly conferences had once embraced the people called Methodist and given structural and dramatic expression (albeit imperfectly) to an egalitarian gospel. Now distinct peoples were structurally differentiated and made the objects of missionary attention. And insofar as quarterly conference extended over different peoples it did so to monitor and administer and control.

Lay Conferencing

In quarterly meetings as well as annual conferences, politics also triumphed over fraternity and revival, especially in the south and on the border. Quarterly conferences were one of the many bodies whose sessions were given over to resolution or decision-making on the sectional issues. And they were, at this point, the official structure within the episcopal churches through which the laity could speak. So the North Carolina Conference appealed to "the reports of quarterly meeting conferences and numerous voluntary meetings" in setting forth "the mind of our people and preachers" on division. South Carolina spoke also of "proceedings of numerous quarterly conference, and other meetings" and Alabama "views expressed . . . both in *primary meetings* and quarterly conferences.[49]

Quarterly conferences did permit laity a voice. Laity had things to say about the fundamental social issues on which the church was then speaking. As conferences increasingly embroiled themselves politically and spoke on national questions, the laity felt restive at having their opinions and influence confined to quarterly conference. So in episcopal Methodism the issue that had animated Methodist Protestants resurfaced, lay representation. A politicized episcopal Meth-odism faced but defeated resolutions for lay representation, the MEC in 1852 and the MECS in 1854. The issue would return, necessitated by the increasing 'locality' of quarterly conference and the divisive issues before the church. The controversy in the Genesee Conference had widened to division through the holding of a succession of Laymen's Conventions, the first in 1858, the second in 1859, the third in 1860, each of them functioning politically. They issued resolutions, circulated petitions, gathered money, organized "Bands." In 1859 a Ministers' and Laymen's Union was formed within the New York Conference, a body dedicated to preserving the status quo on the slavery issue within the MEC. In response, a rival Anti-Slavery group of the New York East Conference, also ministers and laity, pressed for change.

In 1860, Baltimore Conference laity at a camp meeting at Loudoun took matters into their own hands.[50] They called a laymen's conference for December. Other lay or public meetings followed, each expressing itself, often with resolutions on the sectional crisis and recent (MEC) General Conference actions. An important laymen's convention sat concurrently with the annual conference of 1861 at Staunton and nudged it into an act of secession. The first item of business for this annual conference was the memorial from the "Convention of Laymen which assembled in Baltimore in December last, relating to the action on Slavery by the General Conference . . . 1861." Conference also took up memorials from Light Street, Alexandria and Frankford Circuit. On the 10th day, after testy sessions with presiding Bishop Levi Scott, the conference put and passed a motion protesting an 1860 General Conference action on slavery (the New Chapter) (1) as unconstitutional, (2) as breaking the organic law of the constitution of the church, (3) as destroying the unity of the church, (4) as false, heterodox and unscriptural, (5) as mis-interpreting the existing rules on slavery, (6) as a bar to reception of members, ordination of deacons, and ordination of bishops. The conference then acted to break with the MEC:

> 1st. Be it resolved by the Baltimore Annual Conference, in Conference assembled, *That we hereby declare that the General Conference . . . by its unconstitutional action has sundered the ecclesiastical relation which has hitherto bound us together* as one Church, so far as any act of theirs could do so. *That we will not longer submit to the jurisdiction of said General Conference but hereby declare ourselves separate and independent of it*, still claiming to be, notwithstanding, an integral part of the Methodist Episcopal Church.[51]

The next (1862) Baltimore annual conference met in Baltimore rather than in Virginia, that is outside of the Confederacy, and recognized the actions of the previous conference as an act of severance and those not present as withdrawing.

This annual conference entertained but voted down lay delegation, 34 against 22.[52] It had seen the power of lay initiative. So had the southerners. The MECS approved lay representation in 1866. Laity belonged in politicized and business-like conferences that legislated on social issues and stated the church's position and set policy for the whole. And with the collapse of quarterly meeting into station or small circuit, laity demanded a role on more effective conference levels, that is annual and general. The MEC conceded the issue in 1872 but only on the general conference level. Women's rights to representation and ordination lay ahead. Quarterly meeting without revival and annual conference without fraternity but business and politics galore!

Chapter 12

Self-Preoccupation and Ceremony

In the period before and after the Civil War, conferences began to show a more intense self-preoccupation, a preoccupation indicated in procedure and structure, in how they preserved and presented their sittings, and in how they opened.

This self-awareness, which the 1846 MECS "Pastoral Address" noticed as attaching "too much importance to mere matters of form and ecclesiastical arrangement,"[1] derived from several trends. Among them the MECS might have recognized the sectional crisis itself, which induced self-preoccupation by politicizing conferences, by making rules, procedure and structure critical to legislative effectiveness, particularly when presiding bishops resisted conference initiatives. Parties to controversy demanded to be on the record. Accordingly, conferences began to publish their minutes, the Philadelphia Conference in 1838, several of the New England conferences in 1841 and the General Conference in 1844. In that year both the Journal of 1840 and that of 1844 were "Published by Order of the Conference."[2] Partisanship focused attention on the political entity, in this instance on conference.

Self-awareness was not, however, derived from or borne only by parliamentary and political procedure. Self-awareness took liturgical, rhetorical, historical form. And these new conference gestures gave fresh expression to the instincts we have termed revival and fraternity. Indeed, annual conferences which seemingly had driven out revival and sacrificed fraternity, now cultivated religiosity and celebrated fraternity.

Conference Self-Awareness

Conference awareness had many roots, respectability, perhaps being one of the most important. Methodists, especially in the east and in towns and cities, increasingly drew middle class adherents and consequently took their place within society, built more commodious churches, and even experimented (in places) with such un-Methodist institutions as pew-rents and choirs. Methodists participated more in common evangelical Protestant efforts to Christianize society and joined with others in voluntary associations. Both class factors and committee participation fostered Methodist appropriation of the organizational innovations then beginning to revolutionize American society. Among them, the American way prescribed the running of meetings according to procedure and organization by committee.

Such prescription Methodist conferences followed. They opened with elaborate organizational rituals—establishing rules, appointing committees, electing officers, commissioning studies, scheduling reports—then moved on to the Disciplinary questions.[3] The 1853 Baltimore Conference organized itself with "Rules for the Government of the Conference," an elaborate transaction requiring four sections and setting forth the duties of president, secretary, and members, and "Promiscuous Rules." Two bishops were present, Beverly Waugh and Thomas Morris, Morris presiding. The conference appointed the following committees—stewards, necessitous cases, missions, affairs of Dickinson College, colonization, seminaries, memoirs, sabbath schools, Bible cause, temperance, periodicals, post offices, to receive missionary money, tract causes, and Metropolitan Church. Its work included the traditional tasks outlined by the disciplinary questions but also included the hearing and action on reports of committees. Its accomplishments required elaborate statistics.[4]

Conference increasingly ran by reports. For instance, the New England Conference in 1845 heard reports from the following: Committee on Sabbath Schools, Committee on Tract Distribution, Committee on Benevolent Operations, Committee on Peace, Committee on Preachers' Aid Society.[5] And financial reporting no longer covered simply quarterage and the Book Concern. Conferences had to find ways of managing and supporting the institutions Methodists were creating. The same New England Conference sought to calendar its "Benevolent Operations" with a resolution specifying collections dates:

> Bible—2nd S. Aug.
> Sabbath School Union (MEC)—Sept.
> Biblical Institute—2nd. S. Oct.
> Preachers' Aid—2nd. in Dec.
> Missionary cause—last S. Feb.
> Wesleyan Education Society—1st S. April.[6]

Two years later the New England Conference found a way of giving a spatial as well as temporal definition to its monetary concerns. The minutes organized collections in tabular form, in five columns—Bible Society, Missions, Preachers' Aid Society, Sunday School Union,

N.E. Education Society—and thereby graphed the contributions from stations and circuits for the above causes (respectively):

Boston Bennett, Street	$14.00	110.12	25.29	6.50	9.10
Lynn Common	$13.28	150.50	43.61	4.17	5.00 [7]

In another two years, in 1849, New England arrayed its financial statistics on fold out pages (two pages), by district and charge. The first page summarized by columns the following: quarterage, house-rent, traveling expenses, fuel, table expenses, total, receipts and deficiencies; the second page also by columns summarized collections for Sabbath School Union, American Bible Society, Chapel Fund, Preachers' Aid Society, Missionary Society, Biblical Institute, Wesleyan Education Society.[8]

Missions assumed importance in conference activities and commitments, so especially did education, including the conference course of study, collegiate education and increasingly theological education. These educational concerns loomed large in the life of the conference and conference loomed large in these educational institutions.[9] Illustrative was the North Carolina Conference, newly formed in 1838, which devoted much of each session in early years to its various educational ventures. In its first session, for instance, it "recommended the publication of Wesley's Christian Library"; passed legislation on Leasburg Academy, (1) recommending "this School to the patronage of our people," and (2) appointing a committee of trustees "to cooperate with the existing board in the supervision of the School;" requested that the bishop appoint an agent for the school; took action extending similar "patronage" to the Clemmonsville Academy, appointing "5 individuals to be elected as trustees by the present board," and charging the Salisbury presiding elder with the "duty of having the property of said academy properly secured to the trustees appointed from this Conference;" instructed "the committee on the Leasburg and Clemmonsville Academies . . . to report suitable persons to be elected as trustees of those academies;" acted on the nominations of those trustees; took similar action in structuring itself, authorizing, staffing for and pursuing incorporation and land for a Greensboro Female Collegiate Institute;" and dealt in similar fashion with Randolph-Macon College which, as a former part of the Virginia Conference, it continued in relation to.[10]

Education consumed substantial attention in the 1859 Baltimore Conference. It had divided itself the prior year into the East Baltimore and Baltimore conferences and resolved to keep the meeting times separate. Why? for educational purposes, to permit "the President of

Dickinson College to represent the interests of that Institution at both of these Conferences." Of the thirteen standing committees, the following dealt with education: "Affairs of Dickinson College," "Seminaries," (then secondary not post-collegiate-theological institutions), "To Receive Money for Education Board." The "Seminary" report called attention to nine institutions—several beyond the bounds of the conference—and asked for the appointment of visitors to Wesleyan Female Institute, Staunton, Olin and Preston Institute, Blacksburg, Valley Female Institute, Winchester, and Baltimore Female College.[11]

Despite good intentions and in some cases the combined support of several conferences, many of the educational ventures failed. It is not our purpose here to assess the effectiveness of such efforts so much as to acknowledge that education constituted another claim on conference activity that riveted its attention inward, on its own affairs, on administration and finances, on making its structures work.

Minutes reflected this greater conference self-absorption. Conferences increasingly became aware of their own minutes, of their safe-keeping and of their dissemination. In the 1840s[12] and especially in the 1850s, they began to publish their own and not content themselves with the succinct form that went into the yearly general *Minutes of the Annual Conferences.*[13] (The MECS conferences apparently did not publish their minutes regularly until after the Civil War.)[14] Frequently, these early versions did little more than record special actions and reproduce the summations given in answer to the Disciplinary questions:

1. What Preachers are admitted?
2. Who remain on trial?
3. Who are admitted on trial?
etc.

Gradually conferences converted to the "minute" form, recording their actions for both participants and the Methodist membership.

In 1851, the New England Conference diverted from both the minute form and the historic pattern of reporting under the Disciplinary questions. It restructured its minutes into chapters, the first of which served as a summary or digest of the workings of conference. It began with an address to the reader.

> Will the readers of these "Minutes" permit us to introduce them to the New England Conference, and its attendant religious exercise.

This really quite striking presumption—that the conference enjoyed a reading public—led into a highly self-conscious effort at self-presentation. Conference as book! Chapter 1 described the rhythm of the week, touching on the structure of the work day, special services, the anniversary of the N.E. Conference Anti-Slavery Society, the meeting of the Conference Sunday School Union Society, important addresses, including on Saturday Bishop Janes's address to deacon candidates, the evening temperance meeting, Sunday's love feast and preaching, the Monday evening Missionary Meeting and the closing devotional.[15] Chapter II covered the Disciplinary questions; chapter III, Numbers in Society, and Finances; chapter IV, Officers of Conference Societies, General Missionary, Domestic Missionary, Sabbath School, and Anti-Slavery; chapter V, Reports and Resolutions; chapter VI, Appointments; chapter VII, Memoirs; and chapter VIII, Visitors to Literary Institutions, the Course of Study, post office addresses of bishops, the presiding elders and superannuated.[16] These minutes reflected conference's self-preoccupation; indeed, its presumption that a wider Methodism shared in this preoccupation.

This particular set from New England was peculiar in its stage whisper of interpretation. Generally, though, the minutes from that period document annual conferences' concern with themselves, their workings and their self-presentation, a concern that had gradually transformed the intense, communal, revival-like affairs of camp-meeting days into a business-like legislative-judicial-executive organization.

Such organizational efficiency and the 'respectability' that went with it evoked various reactions, from enthusiasm to nostalgia for a simpler day, to opposition. Some concern would, as we note below, find its expression in new conferences, special gatherings on Tuesday or for holiness camp meetings, that would recall Methodism to its roots. Even those enthusiastic for new Wesleyan efficiencies experienced some sense of the loss. Novelty and nostalgia for the Methodism of a simpler day often went together. And both novelty and nostalgia focused attention on the conference as an entity. So did deaths and aging of 'brothers,' men made one in fraternity in the early nineteenth century when conferences had stabilized as geographic entities. Concern with itself derived, too, from conference divisions, boundary issues for conferences split north and south, and the transfer of "brothers" out. Conferences made a point of remembering who was still alive and who was not.[17] In such remembering conferences evidenced intense self-preoccupation. In 1857, Baltimore[18] changed its style of recording and remembering its work. Instead of following the historic questions, it adopted the minute form and identified actions day-by-day. The same conference called for historical sketches of the rise of Methodism.[19] Two years later, the Baltimore secretary prefaced the actual minutes with a list of "Names of Preachers and Date of Their Admission on Trial in the Traveling Connection":

Joshua Wells   1789
Henry Smith   1794
Alfred Griffith 1806

and so on for all the members who had ever served continuing up to 1859.[20] Recollection of the names served perhaps to soften some of the pain caused by the division of the fraternity—the prior year conference had once again divided itself, this time into Baltimore and East Baltimore. Some of the enumerated brothers belonged now to a new fraternity.

Ceremonial Reclaiming Conference

The passion for remembering produced new arrays of charts and tables, business-like procedures by which conference presented itself to itself.[21] It generated biographies of Methodist worthies and new histories of conferences and of Methodism as a whole. Self-awareness and historical awareness were also stimulated by and accommodated in the various centennials and increased interaction with British conferences. The exchange of formal delegates with the English and Irish conferences focused attention on the common heritage, including matters of organization and order. For instance, the MEC fraternal address "To the British Conference of the Wesleyan Methodist Church," amounted to an elaborate "State of the Church" with particular attention to MEC institutions.[22]

Such self-awareness prompted conference discovery of four other liturgical 'traditions'—the semi-centennial sermon, a conference eucharist, the formal opening with the singing of "And Are We Yet Alive," and a memorial service for ministers and spouses who had died in the previous years. All four innovations prospered in the post-Civil War period but "take their rise" amid the pre-war self-preoccupation. In all four, 'revival' and 'fraternity' found new transmuted expression. And in these liturgical expressions, conference preserved reminders of its earlier revivalistic and fraternal substance.

The semi-centennial sermon served such purposes directly and forthrightly. This was a peculiarly conference genre of remembering, a retrospective address delivered by formal conference request[23] before his brethren, by an itinerant who had survived fifty years under appointment.[24] Reviewing the fifty years in the life of the individual and of the conference, these exercises were more historical speeches than sermons.

Indeed, they really diverged sharply from classic Protestant sermonic form. Insofar as they complied with Methodist definition of "taking a text" that did so as pretext. Their text was the life of conference, of circuit, of itinerancy. They were their own scripture, new Chronicles, new prophecy. Jeremiadic in tone, such 'sermons' typically recalled the glories of an earlier Methodism, the excitement of revival and camp meeting, the rigors of the common itinerant life and the vigor of conference brotherhood in the speaker's youth.

Implicitly, if not explicitly, the semi-centennials bewailed the glory that had departed; they celebrated the fraternity that conference had once been. Some were published in conference journals, others independently by request of the body. Some took book form or found their way into one of the *Advocates*.[25] The most famous, *Autobiography of Peter Cartwright* and his *Fifty Years as a Presiding Elder*,[26] the one an implicit semi-centennial of his ministry, the other an explicit semi-centennial of his presiding eldership, have been accorded respect as history and by historians. Respect they indeed deserve, but especially as elaborate instances of this special genre of precious celebration. Cartwright's nostalgic recreations belong to sacred literature, to the semi-centennial sermon. By rhetorical gesture, Methodism reclaimed revival and fraternity.

The eucharist had been once primarily a circuit affair, an office of quarterly conference. With the increase of stations, it took now increasingly more local expression. But it also became an annual conference ceremony. In the early 1850s, Ohio and New England recorded a significant divergence from the historic opening exercises of scripture, hymn and prayer:

> Bishop Janes, after the administration of the sacrament of the Lord's Supper, called the conference to order.[27]

> Bishops Janes was present, and opened the Conference by reading the scriptures, singing, and prayer. After which the sacrament of the eucharist was administered.[28]

The 1850s eucharistic opening did not immediately catch on. Indeed, this venture seemed to be a special experiment by Janes, not replicated by other bishops.[29] And Janes would return to chair a conference and not insist on such an opening.[30] Gradually however, the conferences came to like the more liturgical opening and requested it.[31] For instance, beginning in 1860 New England found an opening Lord's Supper an appropriate ceremony.[32] And by 1867, New England recognized that it had established a tradition. Under the heading of "Opening Session" the secretary noted:

> The sacramental service, by common consent, has come to supersede the more formal mode of introducing the business of our Conferences (reading Scripture selections, singing, and prayer) which was in vogue so long,—and the effect of the change is undoubtedly for

the best. On these occasions, ministers and people unite in com-
memorating the sufferings of our 'blessed, blessed Master,' with
great spiritual profit.[33]

So conferences claimed a liturgical office from quarterly conference,
once the engine of Methodist revival and fraternity.

"And Are We Yet Alive"

Annual conferences appropriated to themselves another ritual
prerogative of local Methodism, particularly of the class meeting, in
choosing to open with the singing of "And Are We Yet Alive." This
Wesley hymn had not been, for the American church, a ritual conference opening and did not really become so, on a widescale basis, until
after the Civil War. Annual conferences had begun simply, with
"Scripture, singing and prayer."[34]

Contributing to the translation of this hymn from class meeting
to annual conference were a complex of factors, including self-preoccupation, a sense of history, nostalgia, the decline of the class meeting,
contact with the British, new hymnbooks, and greater liturgical sensitivity.[35] The hymn, long a favorite, had belonged to local Methodism,
to the class meeting and love feast, and had been so designated in early
nineteenth century hymnbooks. Both the MECS and the MEC put
out new hymnbooks in the late 1840s.[36] The southern church explicitly moved the hymn from its prior location under "Christian Fellowship" and placed it first (# 272) among seven conference hymns and
among three for "Opening Conference."[37] This new placement made
possible a new tradition and a gesture that would claim for conference,
albeit only in song, the intense religiosity of the earlier but fading class
meeting.

The East Genesee Annual Conference went to a more discursive
style of minutes in 1855, with paragraph summaries of each day's
major actions (though modest in comparison with New England's).
In that year, Bishop Beverly Waugh presided. He "conducted the
opening religious service by reading 2d Tim., 2d Chapter, singing the
hymn commencing, 'Except the Lord conduct the plan,' and prayer."[38]
The following year, East Genesee made no indication of its initial
hymn. The conference did receive an Irish delegate and took a special
offering for that church. In 1857, again with an Irish delegate present
and again with Waugh presiding, the conference opened with a
reading of a selection from 1st Peter, "And are we yet alive," and
prayer. One suspects that the international Methodist presence, perhaps reinforced by the British Methodist patterns so close by in
Canada may have been influential. At any rate, the following year, East

Genesee introduced the sacrament and made no mention of its hymn selection.[39]

East Genesee did not immediately establish a tradition. Nor apparently did the General Conference of the MECS. That body chose to sing "And are we yet alive," perhaps as a self-vindicating declaration, beginning with its 1850 session. Southern annual conferences did not immediately follow suit. However, in 1862, the Baltimore Conference of the Methodist Episcopal Church met as two bodies, divided by the war, one in Harrisonburg as "separate and independent" and the other in Baltimore proclaiming loyalty to the MEC, and regarding those not present as withdrawn.[40] The body meeting in Harrisonburg enjoyed a "separate and independent" existence through the war and thereafter voted to align with the MECS. In its first (1862) meeting, and apparently only then, it opened with "And are we yet alive."[41] This the second use as an opening hymn (that I have yet discovered) was probably not known by other conferences and in itself could not have been all that influential. It does, however, nicely situate what would eventuate as a "new" tradition, amid the crises that called into question the very existence of things like "conference" and that shattered fraternity. Slavery, the continuing sectional crisis, war and subsequent "religious" border warfare over turf accelerated conference preoccupation with itself, as conferences naturally cared for themselves in caring for the state of the church. In this context, the new tradition emerged.

By its sentiments, by its celebration of fraternity, by its explicit appeal to gracious revival and by its implicit evocation of the revival and fraternity of class meeting, the hymn served well to give ritual form to what conference was losing:

> And are we yet alive, And see each other's face?
> Glory and praise to Jesus Give For his Redeeming grace!
> Preserved by power divine To full salvation here,
> Again in Jesu's praise we join, And in his sight appear.[42]

In singing that hymn, conferences brought to mind those whom they did not see, who were not alive, who had recently died. Notice of their passing had constituted a ritual from the 1780s, as conferences gave first phrase, then sentence, then paragraph description to the deceased.[43] The ritual had stabilized quite simply. Conferences appointed individuals and/or committees to write memoirs which were read and passed for inclusion in the yearly general *Minutes of the Annual Conferences*. Memoirs constituted (along with statistics) the bulk of the early minutes published by the individual conferences.[44] Composition, reading and approving these memoirs apparently sufficed as ritual. For instance, in 1860 the Philadelphia secretary recorded "A preamble and resolutions expressive of the sense of the Conference respecting the decease of Rev. G. Lacey were offered and adopted." Then two days later, "The Report of the Committee on Memoirs was read and adopted. (*See Memoirs.*)"[45] But conferences were then becoming ever more conscious of the passing of their members, an awareness doubtless reinforced by the deaths and funerals of the Civil War. As we have noted, they constructed elaborate tables which noted those to remember, those members who had died.[46] They also began to turn the committee report into a memorial service. In 1865, New England noted for its fourth day of meeting:

> Services commemorative of the deaths of Epaphras Kibby, Charles Baker, and Chester Field, who have deceased during the past year, were held. Addresses were made by Revs. L. Boyden, A. D. Merrill, and L. R. Thayer.[47]

Then conferences built a memorial service into the fabric of conference life. In 1867, in its organization, Philadelphia voted: "Several of our brethren having died during the year, it was resolved to hold a Memorial Service on Friday, at 10½ A.M." Then

> At 10½ o'clock, the order of the day was taken up, viz: the Memorial Service.
> Hymn 958 was sung, and prayer offered by A. Atwood.
> The name of G. Quigley was called, when a memoir was read by J. Cunningham, and an address delivered by W. L. Gray.
> The name of Joshua H. Turner was called, when a memoir was ready by Jos. Mason, a paper prepared by the class-mates of Bro. Turner was read by T. A. Fernley, and an address delivered by F. Moore.
> The name of Solomon Higgins was called, when a memoir, prepared by Dr. Castle, was ready by R. H. Pattison.
> At the conclusion of the remarks referring to each of these departed brethren, a wreath of Immortells, with their respective names and ages, was presented to the Presiding Bishop, to be placed upon the wall of the church during the session of the Conference.[48]

A pattern gradually emerged.[49] Conference recognized fraternity ceremonially and in formal memorial services gave expression to the memory of the deceased and the ties that bound brother to brother.

The 1877 Ohio Conference brought the liturgical traditions together. It opened with the sacrament of the Lord's Supper, scripture was read, "and the Conference joined in singing the old conference hymn: And are we yet alive, and see each other's face?" Later it passed a resolution inviting Dr. J. M. Trimble to preach a semi-centennial sermon the following year. And the afternoon of the fifth day:

Conference opened by Bishop Haven conducting the memorial exercises, such being the order of the day. Dr. Trimble and C. M. Bethauser read the Scriptures.

The Secretary read the memoirs . . . which were adopted; and brothers . . . spoke briefly, expressing the high esteem entertained of these brethren as men and ministers, after which brothers . . . led the Conference in prayer.[50]

By sacrament and ceremonial hymn, the semi-centennial sermon and the conference memorial service, conferences redefined the meaning of fraternity and revival. By organization, they redefined the meaning of polity.

Chapter 13

The Reconstruction of Methodism

In the period after the Civil War, the quiet organizational revolution through which Methodism and much of American society had been going 'declared itself' so to speak and Methodist conferences found themselves scurrying to make organizational sense of the profound changes which they were experiencing. Most Methodists found the new organization processes and structures congenial, successful, providential, 'Methodistic.'[1] Some, though, like the Free Methodists experienced such accommodation to American society and its organizational preoccupations to be a violation of everything for which Methodists had stood. Each had a point. Methodism had wanted to have it both ways. It had understood itself providentially guided, dynamic, pragmatic, transformative, with a mission to spread scriptural holiness and reform the continent. So it had adapted and adopted as it had found itself more and more invested in and invested with American societal leadership. It had also, since Wesley himself, been abjured to heed our doctrines and discipline. And so it had worried, from the start, about "our Zion" and its preservation. Annual conferences betrayed both the change and the efforts to hold the ancient landmarks, or at least, to remember them.

Conference 'Fraternity,' 'Revival,' and 'Polity'

In the mid-1860s, the New England Conference clearly evidenced both the change through which conferences had gone and the zeal with which members attempted to hold on to what conference had been. This particular annual conference exhibited 'old landmarks' and 'progress' by employing the minutes to give itself not just a record of its eight days of sitting, but even a picture, a daguerreotype, of itself sitting.[2] The minutes provided an "Abstract of Daily Proceedings," an effort at recreative depiction by the secretary, E. A. Manning, who held that office from 1860 to 1879.[3] This is a loving portrayal of the fraternity, doing its work and cherishing its week together. The portrayal is but one of various indices of fraternal self-awareness.

133

Charts and lists galore represented this fraternity and its past to itself. There is, for instance, a list of "Deceased Members of the New England Conference." Also one giving the "Sessions of the New England Conference." The election the preceding year for General Conference prompted a list of Delegates To The General Conference from the New-England Conference, by years, 1804 to 1864. A "Retrospective Register of N.E. Conference" provided a similar history for each living member, charting the successive appointments of each. Another table gave the members alphabetically, indicating addresses, present relation to the conference, year of admission, and years in present appointment. From such data in 1865, the secretary on statistics had computed average service by members to the conference to be 21.25 years. By contrast he estimated the average within Methodism was only 14 years. Of its 190 members, 53 had served more than 25 years, 58 less than 10. It had lost 60 members by death since organization in 1796.[4] And it continued to remember such losses with long memoirs, this year for Epaphras Kibby, Charles Baker, and Chester Field.[5] This fraternity was self-contained and relatively stable, a body bound together by rich memories.

By ritual, especially Disciplinary ritual, the conference sustained the sense that its fraternity remained what it had been. It continued to hear and respond to the bishop's putting of the traditional questions, still numbered: "1. What Preachers are admitted on trial? 7. Who are the superannuated preachers? 17. Where and when shall our next Conference be held?" So prompted, the conference reviewed the character of each member, active or retired. But was this still the closed-doors, no-holds barred searching of one another, the piercing scrutiny that had required the subject under review to leave the room, the accountability to one another that had once bonded and connected itinerants to one another?[6] Conferences seemed to need reassurance that they were. Now isolated problem situations received committee attention and perhaps trial. Within a few years, the secretary felt the necessity of reassuring the reader that the annual examination of character was "no mere farce," that problems did indeed yield charges, charges a committee, a committee formal investigation including testimony.[7] At any rate, increasingly committees constituted the ritual that engaged and preoccupied conference, committees crowded into the polity of the church. The first order of business was constituting the nominations committee[8] and putting it to work staffing the standing committees, the most important of which would require representation from every district. In the mid-1860s the standing committees were Stewards, Necessitous Cases, Education, Bible Cause, Tract Cause, Temperance, Public Worship, To receive

Moneys for Benevolent Operations, Memoirs, Statistics for the General Minutes, Statistics for Conference Minutes, Missions, To nominate Officers for Conference Societies, Preachers' Aid, Benevolent Operations, Observance of the Sabbath, Church Aid, Ministerial Support, Relief Society, Sunday Schools, Slavery and the State of the Country and Conference Minutes. Conference would constitute other committees as it worked.

The committees represented the agency of conference in managing and directing the denomination's work. Committees connected annual conference with the national agents, editors and corresponding secretaries, all of whom would typically be present to make reports. Aside from the publishing efforts and the *Advocates*—aside from the large publishing business, the national agencies or societies—Sunday school, missions, temperance, tracts, Bible—were quite modest endeavors, typically an individual secretary who encouraged activity at conference level. Each secretary was accountable to an annual conference and 'his' agency was effectively under the supervision of that conference or that one and those immediately contiguous.[9] Annual conferences had been the work-horse of the denomination and the 1865 New England Conference reflected that. Its sessions were devoted to reports and actions through which it attempted to take responsibility for the institutions of the church, including its own institutions and particularly both secondary and higher education, the latter including oversight of Wesleyan University and of the church's venture in theological education, the Biblical Institute (late in the decade moved to become part of Boston University).[10] Oversight was exercised through trustees on the institution's board and also visiting committees. Indeed, the year prior General Conference had taken up the question of whether it, rather than annual conferences, should have control and supervision over collegiate education and conceded themselves "unable to fix upon any plan for the organization of a permanent Board of Education which they deem practicable." They affirmed:

> What of ecclesiastical control has been exercised has been by the Annual Conferences. . . . without any established law or uniform plan, and with but little concert between the Conferences or the different institutions. . . .
>
> The committee are confident that the Annual Conferences would not consent to a transfer of the control of the literary institutions under their care to the General Conference, or a board created by its appointment; nor are they sure, could this be done, that the educational movement of the Church would not be robbed of much of its vitality and freedom of action in adapting itself to the peculiar

wants of the different sections of the country by attempting to direct it by a uniform and rigid system.[11]

Annual conference implemented and gave oversight to other ongoing denominational enterprises through permanent conference societies—a Conference [Foreign] Missionary Society, a Domestic Missionary Society, a Tract Society, a Sabbath-School Society. These were auxiliary to national counterparts but had a lively sense of their own agency, met during annual conference, heard reports and sermons, gave direction to the local auxiliaries, and rendered fulsome reports to their members. Most of the denominational dollar was under conference control. Conference trustees and stewards took fiscal responsibility.

Conferences ran the business of Methodism and perforce devoted annual sessions to annual reports. Each agency and each committee reported, in some cases, at great length. In consequence, minutes bristled with complex statistical tables and exhibits. And annual conference did not respect conference boundaries or confine its attention to its own agencies. It looked on the nation, indeed, the whole world as its domain. The New England Conference illustrates this national obsession. It concerned itself, as it had for years, with what was happening in the south, guided by its standing committee "On Slavery and the State of the Country" and appointed an additional committee to think about reconstruction.[12] Accordingly, conference heard a long report on "Reconstruction of the Church."[13] News came during its sitting of the capture of Richmond, eliciting the singing of "Mine eyes have seen the glory" and the Hallelujah Chorus. The attention to the south went hand-in-hand with concern for the whole nation and, in particular, the Methodist connection. Conferences thought for the whole church, vying to set its agenda, formulating resolutions that could be passed to other annual conferences and knowing that through their actions would be carefully covered by the *Advocates*, and for New England, *Zion's Herald*. So New England did not imagine that problems of race relations were just confined to the south. It objected to the action at the recent General Conference (MEC) authorizing the drawing of the color line within the conference structure, segregating by conference, using polity to divide fraternity.[14]

As conference fraternity and polity showed marked changes, so did its spirituality, so did 'revival.' This session of the New England Conference opened with the Lord's Supper, an innovation for American conferences. But was traditional, revivalistic, class-meeting-like spirituality gone? The conference did not want it to be. It devoted the afternoon of first day to a Conference prayer meeting. However, the one ceremony may have been as unusual as the other, or so the secretary's remark would suggest:

> The blessing of God rested upon the Assembly. Why might we not have more such meetings, where we can join our prayers and songs, and offer our testimonies? Oh that the day may come when our Conferences shall prove spiritual Jerusalems, and each minister receive the baptism of the Holy Ghost![15]

Yet there were ample sermons and even on Sunday, a love-feast at 9:00 a.m., prior to the ordination sermons and ordinations. And in the evening conference celebrated the anniversary of the New England Missionary Society. 'Celebration' of such a dynamic institution and celebration of the sacrament and 'celebration' through addresses and 'celebration' in reports produced a spirituality quite distinct from that of earlier Methodism. And conference itself found difficulty in holding that new spirituality within its bounds.

Conference Boundaries and Calendar

Two years later, this same New England Conference took up an issue that would trouble it for several sessions and was then troubling many Methodist conferences: boundaries. How big could and should conferences be? And should conference boundaries follow the lines that the world drew, specifically should they heed state lines? New England thought so, as long it could be done "without injuring our work."

> The reasons in favor of such a re-distribution will strike every mind. We shall thus harmonize our Church with the State, easily arrange our statistics in comparison with other bodies, and thus better learn our position and needs—have a direct and therefore more powerful influence upon our matters of education and politics, temperance and general reform—develop ourselves after the stature of our Commonwealth—and lift that up by our co-operative zeal and power.[16]

This was not a position that had or would meet with universal acceptance and especially troubled conferences that were carved up for such progress.[17] Relatively stable conferences had developed into a conference brotherhood and breaking it up had its costs. Conferences that had been separated would arrange reunions as did New England with Providence in 1867 or as did Baltimore which "paid a visit *en masse* to the Central Pennsylvania Conference at its seat in Chambersburg in 1873.[18] Conference lines may have been etched in sand, good only to the next sitting of General Conference, but conferences knew themselves as bounded entities, as a brotherhood.

Boundaries had sufficiently troubled the prior General Conference (MEC), that of 1864, that it requested the bishops to examine the issue. They did and addressed it in setting agenda for the 1868 General Conference:

> In view of the influence of local legislation upon the corporate wealth of the Church, the benefit of ascertaining from year to year our ecclesiastical statistics within the several States, and the advantages of city, county, and State organizations in carrying on the various benevolent operations, and other collateral interests of the Church, such as the distribution of the word of God, the promotion of the cause of temperance, and the erection of institutions of higher education, it is our deliberate judgment that the General Conference might promote 'the highest welfare of the Church' by readjusting Conference lines.

Such readjusting, the Board of Bishops realized, would affect fraternity, would break bonds—those strong personal attachments which years and decades of common toil and suffering, and pleasant business relations, and delightful social and religious communion" had created. Strong bonds could be respected, perhaps by avoiding "the separation of chief friends." But if not, the bishops hoped "that men of God would cheerfully sacrifice personal feeling upon the altar of religious duty."[19] Fraternity could and must be sacrificed for Methodism's mission and advancement.

Sacrifices upon the altar of duty were being made by the presiding elders, the boundaries of whose districts also proved an important issue and who oversaw, particularly in the east, increasingly large districts.[20] The weight of the enlarged duties can be felt in the written reports of presiding elders, a new feature of conference life (for New England in 1868). For instance, in the 1872 Philadelphia Conference, W. C. Robinson of the South Philadelphia district reported:

> I have been enabled to meet my appointments throughout the year, traveling about 3,600 miles. I have baptized 6 children, solemnized 7 marriages, attended 9 funerals and 14 prayer meetings, and administered the Sacrament of the Lord's Supper 4 times. I have visited 23 Sabbath-schools and addressed them; have held 40 lovefeasts; presided in 165 Quarterly Conferences, and preached 123 sermons.[21]

Striking in this list is the large number of quarterly conferences and the few instances of celebration of communion. Striking in such reports also is the recital of monies raised, buildings erected, net worth of churches and parsonages, numbers in Sunday school—the vast array of statistics and reports that the conferences now demanded of themselves. The presiding elders increasingly played program and executive roles and took especial responsibility for the fund-raising. Symbolizing this new state of affairs, conferences heard the report of collections, by both presiding elder and pastor, and then immediately voted on their characters. So, in the 1872 Baltimore Conference, H. Slicer reported for Baltimore District:

> The names of the Preachers on the District were called, each reported the amount of his Missionary Collection, and their characters were passed.

And the missionary collections, as well as subscriptions, Sunday schools, other benevolent monies (including now amounts contributed to the Woman's Foreign Missionary Society), would be set out in charts on a charge by charge, district by district basis, with the names of pastor and presiding elder clearly displayed by their ritual offerings.[22] Finance and program set the terms, the boundaries, for the church's work.

Boundaries were changing. Annual conference lines were being redrawn to facilitate the program, rather than the conferencing, the circuiting, the itinerating of the continent. Correspondingly, the district and district conference displaced the quarterly conference as the significant unit below the annual conference, the working 'conference' for program purposes. It became especially important in the southern church. And on the local level, the quarterly conference itself, though still named as the operative authority, was given an alter ego, an executive body, a Leaders' and Stewards' Meeting, and later an Official Board (the MECS established a comparable local entity, the church conference in 1866).[23] The first duty delegated to the MEC Leaders' and Stewards Meeting, symbolically significant, was that once carried by the classes and class leaders, the screening of persons for church membership.[24] An official board at the local level and boards up and down the conference structure took over the roles that once had fallen to conferences.[25] Methodist space had been redefined and a new, third dimension, program, gained prominence over the coordinates on the continent.

Similarly, conference time gave way to program time. Setting the rhythms for the Methodist year was the Sunday school. Its new quarterly uniform lessons and Sunday-School Teachers' Quarterly,[26] the interdenominational standard time, displaced quarterly conferences as the de facto time piece of Methodist life. And the Sunday School Superintendent rose to prominence and power, was symbolically and grudgingly given a seat on quarterly conferences, and assumed great significance nationally.[27] John H. Vincent, prominent in the interdenominational effort but also as the head of the new Department of Sunday-School Instruction and Corresponding Secretary of the Methodist Sunday School Union, provided the interdenominational Sunday school cause, Methodist rhythms, with the quarterly publications, the periodic great national conventions and the annual teachers institutes on state and county levels.[28] And Methodism's other institutions and activities—colleges and schools, church extension, temperance, missions—made their own claims on Methodist time and intruded their own rhythms into conference life. Time no longer ran solely on conference patterns. Or perhaps we should say that Methodist life had spilled out beyond the Disciplinary conferences into new conferences, each with its own definition of Methodist time and space.

Conferences Galore: Sorority, Holiness, Sunday School

Conference—quarterly conference, annual conference, general conference—had with the smaller units, class and society, defined Methodist community. And over the years, the activities and programs added into Methodist time and space often had been conference initiatives and certainly had found place and legitimacy within conference. Conferences had tackled missions, Sunday school, the Bible and tract cause, colonization and abolition, and temperance by organizing themselves into such societies and by assigning oversight on local levels to quarterly conferences.[29] By the 1870s, conferences were overwhelmed with quasi-conferences, both within and without, some officially sanctioned and nominally brought within conference orbit, many functioning without official recognition.

Sunday school teachers institutes and conventions were but one of an array of new 'conferences' that had emerged by the time of the Civil War. Women and men, preachers and people met in Tuesday Meetings for the Promotion of Holiness. Preachers meetings stabilized in major cities.[30] Business men gathered weekly in special men-only affairs (out of which came both revival and petitions for lay representation). Indeed, the "business men's revival" of the late 1850s had invigorated and Methodists had participated in a number of important institutions, including the YMCA and Moody- and Moody-type revivals. During the war the Christian Commission had mobilized clergy and laity in channeling support, supplies and medicine to the front.

The Free Methodists had, as noted above, organized with meetings of preachers and laity. Both the MEC and MECS in approving lay delegation provided for lay electoral or district conventions, which found other things to do than just vote. Camp meetings, notably Martha's Vineyard (MA), Round Lake (NY) and Ocean Grove (NJ), had metamorphosed into summer retreats.[31] In the early 1870s, Vincent would transform one of them, Chautauqua, into a summer training institute and thereafter a model, a program, a national scheme for similar gatherings across the country. Other camp meetings moved decidedly away from nurture and endeavored to reclaim historic camp meeting religiosity and the holiness that went with it. A. E. Ballard, George C. M. Roberts, Alfred Cookman and John Inskip called a National Camp Meeting for the Promotion of Holiness for Vineland, New Jersey, in 1867.[32] Its success led organizers to establish a National Camp Meeting Association for the Promotion of Holiness and to call a second national 'conference' for Manheim, Pennsylvania the next year, a gathering that produced an attendance of some 25,000, including 300 preachers and that featured preaching by Bishop Matthew Simpson. Early support from Methodism's leadership moderated as this venture generated other associations; spawned, encouraged and sanctioned a new style of supra-conference holiness itineration; and re-invigorated specifically holiness camp meetings that functioned as both a preservation of earlier patterns and a prophetic judgment against an Israel that had abandoned its covenant. Eventually the tension between these new associations and the church's leadership led to explicit breaks and the founding of new holiness denominations.

Also testing the conference system were the new organizations for women. Some like the Ladies' and Pastors' Union, formally recognized in 1872, would work within existing conference and congregational networks. Others like the Woman's Foreign Missionary Society (MEC), approved the same year, founded 1869, and their counterparts in the MECS (1878) and MP (1879), would early develop patterns of independence, a network of women's conferences paralleling those of the denomination, its own publications (particularly *The Heathen Woman's Friend*), a separate itinerancy (women missionaries), and highly successful fund-raising techniques.[33] Out of such networks, specifically the WFMS but also the Sunday-school institutes and widespread local efforts at mobilization of women for temperance crusades came in 1874 the Woman's Christian Temperance Union, yet another highly complex system of 'alternative' Methodist conferences.[34]

As erosive of the sufficiency of conference were the variety of institutions established by conferences for their work but now demanding more than yearly oversight and therefore necessitating trustees or a board. For instance, in addition to its array of committees, the Philadelphia Conference in 1870 listed officers and, as appropriate, lay and clergy members of the Conference Church Extension Society, Managers, the Conference Missionary Society, the Conference Tract Society, the Trustees of Education Fund, the Philadelphia Conference Education Society, the Trustees of Ministers' Burying Ground, the Trustees of Centenary Fund, the Preachers' Aid Society, and the Historical Society.[35] Such bodies, including the lay and women's organizations, might hold an anniversary meeting in connection with conference, but would in addition meet separately to transact business.[36] More distinct, of necessity, were the boards for the many secondary schools (male and female seminaries), the colleges and the theological seminaries, which conferences staffed but then operated to suit educational rather than ecclesial patterns.

And then (for the MEC) there were the new missionary conferences created abroad through foreign missions and in the South through the Freedmen's Aid Society and the educational and missionary efforts there. The church would be perplexed from the start as to how to treat these new 'conferences,' their delegates and their episcopal leadership.[37] Also new but more immediately suited to the overall conference pattern were district conferences, formed in each Presiding Elders' district, and in the MECS charged with electing the lay delegates to annual conference. These found more of niche, at least initially, and effectively took over the revivalistic functions once the feature of quarterly conferences. These conferences, noted one contemporary commentator, "give prominence to preaching, prayer-meetings, love-feasts, and revival exercises."[38]

In one sense, the district conferences and the new holiness camp meeting associations did re-invigorate conference 'revival'; just as the new men's organizations (clergy and lay) found fresh meaning to 'fraternity' and women's organizations balanced fraternity with 'sorority'; and just as the new boards, nationally and regionally, discovered new vehicles for 'polity.' But, in each instance, the prerogative that had once been conference took new form.

Methodism had simply become too big, too complex, too institutionalized, too wealthy to run itself by conferences that met only periodically. The gravity in Methodism had shifted from conference to its boards and institutions. Conference had once embraced the continent and everything Methodist therein. Conference had once defined time and all Methodist that transpired. Conference had been a new creation, a miracle on the American landscape. Conference, annual conferences in particular, had indeed conferenced the continent. Their sheer number, 76 in the MEC in 1872, plus those in the MECS and the MP, attested that conferencing conquest. That number radically divided Methodist agency and gave it a highly regional orientation. Provincial clerical gatherings had administered Methodist life and work a generation earlier. Now Methodism began the centralization and nationalization and bureaucratization to which American society as a whole was tending.[39]

Chapter 14

Nationalization, Formalization, Incorporation

The organizational revolution affected denominations at the national level more dramatically, perhaps, than at the regional or local levels. Concerned to achieve greater efficiency, order, coherence, consistency, regularity, uniformity in its operations, Methodism increasingly sought those goals by initiatives on the national level. Denominational consolidation perforce centralized prerogatives once the domain of annual conferences. The prerogatives, duties and responsibilities of conference—the nature of this special fraternity— were also to be reshaped and redefined by other general or national processes. Sharpened definitions of membership, formal overtures between churches and negotiations among separated Methodist bodies specified what 'fraternity' should mean. Efforts to recognize the ministry of women and to extend conference membership (and ordination) to them clarified fraternal borders. Preparation for ministry, once through apprenticeship and conference oversight, increasingly would be institutionalized in formal educational programs. Formalization, professionalization, incorporation and nationalization wrought subtle changes in conference.

Consolidation

In 1872 the (MEC) General Conference assembled with lay (men) as full delegates and took action to make the boards of national Methodist societies elective and thus accountable to the church (to General Conference).[1] The MECS had anticipated the MEC on lay delegation and made boards accountable in 1874.[2] Lay participation and denominationally controlled agencies brought to a culmination the long process by which conferences had found themselves regularizing and formalizing administrative duties, had established societies or standing committees to execute and implement these affairs, and had, in effect, transferred to agencies the visions and ideals that it had once summarized and embodied in its own life and which here have

145

been treated as fraternity, revival and polity. The 1872 actions completed that process by centralizing denominational agency on a national level, thus moving to boards what had previously been of necessity effected through annual (and to some extent quarterly) conferences.[3] At the expense of annual conferences, General Conference and general boards acquired executive prerogative and initiative and power.

In these once-societies, now made national, corporate, denominational boards or agencies, Methodist individuals and communities increasingly found common interest, labored, invested themselves, channeled their monies, took pride, defined denominational loyalty, expressed Methodist identity, exercised their corporate will.[4] And from them Methodists received program, publications, direction, guidance. Fittingly, the MEC bishops in 1876 recognized the general agencies as expressions of Methodism's connectional unity.[5] And in 1880, the General Conference rejected a new formula that would have staffed only the more traditional committees, Episcopacy, Itinerancy, Book Concern, Lay Representation and Boundaries, with the traditional formula for significance, power and importance—one member from each annual conference. Instead, by a substitute motion it gave such priority and power to Episcopacy, Itinerancy, *Missions, Education*, Revivals, *Sunday-schools and Tracts, Church Extension, Freedmen and Book Concern*, a list that put the new agencies at the center of General Conference's concern.[6]

Another change, seemingly checked the authority of General Conference, but did so at a national level. This was the provision for judicial review. Here the southern church took the initiative and in 1854 empowered the Bishops, acting collectively and in writing, with the prerogative of challenging a rule or regulation and thereby obliging General Conference to muster a two-thirds majority on the question. This action, consonant with its understanding of conference and episcopacy, the MECS confirmed and clarified in 1874.[7]

Consonant with its understanding of conference and episcopacy, the northern church proceeded in a different fashion, namely by generating from out of conference itself and conference procedure a body with judicial authority. General Conference had served as the supreme court to which appeal was made from annual conference judicial decisions and rulings on the law by presiding bishops. From 1860 to 1872 the General Conference had established a Committee of Appeals and referred such matters to it. In 1876, the MEC established a Judiciary Committee, a body of twelve ("one from each General Conference District") "to consider and report their decision on all questions of law coming up to us from Judicial Conferences."[8]

And in 1884, the body's authority was extended to include "all records of Judicial Conference, appeals on points of law, and all proposed changes in the Ecclesiastical Code."[9]

Both this committee and the southern College of Bishops would thereafter render "court" decisions, thereby leaving a body of *national* law. The MECS actually proceeded in formal fashion to direct its compilation, voting in its 1866 General Conference to request the bishops "to prepare for publication a Commentary on the Discipline, embracing Episcopal decisions, with a view to produce a harmonious administration thereof."[10] That produced Holland N. McTyeiere's *A Manual of the Discipline of the Methodist Episcopal Church, South including the Decisions of the College of Bishops*, a volume regularly updated.[11] The northern church proceeded somewhat later and in less formal fashion to compile a comparable manual. In 1903 Bishop Richard J. Cooke produced *The Judicial Decisions of the General Conference of the Methodist Episcopal Church*.[12] Another major compilation was undertaken in 1924 at the behest of General Conference.[13] Here too then, legitimate concern for order, coherence, consistency, regularity in its body of law led Methodism, north and south, to consolidation at a national level.

'Formal Fraternity'[14]

The creation of judicial structures, the admission of laity into General Conference only and the structuring of once-conference prerogatives into national agencies focused the church's work at the national level and thereby wrought fundamental changes in 'conference' life and work. So also would a set of other 1870s and 1880s developments each of which pressed important and related questions about the nature of this fraternity.

Did the word "laymen," for instance, embrace women? Should they exercise the vote in elections? And were they eligible to serve as lay delegates?[15] Further, now that laity were to be admitted, was it not time to rethink some representation for the local preachers who had gathered for some years in their separate National Association of Local Preachers? What about other groups of ministers, the missionaries and their converts? What status did the mission conferences, their membership and their leadership enjoy? Were they full members of this fraternity? And what about African Americans?

Would the church express fraternity by uniting diverse persons into an annual conference or by employing annual conferences to separate and segregate? To what lengths, in fact, was the church willing to go in distinguishing conferences by race and by language and by gender? How independent might the language conferences and agencies (German and Swedish especially) become? If separated and segregated, what measure of authority would German conferences possess? African American? Mission? Would General Conferences (MEC, MP, and MECS) grant similar autonomy to the 'conferences' for women that it formally recognized—The Woman's Foreign Missionary Society and the Ladies and Pastors' Christian Union (MEC)?[16] Could it imagine the exercise of women's activities extending into the pastoral realm, warranting ordination and conference membership for women? Were women to be included in the fraternity? Were Germans? Were African Americans?

In areas of both north and south, blacks had remained within the MP, MEC and MECS churches, despite the emergence of the AME and AMEZ, despite patterns of segregation and despite white resistance to providing blacks full clergy rights. During the Civil War and especially as northern troops and churches moved south, African Americans exited the MECS in droves, either to establish their own congregations or to align themselves with the MEC or with the AME or AMEZ Churches. The 1866 MECS received a report from its Committee on the Religious Interests of the Colored People that outlined steps recognition of the separation—full ordination, separate quarterly annual and general conferences and black presiding elders. The exact status vis a vis the MECS of such separate entities was ambiguous and the report itself variously understood.[17] Over the next quadrennium the separations continued apace. In 1870 facing the fact of "An African American Exodus, the MECS General Conference made provision for recognition, transfer of property, organization and ordinations. The new Colored Methodist Episcopal Church met the same year, under the presidency of MECS bishops Robert Paine and Holland N. McTyeire, created nine annual conferences, established a publishing house and launched a journal, *The Christian Index*.

The MEC had, as we have noted, made provision in 1864 for black annual conferences and stirred up for itself a hornet's nest of practical, polity and ethical questions. These became more acute as the MEC moved south with missions that initially brought in both blacks and whites. Where black and white had once conferenced together—either from recent missions or long presence—were African American members and preachers to be encouraged into "colored" conferences? In the south should the MEC follow the separatist pattern established by the MECS?[18] Should General Conference therefore elect colored bishops?[19] And how would relations between the MEC and MECS be affected by initiatives with African Americans (and vice versa)?

Would the MEC and the MECS extend 'fraternal' relations to one another? And what about the formal expressions of fraternity and exchange of fraternal delegations—with Canadian, Irish and British Methodists, with the separate German American denominations, with the African Methodists, and with other American communions? What did such declarations of 'fraternity' imply about priorities in fraternity and the meaning and boundaries of Methodist fraternity? These formal gestures took enough general conference time to warrant an enquiry into their importance and the appointment of a Committee on Fraternal Relations, which in 1872 recommended that in the future a specific day be set aside for reception of fraternal delegations and the speeches and sermons confined therein and to as many evenings as needed.[20] Was it not anomalous, given such fraternal excess, that the two bodies that both claimed to be the Methodist Episcopal Church did not enjoy fraternal relations?[21] And if the two episcopal general conferences and the two churches' leadership did re-establish relations and were to privilege that particular fraternal relationship, what implications would follow for these various other dimensions of fraternity, especially for relations with the African Methodist churches and for the internal relations between white and black within the MEC? What, in short, was 'fraternity' to mean? whom did it embrace? how far did it extend? what quality of family did it indicate? what factors of race, language, history would qualify it? These were not new questions but they re-emerged with fresh urgency.

In the 1870s, white Methodists increasingly applied the phrase "fraternal relations," already possessed of a formal, technical force,[22] especially to the two largely-white episcopal bodies, the MEC and MECS, and to international Methodism. In such usage 'fraternity' had more to do with status than with affect, more to do with boundaries than with bonds, more to do with race than with baptism, more to do with exterior than with interior relations, more to do with constitution and polity than with what had earlier constituted the 'fraternal' aspect of conference.[23] Several matters seem striking:

(1) The General Conferences of the 1870s and 1880s (particularly of the MEC) dealt with all these several questions about the shape of and membership in the fraternity (not just relations with the MECS).

(2) Historical treatments have resolved these matters into quite separate stories—the place of mission conferences, the admission of lay*men*, the status of the language conferences, the inclusion of women in 'laymen,' the separations by race, women's organizations and roles and ordination, the relations between and among the African American denominations and between them and the MEC, and the tentative explorations of 'fraternity' between the MEC and MECS.

(3) Fraternity and fraternal relations came increasingly to mean

the relations between north and south, between the white (male) north and the white south.

(4) In acquiring this formal, ecumenical and inter-church force, 'fraternity' lost some of its capacity to denote and sustain the brotherly affection within and certainly the capacity to embrace the various new candidates (even the male candidates) as members.

Brother and sister language would, of course, continue to animate informal discourse, indeed may have become more flowery in informal discourse, but the term 'fraternity,' like so much else in the life of Methodism, surrendered some of its inter-personal, familial intensity as it was pressed into formal, polity usage. And the attention that the MEC and MECS gave to their fraternal relations certainly made difficult the familial, fraternal relations that had pertained between black and white, in both south and north, and may well explain the tentativeness with which the churches dealt with the place and rights in this fraternity of women and of the mission conferences.

Something of the 'conflictual' character of fraternity can be seen in the way in which the relations between the MEC and the MECS were initiated. The impulse really began in overtures made between the AME and AMEZ, both meeting in general conferences in Philadelphia in 1864. The AME made a formal overture to the AMEZ, setting up a committee to explore relations, empowering it to call a convention, if the AMEZ reciprocated, and looking forward to "the combination of the two bodies."[24] The AMEZ did reciprocate, a convention met, it drafted articles "as the basis of a permanent union of the respective bodies," and it dealt with matters of symbolic import like the names for the new church and for its chief officers.[25] In 1868, the AMEZ was moving toward ratification, when informed by a committee from the AME that the latter declined unity on the agreed-upon bases. The AMEZ then overtured the MEC its interest in entering "into arrangements by which to affiliate on the basis of equality, and to become one and inseparable, now and forever."[26] That prompted actions by the MEC General Conference of 1868 to establish a commission "to confer with a like Commission from the African M. E. Zion Church to arrange for the union of that body with our own, be also empowered to treat with a similar Commission from any other Methodist Church that may desire a like union."[27] The overture of the AMEZ to the MEC came to nought, frustrated by relations on bases of caste rather than equality and by some sheep- and shepherd-stealing by the MEC, so alleged the bishops of the AMEZ.[28]

At any rate, the legislation authorizing conversations with the AMEZ or "any other Methodist Church that may desire a like union" became the pretext for an overture by bishops Matthew Simpson and

Edmund Janes in 1869 to the College of Bishops (MECS). Janes also participated in a visit to the 1870 General Conference of the MECS. The 1872 General Conference (MEC) appointed, for the first time, a fraternal delegation to the MECS. In response, the 1874 MECS General Conference empowered a fraternal delegation to carry the proposal of a joint commission to "adjust all existing difficulties" standing in the way of fraternal relations.[29] The MEC reciprocated and a Joint Commission on Fraternal Relations met at Cape May, NJ in August 1876. The first southern demand and the first action recalled the overture made by Lovick Pierce in 1848 and a staple in MECS self-understanding, that "there is but one Episcopal Methodism . . . our two General Conference jurisdictions being each rightfully and historically integral parts of the original Methodist Episcopal Church constituted in 1784." And further that

> Each of said Churches is a legitimate Branch of Episcopal Methodism in the United States, having a common origin in the Methodist Episcopal Church organized in 1784 . . . [they are] one Methodist family, though in distinct ecclesiastical connections.[30]

The southern commissioners convened separately and kept their own record. They noted that "the form of statement in a certain connection would exclude several colored organizations from the classification of Episcopal Methodisms of this country" and concluded that "the omission of reference to them could not be properly construed as an oversight."[31] The larger Methodist fraternity would be bracketed out by careful attention to constitutional, jurisdictional, connectional concerns.[32] A formula for fraternity had been defined that would privilege the relation between the MEC and MECS and keep relations with the AMEZ at very formal levels, the mere exchange of fraternal regards. The Joint Commissioners then went to deal with the contests over property and territory between the two churches, setting out rules and procedures for adjudication of disputes.[33]

Further gestures of fraternity followed in what would be more than a half-century effort at reunion.[34] Both churches thereafter appointed fraternal delegations, both participated in the first international Methodist Ecumenical Conference of 1881,[35] both cooperated in the 1884 centennial of American Methodism.[36] The latter, a major production and gala affair at Baltimore, had been proposed by the MECS in 1878, re-started by the delegations at the Ecumenical Conference, and effectively planned by joint committees from the two churches, with other Methodist bodies invited only by letter. In the preliminary meetings, the record indicated "the utmost harmony prevailed." So also, "The same feeling of brotherly love characterized the Conference." The bonds of brotherhood took expression also in a communion service, a love feast, and a public celebration involving fifty-six Sunday schools, some 25,000 children. Especially important were social events including one at the home of the Rev. John F. Goucher:

> Representative brethren of the Methodist Episcopal Church, and of the Methodist Episcopal Church, South, were brought into closer acquaintance at Mr. Goucher's, and the bonds of fraternity were strengthened by the free and cordial expressions with which brother greeted brother.

Not participating in this greeting of brother and brother were the AME, AMEZ and CME, all of which had sizable delegations present at the conference.[37] Bonds of fraternity could separate as well as unite.

To be sure, these larger gatherings and events, including a second Methodist Ecumenical Conference in Washington, D.C. in 1891, and the many descriptive publications of the churches exhibited the larger family of Methodist churches. And in the 1890s, the MECS and MEC would appoint Commissions on Federation that seemingly had open agenda.[38] But, in fact, they treated with the AME, AMEZ and CME by encouraging their separate unification. Formal fraternity had taken on an all-white aspect.

Defending Fraternal Borders

Geographical borders and boundaries might be reconfigured, might be redrawn to follow state lines, might even be opened somewhat along the once battle-scarred lines between north and south to permit brothers to be together.[39] Flexibility in geographical definitions of conference (and of fraternity) were also achieved through the language and mission conferences that permitted the church to distinguish within a given geographical area communities and peoples for special attention, a formula that had been applied initially to the Native Americans and was now generalized.

On other, non-geographical borders, on boundaries of race and gender especially, Methodism exercised defensive vigilance. The drawing of racial lines we have already noticed. As the churches (MEC and MECS) ordained African Americans, they faced again the issue that had produced the AME and AMEZ, would all-white conferences welcome African American members? A few would and did. The larger pattern almost rehearsed the story of the 1810s—rapidly giving conference boundaries to race, almost totally extruding African Americans in the MECS, permitting southern MEC conferences to organize along racial lines, setting up Black conferences in the north, yet moving slowly on electing African American bishops,[40] and expressing unity across racial lines only at the General Conference (MEC) level.

During the 1870s and 1880s the MEC especially faced questions about gender boundaries as well; such questions also troubled the MECS, MP Church, Evangelical Association, and United Brethren.[41] One resolution, as we have noted, was to form new or give formal recognition to women's organizations. But women's initiatives and experience in running those quickly raised issues of governance, accountability and representation. Given the established principle among MPs and the new opening to lay representation in episcopal Methodism, could and should the latter permit women to stand as candidates for the lay electoral conferences? could and should women be elected as delegates to General Conference? could and should women hold offices in Sunday School and in quarterly conference?

In certain areas, congregations and conferences answered yes to all the above and even to yet another, could and should women's call to ministry be recognized and women accepted as local pastors and then made recommendations of them to ordination as deacon and elder? As early as 1880, the MEC General Conference faced this test in the case of Anna Oliver, a 1876 recipient of the Bachelor of Sacred Theology degree from Boston University School of Theology, briefly a pastor in Passaic, NJ, until displaced by the Newark Annual Conference and by 1879 exercising leadership over a Brooklyn congregation.[42] Having obtained a quarterly conference recommendation, she was presented as a candidate to the New England Conference, as was Anna Howard Shaw, another graduate of Boston. The presiding bishop ruled their recommendations out of order, holding that the law of the church did not authorize the ordination of women.

The matter came to General Conference on appeal, with an accompanying resolution from the New England Conference instructing its delegates "to use their influence to remove all distinctions of sex in the office and ordination of our ministry," with the backing of Boston Alumni, and via a petition from the Willoughby Avenue M. E. Church of Brooklyn petitioning the conference "to make such alteration or alterations in the Discipline as they may consider necessary to remove the disability or disabilities in the way of the *ordination* of our Pastor."[43] On recommendations of its Judiciary and Itinerancy Committees, the conference sustained the bishop's ruling and rejected appeals for a change in the Discipline. Full conference membership and ordination would be a 20th century accomplishment, some seventy-five years later.

Also tested in the 1880s was the issue of whether women might be conference members as laity.[44] Women involved in the missionary organizations and in the temperance cause exercised leadership, garnered resources, demonstrated competence in matters of concern to the denomination as a whole. Should they not be represented where issues of articulation, coordination, authority were resolved? A particularly important test occurred with the 1888 General Conference to which five women were elected, including one with high visibility across the church, Frances Willard. The bishops in their "Address" acknowledged their presence and the constitutional issue it raised[45], the conference refused to seat them, ruling them ineligible under the constitution[46] and then in a close vote referred the matter to the annual conferences by proposing a change to the Restrictive Rule applying to lay delegation—"and the said delegates may be men or women."[47] Both laity and clergy voted majorities in favor, but the latter not with the three quarters required. In response in 1892, the Judiciary Committee ruled, unanimously, that women were ineligible but on an amendment another construction of the Restrictive Rule was proposed—"and said delegates must be male members." The strategy was for this to fail in the annual conference votes, thus entailing the opposite reading of "laymen." The proposal failed decisively but in a quite partial vote, the consequence of some conferences simply not balloting the question, not an outcome that gave conclusive force to the alternative reading.

Women delegates appeared again in 1896 but withdrew amid the ensuing controversy and did not actually take their seats under a compromise. Only with the adoption of a new constitution in 1900 were equal laity rights for women accepted. With the 1904 General Conference (MEC), women could then sit in general conference and in the new lay annual conferences, bodies parallel to the ministerial bodies. (Methodist Protestants, long experienced with lay participation, granted lay rights to women about the same time, in 1892, though permitting them roles in annual conference somewhat earlier.[48] Full lay rights for women in the MECS came later, with approval by General Conference in 1918.)[49]

The new MEC constitution was driven by lay demands for equal representation in general conference, demands that animated annual and general conference sessions from the 1870s on.[50] A 1888 proposed change to allow for no more "lay delegates that there may be ministerial delegates," failed decisively in annual conference votes. But further memorials and requests prompted yet another proposal out of the 1892 General Conference, this one providing that ministers and laity would vote "as one body." It too failed, largely owing to that language.[51] The offensive language was stripped in 1896 but the measure again went down to defeat in annual conference ballots. Later in that quadrennium, a similar resolution (from the Rock River Conference) circulated and passed 9,258 to 1,524. During that same period General Conference had put a Constitutional Commission to work on giving greater precision and clarity to "the organic law of the Church" and the procedures for amendment. The 1900 General Conference concurred on the proposition of equal lay representation and enabling language was therefore incorporated into a new constitution which was thereafter submitted to annual conferences and passed. Once again the church had been pressed, by both procedure and substance, towards thinking of itself, particularly in General Conference assembled, in political terms. Here, too, as in the case of the general boards and agencies with regard to race, the church would work out its problems at the national level. There lay men and women would focus their energy and attention.

Professionalization: Conference and Theological Education

By permitting laity, men and women, roles on the national and local levels, in General Conference and quarterly conferences, but not in annual conference, the church gave a new twist to the meaning of that regional fraternity. Even efforts to introduce lay representation into annual conferences recognized that this body, in particular, had special ministerial roles and recommended that laity, if included, have power to speak or vote on all questions "except those affecting the conduct, character, and relations of traveling elders, and the election of ministerial delegates to the General Conference."[52] Increasingly, especially during the 20th century annual conference would take on the character of a professional organization. Much of that development lay decades ahead. But already in the late 19th century, changes in ministerial preparation occurred that laid the foundations for the later professionalization.

In particular, the church put incredible energy into institution building and made both the church colleges and the new theological seminaries important contexts for ministerial preparation.[53] Because conferences invested themselves in these enterprises, because they viewed them as extensions of their own life and work, because they heard lively annual reports and sent visiting committees, because bishops appointed and they had colleagues appointed to presidencies and to the chairs in Bible (college) and theology (seminary), conferences did not, by and large, experience formal theological education as a loss of their prerogative in preparation of persons for conference membership and ordination.[54] And at this stage the numbers going to seminary remained small and the church had to work to remove the disincentives from attendance (for instance, only in 1884 did the MEC make it possible for a person to attend seminary 'under appointment' and thus not suffer the loss of time earned 'on probation').[55] But formalizing theological education into a seminary program represented a dramatic change in the way that conference had brought persons into ministry.

Previously, ministerial preparation had been a conference affair. In two decisive ways, the conference and its members had formed new members. First, candidates were brought along through the stages of local leadership into itinerancy through an informal, but highly effective mentoring process. The latter preparatory stages included a "traveling with," a supervised apprenticeship while on trial as the junior preacher, yokefellow under a more seasoned itinerant.[56]

Second, during this preparatory phase, the young preacher read from the Conference Course of Study—by the late 19th century a denominationally-approved, four year program of disciplined study.[57] To work effectively the course of study needed the mentoring or apprenticeship relation; it needed someone to travel with the neophyte in his theological journey; it needed a teacher. Changes in the itinerancy, as well as heightened appreciation for what formal theological education might achieve, pointed to increased reliance upon institutionalized instruction, as one observer noted in the 1870s:

> About a generation ago a great change occurred in the practical working of our ecclesiastical system. Through all the older and more settled portions of the Church the circuit system was generally abandoned. The gravity of this change has seldom, if ever, been duly estimated. Measured by its effects upon the whole Church, it is entitled to be designated a radical revolution.
>
> The first and most serious result of this revolution was the practical paralysis of our whole system of ministerial training. The great theological seminary of Methodism was not indeed closed, but it received a blow equivalent to that which would be dealt to a college by abolishing its working faculty. . . .
>
> It effectively deprived our candidates and junior ministry of the instruction, drill, and personal influence which they had been wont to receive from their senior associates upon the district and the circuit. It robbed them of the stimulus and profit of contact with superior minds, the advantages of living models, the blessed contagion of maturer character.[58]

This commentator thought that theological seminaries might take up the role once occupied by the senior itinerant:

> Substantially, they are merely select corps of instructors, conveniently distributed through the Church, to do for our junior ministry what the elders and senior circuit preachers did for them fifty years ago. These seminaries, then, are the providential substitute for the lost teaching agency of our original system.[59]

The capacity of the seminary (and also of the church college) to sustain the fraternal, conference-style instruction and training and the church's ability to keep ministerial preparation integral to conference would prove to be long-term issues.

A professionally trained ministry would come to have a professional self-understanding and professional expectations. Such expectations surface in conference resolutions in the very late 1870s and through the 1880s and 1890s. The Philadelphia Conference, for instance, worried about various matters in the 'professional' interest of its members, including the financial viability of its small charges and the admission of more persons into the conference by trial[60] or by transfer than could be adequately supported. For instance, in 1879 it resolved:

> WHEREAS, There is a full supply of preachers for the demands of the work within the bounds of this Conference; and
> WHEREAS, The crowded condition of this Conference necessitates the assignment of preachers to appointments that cannot adequately support them, therefore,
> *Resolved*, 1. That we respectfully, but most earnestly, request the Presiding Bishop to make no transfers *to* this Conference, at its present session, unless an equal number of men can be transferred *from* this Conference. . . .
> *Resolved*, 3. That no candidate for admission on trial be received at this session of the Conference.[61]

Repeatedly the Conference expressed itself on the financial health of the ministry:

> *Resolved*, That we deprecate the multiplication and continuance of small charges that are not likely to give a fair support to a pastor and his family; and that we deprecate the policy of admitting preachers to such an extent, that true and tried members of the Conference are crowded out."[62]

Philadelphia defended conference rights and the 'professional' interests of its members by expressing concern also over the number of presiding elders each of whom represented a drain on monies that otherwise would go into ministerial salaries,[63] the pursuit by ministers of other business,[64] and processes for selecting the best of those seeking admission.[65] Philadelphia also began to put a higher premium on collegiate and seminary preparation for ministry.[66] Conferences thus began to take on aspects of a professional organization. And conferences would then increasingly traffic with seminaries as one professional agency with another.

Here, as in various dimensions of the life of conferences, complexity and expertise and delegation and specialization and differentiation were drawing new lines, lines that connected, lines that distinguished, lines that compartmentalized, lines that unified. Conferences busied themselves trying to keep track of the great variety of institutions that now served them, including quite large institutions like colleges; attended to initiatives that increasingly flowed out of the new agencies; dealt with local churches themselves becoming wealthy, powerful and complex. Minutes, as we have noted, registered the myriad responsibilities and activities conferences faced. Much remained connected through conference.

And yet the new situation mismatched authority and power. The conferences, which met annually or quadrennially, 'oversaw' entities exterior to themselves that worked day-to-day with strong executive leadership, large budgets and responsibilities that intruded into the life of the church, into conference and congregational affairs. Colleges, seminaries and especially boards, denominational and women's, though not constitutional and merely creatures of conference, exteriorized work that by polity belonged to conference. The new organizational complexities demanded more oversight than the regional body could provide. So conferences, through their delegates initiated the changes that centralized power and authority in denominational boards and agencies.

And in other ways, rights and prerogatives that belonged to conference were exteriorized. The various new gatherings—clergy and lay, male and female—including those specifically committed to holiness, exteriorized revival from conference. And even fraternity had come to have an exteriority as it applied less to relations between brothers than to relations between church bodies.

Is it surprising that conference, annual conference in particular, threw up and defended the boundaries around maleness and whiteness and language and clerical prerogative? What, otherwise, was brotherhood to mean? what would be left of fraternity, revival and polity? where would those vitalities be lodged? and how would they fare when so many definitions, arrangements and structures were determined on a national level to be adopted and applied across the conferences and churches?

Chapter 15

Growth or Decay?

That many changes have occurred in the outward forms of Methodism is obvious. Which do they indicate, growth or decay? The class meeting, for instance, is considerably disued: have fellowship and spiritual helpfulness among believers abated, or do they find, in part, other expressions and other instruments? The rigid and minute Church discipline of former years is relaxed: is this a sign of pastoral unfaithfulness, or is it a sign of growing respect for individual liberty and of a better conception of the function of the Church? The plainness of the early Methodist congregations has disappeared: is this simply vanity and worldliness, or is it, in part, the natural and justifiable development of the aesthetic faculty under more prosperous external conditions? The strenuous contention for this or that particular doctrine or usage of Methodism, once common, is now rarely heard: is this indifferentism, or is it, in part, a better discernment of that which is vital to the Christian faith, and, in part, the result of an acceptance by others of the once disputed opinion?[1]

"Is it growth or decay?" the bishops asked in their 1900 Episcopal Address. They answered in a different fashion than were the holiness groups, then consolidating their protests against Methodist accommodation. Methodists had differing views about the changes through which the movement was passing. Occasion for disagreement about Methodism's change would continue. In the 20th century the long-term patterns that we have been tracing continued. Polity swelled under Methodism's organizational revolution, its growth expressed in the ever larger *Disciplines*. Annual conferences and General Conferences put gargantuan quantities of reports and recommendations on record. Revival and fraternity, squeezed by institutional concerns from the center of conference life, found other niches within the life of the church. Was it growth or decay?

Word, Order, and Sacrament?

Another and related trend brought the ideals of revival, fraternity and polity back into conference life in transmuted form. Revival,

159

fraternity and polity underwent subtle but important alteration, trans-muting themselves into word, sacrament and order. The first and third of these transformations, readily documented, will be covered in this and following chapters and continued 19th century patterns. Polity with accent on politics and policy, as we observed, swelled easily into the role once accorded 'discipline' as Methodism's principle of order. And the instrument and focus of this order seemed to be the board and agency bureaucratic structure. Religiosity (revival) increas-ingly focused within the congregation and in the Sunday service (word). To be sure, Sunday services could be easily replicated in conference and other settings, though without the communal dimen-sions that made them so life-giving at local levels.

The other transformation occurred more within the 20th century. Annual conferences, once racially and linguistically divided ministerial- and male-only, admitted laity (MEC), ordained women and eventually and slowly erased linguistic and racial borders. The church experi-enced these integrative changes as wrenching. In its effort to carry through on building the new conference communities it gave itself little occasion for reflection about the terms, images and metaphors that would replace 'fraternity.' What language could and would rec-ognize, re-create, re-affirm the bonds essential to conference life and work? Community, covenant, profession, inclusivity, pluralism, open itinerancy were among the words that individuals or groups em-ployed in efforts at reclamation. Though self-referential and ecclesial in the fashion of 'fraternity' such terms have not as readily conveyed and re-created its intensity, closeness, spirituality, familial quality. What have, I believe, are terms with more vertical than horizontal force and with no special orientation toward larger collectivities— eucharist, sacrament, liturgy and hymnody. A sacramental unity, I will try to suggest, seems to be taking the place of the bond once main-tained by fraternity. What meaning might such allusions have for Methodism's corporate and connectional life? The same question applied to the other new terms, word and order.

At any rate, word, sacrament and order would eventually become the watchwords for ministry and of conference life and structure. In pursuit of these new ideals, Methodism became more churchly, its leadership more professional, its structure more complex. This trans-formation involved changes in Methodist time and space, in its con-nectional gravity, in the composition and configuration of conferences, and in the profile of their leadership.

The changes, already ongoing, occurred so gradually and with such complexity that it was difficult for those experiencing them and proves difficult even in retrospect to recognize clear points of transition. The engines of change were the processes that we have already noted and denote with technical, social-scientific names—professionalization; centralization; bureaucratization; specialization; even secularization; *but also* processes that seemingly contrasted or conflicted therewith (but do not lend themselves to nominalization as readily)—the church's becoming (eventually) more representative, inclusive, egalitarian; its de-centralizing, regionalizing and localizing; its opening of governance to the laity, to women, to minorities and to youth; its diffusing of functions and responsibility widely; the church's involving itself more actively in community, state and nation. The processes of modernization—if that is the correct term—were conflicting and paradoxical.

The conflictual and paradoxical character of change is particularly striking at the annual conference level. Conferences did become more professional, elitist, clerical, self-preoccupied; they came gradually to function as professional organizations, Methodist counterparts to the A.M.A. and A.B.A. But they also became more inclusive, representative, egalitarian, democratic; grudgingly opened to laity, to African Americans, to women, they had to find new patterns of connection. Change came from above—from the leadership, from boards and agencies, from educational institutions, from general conferences. Change came also from below—from the expectations that laity had of and for ministers, from the challenges that local situations placed upon congregations and ministers and especially from increasingly powerful congregations which had their own way with bishops and conferences. And change came, in some instances, only with great agony and a terrible fight, as in the case of race.

The story of change, then, is not of a conspiracy at the top but of piecemeal developments at all levels which edged Methodism along into a future that no one really foresaw. In this chapter, we will monitor these processes at the turn of the century and in the first decades of the 20th century. Later chapters will pursue the fuller development of the new ideals, word, order and sacrament.

Local, Quarterly, or District Conferences?

Quarterly conferences evidenced both dramatic change and Methodism's unwillingness to give up old structures. The 1872 and 1884 General Conferences (MEC) had made provisions for alternative local structures to the quarterly meeting, one to provide oversight to the presiding elder's circuit, the regional interests of the church—the district conference—and one more clearly internal to congregations or circuits, capable of week-to-week oversight and 'organizational' in its nature—the official board.[2] Both the district conference and the official board took on personnel, functions, purposes that belonged to quarterly meetings.

The district conferences had been eagerly sought by local preachers whose duties and responsibilities had quite literally collapsed as quarterly meetings become increasingly congregational gatherings.[3] In his 1878 presidential address to the National Association of Local Preachers, D. H. Wheeler, D. D. of the N.Y. East Conference had observed:

> Local preachers ought to have *some form of official organization*. There is not now an atom of such organization. There is no Disciplinary provision for the meeting of local preachers, not an atom of work assigned to them as an organized order. They participate in Quarterly and District Conferences, but they have no Conference or Association of their own which is recognized by our law. This condition of so distinct a class of ministers, numbering 12,000, is as remarkable as it is unfortunate. The local preacher needs consultation with his brethren, the inspiration of mutual sympathy and the self-respect that is given by an official responsibility of a collective character.[4]

The official board represented lay interests in governance and moved the polity in the opposite direction, by legitimating, indeed furthering, the internalization of conference within congregation, a development already treated.

Neither district conference nor official board had really displaced the quarterly conference. Neither seemed capable of reclaiming the multi-dimensional purposes (revival, fraternity, polity) of quarterly meetings. The former did sustain some revivalistic flavor (particularly in the south) but lacked a real niche in the connectional system[5] and did not really seem to work (at least in the north). The latter, the official board, *worked* all too well, indeed increasingly claimed the 'polity' roles from quarterly conference but in so doing eviscerated the quarterly conference (and therefore the church as a whole) of what had once been the genius of the Methodist circuit system—its evangelistic outreach, its easy inclusion of 'new work,' its deployment of local preachers into unchurched areas. And the increasingly strong congregational orientation kept even district conferences from carrying through that revivalistic governance role.[6] Indeed, revival and, to some extent, fraternity had found a happy place within the congregation, nurtured as we have noted, in Sunday Schools and the network of women's, men's and youth organizations.

The reality was that the territorial, conferencing character of local Methodism had long since yielded to congregation and building.

Program and even polity oriented attention away from land to edifice. Methodist space had become more interior than exterior. The presiding elders still came and quarterly conferences met but their annual reports—in the last decades of the 19th century and in the first of the 20th—tell of "Church Building, Parsonages, Improvement, Debts Paid, Etc."[7] Passing mention would be made of a district convention and of a camp meeting but these were extrinsic to the day-to-day life of the church. Revivals and conversions belonged to the congregation and were reported charge by charge.[8]

Fittingly, now Methodists gave more prominence on their calendars to the sabbath rather than the quarterly meeting and actually pitted sabbath observance against the camp meetings. Pastors complained, as had A. Rittenhouse to the Philadelphia Conference by formal motion, of Sunday services on camp-grounds as productive of two evils, the drawing "people away from their usual places of worship" and using and implicitly endorsing the desecration of the sabbath by the running of Sunday trains.[9] A similar motion was passed the next year actually opposing holding camp-meetings over the Sabbath which, "occasions the running of Sunday trains and the consequent enforced labor of train hands on that day, and tends to draw people away from their regular church services, and gives rise to numerous forms of Sunday traffic."[10]

Methodists joined other Protestants in campaigns for protection of the sabbath and registered their concerns in the late 19th and early 20th century at both annual and general conferences.[11] Annual conferences added committees "On the Observation of the Sabbath," to their structures and, as was the case for Philadelphia, released one of their members, T. A. Fernley, to serve as Corresponding Secretary of the Philadelphia Sabbath Association.[12]

Methodists also joined other Protestants in another effort that focused locally and often on the congregation, namely to hold their turf in the cities. They rethought and reconfigured ministries and programs as steadfast members moved out and church neighborhoods took on new complexions.[13] Pastors and district superintendents drew support in these campaigns from such organizations as the Philadelphia City Missionary and Church Extension Society. Congregations elaborated an array of social service programs. For instance, for 1908:

> St. Paul's, Rev. C. E. Adamson, pastor.—This church, situated in the section with the largest birth rate and smallest death rate in the city, ministers to an ever-increasing constituency. It employs the regular and institutional methods.

A. The regular services.

Preaching services, class meeting and prayer meeting are held regularly. At the prayer meeting there is an average of ten to fifteen children of foreign birth. . . .

The Banner Epworth League. The early service on Sunday evening crowds the lecture room. By actual count 100 boys and 80 girls are present at the meeting. . . .

B. Institutional work:

Some new lines of work have been undertaken:

1. A millinery class on Tuesday evening. . . .

2. A class in American citizenship on Friday evening. . . .

3. A class in kitchen garden for the teaching of homework. . . .

4. The dressmaking class. . . .

5. Mother's meeting. Every Wednesday afternoon from 15 to 20 mothers, bringing from 15 to 20 small children. . . . Material . . . is sold to them at half price. They sew on children's garments for an hour. Then a talk, recitations of scripture verses and singing of hymns follows. . . .

Old work continued:

The Kindergarten—Every morning . . . probably the largest and finest single kindergarten in the city.

The Girls' Gymnastic Classes, Wednesday evening. . . .

Boys' Gymnastic Classes and Drill, Monday evening. . . .

The Music School, Tuesday afternoon and evening. . . .

The Sewing School, Thursday afternoon . . . attendance of 120, and 10 teachers. . . .

The Outing Club. . . .

The Penny Concert, whose attendance has grown to 800. . . .

The West Philadelphia Auxiliary of St. Paul's, a band of men and women . . . bear the expense of the rent of the apartments of our deaconess, Miss Ella Bateman. . . .

Resume

From 1,800 to 2,000 children are touched each week by St. Paul's in the winter season. It is safe to say that during the year the touch of the church has been laid upon a child 50,000 times. The deaconess in her report said that 15,000 children have been in our industrial classes during the year. The Methodism of Philadelphia has responded nobly to the work which the City Missionary Society is doing in this foreign section.[14]

Such urban institutional churches set the pace for elaborate structuring at the local level and for complex interactions with the surrounding community. But organizational complexity characterized congregations in suburbs, small cities and towns as well. Methodist activity increasingly became community oriented, intense and focussed.

Accordingly, Methodist space and ritual contracted. The rhythms of Methodist life changed from the periodic ministrations of a two week circuit to the weekly leadership of a pastor, from such irregular affairs as camp meeting to the Sunday service, from the circuit structure to the local church and from quarterly meeting to an official board. And yet Methodists could not bring themselves to jettison the quarterly meeting. It remained the legal expression of the church on a local level.

In their 1896 Address, the bishops addressed themselves to this constitutional straddle. In the spirit of the constitutional revisionism of that general conference and the last, they called for a reconstitution, a reconceptualization of conference at the local level. They proposed giving district conferences stronger lay representation and a clear connectional mandate and the replacement of quarterly conferences with 'local conferences.'[15] The bishops clearly saw that new realities demanded a new connectionism.

The church and General Conference found it difficult to let go of the quarterly meeting. As late as 1920, General Conference took up again the proposal, framed it into a constitutional amendment, only to watch it go down to defeat.[16] Instead, General Conference endeavored to hold the straddle and in 1908 agreed not to displace quarterly meetings as the bishops had proposed but to permit a charge to combine or omit the second and third quarterly meetings.[17] And rather than change radically the district conference, General Conference gave the presiding elder a new name, district superintendent, a name which distanced and dissociated 'him' from the local gathering, a name which accented the supervision of the whole rather than the presidency of the local, a name which gave 'him' more organizational than sacramental aura.[18]

At the local level Methodists labored to sustain the straddle with the quarterly conference. The presiding elder on the South District in the Philadelphia Conference reported "By vote of the charges we combined the second and third Quarterly Conferences. . . . This added interest to the third Quarterly Conferences and enabled me to attend two of our camp meetings and to be present at other gatherings where my presence was needed."[19] Two years later the conference proposed "the omission of the second and third Quarterly Conferences for the purpose of holding local conventions to discuss the great question of Methodism . . ."[20] Apparently carrying through on that mandate, the district superintendent of a newly created "Central District" gave out three questions at the first quarterly conference to be addressed by key laity at the combined second and third. He did so to good effect and "Believing that the rejuvenation of the Quarterly

Conference, and its restoration to its former place of inspiring power in the local church, is to-day one of the most vital problems in our polity . . ." He held a district "Fellowship Meeting" for ministers and laity one outcome of which was a District Program, an eight-point platform the first plank of which was "The revivifying of the Quarterly Conference as an inspiring force for the local churches." The "Fellowship Meeting" featured closed sessions, a "Spiritual Retreat" and a "Quiet Hour," sessions devoted to "The Preacher and His Highest Equipment for Service" and "The Church at Work for the Master," and then the eight planks which ranged from the local—the revivifying of quarterly conference—to the district—a summer assembly "modeled on the Northfield lines." Fraternity, revival and polity lived on, here combining the old and the new, revivalistic forms and social gospel language. The District Superintendent spoke of his office as seeking "to create high spiritual ideals and to discover latent leadership in both ministry and laity and to inspire both to intelligent and consecrated effort to greater achievements for our beloved Methodism and Christ's Church everywhere."[21]

The Local Church

Quarterly conference lived on through the 20th century but its revivalist and fraternal ideals continued to flag. Increasingly, Methodism put its focus, not on conference, but on the local church (and the Sunday service). The combined quarterly conferences for the MEC came increasingly to resemble what the MECS knew as the annual church conference and both churches ran their business monthly with an official board, the MEC formally, the MECS more informally.[22] And by the 1920s, "the local church" had become a new norm. Indeed, in their 1928 address, the bishops of the MEC structured the entirety of their remarks in relation to "the local church":

> The local church is taken as the unit in our study of denominational progress, for it is there that we are to test the value of our organization and polity. It is the point of Methodism's contact with humanity. It is our recruiting office for the King's service. It is for us the institute of religious technology, our workshop, our training camp, our spiritual hospital, our home.[23]

The bishops then reviewed, in four sections, the state of the denomination, nation and world in relation to "the local church."

Under "I. The Local Church and What It May Ask of General Methodism," the bishops covered The Church Building, Members, Young People—The Church School, Young People—The Epworth

League, Young People—Finance, Office, The Pastor, Educational Institutions (the whole range), other aspects and tasks of the pastoral office, and several matters concerning laity (they urged admission of laity to annual conference, for instance).

"II. What the Local Church Owes to General Methodism," treated Solidarity and Cooperation and The Local Church and Missions.

"III. What World-Wide Methodism Asks of the World," sought, among other things "credit for honest intention, accuracy in reporting us, and the opportunity to serve" and fairness. And under

"IV. What World-Wide Methodism Owes to the World," the bishops devoted several subsections to youth and addressed The Industrial Problem, Sabbath, Debasing Literature—The Stage—Dress, Divorce, Prohibition, International and Inter-Racial Goodwill, World Peace, Co-ordination and Interdenominational Co-operation, Christian Unity, and The Church.

By conceptualizing the church in terms of its tasks and the local church, the bishops had made irrelevant, or perhaps better made 'subservient,' the entire conference fabric of Methodism. The tasks belonged to the boards and agencies; ministry belonged in the local church. What then of quarterly, district, annual and general conferences?

The bishops would never have conceded the irrelevance of 'conference,' nor could they. The denominational tasks and local ministry were tied together by the layers of conference and through them tasks were distributed, resources garnered and ministry defined and deployed. Nevertheless, the bishops had recognized a new norm at the bottom that went readily with the new bureaucratic norm at the top. Increasingly, the official board at one end and the boards and agencies at the other defined the operative polity of Methodism. Polity had become organizational. Conferences adjusted accordingly.

The Disciplines reflect the change. The 1928 (MEC) Discipline indexed "The Local Church" but spread treatments of it over various rubrics. The 1930 (MECS) Discipline included a subsection entitled "The Local Church" but lodged it under Christian education. The first Discipline of The Methodist Church, that of 1940, devoted a section to "The Local Church" and positioned it last under Part IV, "The Conferences." So placed, it belonged still to the conference order of Methodist reality.[24] By 1944 and from 1944 to 1960, "The Local Church" became Part II of the Discipline, following immediately after "The Constitution" and preceding Part III, "The Ministry" and Part IV, "The Conferences." Within "The Local Church" were embraced treatments of the quarterly conference and the church conference, as well as the official board. "The Local Church" entirely subsumed the once regional quarterly conference. Within that section as well was placed "Church Membership," once a major rubric in its own right.

In the 1968 Discipline of The United Methodist Church (the union of The Methodist and Evangelical United Brethren Churches), "The Local Church" stood first, constituted a major section, and even was made to incorporate the church's calendar. And by 1976 Wesley's ministry—once itinerating and connectional and continental and world-wide—had been embraced by or collapsed into the local church. "The Local Church" demanded fifty two pages of text and followed immediately upon a short theological statement about ministry. Ministry was characterized as local and the Discipline recognized non-local ministry under a new rubric—"Appointments Beyond the Local Church."

Soon thereafter the norm at the top, that defined by boards and agencies, was in deep trouble. Increasingly, Methodists thought not in connectional but in local and parish terms, they spoke of parish ministry and reflected the overall therapeutic and professional changes through which American ministry was passing. By 1990 when the Bishops produced a "Vision for the Church," they rendered it in congregational terms: *Vital Congregations—Faithful Disciples.*[25]

"Nothing Against Them"

Congregations, particularly Methodism's large, upscale, urban and later suburban, multi-staff, institutional affairs, wanted more say in the appointment process, more stable pastorates and more professionalism in their ministers. The same matters concerned annual conferences albeit not always from the same angle. Conferences, by Discipline charged with oversight of the ministry, increasingly exercised that oversight in professional fashion.

Conference scrutiny of their members and particularly of their probationary members underwent seemingly contradictory developments. On the one hand, the annual review of character—the examination of all ministers by the conference as a committee of a whole—became increasingly routinized, stylized and ritualized. On the other, conferences gave more exacting attention to their probationers through specialized committees, courses and institutes, more elaborate examinations and found various ways of encouraging formal theological education. The 1891 Philadelphia Conference expressed these two tendencies with motions. One motion endeavored to give the examination of character some continuing import and protection against disruption by other business:

That, when the call of the districts for the passage of character is begun, it shall not be in order to interrupt the call until all the districts are completed.[26]

Another set of motions (adopted first in 1890) established examining committees during conference, empowered them to meet, divide the work and publish the schedule, and directed the committees "to call the classes together at some convenient point in the Conference at least twice before the next session of the Conference for examination according to the plan."[27] The conference sought thereby to affirm both the older pattern of fraternal apprenticeship and review of character and the new scheme of professional evaluation through committee and schooling.

For some time conferences held together the two processes—the examination of character and professional assessment. In 1900, for instance, the Philadelphia Conference brought its deacons and elders into membership in ceremony that conjoined the two:

> The members of the class of the second year were called before the Conference.
> ADDRESS OF BISHOP.—The Bishop addressed the class, especially emphasizing pulpit preparation, pastoral visitation, and personal communion with God.
> ADMITTED INTO FULL MEMBERSHIP.—The names of the members of the class were called, their characters passed, they reported their missionary collections, the Board of Examiners and the Committee on General Qualification reported, the Presiding Elders represented, and the following were admitted into Full Membership and elected to Deacon's Orders. . . .
> ELECTED TO ELDER'S ORDERS.—The names of the members of the class of the fourth year were called, their characters passed, they reported their missionary collections, the Board of Examiners reported, the Presiding Elders represented, and the following were passed in their Conference Studies and elected to Elder's Orders.[28]
> . . .

The review of character had become except for problem cases, as we have noted in a previous chapter, a stylized endeavor, perfunctory endeavor, nicely captured by the language of the minutes year after year:

> The names of the Effective Elders of the South Philadelphia District were called, they reported their missionary collections, and their characters passed.[29]

The drama no longer lay in the probing of character but rather in the reporting of fiscal success. Indeed, General Conference had mandated that such reports be made, insisting in 1900 that presiding elders and pastors

> shall report in open Conference whether the provisions of the Discipline for the support of the various benevolences of the Church have been carried out in his district

and

> report in open Conference whether he has presented the claims of our benevolent causes according to the requirements of the Discipline.[30]

Now a programmatic and financial ritual, the language changed as the church altered the nature of its apportionments and reporting needs:

> The names of the effective elders on the Northwest District were called, their characters passed, and they reported their collections for Conference claimants.[31]

Gradually conferences dropped the pretense that any real review was going on and asked directly for its reports and whether trial of any member was indicated.

> CHARACTER OF ELDERS ON SOUTH DISTRICT PASSED.— Bishop Warren publicly asked A. G. Kynett the following questions:
> "Are there any charges preferred against any effective elder on the South District?
> "Has each one presented the benevolent causes during the year?
> The Presiding Elder answered: "No charges have been preferred." All the preachers have presented the benevolent causes to the several churches. The character of each effective elder on the South District was then passed.[32]

And as early as 1907 Philadelphia heard in the examination of character the simple exchange that would be the pattern for the rest of the century: "There is nothing against any effective elder on the Northwest District."[33] Passing the characters with a single blanket affirmation by the district superintendent took some time to take hold, perhaps because calling the individual pastor's name and hearing the report of financial receipts got results.[34] Philadelphia continued to hear the individual names called through 1919. Then in 1920

> Bishop Berry asked, "Is there anything against any of the effective elders on the South District? There being nothing against any of the effective elders on the South District, the Conference passed their characters.[35]

Professional Formation and Assessment

The examination of character no longer really served, as it once had, as the tool of assessment, either of those in continuing relation or those in the four-year probationary period. Indeed, the latter had for several decades become an increasingly professionalized process of schooling and examination. Some of that schooling took place in the church's colleges and theological seminaries which gradually became the vehicle of choice for ministerial preparation. These now received aid, oversight and accreditation from the Board of Education, a body much strengthened for such work by the creation in 1892 of a University Senate.[36]

Graduates of seminaries still faced the conference course of study, the mandated route into ministry. The church only gradually recognized seminary as fulfilling the course's expectations. In 1896 for instance, General Conference made one in a long series of concessions in permitting passing of a seminary examination to substitute for the course requirement (except in doctrine and discipline).[37] Conferences, however, did not always immediately concur.[38] Only in 1903 did Philadelphia acknowledge persons admitted "Under Seminary Rule."[39]

One reason for reluctance on the conference's part was that they had developed large scale, well-staffed and innovative training programs of their own. The 1896 General Conference in another action had received from the bishops new guidelines and procedures for the course of study. Included were provisions for a Board of Examiners enjoying a four-year term composed of "men with special qualifications for the work"; a mandate for record-keeping and reporting of academic credits as well as progress under the course; the assigning of individual examiners on each topic on which "he is to give instructions by correspondence and final examinations"; one or two examinations "in locations convenient to the students"; supervision of exams and specification of 70 as a passing grade; and a pre-conference session for the Board for review and examination purposes.[40]

The 1897 Philadelphia Conference carried over the bishops' guidelines with a three page itemization of protocols for Conference Examinations and expanded that to eight pages the following year.[41] Listed were the individual examiners for each specified book in each of the four years, fifteen books and examiners for admission on trial; the dates and places for two two-day examination sessions with the third to be the day before conference; an indication that there would be lectures on the evenings of examination days; an expectation that those who could should attend the monthly Ministerial Institute in

Philadelphia; detailing of exam procedures,including the indication that each exam would be two hours, whether written or oral; specification of writing assignments including an analytical "syllabus" for each book read,[42] exegetical studies, essays and sermons; and directions about submission of work.[43]

Here was a school, a regimented program, with clear classes, assignments and examinations for each year, heightened expectations about growth and learning, some provisions for direct instruction and a faculty. Persons entering the ministry chose, not between school and apprenticeship, but between the conference-correspondence-course-of-study-school and the residential academic year seminary.

The former continued to receive attention, intended to up-grade and professionalize the process and product. The initiatives indicate that gains came slowly. For instance, the Board of Education (MEC) in 1920 complained that Methodist pulpits were filled by and future recruitment for ministry done by men "of whom one half, roundly speaking, have not had the full equipment of a high school education" and only "about one-eighth have had high school, college, and theological education." The Board urged that, "The Conference Course of Study ought to be in the charge of a body of experts, responsible to the Board of Bishops or some other organized authority of the church." They called for master teachers committed full-time to instruction in the courses of study, six months residential programs "modelled upon the officers' training courses used by the army," underwriting of a student's expenses, relief of "students from pastoral obligations during the time of their attendance at institutes and at the training schools," and the production of special textbooks "sufficiently simple and elementary" for this clientele.[44] This same general conference also heard a report from its Commission on Courses of Study, a body established four years prior. It drew more somber conclusions than had the Board of the state of the course:

> The attitude of some Conferences suggests to the student a depreciation of this work. Men are continued year after year in their studies. Boards of Examiners are not supported in their efforts to maintain standards. The young man is often made to feel by those in authority that almost everything else is more important in his work than progress in his studies.[45]

Four years later this Commission issued a major report and outlined further initiatives already under way. These included (1) a series of "handbooks prepared by the Commission," for teachers in the courses, five volumes of which had already appeared; (2) the requiring of written assignments, not just examinations, from students and the (future) development for such assignments of a nationally coordinated correspondence school utilizing Methodist faculties; (3) increase in the number, quality and scope of summer schools of theology, already expanded from thirteen (1921) to forty-two (1923). In this up-grading, the Commission had also brought together to good effect, for purposes of briefing, training and response, representatives from the conference Boards of Examiners and summer schools of theology.[46]

The up-grading of the course of study and of its administration, undertaken by 'progressives,' met mixed reaction. Negative reaction fixed on the selection of books on the course and their liberal cast. Protesting resolutions and memorials to General Conference recur in the second and third decades of the century.[47] During the same period, resolutions and memorials on the course sought relief from the course for those taking formal theological training.

Persons entering the ministry received more exacting and more uniform attention than in earlier days but they received it from an institution or a committee. Gone were the linking of junior to senior preacher on circuit and the oversight by the conference as a whole over the process. Conference dealt with its probationers through committee. To be sure, it so dealt with virtually everything that way. By the turn of the century the journal needed ten pages to describe the structure of conference—officers, commissions, boards, managers and trustees, women's societies, standing committees, visiting committees and special committees.[48] Conference had become a forum for committees and institutions to provide year-end statements; conference sessions featured a series of reports, votes, resolutions, recognitions, certifications, introductions, addresses, sermons (the annual missionary sermon), punctuated by the Disciplinary questions, ordinations, a memorial service and the reading of appointments.

The committee or board oversight of candidacy and admission would become ever more pronounced as the doors of conference were widened to admit first a few and then eventually equal numbers of laity. Committee actions would be reported in a clergy-only executive session. Such a session could never involve the entire body in the probing examination of character, the hazing process applied to every member, that had once knit conference fraternity in close bonds. Conference bifurcated into an annual meeting—a body increasingly open and participated in equally by clergy and laity—and an executive session and structure of committees given over to professional concerns. Through the latter sub-structure, conferences behaved like a professional organization and concerned themselves with raising the minimum salary,[49] controlling admission through higher standards, guaranteeing insurance coverage,[50] protecting pensions.[51]

By 1910 the MEC bishops expressed concern over the "professional" preoccupation of ministers and conferences, a preoccupation they epitomized with the notion of salary. Support, not salary, they insisted was the Methodist pattern. "The Christian ministry is not a profession." and therefore it should not be upheld "on the secular basis of compensation."

> Methodist preachers are 'supported,' not hired. The difference is vital. A 'support' is the sum estimated, *for a pastor already appointed*, by an authorized committee after consultation with the pastor, as sufficient to furnish himself and family a comfortable livelihood. Under this plan consecration is not compromised, and the preacher's message may weigh its full gospel value.[52]

The minister is not under contract "with the Official Board or Quarterly Conference. It is an altar covenant with God alone." They went on then to complain against negotiations, lack of daring and sacrifice, the attention to the dollar value of an appointment, and the commercialization of pulpit service.[53] General Conference concurred and reaffirmed a 1884 resolution deeming negotiations as "contrary to the spirit of our itinerant ministry, and subversive of our ecclesiastical polity."[54] Fundamental change was occurring through professionalization as through localization.

Chapter 16

Jurisdictioned Fraternity

The dynamics of professionalization produced activity at the center—in the general conferences or through the University Senate (MEC) or College of Bishops (MECS)—where standards were set, new selections made for the courses of study, regulatory action or oversight was undertaken, resources garnered and rules and definitions made. Professionalization also produced activity at the periphery—on the local and conference level—where, as we have just noted, boards or committees took charge of implementing, interpreting and applying the standards and congregations made their own application of standards. Professionalization thus reinforced both national standards, *and ironically, by their implementation at the conference level,* reinforced also long-standing patterns of regionalization and localization, walling up the Methodist fraternity ever more within separate conference (fraternal) units.

Also to stimulate and reinforce inertial movement towards regionalization of ministry within conferences and within regions were the efforts at unification of Methodism—those conversations between the MECS and the MEC, eventually involving the MPC, that brought the 1939 reunion. They aimed at making Methodism a more national church and indeed would have that effect particularly insofar as the boards and agencies were concerned. Ironically, the effect on conference and on episcopacy was not centralizing and nationalization but fragmenting by region and race. A constitutional regionalization came with the 1939 union by the addition of yet another conference, the "jurisdictional," to the great iron organizational wheel—quarterly, district, annual, *jurisdictional*, general; by locating all 'white' annual conferences within regional jurisdictions and by placing all African American conferences into a new central jurisdiction; and by empowering the jurisdictions with important authority, including that of electing bishops and of the members of national boards. The effect was a far more regionalized and fragmented fraternity than had existed within the three uniting denominations, each of which had been, in its own way, a national body.

175

Unification: Fraternity by Race and Region

The aspiration for jurisdictions came from the MECS which, in conversations[1] that extended over half a century, held out for a conference arrangement that would (1) accord the minority within a united church (by minority they understood 'southern white') "the power to control its own affairs"[2] and (2) place another minority, namely the African American members of the MEC many of whom gathered in conference in southern territory, into some separate ecclesial structure, preferably one as distinct as the Colored Methodist Episcopal Church.[3] The proposed solution—then termed quadrennial conferences, consisting of another layer of conference between general and annual and providing for regional conferences for whites and a single quadrennial conference of blacks—surfaced in a 1911 round of discussions of a Joint Commission on Federation, comprised by representatives of the MEC, MP and MECS and held at Chattanooga.[4] On this proposal the MP General Conference deferred action pending action of the episcopal bodies. The MECS in 1914 recognized the agreement as containing the "basic principles of a genuine unification . . . by the method of reorganization" but insisted that African American Methodists be "formed into an independent organization holding fraternal relations with the reorganized and united church."[5] The MEC, meeting in 1916, also embraced the plan "as containing the basic principles of a genuine unification" but called for additional "Quadrennial or Jurisdictional Conferences" and conceded that its "colored membership" should be reorganized "into one or more Quadrennial or Jurisdictional Conferences."[6]

These actions led to the constitution of a Joint Commission on Unification representing the two episcopal bodies which met from 1916 to 1920 and left on record three volumes and over fifteen hundred pages of debates and speeches. Central in these negotiations was the racial complexion of any 'unified' Methodist fraternity.[7] On this issue, the southern commissioners were consistent and insistent. Early in the proceedings, for instance, Bishop Horace Du Bose proposed the creation "alongside the white membership of the reorganized Church a connection to bear the same name, perhaps to have some distinguishing description, an adjunct or subjunctive title to indicate that it is a colored connection." This he thought would house both the CME to which the MECS still held relation and the African American contingent of MEC and would enjoy something like the fraternal relations which pertained between the MECS and the CME. Bishop John M. Moore glossed the proposal by hoping that two unifications would occur, that between and among white Methodists and another among the MEC and the three "negro" churches. And Bishop Edwin D. Mouzon added, "The Methodist Episcopal Church, South, in General Conference assembled, recommended that the colored membership of the Methodist Churches be erected into an independent denomination." Then speaking for he southern Commission, he affirmed,

> We are sure that race consciousness, the race consciousness of the colored people and the race consciousness of the white people, the race consciousness of all peoples, must be taken into consideration. We believe that this is better for the colored people. We believe that that is necessary to us.

Northern commissioners, particularly Bishop John W. Hamilton, resisted the notion that race consciousness should govern unification schemes:

> You have all been talking as though these colored brethren were as clay, capable of being molded into a desired form, plastic in the hands of white people, as if we could handle them at our pleasure and do with them as we chose. There are difficulties in this matter that you brethren ought to see. In the first place, we have a body of colored brethren in our Church. . . . We have a constituency of more than a million adherents. We have treated them as men and brothers. We have made no distinction in the rights they sustain of relationship to our membership, just as is the case with you in your foreign mission fields. . . . We have nearly 350,000 colored members within our borders, each of whom has the rights of every white member. They have come into our fellowship through our tuition. Now, are we going to stand up and take each one of these members individually and say to him: 'You go off?' But go off where? . . . I have no more right to tell him to go out of our Church than he has to tell me to do the same. . . .[8]

Such high moral ground proved difficult to hold,[9] particularly since—as the southern commissioners were ever ready to point out—the MEC had itself largely segregated blacks into separate annual conferences and congregations.[10]

Hamilton proved a lonely voice in resisting a race-conscious plan and the jurisdictional scheme gradually emerged through the discussions as a structure (1) that would provide regional configurations among white Methodists thus protecting the southern (white) minority from domination by the northern majority and (2) that would establish a "compromise" between the southern desire for a CME-like solution and northern resistance to a unification that would further divide the church and expel its black membership. Supporting such a compromise were the two African American (MEC) commissioners,

I. G. Penn and R. E. Jones, who viewed jurisdictions as much prefer-able to excision, who did not aspire to union with the other black Methodist bodies, and who welcomed a plan that would, at last, provide for black episcopal leadership. They resisted what became another southern stratagem in the discussions, namely a conference embracing both Africa and the U.S.[11] R. E. Jones affirmed:

> Now, what do we want? . . . First of all, we do not want any caste written in the Constitution. That is fundamental. Second, we do not want any offensive name in whatever arrangement you make . . . And it is fundamental that we should ask for representation in the General Conference. We will agree to the formation of our member-ship from one end of the country to the other in a centralized Conference. . . . I will agree to a reduced representation in the General Conference; I will not agree to elimination. I want the right of the initiative and referendum. . . . We will agree to our bishops having jurisdiction within our territory—that is, that by some proc-ess they shall be limited to our people, so that there will not be any fear that any of our bishops shall ever preside over a white Confer-ence.[12]

That guarantee was reached in the five years of Joint Commission discussions,[13] a scheme for six white regional conferences, one for the "colored people in the United States," and four for membership in foreign countries.[14] African American Methodists would be repre-sented in General Conference, though not in the same proportions as would the white regional conferences and the foreign repre-sentation was even more reduced. To these regional conferences were conferred the rights of episcopal election.[15] In addition, provision was made for a judicial council and for a brake on general conference action by vote of two regional delegations.[16]

To the 1920 MEC General, the bishops posed four questions to ask of union or federation:

> 1. Does the movement make for a real brotherhood of Christian people? 2. Does the movement make for the real unity of all sections, races, nations, and classes within Christ's Church? 3. Does the movement make for unity of life, unity of sacrificial, atoning purpose toward men, unity in the holiness and passion of the church's life, like the unity between Christ and the Father? 4. Does the movement make for evangelistic efficiency and the triumph of the cross among all peoples, all classes, all races, and on all continents?

They went on to say:

> For the Church of Christ is not a racial church. The Church of Christ is not a national, sectional, or class church. Plans of union that

sectionalize, that nationalize, that racialize the church are not plans for Christian union.[17]

The conference found other aspects of the plan troubling and, while reaffirming its commitment to unity, continued its Commission and called for the convening of a Joint General Convention (of the MEC and MECS) to iron out problems.[18]

Where the MEC saw problems, the MECS experienced crisis. Virtual warfare broke out in the South over unification, warfare that badly divided the College of Bishops, that roiled annual conferences, that became the consuming passion of certain papers and that politicized the entire church. Progressives supported the commission's plan; to oppose it, conservatives formed organizations like the League for the Preservation of Southern Methodism. The lines were clearly drawn and honored over a variety of controversies during the 1920s and 1930s, (touching reorganization, the Klan, prohibition, fundamentalism, evolution and Al Smith).[19] Each of the issues seemed to entail the others and unification certainly served to emblem conservative fears of the Negro, the north, change, modernism and secularism.

By its temporizing action of 1920, the MEC took the MECS (1922) off the hook. It did not have to act on the plan and bring the swelling controversy to focus. The MECS rejected the notion of such a Joint General Convention but also continued a commission and authorized the calling of a special session of its General Conference if the commissions were able to work out a viable plan.

This new Joint Commission met in early 1923 and adopted a new plan, which continued some features of the 1916–20 proposal, but addressed southern racial and regional concerns by establishing just two jurisdictions, one embracing the MEC, the other the MECS. The MEC General Conference adopted it with little fanfare, as did its annual and lay conferences. By contrast, the MECS General Conference experienced a tense special session, marked by prolonged debate over a procedural amendment proposed by A. J. Lamar and supported by four of the bishops challenging the legality of the special session and calling for a year's delay.[20] The southern church eventually defeated the Lamar Resolution and passed the plan but not before the opposition to unification had scored its points, many of them detailed in a twenty-five Minority Report that insisted that the issues of 1844 were not dead, that the plan surrenders the liberty and independence of the church, that it "practically strips the Annual Conferences of all power in the government of the Church" and confers it on "the Super-General Conference," and that "it established a relation with the negro race not best for him, not possible for us."[21]

Such sentiments carried the day when the plan was submitted, as such fundamental constitutional changes required, to the MECS annual conferences. New organizations emerged, the "Friends of Unification," and the "Association to Preserve the Methodist Episcopal Church, South by Defeating the Pending Plan of Unification," each with its backing within the church press and its patrons on the College of Bishops. The southern *Advocates*, twenty for unification, six against, hoisted the battle banners and the bishops in their teaching office and as the appointive power weighed in for the two causes. Presiding bishops used and abused their power to sway the annual conference votes. As leaned the presiding bishop so voted the conference, with but one exception.[22] The plan went down to defeat, 4,528 for 4,108 against, far short of the required 75 percent and indicative of how badly divided the southern church found itself. Convening again two years later in regular session, the MECS accepted the recommendation of its Committee on Church Relations "That there be no agitation, discussion, or negotiation concerning unification during the ensuing quadrennium."[23]

The MECS found further reason for reticence in the 1928 action of the MEC in resolving that it would hold General Conference only where its white and black delegates could be entertained on the same basis.[24] In response, Bishop Edwin D. Mouzon (MECS) proclaimed that this action "postponed the union of the Church South and the Church North indefinitely."[25] The MEC and MP did continue conversations in the late 1920s and early 1930s and the MECS rejoined in 1934, the resumption preceded by national youth gatherings, informal meetings of interested leaders and exploratory sessions of standing commissions on union. The three churches formally authorized negotiations in general conferences of 1932 and 1934. Yet another Joint Commission met in 1934 and 1935, accepted the principles of jurisdictional governance and full lay representation, and appointed a drafting subcommittee.

1939: Ensmalling the Church?

The new committee's plan reverted to the 1916–20 conception of multiple (white) regional jurisdictions and one central (black) jurisdiction. It provided for equal representation of laity and clergy in annual, jurisdictional, and general conferences, the retention of bishops and the establishment of a Council of Bishops, a Judicial Council related to General Conference and the Council of Bishops, and a new name—The Methodist Church.

This plan passed in general and annual conferences in all three churches, again eliciting opposition in the South[26] and this time producing considerable anguish in African American conferences and among others committed to more genuine Methodist fraternity. African Americans contributed 36 of the 83 "no" votes in the 1936 MEC General Conference, 11 others abstaining. They sat in silence while the conference sang "We're Marching to Zion." Seven of the nineteen black conferences defeated the proposal, a few others refusing to vote, the remainder resigning themselves to the inevitable.[27] Just as the nation was becoming more sensitive to its racial inequalities and to segregation as a blight on democracy, Methodism had made more visible and constitutional the color line it had long drawn within its fraternity.

Jurisdictions divided Methodist fraternity by race—gathering all the African American conferences into one Central Jurisdiction. Jurisdictions also divided the white fraternity by region. And it located within the Jurisdictions critical 'connectional' powers—namely the election and deployment of bishops and the election of the governing board members of the national agencies.

One other 'connectional' power was stripped from General Conference at the Uniting Conference of 1939—the election of the general secretaries of the national agencies.[28] The proposal honored professionalism—election of agency staff by its own board was, as one proponent put it, in accordance with "the usual practice when you are seeking experts as these boards will require to perform an expert job." Would the nearly 800 members of the new General Conference have the competence, leisure and judgment to choose as wisely?[29] A few thought that staff professionalism sacrificed important denominational values. J. M. M. Gray (Detroit) insisted

> . . . In some fashion we must combat effectively the disintegrating influence of Jurisdictional lines upon our general connectional influence. And when we elect all our secretaries by boards and elect all our boards by Jurisdictions we have flung away the last of the great influences that have bound us together as a connection.
> I am in favor of the election of the Secretary by the General Conference.

Agreeing, Harold Paul Sloan (New Jersey) spoke against the tendency to "ensmall" the church and of the divisive potential of elections by the boards of their staff.

> (1) I feel there is grave danger of breaking our great American Methodism up into a lot of small groups, each Board will be a group, each Jurisdiction will be a group, and the large interests of the Church instead of coming into focus in the great United General

nce, will never come to focus at all, but will be in expression
small groups.

The responsibility in most instances with these executive
s is a responsibility in which they can commend themselves to
the Church as a whole. A man who has not made an impression upon
the Church as a whole as an effective leader for a Board ought not
to be elected to that place.[30]

The Uniting Conference was in a festive, celebrative, even revivalistic mood, not in the frame of mind to test elements of the new
bond of fraternity, jurisdictionalism and professionalism, even in the
name of what had been essentials of Methodism—connectionalism
and accountability to conference (polity and fraternity). Nor could the
delegates be expected to anticipate the consequences of the many
changes that it authorized—

- the dramatic enlargement of general conferences, through the
  uniting itself, and of annual conferences, through full lay representation and equalization—enlargements that affected capacities for oversight, decision-making, governance;

- the reduction of bishops from itinerating general superintendents to regional and eventually diocesan officers;

- the establishment of regional/racial authority, through jurisdictional elections, as the office-making principle;

- the diffusing of power and responsibility through the various
  conference levels (general, jurisdictional, annual);

- the concession to the national boards, themselves increased to
  what had once been 'conference' size, of new powers of self-determination; and

- the establishment of a body with powers of judicial review—the
  Judicial Council.

The consequence of so diffusing authority was to leave the boards
and agencies as *the* connectional principle in the church. If the plan
did not exactly "ensmall" the church, it did decentralize both conference and episcopacy so as to "enlarge" the place for bureaucracy.

In the churches produced by the 1939 and 1968 unions, jurisdictions functioned as a electoral colleges in the Methodist polity. Three
of them evolved in significant fashion into genuine conferences,
developed an on-going apparatus and played key roles in conference
economy. The two southern jurisdictions, the Southeastern and South
Central, did so by design, effectively carrying into their operations the

personnel, relationships, papers, schools, camps, style and ethos of the southern church. The Southeastern owned the Lake Junaluska Assembly and Emory University, developed a kind of axis between Junaluska and Atlanta, employed two executive secretaries, established program committees covering the major areas of the church's life, carried on promotional campaigns within the jurisdiction.[31]

The Central Jurisdiction was symbolically problematic from the start. It dissociated black Methodists from their cross-town or -countryside white counterparts. It also created some large and unwieldy conferences and forced leadership to cover great distances. Never did it garner the resources nor claim the denominational attention that its proponents had envisioned.

It did nevertheless connect African American Methodists in ways that they had not been previously connected. It became a national structure that provided for the identification, development, selection and exercise of black leadership. The Central Jurisdiction guaranteed black representation on national boards and committees (denominational and women's); produced national leadership for the church; continued as the *Central Christian Advocate* a denominational paper with a significant black readership; gave sustained national attention to the denomination's black colleges; and from the start witnessed prophetically against the very racism that it emblemed.[32]

For black women the Central Jurisdiction's Women's Society of Christian Service proved an effective vehicle for 'sorority.' for witness, for action and for collaboration. The Women's Society, working with their white counterparts and through the Board of Missions, played particularly important roles, from the early 1940s, in promoting interracial concord, campaigning for African American staffing and representation in denominational missions, and protesting segregation.[33]

An artifact of white racism and a vehicle for black empowerment, an expression of ethical failure and an instrument of social witness, an emblem of a divided community and a structure for black fraternity and sorority, the Central Jurisdiction lived a far more complex existence than the other jurisdictions. It began the campaign to end its own life, from within and virtually with its constitution, and continued it as a quest for a fuller affirmation of Methodist fraternity throughout the 1950s and 1960s.

Towards an inclusive fraternity, the church made slow progress—

- expressing a commitment to "the ultimate elimination of racial discrimination in The Methodist Church" in 1944;

- redrawing some western boundaries in 1948 to make easier the voluntary transfer of black churches out;

- easing such transfer in 1952;

- establishing a constitutional principle in 1956 (Amendment IX) of voluntary transfer of entire conferences or parts of conferences as well as congregations;

- embroiling itself in 1960 in a major debate over elimination of the Central Jurisdiction but failing to agree on a deadline, studying the matter in Commissions over the 1960–64 quadrennium; and

- resolving in 1964 with respect to projected unity with the Evangelical United Brethren that "no racial structure[s] be carried over into the Constitution of the new United Church."

The Central Jurisdiction met last in a special session in 1967 and the final transfers and mergers were completed by 1973. Some of its energy and vision live on in Black Methodists for Church Renewal, a caucus expression to jurisdictional life and yet, as we shall see, another form of Methodist 'fraternity' and 'conference.'[34]

Jurisdictions did not create Methodism's racial and regional divisions. Racial divisions survived the elimination of the Central Jurisdiction on a congregational level and in appointment patterns. Jurisdictions did give such divisions constitutional and conference expression. They legitimated a fraternal exclusivism that had been in Methodism from the start and that yielded grudgingly at admission of laity, local preachers, women, people of color. They put in place a principle of representation by category (by region and race) that would, as it came to be applied to more and more self-identifications, build division into denominational workings. By legitimating, indeed, equating the connection of annual conference with region, by dividing conferences jurisdictionally, by locking conferences into space, they made it difficult to reclaim the notion of conferences as provisional and missional expressions of a collective Methodist ministerium. It would be henceforth unthinkable to imagine redrawing conference lines to cross jurisdictions. It became less and less thinkable to imagine recarving conferences within jurisdictions. Combining conferences seemed, however, to be everybody's gain—bigger fraternities, capable of greater things.

Chapter 17

Conference to Caucus:
Mergers and Pluralism

1939 brought unity and division, unity in a larger general conference, now combining the three branches of Methodism into a truly national church, and division into jurisdictions of region and race. That story line—of mergers producing ever-larger 'fraternities' and of new institutions for division and diversity—also defined the drama for annual conferences from 1939 to the 1990s. Conferences grew larger by the unifications of 1939 and 1968, by the inclusion of laity in equal numbers, by dissolution of the Central Jurisdiction, by actions to merge contiguous conferences. Unity and integration were the slogans of the day, internally echoing the ecumenical gospel and the Civil Rights impulse. Growth also had much to do with professional interests, interests both of clergy and of episcopacy.

The slogan of unity and the fact of larger, more inclusive conferences made division by conference, segregation by conference, ever more problematic. Increasingly Methodists objected to dividing out conferences by language and race, a pattern practiced and sanctioned for over a century in the interest of the older (European) ethnicities but problematic when imposed upon a race. The Central Jurisdiction, in particular, became Methodism's public scandal. Ironically, by its creation, by giving segregation the ultimate sanction—making it connectional and constitutional—1939 laid foundations for dissociation of conference and particularity. Aversion to division and distinction by conference became a principle, so when in the 1970s and 80s Americans again found ethnicity essential, new particularities could not be accorded 'conference' status. And lacking conference as a vehicle for fraternity, revival, and order, Koreans, other Asian Americans, Hispanics, Native Americans, African Americans, women, and gays experimented with other forms of community in the last decades of the century. One of the alternatives to conference that emerged was the caucus.

Conference 'Brotherhood'?

The 1939 Uniting Conference did not really debate the Central Jurisdiction and its racial boundaries of Methodist fraternity. Nor was it willing to address another boundary issue, namely full clergy rights for women. Florence Resor Jardine (Northern Minnesota) had presented a minority report specifying "Women are included in all provisions, both for the local and the traveling ministry." Appeals to the ministerial roles (short of full ordination) already conceded by the MEC, to the century of Methodist Protestant experience, and to the women clergy within that communion proved of no avail. The latter would be 'grandfathered' in.[1] Other women would wait until 1956 for full clergy rights and admission to annual conference on those grounds. Lay women, however, retained rights of annual conference membership in the new church, as they had in the MP and MECS (the latter only since 1918).

For former annual conferences of the MEC, both the admission of laity and the inclusion therein of lay women, represented changes to what had been once an exclusive brotherhood. The addition of laity, male and female, in numbers proportional to the clergy changed MEC conferences dramatically (MECS to a lesser extent; MP not at all), perhaps easing the way to full ordination of women. Bodies of male clergy, tenured for life, now welcomed lay representatives, individuals who might or might not be elected for more than one session and simply did not 'belong' in the same fashion.[2] What now might bond conference?

As significant a change in that brotherhood, but one less easily recognized, was its increased size. To put the matter bluntly, the 1939 conference mergers produced bodies so large as to make difficult, if not impossible, the kinds of personal bonds of each with all that once had characterized the brotherhood. And 1939 only set the stage for a series of other mergers.

The change induced by size escaped and continues to escape remark for various reasons, particularly because other adjustments claimed immediate attention—to the merging of these old fraternities, the conferences; to the new faces, the strangers now 'brothers'; to the new jurisdictional order; to different ways of doing business requiring harmonization; to new leadership (and for MP's to bishops); to a new class of membership, the laity (for MEC's); to a new identity as a conference of The Methodist Church; and, of course, to the regimens and austerities of yet another World War, a war that brought massive numbers of women into the work force and made their presence in conference hardly remarkable.

Another reason that the new size escaped extensive comment was that conferences, in older areas of Methodist labors, had been growing all along. The churches had gradually eased away from the early 19th century practice and policy of routinely reducing the size of conferences by division. Or perhaps it would be more accurate to say that the practice of dividing off conferences, had, as it were, moved west (and abroad) with the frontiers of Methodist growth. Increasingly, the churches left the older conference intact. In a few instances there had been some mergers of small contiguous conferences. In consequence, older conferences had experienced growth as the Methodist population itself grew. The growth can been visualized through the opening roll calls of two of the older conferences (MEC):

	Baltimore[3]		Philadelphia	
	Clergy	Laity	Clergy	Laity
1860	73	0		
1870	115	0	118	0
1880	146	0	155	0
1890	144	0	156	0
1900	160	0	240	0
1910	178	0	215	0
1920	217	0	254	0
1930	202	0	217	0

Even for these rather large conferences, however, unification represented change. Both doubled[4] just by the admission of laity to become quite large bodies. Compare the following combined clergy and laity numbers with those of 1930:

	Baltimore		Philadelphia	
	Clergy	Laity	Clergy	Laity
1940	294	233	258	232

Only former MEC conferences experienced doubling merely through the admission of laity (or to put the matter differently by the uniting of the lay conference and the annual conference). From its inception, the MP had accorded laity full membership as had the MECS more recently.[5] But conference members from those churches also experienced dramatic growth in the 1939 unification. Many of the MP conferences had been small. Note, for instance, the MP conferences of Indiana and Ohio:

	Clergy	Probationers	Laity
Indiana			
1937	51	5	36
1938	48	8	36
1939	56	12	50
Ohio			
1937	53	7	48
1938	58	7	50 [6]

The MECS conferences which had not accorded the laity parity grew but less dramatically.

Further, many conferences from these two traditions felt the change in scale where conferences from all three churches were joined. Such mergers occurred across the Methodist heartland, from the upper South and middle Atlantic states to the west coast. The Virginia Conference of the new church grew dramatically over its primary predecessor body, that of the MECS. In 1939, it had convened with 269 ministers and 127 laity in attendance. The new (MC) conference meeting that same year experienced difficulty in opening, determining its new membership and adjusting lists from the MEC, MP and MECS. The first general conference ballot revealed its new size, 401 clergy and 276 laity. The next year (1940) the roll call was answered by 477 clergy and 179 laity.[7] In future years the laity would turn out in better proportions. The new Virginia conference had more than doubled.

The new West Virginia Conference of the Methodist Church drew even more dramatically. It brought together West Virginia conferences of the three churches and drew also from Baltimore and Holston. In its first meeting in 1939, the leadership also apparently despaired of straightening out membership and attempted no roll call. The first ballot for General Conference elections showed 353 clergy and 224 laity in session. The next year a roll call indicated 415 clergy and 286 laity. The predecessor conferences had simply not been of that scale. In the 1938 MEC conference 156 ministers (plus 23 supplies) had answered roll call. In the 1938 MECS conference 109 clergy and 44 laity answered. The MPC was of roughly the same size by of equal numbers of laity and clergy (69 and 69).[8] Fraternities of 150 had become an institution of roughly 700.[9] Roll calls for such a crowd were too time consuming and difficult. Not surprisingly, many conferences that had not already done so abandoned yet another fraternal ritual and resorted to registration cards.

West Virginia's experience did not typify those of conferences more remote from the swath across the country where the MEC and MECS competed or where episcopal Methodism overlapped with MP strongholds. Some conferences remained small. In the Northeastern Jurisdiction, in fact, only West Virginia and Baltimore were of this scale. New York East, Newark, Philadelphia, New Jersey, Central Pennsylvania and Pittsburgh had ministerial membership of 200 or so. And two New England conferences, New Hampshire and Vermont, were under 100.[10] In the Western Jurisdiction, Southern California had 285 ministers in effective relation and California had 225, with other conferences, including the Japanese, Hawaiian, and Latin American being quite small. Still for all the prior MEC conferences, unification doubled their numbers and did so including people (the laity) whose membership was good only one year at a time. Clergy registered their sense that the fraternity had been fundamentally changed with complaints about conference size, as Nolan Harmon notes:

> The unwieldiness of present Annual Conferences in The Methodist Church has been much complained of. This is, of course, due to the doubling of conference membership in those conferences largely made up of former Methodist Episcopal or/and Methodist Episcopal Church, South units. The admission of one layman for every charge had the effect of doubling such bodies, and at once presented conference entertainment committees, and those in charge of conference program with a problem in housing, feeding, and organizing such largely increased bodies. The expense of entertaining each Annual Conference leaped accordingly, and as a consequence there has been a tendency to cut to a minimum the actual time of holding such conferences.[11]

Perhaps because the principle of fraternal intimacy had been sacrificed in the interests of a higher good—broader lay participation in governance, in the establishing of budgets, in the setting of policy and in the determining of program—perhaps because the gains so clearly offset the loses, conferences could take advantage of increased size for still other gains. Larger conferences could afford a larger staff to program more effectively and duplication might be curtailed and efficiencies achieved. Larger conferences permitted a greater array of possible appointments, making it easier for cabinets and bishops to move clergy around and making itineration seem more like progress to better and better appointments.

So in the last half of the 20th century, smallness was no longer prized and a new pattern of conference unifications was set, reversing what had been the nineteenth century policy—dividing conferences.

Over the next decades clergy (and bishops) sought to enlarge conferences—to increase the appointment or career options for ministers, to make appointment-setting easier on cabinets and bishops, to reduce, preferably to one, the number of conferences over which a bishop had to preside, to develop stronger conference programs, to increase the financial base for pension programs, to achieve efficiencies (and savings) by merging conference staffs and, toward the end of the century, to make easier women's, double career, ethnic and cross-racial appointments.[12]

Gains for efficiency, episcopal convenience and clergy careers came with a price. Annual conference sessions outgrew the churches or chapels in which they had met, where business flowed easily into worship, and where every architectural detail reminded the body of why it met and whom it served. By 1970 when yet another merger had taken place (with the Evangelical United Brethren), the ministerial membership (in full connection) of the Baltimore Conference had reached 662, Eastern Pennsylvania (Philadelphia) 559, West Virginia 541, and Virginia 887. Texas was by then 657, Southern California-Arizona 828, East Ohio 799, Iowa 813, West Ohio 1,190, Western North Carolina 834, and Florida 854.[13] With roughly equal numbers of laity present, such conferences strained the facilities of even the largest churches and college chapels. To accommodate their numbers conferences resorted to gymnasiums and civic centers.

The Whole in the Part

With a premium now on inclusion, with representation as a constitutive principle and with conferences of such size as to make exclusion anomalous, the church struggled after 1939, as we have noted, with the segregation that it had institutionalized in the Central Jurisdiction. Other conference particularities and 'conferenced' particularity had given way with less resistance.

Notable was the decline of the ethnic-language conference. In the 1920s, the MEC had divided itself ethnically—ten German conferences, six Swedish, two Norwegian-Danish, two Hispanic, a Japanese, a Chinese, twenty African American (plus missions and mission conferences abroad). The MECS lacked the African American conferences but did feature Native American, Hispanic and German mission conferences. The MP had had African American, German and Native American conferences. The EUB and its conferences, of course, represented two German-speaking traditions. Well into the 20th century, then, ethnicity was valued positively, ministry along language and racial lines thought imperative, and conferences utilized as the structures for such purposes.

This older conference ethnicity succumbed, a casualty of the integrating and unifying tendencies of 20th century America. The conferences and congregations gradually moved to English and welcomed (or accepted) unity with other Methodist conferences. German Methodism (within the MEC and MECS) suffered in the anti-German fervor of the First World War, churches gave up language particularities and German conferences merged with over-lapped English-speaking counterparts, for the MECS in 1919, for the MEC over the next decade. Also in the 1920s, some Swedish, Norwegian and Danish conferences united with English conferences. Others continued through unification, but merged among themselves and then with English-speaking counterparts in the 1940s. A distinct Chinese conference remained until 1952 and a Japanese one until 1964. The major exception to this pattern of ethnic merger were Native Americans and Hispanics who, though merged with English conferences elsewhere, in the southwest and Puerto Rico had sufficient territorial rootedness as well as ethnic-linguistic staying power to retain their conference structures, surviving the unifications of 1939 and 1968 and the abolition of the Central Jurisdiction. The Rio Grande Conference, the Puerto Rico Conference[14] and the Oklahoma Indian Missionary Conference remain as testimony to the importance the churches once accorded conference particularity.

Illustrative of this integrating and unifying (ecumenical) tendency was the 1968 unification of English-speaking Methodism with the former German-speaking denomination, The Evangelical United Brethren, itself the product of complex mergers including particularly the Evangelical Church and the Church of the United Brethren in Christ. Fittingly, the EUB insisted, as one condition for unity, on the full dismantling of the Central Jurisdiction and the uniting of the remaining black and white conferences.

The process in the case of the Central Jurisdiction was more agonizing and conflicted than in the other unifications but shared the common pattern. Unifications had meant aggregation and absorption, the smaller language or racial conferences and churches being integrated into the larger and existing Anglo or English-speaking entities. A notable exception to this larger trend was South Carolina, where white and black conferences were of similar size. Over all, though, African American congregations and ministers were but the last to be absorbed in a church that had put unity in its name.

Ironically, inclusion and unity bred new alternative quasi-conferences. African Americans were among the first to re-establish another members-only form of conference, the caucus, and were to be among the intended beneficiaries of a new modality of connectionalism, what in American society generally would be known as the monitoring or regulatory agency. Black Methodists for Church Renewal (BMCR) dates from a national organizing conference in February 1968, which in the mood of Black power, called for self-definition, self-determination and black solidarity.[15] In that same year, General Conference established the Commission on Religion and Race as a general agency for the new church.

BMCR and, to a lesser extent, the Commission, which had a multi-ethnic mandate, continued and gave fresh expression to the conference and connectional life that African Americans had experienced in the Central Jurisdiction. And they signalled what would be a common pattern for the remainder of the century, namely the emergence of affinity groups, organized locally, on a conference level, regionally and nationally.

Other groups and commissions, with similarly particularized agenda and membership, emerged about the same time—some like the Good News Movement (1966) to remain an association, others like the Commission on the Status and Role of Women (1970) to gain agency status. In the same year as COSROW was established, emerged the Native American International Caucus,[16] in 1971 Methodists Associated Representing the Cause of Hispanic Americans,[17] in 1974 the National Federation of Asian American United Methodists[18] and in 1975, Affirmation, a gay and lesbian caucus.

Such bodies were by no means new, as we have seen. Groups of local preachers, for missions, against slavery, for holiness, for Sunday schools, for temperance—for or against the issues that concerned the church—had prospered in the 19th century. And, as we have noted, such bodies played conference-like roles for their adherents. However, such entities functioned in relation to the whole, in a different fashion, not as 'brother' or 'sister' conferences in the larger family but as assemblages of prophets who wanted the family reformed.

The prophetic mood and form prospered in the late 20th century, perhaps because unity had become the norm, perhaps because church gatherings had become so large, perhaps because the church no longer could give new missional endeavor its own conference, perhaps because the caucus form served well in a society ideologically conflicted. At any rate, the new bodies—whether organized from the affinity group as a caucus or accorded commission status by the denomination—often find themselves in a prophetic relation to conferences and the rest of the church. They behave like monitoring, watch-dogging, advocacy, special-interest agencies, the religious

counterpart to the political action group. Such ⌐
operate with a hermeneutic of suspicion, powers or ⌐
investigation and report, a mandate to correct chur⌐
eventually the warrant of official or quasi-official accepta.

The caucuses have functioned like political action gro
have also functioned like conference or mission agencies—ı.
fying and developing leadership, in urging its recognition ¸ the
church as a whole, in representing the interests of their membership,
in demanding the resources requisite for effective ministry and mission, in serving as spokespersons for their membership.

The caucuses have become alternative Methodist conferences—
with conference's revivalistic, 'fraternal' and organizational roles.
National and regional gatherings feature fervent, celebrative worship
and especially singing. Some groups (Good News, BMCR, Korean
caucus) offer explicitly and traditional revivalistic fare, more in touch
with conference's revivalistic heritage than annual conferences themselves. Others experiment liturgically but with comparable intensity,
joy, involvement, expressiveness. The latter's spirituality functions to
continue the transformation of revival into word.

The intense spirituality affects the quality of the relationships
within and among the group. Gatherings evidence the joyful hugs of
meeting and the painful physical parting of early conferences. Individuals network with brothers or sisters sharing the cause, culture,
heritage or language. Publications, phone-calls and computer-con-
nections sustain those networks between meetings. Fraternity has
become sorority and community, albeit developed and expressed
most fully intra-rather than inter-group. Such communalism, ecclesial
and eucharistic, furthers Methodism's search for alternatives to 'fraternity,' new styles, modes, structures of reclaiming conference's affective dimension.

Such search for a new order, for new order, is often taken to be
the preoccupation of the affinity groups. And, at times, they do seem
consumed with a passion for order for polity. They envision a new
church. Towards that end, collectively the members dream, plan and
labor in building effective and faithful institutions. The caucus may
itself be structured to model the new order. Or the caucus may devote
its energies to structuring United Methodism as a whole. They typically garner resources to institutionalize and to staff for such program-
ming. Caucuses have become among the most obvious and effective
expressions of Methodist connectionalism (though obviously they
divide as well as unite).

The Part in the Whole

United Methodists had no premium on the caucus, political action group and regulatory agency. They became standard features and action modalities of American political and religious life in the 1970s and 80s. In national life as within the denomination, the unitive, integrating and consensus trends triumphed only to elicit and confront a revived ethnicity. In part, the one bred the other. Efforts to achieve full integration required attention to past discriminatory practice and hence to the particularities that divided. Affirmative action, utilization-analyses, court-appointed quotas became accepted procedures for achieving representation and overcoming past discrimination. Such integrative efforts ran on ethnic- and gender- and handicapping-consciousness. A revived particularity, however, derived only in small part from such U.S. exigencies. Across the globe a revived ethnicity challenged the homogenizing and unifying post WW II commitments. Affinity organizations became the order of the day.

The Methodist Church and United Methodism discovered, also, that unity required structuring for particularity. Methodism had, for a century and a half, organized itself politically through conferences. And when gathered in plenary meetings, as in General Conference, it had cared for representation through conference delegation. With ethnic conferences all but gone and, in principle, unacceptable, the church discovered that organization solely on the basis of conference no longer guaranteed that the various interests would be represented. The new affinity groups became essential to the organizational grammar and particularity the operative criterion for order.

The 1939 union had put regional, jurisdictional quotas into play. The 1968 union mandated percentages in general and jurisdictional agency membership for representation from the former EUB and MC bodies and stipulated that agencies staff themselves "without regard to race, color or sex" *but also* achieve adequate representation with respect to such categories and also with regard to "laymen and laywomen." The church extended the mandate for racial representation from the general down to the local level and authorized "boards, committees, and agencies" when the normal procedures of election did not so provide "to elect as many additional members at large as may be necessary to meet this requirement."[20]

In 1976, the church gave representation by particularity a formulaic expression. The working of the new formulae can best be seen in the mandates for the boards and agencies. Program boards were to be constituted through the usual jurisdictional mechanisms and with the required jurisdictional representation. Percentage membership for former EUBs was continued. Now jurisdictional slates were to have four laymen, four laywomen and four clergy in full connection (one of the latter "shall be a woman") so that the boards were one-third laymen, one third laywomen and one third clergy. If that process did not result in sufficient representation by ethnic minorities, women, youth and young adults, then boards were "to perfect the representation" with at-large members, while maintaining the one-third principle. Further, boards were exhorted to have "no less than two (one woman and one man) of each of the following: Asian Americans, African Americans, Hispanic Americans, and Native Americans" and no less than 20 percent under thirty-one.[21] To achieve nominees for such an elaborate organizational expectations, the *Discipline* authorized each agency to establish special at-large nominating committees empowered to consult with the Rio Grande, Puerto Rico, and Oklahoma Indian Conferences, with the caucuses and with other appropriate groups.

Observing the General Conference that produced this formula and the nominating process that ensued, Robert Wilson and Paul Mickey spoke of "institutional crisis" and charged that staffing of agencies by category, rather than serving programmatic and missional purposes, had made selection an end in itself.[22] That perhaps overstates the negative consequences of the new procedures of recognizing leadership, fails to recall the particularities that ordered Methodism in the past, and understates the symbolic significance previously associated with service on general agencies. Nevertheless, the new particularity and representational schema did change conferences and conference life. Most obviously, this formula governed representation—who represented conferences on boards and agencies. But since it applied to conference agencies as well as national and jurisdictional, formula representation increasingly affected the church at all levels. Conferences, as well as jurisdictions and the general church, staffed their committees and agencies and filled cabinets and program positions under the mandate to achieve inclusivity. Warranting this new inclusivity were a heightened self-consciousness that the church's leadership must be as pluraform as the church itself[23] and new theologies of the laity, of liberation, of pluralism.[24] Enabling it were the entry of women into professional roles and, in particular, into the ministry and new resources poured into ethnic ministry, particularly through missional priority given the Ethnic Minority Local Church (from 1976 to 1988). Conferences indeed struggled to became as pluraform and diverse as the church itself and to find some unity of purpose amid the pluralism.

New slogans—empowerment, open itinerancy, pluralism—served

to image the diversity as a new norm of community and to establish living and thinking amidst diversity as the goal ahead. Nowhere did the normative quality of pluralism come to more powerful expression than in the 1972 *Discipline*. Under the guidance of Albert Outler and his Theological Study Commission, General Conference adopted and added to the *Discipline* a statement entitled "Our Theological Task." It set forth "theological pluralism . . . as a principle," a Wesleyan standard and Gospel for a new and ecumenical age. Methodism's "theological spectrum" and "our history of doctrinal diversity" were recognized, if not celebrated. Indeed, they were contemporary expression of Wesley's own catholic spirit. Making the church equal to his purposive vitality was a newly (re)discovered Wesleyan way of doing theology—with the quadrilateral of scripture, tradition, experience and reason.[25]

The church structured and ordered itself by attention to particularity. The part made the whole whole. Unity with such attention to inclusivity and particularity was precarious. Potentially, conferences and the church generally might fragment along caucus lines. And some observers experienced a church organized by such self-conscious attention to particularity as already fragmented. To them, fragmentation resulted from the caucuses serving as primary membership units, operating with a exclusive or quasi-exclusive criterion of membership, claiming loyalty from adherents, holding meetings in connection with conference gatherings and defining and pursuing their own agenda in relation to the conference as a whole. Such worries over fragmentation and over the pluralistic spirit that seemed to celebrate it led, in part, to a new Committee on "Our Theological Task" and the recasting in 1988 of the Disciplinary doctrinal statement, a process shepherded by Richard Heitzenrater.[26] The new statement nuanced the quadrilateral so as to accord primacy to scripture and sought consensus amid the pluralism. The caucus spirit it could not exorcise.

With its prophetic and judgmental stance on the church as a whole, the caucus elevates its own structures and principles into an alternative order. And dividing the world into adherents and non-adherents, its efforts to replace or remake the whole may seem threatening. Where the caucus runs on ideological bases, where it develops its alternative order into a shadow church, where it operates with a highly adversarial style, where it actively evangelizes—the threat of schism may be quite real, especially given the ideological fracturing of American society. The revived particularity and the caucus or struggle groups in a church where large, impersonal conference gatherings and commitments to inclusion, unity and pluralism hold sway do result in some nostalgia for the fraternity, revival and order of earlier Methodism.

The Unconferencing of Ministry

From the days of Wesley ministry had been a conference affair. Conferences had determined the conditions and expectations for admission on trial and full connection in the traveling ministry; it decided who would be admitted and ordained; every year it examined the characters of all in connection; it tried and disciplined any who strayed from the path to holiness; it did the business of the church; it also spent its sessions in preaching and worship, in conversation and dialogue, renewing and reviving fraternity and spirituality; and with the concluding reading of appointments by the bishop, it accepted or re-accepted a place of ministry in the Methodist connection.

In the late 20th century, annual conferences were neither capable of exercising, nor expected to exercise these offices. Large bodies, equally lay and clergy, they like the other levels of conference seemed too cumbersome to work. The shape of ministry had become an issue of definitions and the office of General Conference commissions which dealt with ministry directly in a series of studies.[27] Admission and other ministerial relations belonged to a committee which reported to an executive session, a session programmatically and emotionally divorced from annual conference as a whole. Discipline turned into counseling and counseling out, an affair for the conference psychologist and a subcommittee of a committee. The conference's business became the province of a professional conference staff, working out of conference headquarters and bringing to meetings the agenda and actions to be taken. Dialogue and conversation could be found away from the conference floor, in the crowded meal halls or around the bookstalls, but fraternity had become not the one with the whole but the one with his/her tribe or kin. Preaching and worship, confined to the conference itself and no longer regional in its outreach, struggled against the tide of business, reports, appearances, promotions, elections and struggled in buildings often ill-suited to the worship occasion. Logistics and liturgical sensibilities fought to control how communion would be celebrated and other services 'staged.' Fraternity booked special meals for each caucus and cause to convene and for seminaries to gather their own. Appointments were made long before conference itself, by elaborate, increasingly mandated procedures of consultation, and were widely known before conference convened. Bishops in places gave up the reading of appointments, a convention imparting no information and lacking drama.

Conferences still opened with the singing of "And are we yet alive". It was a good question. And conferences as a means of grace? Was it an oxymoron? Had pluralism and inclusivity become the new revivalism, boards the new polity, professionalism the new fraternity? What of the earlier ideals and their bearing on conferences?

What of the ideals in transformed expression? We have suggested that the 20th century processes had given fraternity, revival and order new form, but form that did not fully animate the conference structure. Revivalism as word had its most lively expression below the conferences in the local church. Polity as order remained ultimately in General Conference hands but more as policy and politics than practice. The connectional and disciplining force of polity belonged, on a day to day basis, to the boards and agencies or to General Conference's commissions which also seemed to take on a life of their own. And fraternity as community, as we have seen, was most vitally expressed in the new smaller groups and caucuses. A new unity for annual conferences proved difficult through formal worship services and eucharistic occasions. Could these new ideals—word, order and sacrament re-animate conference life?

Chapter 18

Conference as a Means of Grace:
A Theological Afterword

By the late 20th century, conferences seemed no longer a means of grace and, at times, no longer very serviceable entities. The quarterly conference, once a primary vehicle of Methodism's revival and of its evangelistic mission on a local level, had been subsumed within congregations and transformed into an annual business meeting. Its drama now focussed on the setting of salaries and accepting of apportionments. General conference, once the primary expression of Methodism's connectional polity had lost key elective responsibilities to jurisdictions (and to boards and agencies), had seen the boards rise to connectional prominence, and had increasingly turned its work over to commissions. It had become a forum in which the denomination's acute conflicts came to focus in the drafting of resolutions and recasting of the *Discipline*. Annual conferences once the primary locus of Methodism's fraternity had, as we have just noted, embraced new members and grown to bloated size. They struggled with procedures and structures that would make large, pluralistic lay and clergy affairs genuine community. Were conferences a means of grace?

Intimations

Historians have difficulty with the present and recent past. So it is not easy for this one to answer questions about conferences as a means of grace and the present expressions of revivalism, fraternity and polity. However, we have already suggested that, in fact, new modalities of these ideals have been gradually emerging over the course of the century. At this writing, the questions seem to be answering themselves and those ideals seem to have some potential for refashioning conferences as means of grace.

The Wesleyan spirit appears to be at work in a variety of new efforts that work vitally at local levels but re-connect Methodism nationally in new dynamic forms of gathering and witness. Such re-conceiving and re-anchoring the connection can be seen in the

199

Disciple Bible Study, Emmaus Walk, Covenant Discipleship, the Academy for Spiritual Formation, Chrysalis, Volunteers in Mission, Good News and the several caucuses, Reconciling Congregations and a variety of efforts, particularly in urban ministry, some specifically Methodist, others ecumenical. Each has connectional leadership and powerful local expression. Each moves beyond the walls of our buildings to find "new homes" for religious expression. Each draws in and equips fresh leadership. Each beckons the whole of Methodism to a new spirit and to renewal. These are not revivalism in the old mode. But each in its own way is a disciplined spirituality, a refashioning of the Wesleyan word. They do not yet have the structural, formal and official role that quarterly conference once accorded revival. But they do have denominational sponsorship. And they do attempt to recover something of earlier Methodism's expansive sense of space.

Annual conferences across the church have, in one way or another, recalled that conference was once a means of grace. They experiment with new ways of freshening up the annual event—giving featured time to Bible study, holding meals together, accenting serious theological enquiry, including a greater range of special worship services, putting mission before business, endeavoring to conduct themselves mindful of the end for which they gather. Self-conscious in efforts to broaden leadership and include women and ethnic persons in key slots, they struggle for new terms and images for their community. Such struggles come to pointed expression in worship, where conferences know they most dramatize, to the fullest extent possible, both knowledge of God and knowledge of self. There efforts veer from the effervescently evangelical to the scrupulously liturgical and with every possible accommodation of diversities of interest and person. The latter, a sacramental and explicitly eucharistic self-expression seems, we have suggested, to represent one tendency and one that might well hold together the typical annual conference's many diversities. Fully eucharistic communities most conferences have not really yet become. But that is certainly one direction of movement. We have noted, for instance, that in their smaller units—the affinity groups described above and the conference boards, including hard-working bodies like Boards of Ordained Ministry—conferences do partake of a eucharistic style and model new forms of community. So far such new community is eucharistic for the smaller unit not the whole.

And on the general church level serious connectional enquiry, study, planning and modelling goes on through the Council of Bishops, the general boards, commissions of General Conference, the seminaries and special studies. The order or form that the church might take—one renewing and energizing—is the object of virtually all the studies. Some propose to downsize the organization; others want to make the connection global; a few, including a major board, propose both; still others would abandon organizational uniformity to free churches and conferences, at all levels, to experiment with new forms and processes; many want more vigorous leadership but without authoritarianism; some want a much strengthened episcopacy; others want to revisit the nature and role of the district superintendency; a few whisper of dropping jurisdictions; some give up connectionalism and empower the local church.

Whether re-organization will renew Methodism connectionalism, whether these studies and plans have grasped what connectionalism was and might be, is hard to say. Sometimes clearer and more expressive connectionalism can be seen in efforts that are organizationally less self-preoccupied but that undertake action in purposive and mission-oriented fashion. An example might be the United Methodist Publishing House's success with the new *United Methodist Hymnal*.[1] Some have recognized its connection-wide interactive reporting and listening procedures as promising and worth studying. While it certainly modelled a fresh 'conferencing,' it made only casual use of and had minimum impact upon the existing conference structures and has not established a new order. The question remains, if the connection is to be renewed and reformed, will that new order be conferences or conference-related?

Time, Space, and Gravity

Word, sacrament, order—these new ideals do have some rough approximation to the processes on-going in the various levels of the church, the levels once governed by conference revival, fraternity and polity. I have here characterized the new ideals with respect to the different conference levels, word at the local church (once quarterly conference) level, sacrament at the annual conference level, order at the general church level. One might as readily speak of word on the general church level, sacrament for the local church and polity for annual conferences or all three at each level. The new ideals do have a certain currency in United Methodist life.

Theologically United Methodists, as good Protestants, are clear that to speak of word, sacrament and order is to speak of several ways in which God's grace operates in human lives. They will also recognize those as classic marks of the church, marks mediated to Methodists through Wesley and the Anglican tradition. Methodists also, following Wesley and Anglicanism, have viewed those marks as identifying where the Spirit of God is at work not locking God into one form of the church. No one church form is prescribed in the New Testament; no one mode of governance or organization guarantees that the Spirit is present; no structure, including that of the historic episcopate, in and of itself, guarantees apostolicity; form belongs to the realm of adiaphora, of discretion.

What then of conference as a means of grace? of revival, fraternity and polity? of word, sacrament and order? Though Wesley may not have put it this way, to speak, as he did, of Christian conference as one of the instituted means of grace, to surround it with other instituted gracious means, to identify additional prudential means clearly evocative of Wesleyan structure, to call his governing gatherings 'conference.' and to conduct his business in a conferencing mode was to say something very profound—not about form—but about *style*. No one form of the church may be biblical. No one organization or structure guarantees the Spirit's presence. But to be the body of Christ must not the church be gracious in its style, in its way of doing and being, in its way of conducting business?[2] Must not ends and means link closely? Indeed, must not means be proximate ends? Must not our way of doing church *be* church? Must not our forms operate spiritually/Spiritually?

Early Methodists, we have suggested, did church, conducted business, shaped themselves in a gracious, conferencing fashion. Conference was spirituality, community, God's order. It was revival, fraternity and polity. Those older ideals, adequate for their day, have given way, we suggest to word, sacrament and order, terms theologically more precise, traditional, ecumenical. What is unclear is whether and to what extent these new ideals shape the style of our doing and being, shape the day-to-day forms within which we live and work, shape the structures that, in fact, govern United Methodist lives. What is unclear is how fully conferences, local churches and boards are animated by these new ideals and how fully these United Methodist structures express what Methodists intend by the ideals. What is unclear is whether our forms are gracious, spiritual!

For earlier Methodism, conference spirituality so defined Methodist life that we spoke of it as a kind of gravity; conference so determined Methodist activity—so set the rhythms for all that Methodists did—that we referred to as time; conference so encompassed Methodist purpose that we termed it space. As a new creation, conference imprinted Methodist design on the American continent, reordering it according to conference rhythms, so as to achieve spiritual gravity. Geographic (spatial), historical and yet eschatological (temporal), redemptive and missional (gravitational), Methodists sought Zion on the American continent.

Those high ends Methodist revival, fraternity and polity served and served quite well. Ends and means were tightly linked. Methodist structure was what it purposed, it was gracious. Conferences indeed revived. Christian conference in Wesley's sense of Christian engagement and conversation went on through the formal governing organization of conference—general, annual, quarterly—and through its local counterpart, the class. That we have forgotten these gracious aspects of conference is, I hope, after these many pages, very understandable. The unraveling of conference as a means of grace has been gradual and long-term. We can be forgiven, I am sure, that we forgot that spiritual gravity belonged in our organization, that we forgot to fashion our structures and procedures to fit our new ideals, that we forgot to re-create the Wesleyan linkage of means and ends.

At any rate, somehow that linkage of means and ends, of structure and purpose, of grace and form has not been re-established. Word, sacrament and order do not yet generate the bonds, the energy, the vision, the tactics that would enliven our structures and through enlivened structures shape our world(s). Through these new ideals Methodists do not yet seem prepared to again conference the continent or, for that matter, even the neighborhood. New Methodist spatiality need not, cannot, must not be imperialistic, colonial, civil religious, conquering. But then "reforming the continent" had no such script. A new creation or renewed creation would be quite spatial enough.

And Methodist time? That conference no longer bonds, energizes, stimulates, orders or choreographs Methodist effort is manifestly evident in calendar. Earliest Methodism indeed ran on conference time and Methodist rhetoric still evokes that conference temporality—quadrennial, annual, quarterly. Time seemed almost to stop for conference, certainly for annual and quarterly conference. It started again when appointments were announced and conference released leaders and preachers to the circuits.

By the late 19th century, as we have noted, the weekly clock hand of the Sunday school, of the sabbath, and of program increasingly defined the rhythms of Methodist life. Only recently has yet another clock hand taken hold in Methodist affairs—that of the liturgical year, of word, sacrament and order.

It would be wonderful to report that a new Methodist time had displaced program time, had enlivened us spiritually, and had set conferences, indeed all of Methodism, running again in gracious fashion. The truth is that the typical United Methodist does not live by the liturgical year but instead by a host of calendars that leave a minister or local church reeling. A conference year might start in late

May, the fiscal year July 1, the program and educational year after school resumes in September, the local church year in early October with charge or church conference, the financial campaign year late in that month, the governance year January 1 when committee and church officers change, the new tax year at the same time, the memorial year in April with home-coming and dinner on the grounds. With calendars galore, churches have some difficulty in knowing what time it is and great difficulty in gearing up for anything in particular. No calendar dominates. None establishes our priorities.

The liturgical year—the year of word, sacrament and order—simply does not order Methodist life as did either conference or Sunday school time. A recently trained minister might follow the lectionary, attend to liturgical colors, and urge her congregation to observance of Pentecost or Epiphany. But the Christian year has not yet fully captured Methodist life. Indeed and sadly, some of the most precious days, as for instance Christmas, belong as much to the civil, commercial, educational and vacational calendar as to the Christian.

Calendar is one way of establishing priorities, emphasis, purpose. To a single conference calendar and its earlier simplicities, Methodism cannot, perhaps, return. But United Methodism can and should ask what has primacy? whether its rhythms do indeed serve its priorities? whether its orientation to building, neighborhood and community register its proper emphases? whether its conduct of its business reflect its purpose? whether its structures accord with their end. To speak, as we have, of conference as a means of grace is to say that the Methodist genius has been to make structure serve its end; to conduct business in a gracious fashion; to orient Methodists out in mission and service to their neighborhood, community and world; to establish its priorities through its rhythms; to orient in space and time to what had most gravity—namely the Holy Spirit.

For conference to be again a means of grace, must not a gracious calendar gain prominence, must not its ideals truly animate Methodist life, and must not conference itself fully express its own ideals? Can conference be again a means of grace? If not, what might? And if something else, some other permanent aspect of Methodist life, has or can become Methodism's means of grace, then what should we do with conference?

Abbreviations

Baker, *Methodists*

Gordon Pratt Baker, ed., *Those Incredible Methodists: A History of the Baltimore Conference of The United Methodist Church* (Baltimore: Commission on Archives and History, the Baltimore Conference, 1972).

Baltimore *Minutes*

Refers to the *Annual Minutes of the Baltimore Annual Conference of the Methodist Episcopal Church* (before 1856, *Annual Register*) for the year indicated.

Bangs, *History*

Nathan Bangs, *A History of the Methodist Episcopal Church*, 12th ed., 4 vols. (New York: Carlton & Porter, 1860).

Behney/Eller, *History*

J. Bruce Behney and Paul H. Eller, *The History of the Evangelical United Brethren Church*, ed. Kenneth W. Krueger (Nashville: Abingdon Press, 1979).

Buckley, *History*

James M. Buckley, *Constitutional and Parliamentary History of The Methodist Episcopal Church* (New York: The Methodist Book Concern, 1912).

Drinkhouse, *Reform*

Edward J. Drinkhouse, *History of Methodist Reform: Synoptical of General Methodism 1703 to 1898 with special . . . reference to the History of the Methodist Protestant Church*, 2 vols. (Baltimore: Board of Publication of the Methodist Protestant Church, 1899).

Elliott, *Secession*

Charles Elliott, *History of the Great Secession from the* Methodist Episcopal Church (Cincinnati: Swormstedt & Poe, 1855).

Emory, *Discipline*

Robert Emory, *History of the Discipline of the Methodist Episcopal Church*, rev. W. P. Strickland (New York: Carlton & Porter [1857]).

HAM

The History of American Methodism, ed. Emory S. Bucke, 3 vols. (New York and Nashville: Abingdon Press, 1964).

JLFA — *The Journal and Letters of Francis Asbury*, ed. Elmer T. Clark, 3 vols. (London: Epworth Press, and Nashville: Abingdon Press, 1958).

JGC/MEC — Refers to the *Journal of the General Conference of the Methodist Episcopal Church* for the year indicated.

JGC/MEC 1796–1836 — *Journals of the General Conference of the Methodist Episcopal Church, 1796–1836* (New York: Carlton & Phillips, 1855). Year indicated in parentheses.

JGC/MECS — Refers to the *Journal of the General Conference of the Methodist Episcopal Church, South* for the year indicated.

JGC/MECS 1846–1850 — *Journals of the General Conference of the Methodist Episcopal Church, South, held 1846 and 1850* (Richmond: Published by John Early for the Methodist Episcopal Church, South, 1851). Year indicated in parentheses.

Lee, *Short History* — Jesse Lee, *A Short History of the Methodists* (Baltimore, 1810; Rutland, Vt.: Academy Books, 1974).

Mathews, *Slavery* — Donald G. Mathews, *Slavery and Methodism* (Princeton: Princeton University Press, 1965).

MEC — Methodist Episcopal Church

MECS — Methodist Episcopal Church, South

MPC — Methodist Protestant Church

Minutes MC — *Minutes of the Methodist Conferences, Annually Held in America; From 1773 to 1813, Inclusive* (New York: Published by Daniel Hitt and Thomas Ware for the Methodist Connexion in The United States, 1813).

Minutes NE — *Minutes of the New England Conference of the Methodist Episcopal Church . . . 1766 to . . . 1845*, 2 vols. (typescript prepared by George Whitaker for New England Methodist Historical Society, 1912).

Mudge, *New England* — James Mudge, *History of the New England Conference of the Methodist Episcopal Church, 1796–1910* (Boston: Published by the Conference, 1910).

Neely, *Conference* — Thomas B. Neely, *A History of the Origin and Development of the Governing Conference in Methodism* (Cincinnati: Curts & Jennings, 1892).

New England *Minutes* Refers to the *Minutes of the New England Conference of the Methodist Episcopal Church* for the year indicated.

N. Carolina *Minutes* "Minutes of The North Carolina Annual Conference, 1838–1885," 2 vols. (photocopy of original handwritten Minutes, Duke Divinity School Library). Year indicated in parentheses.

Norwood, *Sourcebook* Frederick A. Norwood, ed., *Sourcebook of American Methodism* (Nashville: Abingdon Press, 1982).

Norwood, *Story* Frederick A. Norwood, *The Story of American Methodism* (Nashville and New York: Abingdon Press, 1974).

Ohio *Minutes* Refers to the *Minutes of the Ohio Annual Conference of the Methodist Episcopal Church* for the year indicated.

Organization MECS *History of the Organization of the Methodist Episcopal Church, South, with the Journal of its First General Conference* (Nashville: Publishing House of the Methodist Episcopal Church, South, 1925).

Paine, *M'Kendree* Robert Paine, *Life and Times of William M'Kendree,* 2 vols. (Nashville: Publishing House of the Methodist Episcopal Church, South, 1874).

Philadelphia *Journal* Refers to the *Official Journal and Year Book of the Philadelphia Annual Conference of the Methodist Episcopal Church* for the year indicated.

Philadelphia *Minutes* Refers to the *Minutes of the Philadelphia Conference of the Methodist Episcopal Church* for the year indicated.

POAM Russell E. Richey, Kenneth E. Rowe, and Jean Miller Schmidt, eds., *Perspectives on American Methodism: Interpretive Essays* (Nashville: Kingswood Books, 1993).

Redford, *History MECS* A. H. Redford, *History of the Organization of the Methodist Episcopal Church, South* (Nashville: A. H. Redford, for the M.E. Church, South, 1871)

Sweet, *Methodists* William Warren Sweet, ed., *Religion on the American Frontier, 1783–1840: The Methodists, A Collection of Source Materials* (New York: Cooper Square [1964]; reprint of 1946 ed.).

Sweet, *Rise*

William Warren Sweet, ed., *The Rise of Methodism in the West, Being The Journal of the Western Conference 1800–1811* (New York and Cincinnati: The Methodist Book Concern, 1920).

Tigert, *History*

Jno. J. Tigert, *A Constitutional History of American Episcopal Methodism*, 3d ed., revised and enlarged (Nashville: Publishing House of the Methodist Episcopal Church, South, 1908).

Tigert, *Methodism*

Jno. J. Tigert, *The Making of Methodism: Studies in the Genesis of Institutions* (Nashville: Publishing House of the Methodist Episcopal Church, South, 1898).

Unification

Joint Commission on Unification of The Methodist Episcopal Church, South and The Methodist Episcopal Church, 3 vols. (Nashville: Publishing House Methodist Episcopal Church, South; and New York: The Methodist Book Concern, 1918–20).

Wesley, *Works*

The Works of John Wesley; begun as "The Oxford Edition of The Works of John Wesley" (Oxford: Clarendon Press, 1975–1983); continued as "The Bicentennial Edition of The Works of John Wesley" (Nashville: Abingdon Press, 1984—); 15 of 35 vols. published to date.

Wesley, *Works* (Jackson)

The Works of John Wesley, ed. Thomas Jackson, 14 vols. (London, 1872; Grand Rapids: Zondervan, 1958).

West, *Debates*

Robert A. West, reporter, *Report of Debates in the General Conference of the Methodist Episcopal Church . . . 1844* (New York: G. Lane & C. B. Tippett, 1844).

Notes

Notes to Chapter 1

1. See Russell E. Richey, "History as a Bearer of Denominational Identity: Methodism as a Case Study," *Beyond Establishment: Protestant Identity in a Post-Protestant Age* (Louisville: Westminster/John Knox, 1993), 270–95, and *POAM*, 480–97, 588–96. See also "Methodism and Providence: A Study in Secularization," *Studies in Church History*, 26:51–77.

2. The references to 'conference' in standard Methodist bibliographies, subject indices and reference works are quite modest. For instance, *The United Methodist Periodical Index* does not employ 'conference' as an entry (note the volumes for 1961–65, for 1966–70, for 1970–75, and for 1975–80). The *Methodist History Index*, Volumes 1–22 (Oct., 1962–July, 1982) does contain four references to 'conference' but only one of them deals explicitly and directly with the conference. *The Encyclopedia of World Methodism*, ed. Nolan B. Harmon, 2 vols. (Nashville: United Methodist Publishing House, 1974), 1:558–61, offers several short articles with 'conference' in the title. Only one of the essays, "Conference, British Methodist," really focuses on the conference as a Methodist phenomenon. The pattern is not new. Matthew Simpson rendered only very passing remark on conference in *Cyclopaedia of Methodism*, 5th ed. (Philadelphia: Louis H. Everts, 1883).

The invaluable multi-volume *Methodist Union Catalog: Pre-1976 Imprints*, edited by Kenneth E. Rowe (Metuchen, N.J. & London: Scarecrow Press, 1975—), Vol. 3, does not index by subject and so gathers under 'conference' only items with that as the initial word in the title. Even so, one might expect a considerable array of books devoted to this central feature of Methodist polity. Instead 'conference' is used primarily (1) in adjectival fashion [i.e. *Conference Legislation*] or (2) independently of its Methodist meaning [i.e. *Conference on Human Relations*]. Rowe's exhaustive inventory tells the story. Methodists have been strangely uninterested in interpreting their most basic ecclesial feature.

This is not to say that we want for books having to do with the conference. Methodist libraries teem with conference histories. However, these treat specific conference sagas. Seldom do they step back to analyze the conference as a phenomenon. The main resources remain Thomas B. Neely, *A History of the Origin and Development of the Governing Conference in Methodism* (Cincinnati: Curts & Jennings, 1892); Jno. J. Tigert, *A Constitutional History of American Episcopal Methodism*, 3d ed., revised and enlarged (Nashville: Publishing House of the Methodist Episcopal Church, South,

1908); and James M. Buckley, *Constitutional and Parliamentary History of The Methodist Episcopal Church* (New York: The Methodist Book Concern, 1912).

One looks in vain for intellectual or theological assessments. Conference belongs to the category of polity and that alone. That is graphically illustrated in the *Index to the Methodist Quarterly Review . . . 1818–1881* by Elijah H. Pilcher (New York: Phillips & Hunt, 1884), perhaps the best indication of 19th century Methodism's reflection on itself. It arrays topics under a variety of headings, biblical, theological, ecclesiastical, philosophical, biographical, religious intelligence, miscellaneous. Conference belongs clearly to the category of 'ecclesiastical' and that only.

3. Although the estimate which best captures the nuances of conference, W. L. Doughty, *John Wesley: His Conferences and His Preachers* (London: City Road, 1944), focuses entirely on the British conference, its findings apply to the American as well.

4. For the emergence of conference forms among German pietists as the United Brethren and Evangelical Alliance, see below. That placement derives from the conviction that on this aspect the Methodist movements are particularly indebted to Wesley.

5. For the larger contours of this movement as well as its distinctive emphases see Ted A. Campbell, *The Religion of the Heart* (Columbia: University of South Carolina Press, 1991). I am indebted to Campbell for a number of helpful suggestions.

6. Richard P. Heitzenrater, *Wesley and the People Called Methodists* (Nashville: Abingdon Press, 1995). On the beginnings of conference, see 141–46.

7. John Wesley, "Thoughts Upon Some Late Occurrences" [1785], *Works* (Jackson), 13:248. Compare the formulation within the formalized collection of minutes, called "The Large Minutes," which functioned as the constitution of the movement: "In 1744 I wrote to several Clergymen, and to all who then served me as sons in the gospel, desiring them to meet me in London, and to give me their advice concerning the best method of carrying on the work of God. . . . Observe: I myself sent for these of my own free choice. And I sent for them to advise, not govern, me." Wesley, *Works* (Jackson), 8:312. Neely observed, "But let it not be supposed that the Conferences which Mr. Wesley called had any governing power. The members discussed, but Mr. Wesley decided. They debated, but he determined. Mr. Wesley was the government; and, though he invited the preachers to confer with him, he did not propose to abandon any of his original power. They had a voice by his permission, but he reserved the right to direct." Neely, *Conference*, 9–10.

8. This point and the statement cited derive from Frank Baker, "The People Called Methodists—3. Polity," in Rupert Davies and Gordon Rupp, eds., *A History of the Methodist Church in Great Britain*, Vol. 1 (London: Epworth Press, 1965), 211–55. Baker observes, "In origin the Methodist Conference was far from being the supreme doctrinal, legislative, administrative, and disciplinary court which it eventually became" (242).

9. "Minutes of Some Late Conversations Between The Rev. Mr. Wesleys and Others," Wesley, *Works* (Jackson), 8:275.

10. Among the papers left by John Wesley's mother was one entitled, "A Religious Conference Between M. and E." The letters stood for Mother and Emilia; the conference unfolded in a catechetical manner of question and answer; John Wesley endorsed the document "My Mother's Conference with her Daughter," and the paper bore within its subtitle, "WRITTEN FOR THE USE OF MY CHILDREN." See "Mrs. Wesley's Conference with Her Daughter. An Original Essay by Mrs. Susannah Wesley." *Publications of The Wesley Historical Society,* III (1898).

11. These questions were themselves introduced by a question, "What is the method wherein we usually proceed in our Conferences?":

> A. We inquire,
> (1) What Preachers are admitted? Who remain on trial? Who are admitted on trial? Who desist from travelling?
> (2) Are there any objections to any of the Preachers? who are named one by one.
> (3) How are the Preachers stationed this year?
> (4) What numbers are in the society?
> (5) What is the Kingswood collection?
> (6) What boys are received this year?
> (7) What girls are assisted?
> (8) What is contributed for the contingent expenses?
> (9) How was this expended?
> (10) What is contributed toward the fund for superannuated and supernumerary Preachers?
> (11) What demands are there upon it?
> (12) How many Preachers' wives are to be provided for? By what societies?
> (13) Where and when may our next Conference begin?

"The Large Minutes" (1789), Wesley, *Works* (Jackson), 8:326. This question first appeared in the 1770 Minutes.

12. See Baker, "The People Called Methodists—3. Polity," 243; Tigert, *History,* 27 ff.

13. Wesley, *Works* (Jackson), 13:242–43. Also cited in Tigert, *History,* 25–27, from the British *Minutes,* ed. 1812, 1:87–89; ed. 1862, 87–89.

14. Wesley, *Works* (Jackson), 8:243. Baker, "The People Called Methodists—3. Polity," 244–45; Tigert, *History,* 27–44. This 1784 document, known as the "Deed of Declaration," was a legal instrument entered in Chancery which formally transferred Wesley's authority and rights to Methodist property to a conference of individually named persons. See also Henry W. Williams, *The Constitution and Polity of Wesleyan Methodism* (London: Wesleyan Conference Office, [1880?]), 14–19.

15. Neely, *Conference,* 70. Heitzenrater reminds us that such efforts to secure the authority of Conference were contested and that the power of Conference was challenged in the 1790s after Wesley's death.

16. These points are made in different form by Doughty, *John Wesley: His Conferences* (27):

> The Conference steadily grew in influence and popularity and speedily became the focal point of Methodist religious life. . . . Its

meeting places were London, Bristol, and Leeds, and the Methodists in those areas eagerly anticipated its coming and shared joyously in its many public ministrations. Round it gathered the loving, reverent thoughts and for it rose the prayers of the Methodist people everywhere. It became the symbol of their unity; the grand climax of their year; an incentive to more intense missionary enterprise and the fount of inspiration for a deeper personal consecration.

17. "John Bennet's Copy of the Minutes of the Conferences of 1744, 1745, 1747 and 1748; With Wesley's Copy of Those for 1745," *Publications of The Wesley Historical Society*, I (1896), 39.

18. Ibid., 49–50. In the Large Minutes this question was recast: "Do we sufficiently watch over our Helpers?" The first American Discipline reshaped that into "Do we sufficiently watch over each other?" The Large Minutes continued with the sentence about helper as pupil. The American Discipline omitted that. Both then continued with a recast version of the counsel; the British version continued the Wesleyan oversight; the American persisted in rendering Wesley's paternal venture in fraternal language:

> Should we not frequently ask each-other, Do you walk closely with God? Have you *now* Fellowship with the Father and the Son? At what Hour do you rise? Do you punctually observe the Morning and Evening Hour of Retirement? Do you spend the Day in the Manner which the Conference advises? [British version "which we advise?"] Do you converse seriously, usefully and closely?

Tigert, *History*, 575. In the Large Minutes this question was expanded to include also the query about use of the Means of Grace: "Do you use all the Means of Grace yourself, and inforce the use of them on all other persons?" Then followed the distinction:

> They are either *Instituted* or *Prudential*.
> I. The Instituted are,
> 1. Prayer . . .
> 2. Searching the Scriptures . . .
> 3. The Lord's Supper . . .
> 4. Fasting . . .
> 5. Christian Conference.

The first Discipline followed on the latter points. See Tigert, *History*, 575–76.

19. "Bennet's Minutes," 53-4:

> Q. What further advice can be given to our Assistants in order to their confiding in each other?
> A. Let them beware how they despise each other's gifts, and much more how they speak anything bordering thereon. 2. Let them never speak slightly of each other in any kind. 3. Let them defend one another's character in every point to the uttermost of their power. 4. Let them labour in honor each to prefer the other to himself.

In the Large Minutes and the First Discipline of the MEC (Q. 67 of the latter), the above and those cited in the text were worked into an eight point answer. See Tigert, *History*, 578.

20. John Lawson, "The People Called Methodists—2. 'Our Discipline'," in Davies and Rupp, eds., *A History of the Methodist Church in Great Britain*, Vol. 1, 185.

21. See Tigert, *History*, 575–76. This section of Tigert's work parallels the 1780 British Large Minutes with the first Discipline of the American church. The five means of grace were taken over intact into the Discipline.

22. See note 7 above.

Notes to Chapter 2

1. Norwood, *Story*, 70, breaks the development of Methodist structure at the Christmas Conference (1784) and therefore discerns three periods prior to that: 1769–73, 1773–79 and 1779–84.

2. *JLFA*, 1:59–60 (December 22, 1772). For the next quarterly meeting (conference) Asbury minuted this summary, "The whole ended in great peace" (1:75).

3. Neely, *Conference*, 99.

4. *JLFA*, 1:80 (June 3, 1773).

5. "The Life of Mr. Thomas Rankin," in *Lives of Early Methodist Preachers*, ed. Thomas Jackson, 4th ed., 6 vols. (London, 1872), 5:193.

6. *Minutes MC*, 5. Cited also in Bangs, *History*, 1:78–79. Dividing the business of this first conference into three categories—constitutional, legislative and executive—Tigert terms these first questions 'constitutional'. He argued, however, "The proposal of the questions hardly involved the right of the body to reach a contrary conclusion" (62). Tigert conceived of Rankin's authority as derivative from but quite analogous to that of Wesley. He possessed the superintending and appointive power and the conference constituted "the *consulting* element, with limited *legislative* privileges" (65). The legislative power of the conference was exercised in the passing of a number of regulations which tightened discipline and curbed the printing of Wesley's books and the celebration of the sacraments. The executive power was expressed in stationing of the preachers and assessing the state of the Methodist effort. Tigert, *History*, 65–70. Neely states the matter more forthrightly: "[T]he Conference did not have inhering in it any legislative, judicial, or executive power, but simply carried out what the Large Minutes set forth or what Wesley declared." Neely, *Conference*, 104.

7. Ibid.

8. *JLFA*, 1:85 (July 14, 1773). Otherwise Asbury's wording parallels that of the official minutes. For the first two questions Asbury had simply, "The old Methodist doctrine and discipline shall be enforced and maintained amongst all our societies in America."

9. See note 6 above.

10. *JLFA*, 1:116 (May 25, 1774). William Duke noted, "I came to Philadelphia to the Conference. I have seen this Day much need of the

Meek and Lowley Mind of Jesus" (manuscript Journal, May 24, 1774). For actions of conference, see *Minutes MC*, 7–8.

11. Note Asbury's complaints elsewhere, for instance *JLFA*, 1:127 (August 12, 1774); *JLFA*, 1:130 (September 10, 1774); *JLFA*, 1:140 (December 4, 6, 1774); *JLFA*, 1:145–46 (January 2, 12, 18, 1775).

12. *JLFA*, 1:156 (May 16, 1775). For conference see *Minutes MC*, 9–10.

13. *The Experiences and Travels of Mr. Freeborn Garrettson* (Philadelphia, 1791). Reprinted in *American Methodist Pioneer: The Life and Journals of The Rev. Freeborn Garrettson, 1752–1827*, ed. Robert Drew Simpson (Rutland, VT: Academy Books, 1984), 55. Compare Jesse Lee on his first conference that of 1782 meeting at Ellis' Meeting House, Sussex:

> The union and brotherly love which I saw among the preachers, exceeded every thing I had ever seen before, and caused me to wish that I was worthy to have a place amongst them. When they took leave of each other, I observed that they embraced each other in their arms, and wept as though they never expected to meet again. Had the heathen been there, they might have well said, "See how these Christians love one another!" By reason of what I saw and heard during the four days that the Conference sat, I found my heart truly humbled in the dust, and my desire greatly increased to love and serve God more publicaly than I had ever done before.

Minton Thrift, *Memoir of the Rev. Jesse Lee. With Extracts from his Journals* (New York: N. Bangs and T. Mason for the Methodist Episcopal Church, 1823), 42.

14. *JLFA*, 1:178 (February 5, 1776).

15. Cited by Tigert, *History*, 85.

16. *Minutes MC*, 7.

17. *JLFA*, 1:239 (May 12, 1777).

18. Ibid. For official gathering, see *Minutes MC*, 13–15.

19. Ibid.

20. "Minutes of a Conference held in Baltimore, May, 1777," a version kept by Philip Gatch and originally printed in the *Western Christian Advocate* (May 19–26, 1837) and reproduced in Norwood, *Sourcebook*, 56.

21. Asbury's rank among the American preachers is indicated in his placement on the list of "assistants." During Rankin's tenure, Asbury's name came second. See the Minutes of 1774, 1775, 1776 and 1777, *Minutes MC*, 7, 9, 11, and 13.

22. Tigert, *History*, 94.

Notes to Chapter 3

1. The most notable exception to this historiographical tradition is the great historian of the Methodist reformers, Edward J. Drinkhouse. See his *History of Methodism Reform*, 2 vols. (Baltimore: Board of Publication of The Methodist Protestant Church, 1899), 1:212–25. Tigert, *History*, also evidences great sympathies for the Southern or Virginia side. See chapter 7. Norwood views this a crisis which "involved not only the sacraments, but also the relation of Methodists to the Church of England and the

authority of Asbury as general assistant—to say nothing of the authority of Wesley. . . ." Norwood, *Story*, 91.

2. *Minutes MC*, 19–20.

3. Portions of the manuscript minutes are reproduced in *The Life and Times of The Rev. Jesse Lee* by Leroy M. Lee (Charleston: John Early for the MECS, 1848), 79–81 and also by Tigert, *History*, 106–7. A fuller version can be found in the *Western Christian Advocate*, 4 (May 26, 1837), 18. Jesse Lee reported that for the most part the Methodist people received the sacraments happily; see Lee, *Short History*, 69–70.

4. The connective links here are ones of theme rather than influence or indebtedness. The essential point is that conference as experience (rather than simply as idea, whether of theology or polity) generated powerful habits, beliefs, and expectations that from time to time precipitated themselves as movements for reform.

5. *Minutes MC*, 26.

6. Ibid, 26. The Northern conference also reaffirmed Asbury's position as general assistant, requiring his signature on licenses thereby warranting good standing in the Methodist connexion. It also reasserted its intention to remain within the Anglican Church (Questions 8, 9, 12, and 13, pp. 24–25).

7. Ibid., Questions 7, 24, pp. 24, 26.

8. See Asbury's account of that meeting, *JLFA*, 1:348–50 (May 3–10, 1780).

9. *American Methodist Pioneer*, 175–76, entries from Garrettson's mss. journal. The version published in *Experience and Travels* was much more staid and less effulgent in its spiritual and fraternal expressions. See *American Methodist Pioneer*, 104. Asbury noted a similar pattern to the meeting. *JLFA*, 1:349–50 (May 9–10, 1780). Cf. also William Watter's version which is highly expressive. Tigert cites from it liberally in *History*, 119–20.

10. Frederick Norwood so entitles his chapter which covers these developments. See "From Society to Church," *Story*, 94–110. His sense of this development is rendered with different images than those employed here, but also suggests that accidental and inertial factors were important. He speaks for instance of "Methodists," stumbling "their way from society to church" (101).

11. Early Methodists, for instance, spoke of the transition in similar terms. See *Sketches of The Life and Travels of Rev. Thomas Ware, Written by Himself* (New York: G. Lane & P. P. Sandford for the Methodist Episcopal Church, 1842; reprinted by Holston Conference Task Force on the Bicentennial, 1984), 110–12.

12. *Short History*, 75. The next year two circuits were taken in and in 1783, eleven. 79, 82.

13. *Minutes MC*, 28–29 (1781). The title of that conference specified "Held at Choptank, State of Delaware, April 16, 1781, and adjourned to Baltimore the 24th of said month." Quest. 2 asked, "Why was conference began at Choptank?" The answer: "To examine those who could not go to Baltimore, and to provide supplies for the circuits where the Lord is more immediately pouring out his Spirit" (29). Tigert termed this devel-

opment, "the germ of the modern American Annual Conference." *History*, 122. See also his discussion of "The Baltimore Conference System of Government," ibid., 523–31.

14. Tigert (*History*, 123–34) observed:

> To this day, according to the language of the Discipline, a preacher is "admitted on trial," not into a particular Annual Conference, but "into the traveling connection." The Annual Conferences arose and continue to arise from subdivisions of the Church, its territory, and its one body of ministers, who form what is technically called the "travelling connection." The Church did not arise from the amalgamation of Annual Conferences. The Annual Conference is thus a unit of administration, created first by the Superintendents for their convenience and that of the preachers, and later by the authority of the General Conference. This unit of administration is territorial, for, within its prescribed boundaries, every Annual Conference, great or small, exercises precisely the same powers, under the same rules and regulations.

15. *Minutes MC*, 30–31.

16. Beginning with 1779, the question would be posed (as needed) "Who desist from travelling?" *Minutes MC*, 18.

17. *Minutes MC*, 48. The next year, conference began a practice still honored of entering a biographical sketch of the 'brother' who had died. Initially they were no more than a sentence. Lee observed of the initiation of the notice: "This was a new plan, and it was a very proper and profitable one. By it we might know when our preachers left the world. Previous to this we had taken no account in our minutes of the death of any of our travelling preachers" (*Short History*, 87).

18. General Conferences could also possess such intense spiritual 'gravity'. For instance, that of 1800 drew extensive comment in Methodist literature for the revival that accompanied it. See J. B. Wakeley, *The Patriarch of One Hundred Years; Being Reminiscences, Historical and Biographical of Rev. Henry Boehm*, (New York: Nelson & Phillips, 1875; reprinted Lancaster, PA: Abram W.Sangrey, 1982), 35–42. That of 1808, he described as "like one great love-feast from beginning to end." (180) The General Conference of 1812 did not reach such heights, though Boehm attended to its evangelical outreach (394–98). In 1816, General Conference possessed a peculiar spiritual gravity owing to the recent death of Asbury and the ill health of McKendree. Boehm actually described the Philadelphia Annual Conference which labored under the same conditions "a gloomy one" (430–37).

19. *JLFA*, 1:386–87 (November 3 and 6, 1780). Samuel Magaw was one of several clergy members of the Church of England who supported the Methodist movement. Compare the accounts Freeborn Garrettson provided for quarterly meetings, as for instance this one for a Dover meeting of May 1783 (*American Methodist Pioneer*, 221; this portion derives from his mss. journal):

> *Saturday 17.* Quarterly Meeting began at T(homas) W(hite's).
> *Sunday 18.* Was a very high day to many souls. I do not think there

were less than two thousand souls. After the house was filled, three of the preachers took the remainder of the people in the woods. Two of my brethren spoke in the house before me. Just as I began, they were dismissed in the woods, so that I had the whole congregation. I was obliged to speak so loud in order for all to hear, I got somewhat hoarse, but glory to God; it was a sweet time to me and many others.

20. Tigert, *History*, 535. Tigert reproduced the first Discipline and Wesley's Large Minutes in parallel columns, making American editorial changes easy to spot. The question had been carried over verbatim from the Large Minutes. In the answer, American Methodists made a significant change in the wording. The change attested the different social/physical context within which they worked, the fact of the new nation and perhaps also something of their ambition. Wesley had said, "To reform the Nation, particularly the Church; and to spread scriptural holiness over the land." American Methodists changed "the Nation, particularly the Church" to "the Continent" and changed "land" to "Lands."

21. *JLFA*, 1:606 (July 31, 1789). *JLFA*, 3:109 (January 1, 1792). For discussion of this as a Methodist and evangelical commonplace, see Richey, *Early American Methodism* (Bloomington and Indianapolis: Indiana University Press, 1991), 42–46.

22. *The Arminian Magazine*, 2:202, "An Extract of a Letter from James Haw, Elder . . . to Bishop Asbury."

Notes to Chapter 4

1. *JLFA*, 1:471 (November 14, 1784).

2. *Minutes MC*, 37, Quest. 19. The Ans. was "Yes." This formulation warrants Asbury's authority on two grounds (1) appointment by Wesley and (2) selection by conference. See Tigert, *History*, 136. Its twofold derivation was reasserted in the (regular) annual conference of 1784 in the formula by which European preachers were to be deemed acceptable. They were, among other qualifications, to have standing if they would "be subject to Francis Asbury as General Assistant, whilst he stands approved by Mr. Wesley, and the conference" (*Minutes*, (1784), 48, Quest. 21).

3. In his mss. journal, Freeborn Garrettson reported meeting Coke and hearing of Wesley's provisions for the American movement. He continued: "I thought it expedient to return with him to a Quarterly Meeting held in Kent county, where I expected to meet Mr. Asbury, and a number of the preachers. About fifteen met. "We sat in Conference. It was thought expedient to call a General Conference to Baltimore. I was appointed to go and call the Conference" (*American Methodist Pioneer*, 243). Compare this formulation with that Garrettson published in *Experience and Travels*, 122.

4. *JLFA*, 1:427.

5. Tigert (*Methodism*, 86) summarized the matter brilliantly:

(1) The Christmas Conference was a called Conference, unexpectedly intercalated between the regular annual sessions of the American Conference of 1784 and 1785; (2) it was no part of Mr.

Wesley's plan either for the organization or the government of the American Methodist Episcopal Church, that government continuing to rest, after the Christmas Conference as before . . . in an annual assembly known as the "Conference"; (3) it was not provided for by an action of this existing American Conference; (4) its necessity was not foreseen by Dr. Coke, either on the basis of his instructions from Mr. Wesley or on that of his personal or official position; (4) it was not called by Mr. Asbury acting individually or officially; (6) it was called by a council of preachers, assembled for Quarterly Meeting purposes, but specially convened as a council, at Barratt's Chapel, Asbury and Coke both concurring; (7) its purpose was to pass on "the design of organizing the Methodists into an Independent Episcopal Church," or to take action on 'Mr. Wesley's plan". . . .

6. Frank Baker, in *From Wesley to Asbury* (Durham: Duke University Press, 1976), 162, observes that "The hastily summoned Methodist preachers who huddled together in a wintry Baltimore that Christmas of 1784 issued their own declaration of independence."

7. Journals and memoirs of participants provide the detail. See especially that of Bishop Thomas Coke excerpted in *The Arminian Magazine*, I (1789), 290–92. Coke's account indicates that even this conference, though preoccupied with its organizational and legislative duties, took seriously its responsibilities to the Methodist populace:

At six every morning one of the prachers gave the people a sermon: the weather was exceedingly cold, and therfore brother Asbury thought it best to indulge the people: and our morning congregations held out and were good to the last. At *noon* I preached; except on the Sundays and other ordination-days, when the service began at *ten* o'clock, it generally lasting on those occasions four hours: and the chapel was full every time. At *six* in the evening, a travelling-preacher preached in the *Town* chapel, anoother in the *Point* chapel, (a chapel about half a mile out of town) and another in the *Dutch* church, which the pious minister (Mr. *Otterbein*) gave us the use of in the evenings during the conference. (Brother *Asbury* has so high an opinion of Mr. *Otterbine*, that we admitted him, at brother *Asbury's* desire, to lay his hands on brother *Asbury* with us, on his being ordained bishop.) (291)

8. See Norman W. Spellman's discussion in *HAM* 1:215–16.

9. *JLFA*, 1:474–76 (December 18, 1784). Compare the account in *The Life and Travels of Rev. Thomas Ware*, 105–7.

10. The handiwork of the Christmas Conference can best be observed in Tigert's parallel reproduction of the Large Minutes and first Discipline, in *History*, 532–602. The American conference *disposed* of these changes by vote. They were apparently *proposed* by a little group of English Methodists who convened to prepare for the conference. Richard, later Bishop, Whatcoat reported that delimitation of conference's actual power in his Memoirs:

December 19th, I preached in Hunt's chapel and rode to Mr. Henry Gough's; spent the evening with Dr. Coke, Mr. Asbury, and brother Vasey, in great peace. Twentieth, my rheumatism returned; we began to prepare for our conference, and to consider some of our rules and minutes, as necessary to the helping forward the Lord's work in our connection, with great deliberation and impartiality, in the fear of God, may we hope to the end—21st, we went through some more of our minutes— 22d and 23d, we continued in the same exercise—24th, we rode to Baltimore.

P. P. Sandford, *Memoirs of Mr. Wesley's Missionaries to America* (New York: G. Lane & P. P. Sandford for the Methodist Episcopal Church, 1843), 365–66.

11. Whether American Methodism had a constitution at this stage and, if so, in what it consisted is a matter of some debate. See, for instance, Buckley, *History*, 121–27. It is instructive that the second Discipline, published in *The Sunday Service of the Methodists In the United States of America* (London, 1786), 322–55, carried this title: "The General Minutes of the Conferences of the Methodist Episcopal Church in America, forming the Constitution of the said Church."

12. This is, of course, the title and theme of Thomas B. Neely's volume, *A History of the Origin and Development of the Governing Conference in Methodism*.

13. Tigert, *Methodism*, 120–21. It would be more accurate to say that the Christmas Conference granted authority to conference, for the Christmas gathering was a special assembly and not the annual meeting to which authority was conferred. Yet that technicality should not obscure the reality that a conference acted very much in its own interest.

14. "[W]ho have Power to expel him for improper Conduct, if they see it necessary." Tigert, *History*, 549.

15. The first Discipline queried:

> Q. 2. What can be done in order to the future Union of the Methodists?
> A. During the Life of the Rev. Mr. Wesley, we acknowledge ourselves his Sons in the Gospel, ready in Matters belonging to Church-Government, to obey his Commands. And we do engage after his Death, to do every Thing that we judge consistent with the Cause of Religion in *America* and the political Interests of these States, to preserve and promote our Union with Methodists in *Europe*.

Tigert, *History*, 534. That oversight was also implicitly recognized in the acceptance of Wesley's provisions for the new church—"The Sunday Service," "A Collection of Psalms and Hymns," and "The Articles of Religion." It was explicitly exercised in Wesley's letter to "Our Brethren in America" granting independence, conveying the above provisions, specifying an episcopal form of government and designating Coke and Asbury as "Joint Superintendents." This is much reproduced. See *JLFA*, 3:37–39, or Wesley, *Works* (Jackson), 13:251–52.

Tigert (*History*, 184–94) argued, quite persuasively, that Wesley intended that oversight to be effectual and made no provision for the political and legislative autonomy that the Americans, in fact, asserted. He expected to exercise that oversight and did so later by directing the appointment of superintendents. The Americans rejected those directions and actually stripped the Discipline of the the above proviso.

16. Lee, *Short History*, 89, 100. The manuscript minutes from 1773 to 1784 were gathered with the subsequently published minutes in several compilations, as for instance *Minutes MC*, recently reprinted by the Strawbridge Shrine Assn. Inc. New Windsor, Md.

It is worth noting that the first published minutes, those of 1785, extracted Wesley's letter "To Dr. Coke, Mr. Asbury, and our Brethren in North America," which outlined Wesley's reasons for putting them "at full liberty, simply to follow the scriptures and the primitive church." *Minutes MC*, 49–50.

17. This is Tigert's formulation and the title of a chapter in his *Methodism*.

18. Lee, *Short History*, 118.

19. Lee (*Short History*, 78–79) observed of the 1782 division of the conference into two sessions:

> The work had so increased and spread, that it was now found necessary to have a conference in the south every year, continuing the conference in the north as usual. Yet as the conference in the north was of the longest standing, and withal composed of the oldest preachers, it was allowed greater privileges than that in the south; especially in making rules, and forming regulations for the societies. Accordingly, when any thing was agreed to in the Virginia conference, and afterwards disapproved of in the Baltimore conference, it was dropped. But if any rule was fixed and determined on at the Baltimore conference, the preachers in the south were under the necessity of abiding by it. The southern conference was considered at that time [1782] as a convenience, and designed to accommodate the preachers in that part of the work, and to do all the business of a regular conference, except that of making or altering particular rules.

20. Tigert, *Methodism*, 147–57.

21. Cited in *JLFA*, 3:49. Asbury accepted Wesley's direction. He wrote Whatcoat: "My dear Brother: Hereby I inform you that Mr. Wesley has appointed you a joint Superintendent with me. I can, therefore, claim no superiority over you." (*JLFA*, 3:49)

22. *JLFA*, 3:53. The letter extends from pp. 51 to 53.

23. Q. 2 in Tigert, *History*, 534.

24. *JLFA*, 3:54 (May 2, 1787). The minutes for that year reflect Coke's abdication: "*Quest. 1. Who are the Superintendents of our church for the United States? Ans.* Thomas Coke, (when present in the States) and Francis Asbury." *Minutes MC*, 62. Tigert (*Methodism*, 156) observed: "Thus in 1787—not in 1784—the American Methodist Episcopal Church fully and finally asserted its autonomy. . . ."

25. Lee, *Short History*, 126.

26. *Minutes MC*, 64 (1787).

27. Ibid., 62–64.

28. Something of the character and function of conference's probing and testing can be gleaned from this counsel of Asbury to one of his presiding elders, Nelson Reed of the Baltimore district, counsel that extended to quarterly meetings and other gatherings the regimens of conference (*JLFA*, 3:100–1 [May 29, 1791]):

> Examine your preachers at every two months, like a conference, of their growth in grace, and walk with God and be very particular to know how the classes' meetings are, and establish bands. I wish you to take about a day in conference or a day when the people are gone. Call the leaders, stewards and local preachers and exhorters, know the state of their souls and their classes. Inquire of local preachers about their congregations and the work under them, let them speak of the exercises of their souls. Every circuit wants a conference, as well as every district, and get all your men together, let them witness for or against each other. If you have any doubts of an exhorter or local preacher desire him to bring a recommendation from the society where he lives, of his piety, and do not proceed to authorize any unless recommended, if doubtful. If the societies have to complain, let them send their witness or sign their letters of complaint to the elder. Any local deacon, or elder, must come before such a court, if unfaithful. It would not be amiss to list their names, and if they do not appear inquire if they stand clear, so you must judge Israel as Samuel did.

29. Lee, *Short History*, 129–33.

30. Ibid., 138–40. In his Memoirs, Richard Whatcoat renders comparable accounts for quarterly meetings the following year:

> The 26th of April, 1789, at a quarterly meeting, held at the old meeting-house, near Cambridge, Dorchester country, the Lord came in power at our sacrament; the cries of the mourners, and the ecstasies of believers were such, that the preacher's voice could scarcely be heard, for the space of three hours: many were added to the number of true believers. At our quarterly meeting, held at S. Michael's, for Talbot circuit, the power of the Lord was present, to wound and to heal. Sabbath following, our quarterly meeting, held at Johnstown, for Caroline circuit, was yet more glorious; the power of the Lord came down at our love-feast. The house was filled with the members of our societies, and great numbers of people were on the outside; the doors and windows were thrown open, and some thronged in at the latter. Such times my eyes never beheld before.
>
> May 5th and 6th, we held quarterly meetings for Dover circuit, at Duck Creek Cross Roads; the 7th and 8th, at Dudley church, for Queen Ann's circuit; and on the 10th and 11th, at Georgetown, for Kent circuit. The power of the Lord spread from circuit to circuit. O, how delightful it is to preach glad tidings, when we see souls "coming home to God, as doves to their windows"!

P. P. Sandford, *Memoirs of Mr. Wesley's Missionaries to America* (New York: G. Lane & P. P. Sandford for the Methodist Episcopal Church, 1843), 367–68.

31. These are entries for conferences in N.C. (March 30), Petersburg (April 20), Duck Creek, Md. (May 10), Chester (May 17), Trenton (May 22), New York (May 26), *JLFA*, 1:671–75. Asbury took careful measure of the peace and harmony of each meeting because of the lingering controversy over the council. See the discussion in the next section.

32. See Carol V. R. George, *Segregated Sabbaths. Richard Allen and the Rise of Independent Black Churches, 1760–1840* (New York: Oxford University Press, 1973); *The Life Experience and Gospel Labors of the Rt. Rev. Richard Allen* (2nd ed., New York: Abingdon Press, 1960); Will B. Gravely, "African Methodisms and the Rise of Black Denominationalism," in *POAM*, 108–26.

33. George, *Segregated Sabbaths*, 43, casts doubt on this possibility.

34. Lee, *Short History*, 149–50. Thomas Ware shared Lee's opposition, though otherwise holding "the profoundest veneration" for Mr. Asbury, an esteem widely shared. "[A]n unwillingness to oppose Bishop Asbury led a majority of the preachers to yield, so far as to permit the experiment to be made." Ware continued, "A minority, however, opposed it from the first; and I happened to be one of that number. I had ventured to say, if there must be a council to consist of bishops and presiding elders, the latter should be chosen, not by the bishops, but by the conferences, and every thing done in council should be by a simple majority." *The Life and Travels of Rev. Thomas Ware*, 181–82.

35. Tigert (*History*, 244) noted that this "virtually gave Bishop Asbury—for Bishop Coke was not present at either of the sessions held—an absolute veto on all proposed legislation." Of course, it gave every member such a veto, but since the elders, "presiding elders" in the language of the plan, served at the bishop's pleasure, the power of the bishop was effectively magnified.

36. Lee, *Short History*, 150. Tigert (*History*, 245) used the term "nullification" to describe the potential effect of this provision. Lee excerpts liberally from the minutes of the 1789 and 1790 meetings of the Council, 151–59. See also the published versions, seven and eight page documents, entitled differently each year—*The Proceedings of the Bishop and Presiding Elders of the Methodist-Episcopal Church, in Council Assembled, at Baltimore, on the First Day of December, 1789* (Baltimore, 1789) and *Minutes Taken at a Council of the Bishop and Delegated Elders of the Methodist Episcopal Church: Held at Baltimore in the State of Maryland, December 1, 1790* (Baltimore, 1790).

37. Lee, *Short History*, 151–55. Legislation so passed "shall be received by every member of each conference" (153).

38. *JLFA*, 1:614–15 (December 3, 1789). Freeborn Garrettson reported (*American Methodist Pioneer*, 265):

> *Wednesday 9*—Sweet conversation—every night we had a sermon and several exhortations. Among the rest, I found freedom to speak. O how wonderful the power of God came down—I suppose there were more than a thousand people present, and the whole congregation agitated, the voice of singing, praying, exhorting and crying for mercy and singing the praises of God, and most exultant strains were heard in every part of the church. This continued 'til three in

the morning. I know not how many were converted, or how many sanctified.

Thursday, December 10, 1789—This was to be the concluding day of our council. Part of it was spent in telling our experiences and giving ____ of the work of God in our Districts. At night we had another blessed meeting which continued until after midnight.

39. Neely, *Conference*, 304.

40. *JLFA*, 1:620 (January 12, 1790). Asbury registered his own sense of the constraints on his power and influence.

41. *JLFA*, 1:625 (February 14, 1790).

42. *JLFA*, 1:642 (June 14, 1790). James Meachem, a young preacher at that conference, noted in his journal for September 1, 1790, the opposition to the council in southern Virginia, an opposition which he thought would lead either to expulsions or separation. Four days later he reported receiving "4 Letters from the Travelling Preachers, they are much oppos'd to the Council." Meacham, "Journals" IV for September 1–5, 1790, in James Meacham Papers, 1788–1797 (Manuscript Department, Duke University Library, Durham, NC.; used with permission).

43. *JLFA*, 3:87 (commentary on letter "To the Virginia Preachers" dated Autumn, 1790).

44. *JLFA*, 1:649 (August 25, 1790). Sentiment against the council was far from uniform. Most of the conferences supported the plan. Asbury noted for the conference on the eastern shore of Maryland, "One or two of our brethren felt the Virginia fire about the question of the council, but all things came into order, and the council obtained." *JLFA*, 1:650 (September 13, 1790).

45. Paine, *M'Kendree*, 1:61, 113, 129. McKendree then possessed great confidence in O'Kelly whose word "was next to gospel with me" (61).

46. Its first apparent action showed sensitivity to the widespread concern about the limits of the council's power but nevertheless carved out clear areas for initiative:

> Q. What power do this council consider themselves *invested* with by their electors?
> A. First, they *unanimously* consider themselves invested with *full* power to act *decisively* in all temporal matters. And secondly, that of *recommending* to the several conferences any new canons, or alterations to be made in any old ones.

Minutes Taken at a Council of the Bishop and Delegated Elders, 3; also in Lee, *Short History*, 155.

Notes to Chapter 5

1. *JLFA*, 1:667–68 (February 23, 1791). At the Petersburg conference, Asbury noted, "The affair of the council was suspended until a general conference." *JLFA* 1:672 (April 19, 1791).

2. The framing legislation for the council had begun, "Whereas the holding of general conferences on this extensive Continent would be

attended with a variety of difficulties, and many inconveniences to the work of God." Lee, *Short History*, 149.

3. *JLFA*, 1:687 (July 1, 1791). Compare the account in Leroy Lee, *The Life and Times of The Rev. Jesse Lee*, 268–71. Jesse Lee had made a similar proposal when the council met (though not a member of that body). He had been sharply rebuffed. The council responded (ibid., 282):

> Very dear Bro.: We are both grieved and surprised to find that you make so many objections to the very fundamentals of Methodism. But we consider *your want of experience* in many things, and therefore put the best construction on your intention.

4. Lee, *Short History*, 177.

5. Lee reported: "At that general conference we revised the form of discipline, and made several alterations. The proceedings of that conference were not published in separate minutes, but the alterations were entered at their proper places, and published in the next edition of the form of discipline." *Short History*, 180. A reconstruction of the minutes, effected by Thomas B. Neely, can be found in Lewis Curts, ed., *The General Conferences of the Methodist Episcopal Church from 1792 to 1896* (Cincinnati: Curts & Jennings; New York; Eaton & Mains, 1892). For a recent analysis of the conference, see Frederick A. Norwood, "A Crisis of Leadership: The General Conference of 1792," *Methodist History*, 28 (April 1990), 129–201.

6. Lee, *Short History*, 193.

7. Tigert, *Methodism*, 145.

8. Buckley, *History*, 68–69.

9. Tigert, *History*, 263.

10. Lee, *Short History*, 181. Tigert, *History*, 263–64. For a brief period "annual conferences" were called "district conferences." Elsewhere Tigert (*Methodism*, 123) observed:

> The facts of our history are that General and Annual Conferences are complementary: each implies the other. The body in which were lodged, and which actually exercised, the supreme governmental powers of the Methodist Episcopal Church—electoral, disciplinary, legislative—between 1785 and 1792 was neither a General nor an Annual Conference. It was a yearly assembly or assemblies which combined the functions of both. General and Annual Conferences, in the sense of the Discipline from 1792 to the present, had not existence prior to that date. The functions of the two—General and Annual—have been differentiated and defined out of the undivided powers of a primitive body known as "Conference," recognized and set up—constituted if one please, since many powers necessary to its supremacy were added, previously unknown in American Methodism—by the Christmas Conference at the time and in the act of organizing the Church.

11. Lee, *Short History*, 183.

12. Tigert, *History*, 264–65.

13. Lee, *Short History*, 178.

14. Ibid.,178–79.

15. For discussion of this ideology and its play in American Methodism, see Russell E. Richey, "The Four Languages of Early American Methodism," *Methodist History*, 28 (April 1990), 155–171. The literature on republicanism is extensive. See helpful delineations of earlier phases of the debate by Robert E. Shalhope, "Republicanism and Early American Historiography," *The William and Mary Quarterly*, 3rd ser., 39 (April 1982), 334–56, and "Toward a Republican Synthesis," *The William and Mary Quarterly*, 3rd ser. 29 (January 1972), 49–80. See also Isaac Kramnick, "Republicanism Revisionism Revisited," *The American Historical Review*, 87 (June 1982), 629–64, and the various essays in *Three British Revolutions: 1641, 1688, 1776*, ed. J. G. A. Pocock (Princeton: Princeton University Press, 1980).

16. In a letter that December to a local preacher, James O'Kelly explained his position (*JLFA* 3:114, "To Jesse Nicholson"):

> What have I done? Overturned government? What? the Council—not Methodism. I only say no man among us ought to get into the Apostle's chair with the Keys, and stretch a lordly power over the ministers and Kingdom of Christ. 'Tis a human invention, a quicksand; and when my grey hairs may be preserved under bound, I may be remembered. We ought to respect the body before any mere man. A consolidated government is always bad. We have published that we believe a General Conference to be injurious to the Church. District Conferences have lost their suffrages; men of wit will leave the travelling connection. Boys with their Keys, under the absolute sway of one who declares his authority and succession from the Apostles—these striplings must rule and govern Christ's Church, as master workmen; as though they could finish such a temple. People are to depend on their credibility. These things are so; I know what I say; I am able when called upon to answer it. I am a friend to Christ; to his Church, but not to prelatick government.

17. *The Life and Travels of Rev. Thomas Ware*, 220–21. Ware (220) affirmed, "Had Mr. O'Kelly's proposition been differently managed it might possibly have been carried. For myself at first I did not see any thing very objectionable in it."

William McKendree, who sided with O'Kelly, lodged with him at general conference, but later reverted to the Methodist Episcopal Church (and even later was elected bishop) caught the republican resonances in a retrospective assessment: "Evil was determined against the Connection, justified by the supposition that the Bishop and his creatures were working the ruin of the Church to gratify their pride and ambition" (Paine, *M'Kendree*, 1:64). McKendree's return to the connection had much to do with the excesses in this republican rhetoric. In particular, he found Asbury not to be the tyrant that O'Kelly alleged him to be.

18. Critical to the change in sentiment was an adroitly crafted letter that Asbury, sick in bed, sent to the conference. It suggested a very contrary view of Methodist political reality (*JLFA*, 1:734 [November 8, 1792]):

Let my absence give you no pain—Dr. Coke presides. I am happily excused from assisting to make laws by which myself am to be governed: I have only to obey and execute. I am happy in the consideration that I never stationed a preacher through enmity, or as a punishment. I have acted for the glory of God, the good of the people, and to promote the usefulness of the preachers.

19. William Warren Sweet estimates that the overall losses suffered in the 1790s to the Republicans, to William Hammett and to other causes amounted to some 10,000. See his *Methodism in American History*, rev. ed. (New York: Abingdon Press, 1953), 134. The Hammett movement, centered in Charleston and taking the name Primitive Methodists, made less of an impact on the movement. Buckley (*History*, 76) regarded the loss as only that shown in the minutes, some 7,352, which he too spreads over various causes.

20. For an analysis of that process, see Will B. Gravely, "African Methodisms and the Rise of Black Denominationalism," in *POAM*, 108–26.

21. The historiographical tradition was shaped by the effective reply to O'Kelly of Nicholas Snethen, *A Reply to an Apology for Protesting Against the Methodist Episcopal Government: Compiled Principally from Original Manuscripts* (Philadelphia: Printed by Henry Tuckniss, 1800). See pp. 28, 32, 51–3.

22. Buckley, *History*, 76.

23. Meacham, "Journals," VI for Nov. 6, 1792, in James Meachem Papers, 1788–1797 (Manuscript Department, Duke University Library, Durham, NC.; used with permission).

24. Snethen (*Reply*, 38) represented O'Kelly's movement as a fraternity: "Mr. O'Kelly finds himself only one among so many; the majority will govern; he cannot make them see out of his own eyes; he leaves the conference, exclaiming 'O Dort! Dort!' and writes 'To the synod, a mournful farewell.' He calls together his fraternity, in a conference at Piney-Grove."

Notes to Chapter 6

1. One that does so quite evocatively and successfully is Mudge, *New England*. Note especially the chapter entitled "Life in the Conference."

2. The revivalistic character of conference has been already noted and will be discussed also below. See also "From Quarterly to Camp Meeting: A Reconsideration of Early American Methodism," *Methodist History*, 23 (July 1985), 199–213.

3. *Short History*, 174–75. Lee actually said eighteen but numbered the general conference among them.

4. "In consequence of reducing the number of annual conferences to seven, some of the preachers, who labored in the frontier circuits, had to come from two to four hundred miles to attend the conferences, which obliged them to leave their regular work from three to six weeks, during which time the people were unsupplied with the word and ordinances of the gospel." Bangs, *History*, 2:20.

5. Ibid, 2:19.

6. Lee, *Short History*, 194–95.

7. Entries from Freeborn Garrettson's manuscript journal illustrate the "traveling together":

> *Thursday 27*—After an agreeable time with Brother and Sister M___y the young preacher rode with me to Sharon (Conn.). . . .
>
> *Saturday 28 and Sunday 29*—was our Quarterly Meeting in Pittsfield (Mass.). . . .
>
> *Monday, December 31*—was a remarkably stormy day. I rode in a sleigh accompanied by three preachers and others, to Lanes-Borough. . . .
>
> *Tuesday evening, January 1, 1793.*—We rode to Adams, (Mass.). . . .
>
> *Wednesday 2*—In Williamsstorn (Mass.) the room was crowded . . . .
>
> *Thursday 3*—Brother (D. or B.) and I continued together. . . .
>
> *Friday 4*—We went on to Ashgrove (N.Y.). . . .
>
> *Saturday 5*—Quarterly meeting began. Five preachers were present. . . .
>
> *Sunday 6*—Our love feast began a little after sunrise. . . .
>
> *Monday 7*—We rode 15 miles and there were four preachers with me. The following day we had a solemn sacramental occasion at B___d's, Esq. As the preachers continued with me, I again gave up the evening meeting to them. I suppose 200 were present, we had two sermons, and an exhortation. . . .
>
> *Wednesday 9*—This morning I parted with three of the brethren, and Brother Dillon and I set out for Albany. . . .
>
> . . . .
>
> *Monday 14*—Two of the preachers left me. . . .
>
> *Tuesday 15*—We rode to Johnstown and I preached. . . .
>
> *Wednesday 16*—I was accompanied in a sleigh by two preachers, and one young convert 30 miles to Springfield. . . .
>
> *Thursday 17*—We are now five in number, four in the sleigh and one on horseback. We traveled through a severe snow storm about 11 miles. . .
>
> *Friday 18*—We still pursue our journey to the west. . . .
>
> *Saturday 19*—We still pursue our journey to the west, our number has increased to seven. . . .
>
> . . . .
>
> *Tuesday 22*—At present we are only four in company. . . .
>
> . . . .
>
> *Thursday 24*—I have only preacher with me, and we turned our faces toward the Delaware. . . .
>
> *Friday 25*—Nine of us set out for Quarterly Meeting. . . .

American Methodist Pioneer, 282–88. In the omitted entries, Garrettson did not indicate whether others traveled with him.

8. Meacham, "Journals," VI for May 26, 1792, in James Meachem Papers, 1788–1797 (Manuscript Department, Duke University Library, Durham, NC.; used with permission).

9. "The Letters Written to Daniel Hitt, Methodist Preacher, 1788 to 1806" (given by the Stevenson family to Ohio Wesleyan University; transcript made by Miss Annie Winstead, Upper Room; Notes and Introduc-

tion by Raymond Martin Bell, 1967). Copy in the Drew University Library. The citations are from pp. 18 and 26 and are respectively dated January 21, 1789 and January 28, 1790.

These sentiments recur throughout the correspondence. Two other plaintive statements should suffice in showing how much these letters from one another meant to the preachers:

> Give my respects to Br. Conway. I suppose, he'll not leave that district now. . . . Give my respects to all enquireing friends, tell them not to be so choice of their ink & paper.

> I receiv'd your missive; & kindly thank you for the Love & friendship contained therein; and I am truly sorry that it has been out of my power to answer it untill now: but be well assured you lie near my heart, & have a place in my affections; I well remember the sweet moments we have spent together; & hope to spend many more with you in our Father's house above.

Ibid, p. 158; letters from Seely Bunn and Thos. Bell dated respectively August 16, 1795 and February 6, 1796.

10. "Autobiography of Rev. William Burke," in James B. Finley, *Sketches of Western Methodism*, ed. W. P. Strickland (Cincinnati: Methodist Book Concern, 1857), 68.

11. In so doing, General Conference gave reasons that approximated those cited later by Lee; see *JGC/MEC 1796–1836*, 11–12 (1796):

> N.B. For several years the annual conferences were very small, consisting only of the preachers of a single district, or of two or three very small ones. This was attended with many inconveniences:—1. There were but few of the senior preachers whose years and experience had matured their judgments, who could be present at any one conference. 2. The conferences wanted that dignity which every religious synod should possess, and which always accompanies a *large* assembly of gospel ministers. 3. The itinerant plan was exceedingly cramped, from the difficulty of removing preachers from one district to another. All these inconveniences will, we trust, be removed on the present plan; and at the same time the conferences are so arranged that all the members respectively may attend with little difficulty.

> To all which may be added, that the active, zealous, unmarried preachers may move on a large scale, and preach the ever-blessed gospel far more extensively through the sixteen states, and other parts of the continent; while the married preachers, whose circumstances require them, in many instances, to be more located than the single men, will have a considerable field of action opened to them; and also the bishops will be able to attend the conferences with greater ease, and without injury to their health.

12. Wallace Guy Smeltzer, *Methodism on the Headwaters of the Ohio: The History of the Pittsburgh Conference of the Methodist Church* (Nashville: Parthenon Press, 1951), 73: "Though the geographical boundaries of the Conferences were set in 1796, it is not until after the General Conference of

1804 that the membership of the Preachers came to be considered as belonging to specific Conferences."

13. For these boundary actions, beginning with 1796, see *JGC/MEC 1796–1836*, 12 (1796), 43 (1800), 52–53 (1804), 107–9 (1812), 152–54 (1816), 215–17 (1820), 273–75 (1824), 304, 324 (1828), 364, 388–90 (1832), 428, 458, 460, 465, 469–72 (1836). The 1808 Journals suggest there was little or only minor change.

14. Ibid, 12 (1796).

15. The description of the Western Conference carried this proviso: "That the bishops shall have authority to appoint other yearly conferences in the interval of the General Conference, if a sufficieincy of new circuits be anywhere formed for that purpose." Ibid., 11 (1796).

16. And, of course, also an all-male affair. A less open conference moved women further from the political center of the movement.

17. Lee, *Short History*, 270–71. For discussion of efforts by African American congregations to obtain ordination of their leadership and the church's resistance to that, see Gravely, "African Methodisms and the Rise of Black Denominationalism," *POAM*, 113.

18. The New England Conference appointed such an officer in 1812. See *Minutes NE*, 1:161–62.

19. Appealing to Philip Gatch's *Journal* and minutes of the South Carolina Conference, Tigert hypotheosized that annual conferences had already initiated the office and General Conference standardized the practice. Tigert, *Methodism*, 93, 93n.

20. *Minutes NE*, 1:29–31 (1800). The mss. of early New England Conference minutes are at Drew University.

21. Ibid., 1:36–37 (1801).

22. Ibid., 1:45 (1802). A rather different assessment came for a Mr. Wall the following year:

> Oliver Wall, having travelled two years, was examined; there were objections. Br. Snelling & Smith said that he had not been acceptable on Readfield Ct. Br. Heath said that he was not acceptable on Falmouth Ct. when he rode with him, but thought it owing to his slowness of thought & ungracefullness of speech, as he was correct in his doctrines; Br. Emery gave nearly the same testimony Br. Taylor expressed doubt about his being qualified for a travelling preacher. It was however hoped & rather concluded by all that he was pious.

Ibid., 1:57 (1803). The conference therefore voted that he be not admitted and not continued on trial, but reconsidered later in the session and continued him on trial.

23. Ibid., 1:94 (1806).

24. "The high taste of these southern folks will not permit their families to be degraded by an alliance with a Methodist travelling preacher; and thus, involuntary celibacy is imposed upon us: all the better." *JLFA*, 2:591 (Febrary 1, 1909).

25. *Minutes NE*, 1:50 (1802).

26. See Lee, *Short History*, 271–73. The revival was stimulated also by the annual conference that followed immediately at Duck Creek. The "Memoirs of the Rev. Richard Whatcoat" also report this phenomenon:

> At our General Conference, held at Baltimore, in Maryland, May the 6th, 1800, I was elected and ordained to the episcopal office. We had a most blessed time and much preaching, fervent prayers, and strong exhortations through the city, while the high praises of a gracious God reverberated from street to street, and from house to house, which greatly alarmed the citizens. It was thought that not less than two hundred were converted during the sitting of our conference.
>
> On the 1st of June we held a conference at Duck Creek Cross Roads, in the state of Delaware. This was a glorious time; such a spirit of faith, prayer, and zeal, rested on the preachers and people, that I think it exceeded any thing of the kind I ever saw before. O, the strong cries, groans, and agonies of the mourners! enough to pierce the hardest heart; but when the Deliverer set their souls at liberty, their ecstasies of joy were inexpressibly great, so that the high praises of the Redeemer's name sounded through the town, until solemnity appeared on every countenance: the effect of which was, that on the Thursday following, one hundred and fifteen person joined the society in that town, while the divine flame spread greatly through the adjacent societies. We visited our societies, and passed on through Philadelphia.
>
> Our conference began at New-York the 19th of June, 1800, and closed the 23d; a few souls were converted.

P. P. Sandford, *Memoirs of Mr. Wesley's Missionaries to America* (New York: G. Lane & P. P. Sandford for the Methodist Episcopal Church, 1843), 372–73. There is also a very thorough discussion in Baker, *Methodists*, 88–90.

27. See the standard treatment, Charles A. Johnson, *The Frontier Camp Meeting* (Dallas: Southern Methodist University Press, 1955); my "From Quarterly to Camp Meeting," *Methodist History*, 23 (July 1985), 199–213; Kenneth O. Brown, "Finding America's Oldest Camp Meeting," *Methodist History*, 28 (July 1990), 252–54; Dickson D. Bruce, Jr., *And They All Sang Hallelujah: Plain-Folk Camp-Meeting Religion, 1800–1 845* (Knoxville: University of Tennessee Press, 1974); John B. Boles, *The Great Revival, 1787–1805: The Origins of the Southern Evangelical Mind* (Lexington: University of Kentucky Press, 1972); Leigh Eric Schmidt, *Holy Fairs: Scottish Communions and American Revivals in the Early Modern Period* (Princeton: Princeton University Press, 1989); Marilyn J. Westerkamp, *Triumph of the Laity: Scots-Irish Piety and the Great Awakening, 1625–1760* (New York: Oxford University Press, 1988); Roger Robins, "Vernacular American Landscape: Methodists, Camp Meetings, and Social Responsibility," *Religion and American Culture*, 4 (Summer 1994), 165–91; and Ann Taves, "Methodist Enthusiasm" in her forthcoming *The Making and Unmaking of Religious Experience: Psychological Theory and Religious Revivals*.

28. For one among the many contemporaneous 'recognitions' of the phenomenon, see the "Journal of Benjamin Lakin," in Sweet, *Methodists*, 215–225.

29. The magazine had only recently acquired that title. It had been launched by Wesley as *The Arminian Magazine* and continued under that title after his death.

30. *The Methodist Magazine*, 25 (London, 1801), 217 (letter dated Aug. 20, 1801). The person identifying the revival of religion, J. Chappell, went on to say: "It is said there never was such an outpouring of the Spirit, as there is at present thro' most parts of the Continent." Ibid., 262 (letter dated Oct. 23, 1801). He like Asbury connected revivals around Baltimore with those in Kentucky and Tennessee. He noted of the western gatherings, "They encamp on the ground, and continue praising God for a whole week, day and night." Ibid., 263. The latter was one of a number of letters republished as information for British readers, but most were originals directed from the Americans to Coke.

31. "There is," wrote Ezekiel Cooper to Coke, "a great and glorious Revival in Tennessee and Kentuckey, among both Presbyterians and Methodists, who join in christian fellowship, and help each other in the blessed work. Some of our Ministers, and some of the Presbyterian Clergy, join as a band of brothers to make war against the kingdom of the Devil; and the fruit of their joint labours is wonderful. Their meetings continue for days together; the people come from far in their waggons, &c. to their great meetings: They bring provisions with them, pitch their tents in the woods, and there continue for days, worshipping the Lord together." Ibid, 424 (letter dated September 7, 1801).

32. Ibid., 422–23 and 523.

33. *JLFA*, 3:255 (December 30, 1802). Zachary Myles of Baltimore wrote Coke (Jan. 11, 1803), "Mr. Asbury wrote word to our preachers, to make preparation for the erection of a Camp within two miles of this City, at our next Conference in April." *Methodist Magazine* 26 (1803), 285.

34. Johnson, *Frontier Camp Meeting*, 6, 82; compare Lee, *Short History*, 362. Methodists did, of course, legislate on and regulate the phenomenon. For instance, the Baltimore Conference in 1811 decreed that they should be held only "under the direction and approbation of the Presiding Elder." The conference also called upon state for help, obtaining a 1812 law from the Maryland Assembly imposing a $20 fine "for erecting booths for selling liquor within two miles of any Methodist camp or quarterly meeting." Baker, *Methodists*, 54, 96.

35. The emergence of the pattern can be seen in Wakeley, *Henry Boehm*, 128–36, 147–54, 163–69, 210, 213, 255, 282, 290, 302, 312–13, 315, 317, 363, 417, 460–61, 467. Boehm traveled with Asbury, "longer than any other man,"(438) and with those entries reported on and described camp meetings and incidentally noted their increasing connection with conference, particularly quarterly conference. The pattern continued well into the century, prevailing longer in the west. Jacob Lanius, for instance, reported Missouri camp meetings during conference for 1832 and 33. *The Journal of the Reverend Jacob Lanius, An Itinerant Preacher of the Missouri Conference . . . from 1831 A.D. to 1841 A.D.*, typescript ed. Elmer T. Clark, 1918, 6–7.

36. "The Journals of the Illinois Conference," in Sweet, *Methodists*, 261–366, p. 266. The role that camp meetings played in taking over the

spiritual dimension of conference was indicated in a motion that followed (267): "Brother Scripps then introduced a resolution in writing seconded by Brother Armstrong, respectfully requesting Bishop Soule to preach at the Camp Ground tomorrow at Eleven O'Clock a.m. a Funeral Sermon in Memory of our much revered Father in Christ William Beauchamp."

37. Paine, *M'Kendree*, 2:380.

38. Johnson dates the practice from 1806 (*The Frontier Camp Meeting*, 86–7). For an illustration see the following in Sweet, *Methodists*: the "Journal of Benjamin Lakin," 230, 252–54; "Journal of James Gilruth," 440, 442–43, 447; references to camp meetings in Ohio, 172, 179, 183–85, 193, 197, 198–99. For conjunctions of conference and camp meeting, see 266, 279, 337.

39. Asbury wrote Elijah Hedding, *JLFA*, 3:380–81 (December 14, 1807):

> I have either seen, or heard, directly, or indirectly from most of the 35 districts, but some great official letters, are not come to hand. But from what I have collected, campmeetings are as common now, as quarter meetings were 20 years back, in many districts, happy hundred have been converted; in others happy thousands. Glory! Glory! Glory! Reputable report says, in the east of Maryland, last August, campmeeting 10 days, 2500 or 3000 converted. Oh my brother, doubt not, the good news you bring, will come to be general, and not only general but universal. . . .

40. *JLFA*, 3:452–53 (September 1, 1811). The next day he wrote Coke (*JLFA*, 3:455):

> My dearly beloved in the Lord:
> May great grace rest upon us and the church of God, and the ministry in which we are engaged. Next month, by divine permission, I shall close my fortieth year in America. When I came hither in 1771, we had 400 in society, who were more nominal than real members, and now we number 185,000. Our former circuits are become districts, and our present ones are like little parishes! Our campmeetings, I think, amount to between four and five hundred annually, some of which continue for the space of six or eight days. It is supposed that it is not uncommon for then thousand persons, including all who come at different periods, to be present at one of those meetings. On such occasions, many become subjects of a work of grace, and many experience much of the sanctifying influences of the Holy Spirit; backsliders are restored, and the union of both preachers and people is greatly increased.

41. John F. Wright, *Sketches of the Life and Labors of James Quinn* (Cincinnati: The Methodist Book Concern, 1851), 109.

42. "Brother M'Caine moved, that the quarterly meeting conference shall appoint a secretary to take down the proceedings of the quarterly meeting conference, in a book kept by one of the stewards of the circuit for that purpose. Carried." *JGC/MEC 1796–1836*, 55 (1804). Examples of those can be found in Sweet, *Methodists*, 552–639. The minutes cover church business, fiscal matters, juridical proceedings.

Notes to Chapter 7

1. *JGC/MEC 1796–1836*, 51 (1804).

2. Wakeley, *Henry Boehm*, 182–82: "There was not only preaching on Sunday, but three times every day in the Light-street Church, and every evening in the four other churches, namely: The Point, Oldtown, African, and the New Church (Eutaw)."

3. Ibid., 395–97.

4. *JGC/MEC 1796–1836*, 80–81 (1808). The language seems to be wholly absent from 1812, when Daniel Hitt secretary; occurred occasionally in 1816 (Lewis Fechtig sec.) and 1820 (Alexander M'Caine sec.); was almost wholly absent from 1824 (R. R. Roberts sec.) except as imbedded in a motion; appeared very occasionally in 1828, pp. 318–19 (Martin Ruter sec.); and the same holds in 1832 and 1836.

5. Buckley, *History*, 93.

6. Mudge, *New England*, 56 ff.

7. *JGC/MEC 1796–1836*, 48 (1804). This differs from the enumeration given by Lee, *Short History*, 297.

8. Lee, *Short History*, 297.

9. Buckley, *History*, 94–5.

10. Tigert, *History*, 293–96; Buckley, *History*, 95–6. "A plan," said Lee (*Short History*, 345–45) "which would have overset and destroyed the rules and regulation of the Methodists, respecting the election and ordination of Bishops."

11. Lee, *Short History*, 345.

12. Tigert, *History*, 299. Tigert reproduced the "material part" of the Memorial. The *Minutes NE*, 1:105 (1807), indicate that letters concerning this legislation were read to the New England Conference. In accordance with this action, New England voted the following year to send seven delegates.

13. This is the conclusion that Tigert reached in *History*, 299–300.

14. Buckley, *History*, 101–2. New England had "Voted that this Conf. judge it expedient to send delegates to the general Conf. Voted that seven be considered a sufficient number to represent this Conf. in the general Conf." *Minutes NE*, 1:118 (1808).

15. *HAM*, 1:475–76; Tigert, *History*, 301.

16. Tigert, *History*, 305–6.

17. *HAM*, 1:476.

18. "Carried by a very large majority." *JGC/MEC 1796-1836*, 88 (1808).

19. Ibid.

20. Ibid., 89. Lee's concern for seniority was cared for explicitly by a later motion: "Moved by Joseph Totten, and seconded by Stephen G. Roszel, that no preacher shall be sent as a representative to the General Conference until he has travelled at least four full calendar years from the time that he was received on trial by an annual conference, and is in full connexion at the time of holding the conference. Carried." Ibid., 95.

21. The editors of the Discipline reshaped the legislation that passed General Conference, putting items into a logical sequence and, in certain

instances, reverting to formulations of the drafting committee. For analysis of the changes, see Neely, *Conference*, 363–73. For interpretation of the
separate provisions, especially the Restrictive Rules, see Buckley, *History*,
chapters 19 through 29.

22. Neely termed the delegated Conference "a new epoch in the
development of Conference government." It "was to be a ministerial body
composed of a proportionate number of ministerial delegates from the
Annual Conference, that it was to be the law-making body of the Church,
that it was to have a supplementary or concurrent share in the constitu-
tion-making power, and that it was to exist and act under a constitution
of which no part could be changed except by compliance with the process
laid down by the power that created the constitution, and that this process
required the recommendation of all the Annual Conferences, and then
the concurrence of the General Conference." Neely, *Conference*, 373, 388.

23. Tigert, *History*, 323–24.

24. *JGC/MEC 1796–1836*, 93 (1808).

25. On this see Mathews, *Slavery*, and H. Shelton Smith, *In His Image,
But . . .* (Durham: Duke University Press, 1972). The church had, as we
have noted, already in 1804 printed separate Discipline for the South
minus the anti-slavery rubric. See Mathews, *Slavery*, 30 ff.

26. There ironically slavery could not be 'depended' upon to distinguish black from white. So churches segregated to distinguish white from
'freedman' and slave.

27. Considerable tension occurred over property, title, access to the
pulpit and other intra-congregational matters treated elsewhere in this
volume. See Gravely, "African Methodisms and the Rise of Black Denominationalism," in *POAM*, 108–26.

28. See Carol V. R. George, *Segregated Sabbaths. Richard Allen and the
Rise of Independent Black Churches, 1760–1840* (New York: Oxford Univer-
sity Press, 1973); Howard D. Gregg, *History of the African Methodist Episcopal
Church* (Nashville: AMEC Sunday School Union, 1980).

29. *Discipline of the African Methodist Episcopal Church*, 1817.

30. Lewis V. Baldwin, *"Invisible" Strands in African Methodism: A History
of the African Union Methodist Protestant and Union American Methodist Episcopal Churches, 1805–1980* (Metuchen: Scarecrow Press, 1983).

31. David H. Bradley, *A History of the A.M.E. Zion Church 1796–1968*,
2 vols. (Nashville: A.M.E. Zion Publishing House, 1956, 1960). William J.
Walls, *The African Methodist Zion Church: Reality of the Black Church* (Charlotte: A.M.E. Zion Publishing House, 1974).

32. At one stage African congregations proposed the establishing of
Black conferences if ordination and the measure of authority and integrity
that entailed would be granted. Even that had been denied.

33. The label of 'Methodist' perhaps overstates the unity existing at
this point but serves to suggest the possibility that events would frustrate.
For the developments that brought the German movements into being see
Behney/Eller, *History*.

34. Behney/Eller, *History*, 97–111.

35. R. Yeakel, *Jacob Albright and His Co-Laborers*, trans. from the German (Cleveland: Publishing House of the Evangelical Association, 1883), 102.

36. Ibid., 83; Behney/Eller, *History*, 75–76.

37. Yeakel, *Jacob Albright*, "Life Experience and Ministerial Labors of George Miller," 244–45; Behney/Eller, *History*, 78–79. Using the 1804 Discipline rather than that of 1808, Miller and company did not put the "Restrictive Rules" into their constitutive order.

38. "Die soggenannten Albrechtsleute." Another phrase used was "Die sogenannten Albrechts." Behney and Eller rightly prefer the translation given to the more frequently seen,"The so-called Albright's people" or "The so-called Albrights." Behney/Eller, *History*, 91.

39. R. Yeakel, *Jacob Albright*, "Life and Labors of John Dreisbach, Evangelical Minister and the First Presiding Elder in the Evangelical Association," 294–96.

40. The Evangelicals, like the Methodists, wanted only itinerants to be members. Behney/Eller, *History*, 94.

Notes to Chapter 8

1. *JGC/MEC 1796–1836*, 11 (1796).

2. These can be followed in the successive Journals, but may be most conveniently visualized in Emory, *Discipline*. His section, "Of the Boundaries of the Annual Conferences," 246–94, details the changes in General Conference legislation, for each successive General Conference, including the specific wording of provisos.

3. The last included "an annual conference on the western coast of Africa, to be denominated The Liberian Mission Annual Conference." See Emory, *Discipline*, 246–60.

4. See the earlier discussion in chapter 3, part B.

5. "An Appeal to the Methodists, in Opposition to the Changes Proposed in Their Church Government," (1827) in Thomas E. Bond, *The Economy of Methodism Illustrated and Defended* (New York: Lane & Scott, 1852), 9–56, p. 19.

6. This pattern is well described by Wallace Guy Smeltzer, for *The History of United Methodism in Western Pennsylvania* (Nashville: Parthenon Press, 1975), 69 ff. The latter stages in the emergence of conference there included Asbury's formation of the Redstone circuit (documented in Robert Ayres' Journal), Asbury's own trips through, (1784, 85, 86 and some twenty through the region between 1784 and 1815), the division of the circuit (1787, Redstone divided into 3) and then quarterly meetings and annual conferences in region.

7. Examples of these could be entered endlessly from the journals and memoirs of western itinerants. They spent a considerable portion of their time, particularly in the summer, in going to or conducting camp meetings. For instance, Jacob Lanius began July 28 [1836] a series of successive camp meetings (in different places) which continued to September 10, concluding "in order to get to conference in time." He left conference "in company with Brother Waugh, in order to attend a camp

meeting on my circuit at Mud Town the seat of our revival [Sept. 15]." He was *effectively two months in camp meetings* and then began another on Oct. 7. See *Journal of Jacob Lanius*, 270, 275, 277–80. The next year the season of camp meetings began later for Lanius, in early August; he attended only three; then broke for conference which began in St. Louis on Sept. 13.

These continued to be highly 'fraternal affairs'. For instance, William Burke spoke of the gathering of traveling preachers, "with worn and tattered garments, but happy and united like a band of brothers. The quarterly meetings and annual conferences were high times. When the pilgrims met they never met without embracing each other, and never parted at those seasons without weeping. Those were days that tried men's souls." "Autobiography of Rev. William Burke," in James B. Finley, *Sketches of Western Methodism* (Cincinnati: Methodist Book Concern, 1854), 22–92, 68.

8. Smeltzer (*History of United Methodism in Western Pennsylvania*, 83) summarized the process:

> Religion was destined to prove itself as the greatest civilizing force for law and order and decent community life in the new frontier settlements. And highly organized Methodism, with its system of spiritual oversight and Christian nurture, literally seemed made for the times.
>
> When the Methodist itinerating preachers were assigned to carve out a new Circuit in virgin territory they would seek out cabin homes where they would be welcomed, located at intervals of from five to ten miles apart. . . . If one preacher was assigned to the new territory he would endeavor to set up a two-week Circuit, that is, a territory with up to a dozen preaching places in it that he could cover in a round of two weeks, preaching daily, or almost daily, that would cover about one hundred miles in a single round. If two preachers were assigned the extent and number of preaching places would be doubled, and the preachers would follow each other around the Circuit at two week intervals, giving preaching at each point every two weeks.
>
> The itinerating Circuit Rider did more than preach. He was also an organizer. At the close of his first sermon at a place he would explain the Methodist system, organize the professing Christians who agreed to it into a Methodist Class, and appoint a Class Leader. . . . In his setting up of the Circuit the preacher would explain the nature and function of the Quarterly Meeting for all the Classes on the Circuit, and the system of financial support. . . .

Smeltzer also spoke of Methodism as having four cornerstones—the class meeting, lay preaching, the circuit system and annual conferences. Elsewhere he identified six features of early Methodism—the class and class leader, the circuit system, quarterly meetings, the presiding elder and district, annual conference and quarterly conference. See his *Methodism on the Headwaters of the Ohio: The History of the Pittsburgh Conference of the Methodist Church* (Nashville: Parthenon Press, 1951), 54–5.

9. See Theodore L. Agnew, "Methodism on the Frontier," *HAM*, 1:488–545; Nathan O. Hatch, *The Democratization of American Christianity* (New Haven: Yale University Press, 1989).

10. Sweet, *Rise*, 101–9. This particular conference exhibited, incidentally, quite striking spiritual dimensions.

11. *Minutes NE*, 1:92 (1806). After the letter was drafted and read, Conference "Voted that Mr. Asbury be desired to convey a copy of the letter to Bishop Coke to the several annual Conf" (96). A subsequent motion suggested that the letter be not sent but apparently carried.

12. The text of one version, that to the New York Conference dated June 1, 1805, is in *JLFA*, 3:333–39.

13. Sweet, *Rise*, 107.

14. "Up to the year 1828 all the Annual Conferences sat with closed doors, none being admitted except full members. This was convenient and almost necessary considering the extremely close and searching personal examination to which the members were subjected and the rigid scrutiny of all the candidates for admission or orders. But as the numbers grew larger and customs changed a little the rigidity of the rule was gradually relaxed. Yet there are many traces of it throughout the thirties." Mudge, *New England*, 98.

15. Sweet, *Rise*, 107. "The *Journal* did not indicate but Asbury did that he preached the Sunday of conference week 'to about three thousand souls'." Sweet's note, 108.

16. *Minutes NE*, 1:105, 110 (1807). The following year, that conference "Voted unanimously, that we keep all Friday's in the year as days of fasting or abstinence, and recom'd. it among our brethren." Ibid., 123 (1808).

17. See "The Evangelical Movement and Political Culture during the Second Party System," *The Journal of American History* (March 1991), 1216–39, and "Religion and Politics in the Antebellum North," in Mark Noll, ed., *Religion and American Politics* (New York: Oxford University Press, 1990), 121–45.

18. These the annual or general minutes have been aggregated, a practice begun when the conference was one or considered one, but continues to this day, a further indication of unity of this fraternity. See for *Minutes MC*, 405–35 (1808).

19. The answer to which the conferences had struggled: "Francis Asbury, William M'Kendree. . . . Doctor Coke, at the request of the British Conference, and by consent of our General Conference resides in Europe: he is not to exercise the office of Superintendent among us, in the United States, until he be recalled by the General Conference, or by all the Annual Conferences respectively." *Minutes MC*, 411 (1808).

20. Compare this list with that of Wesley's in chapter 1, note 11. Often this structure governed proceedings but remained implicit in the minutes. Sometimes, however, the secretary would indicate the movement of business.: "The Conference proceeded to take up & answer the 3rd Question. Who are to be admitted into full connection." Sweet, *Rise*, 192 (1811). "Took up the second question, "Who remain on trial?" *Minutes NE*, 1:272 (1819).

21. In 1802, the Western Conference elected "A Committe of Claimes," then a committee "to waite on the next Assembly, at Frankfort, in Kentucky, to attend to the business of Bethel Academy." By 1804, the former had been renamed "Committe of Appropriations," and remained the only one established at the organization of the conference. In 1805, as we have seen, organization involved also a Committee of Address. Conferences created ad hoc committees as needed. Sweet, *Rise*, 81, 92, 101.

22. Sweet, *Rise*, 174.

23. Sweet, *Rise*, 175, 192.

24. Baltimore did in 1810. "For the first time in the history of the Conference, a schedule of rules was adopted for the government of the body 'in their sittings.'" James Edward Armstrong, *History of the Old Baltimore Conference* (Baltimore: Printed for the Author, 1907), 160. These were then detailed.

The New England Conference, on the other hand, established in 1808 a committee of business (along with "a committee to examine a manuscript collection of hymns," and "a committee for examination of publications." In 1814, Stewards were established. Apparently only in 1819 did New England move to rules.

> On motion Voted Brothers Pickering & Hedding superintend the appointments for preaching. Proceeded to appoint the Stewards of the Conference, S. Sias, M. Ruter, & J. Sanborn chosen. Voted a Committee be appointed to draft rules & by-laws for the government of this Conference during the session, M. Ruter, E. Mudge, & T. Merritt chosen. On motion, Voted Brothers Merrill, Hyde & Frost be reappointed a Committee on the book business. A Committee was appointed to write memoirs of those preachers who have died this year, T. Merritt, E. Mudge, & S. Sias the persons. Geo. Pickering, E. Hedding, & M. Ruter appointed a Committee to examine the candidates for full connexion.

Minutes NE, 1:118, 122, 153, 271–72. The General Conference of 1812, the first delegated conference, constituted a committee of rules and various other committees in organizing. *JGC/MEC 1796–1836*, 98–104 (1812).

25. Sweet, *Rise*, 175–87. One of these cases eventuated in a committee "to take evedence (sic) and Prepare the business for next Annual Conference." In 1811, the conference established the first day a committee of appropriation and a book committee; it read and adopted rules without amendment; and created also a committee to draft a letter to local preachers, a committee which reported on the case carried over from the previous conference, and a committee to give advice in case of ownership of a fourteen year old slave.

26. Mudge (*New England*, 158), himself a conference secretary, indicated that the role involved more than keeping "a truthful, well written record":

> Necessarily becoming very familiar, especially if his term is a protracted one with all the Conference business, he can do much to expedite it. By keeping his eye on every part of it, seeing that the

proper committees are appointed and instructed in their duties, and that no item is forgotten or neglected, he lends valuable aid. This is particularly the case where, as in our Methodist arrangements, the president is usually a stranger, ignorant of local customs and traditions, and almost wholly unfamiliar with the hundreds of faces that confront him. The secretary must coach him as to these things, and be a right arm on which, if need be, he can heavily lean. The secretary also has charge of the roll of membership, looks after the archives which, when they run back over a hundred years, are of priceless value, and edits the printed Minutes. This latter task requires work before, during and after the session, requires some literary skill as well as patience, industry, information and enterprise. The secretary is the one man who represents the entire Conference in many ways during the interval between the sessions, and is given by the law of the Church a variety of inter-sessional duties. . . .

27. For the entire list see the *Minutes NE* and particularly the section frequently included, "Sessions of the New-England Conference," which identified both bishop and secretary. See also Mudge, *New England*, 159–68.

The Baltimore Conference evidenced a similar pattern, though the terms tended to be five to ten years, rather than ten to twenty, as in the case of New England. See Baker, *Methodists*, 112–13 and 271 for a brief discussion of the role; 491–93 for the MEC conferences; and 494–99 for other contributory conferences.

28. "Journal of James Gilruth" (August 1835), in Sweet, *Methodists*, 456. McKendree had complained in 1818 during a period of incapacitation; see Paine, *M'Kendree*, 1:381–82n:

> During this affliction, I was brought to examine my life in relation to eternity closer than I had done when in the enjoyment of health. 'The spiritual and temporal business of the Church' has become so complicated, spread out over so vast a territory, and involves so many responsible and delicate official acts, that I have been almost constantly mentally employed, and frequently greatly perplexed and distressed in its management. . . .

29. *The Democratization of American Christianity* (New Haven: Yale University Press, 1989); Jon Butler, *Awash in a Sea of Faith* (Cambridge: Harvard University Press, 1990).

30. Charles W. Ferguson, *Organizing to Beat the Devil: Methodists and the Making of America* (Garden City: Doubleday & Company, Inc. 1971).

Notes to Chapter 9

1. Something of Asbury's style and self-understanding can be seen in his valedictories, for instance that given before the Genesee Conference to McKendree, *JLFA*, 3:475–92 (August 5, 1813).

2. Paine (*M'Kendree*, 2:219–20) characterized him (and Asbury): "He was the first native American Bishop in the Methodist Episcopal Church, and inferior in the aggregate of those qualities which the office requires

to no one before or since his day. No man can *ever* fill the niche of Asbury—he was, under God, the father of American Methodism—he was superior to McKendree only in priority of time, length of life, and service."

3. McKendree wrote Asbury in October, 1811, proposing that he collaborate with Asbury in appointments, taking Asbury's plans for stationing to "a council of Presiding Elders" (Paine, *M'Kendree*, 2:260– 61). The address is reproduced by Bangs, *History*, 2:308–12. McKendree submitted the address in writing. His biographer reproduced the address and also reported this exchange between McKendree and Asbury (Paine, *M'Kendree*, 2:265–70):

> His address was read in Conference; but as it was a new thing, the aged Bishop (Asbury) rose to his feet immediately after the paper was read, and addressed the junior Bishop to the following effect: "I have something to say to you before the Conference." The junior also rose to his feet, and they stood face to face. Bishop Asbury went on to say, "This is a new thing. I never did business in this way, and why is this new thing introduced?" The junior Bishop promptly replied, "You are our *father*, we are your sons; you never have had need of it. I am only a *brother*, and have need of it." Bishop Asbury said no more, but sat down with a smile on his face.

4. The second Discipline was entitled, *The General Minutes of the Conferences of the Methodist Episcopal Church in America, forming the Constitution of the said Church* (London, 1786), 11. See also Emory, *Discipline*, 137. Here, as for other topics, Emory's compilation of all the legislation concerning the office, in sequential order, proves helpful in visualizing its growth in power and authority. Tigert (*Methodism*, 34–35) defined its duties from the start as "(1) the administration of the sacraments; (2) the official visitation of the Quarterly Conferences; and (3) the exercise within an assigned district of all the powers of the general superintendents for the government of the Church during their absence, extending to the ordinary enforcement of law and the prompt administration of discipline." Lee (*Short History*, 120–21) had observed for the prior year:

> The form of the minutes of conference was changed this year, and all the *Elders*, who were directed to take the oversight of several circuits, were set to the right hand of a bracket, which inclosed all the circuits and preachers of which he was to take charge.

This may be considered as the beginning of the presiding elder's office; although it was not know by that name at that time; yet, in the absence of a *Superintendent*, this *Elder* had the directing of all the preachers that were inclosed in the bracket against which his name was set.

5. Tigert, *Methodism*, 37:

> The chronology of the name is as follows: (1) It occurs first in the plan of the Council as given by Jesse Lee in 1789; (2) it occurs nowhere in the first edition of the General Minutes, published by John Dickins in 1795, embracing the official records of all the Annual Conferences from 1773 to 1794, including the Christmas Conference; (3) in the reprint of 1813, the title is used in the appointments

of 1789, probably to conform the Minutes to the Plan of the Council—it then disappears from the Minutes until 1797, after which it continues in general use; and (5) it occurs in the first extant journal of a General Conference, namely, that of 1796.

6. *The Doctrines and Discipline of the Methodist Episcopal Church ... 1792* (Philadelphia, 1792), 18. See *The Doctrines and Discipline of the Methodist Episcopal Church, in America: With Explanatory Notes, by Thomas Coke and Francis Asbury* (Philadelphia; 1798. Reprinted in facsimile. Edited by Frederick A. Norwood. Rutland: Academy Books, 1979), 46–53, for the legislation, a description, and the bishop's interpretation of the office. Defense was already deemed necessary. By appeal to Scripture, tradition and the example of Wesley, the bishops insisted that "the presiding elders must, of course, be appointed, directed, and changed by the episcopacy." (50)

7. Much of the discussion, quite rightly, focusses on the matter of election, the controversial issue. It is worth noting that the church (the bishops?) could have found some ritual/liturgical way of investing the presiding elders with the authority so mysteriously conferred by appointment. That it did not is hardly surprising. The church, at that point, had little appreciation for formal ceremony, though it put high value on informal ceremony.

8. See *JGC/MEC 1796–1836*, 140 (1816). Actually a reformulation, accepted as a friendly amendment, it read:

> The bishop, at an early period of the Annual Conference, shall nominate an elder for each district, and the Conference shall, without debate, either confirm or reject such nomination. If the person or persons so nominated be not elected by the Conference, the bishop shall nominate two others for each of the vacant districts, one of whom shall be chosen. And the presiding elder so elected and appointed shall remain in office four years, unless dismissed by the mutual consent of the Bishop and Conference, or elected some other office by the General Conference. But no presiding elder shall be removed from office during the term of four years without his consent, unless the reasons for such removal be stated to him in presence of the Conference, which shall decide, without debate, on his case.

9. On this matter, see Drinkhouse, *Reform*, 1:525. Drinkhouse provides a distinctively 'reform' perspective on the whole issue before us.

10. All published in New York, respectively in 1815, 1816, 1817, and 1820.

11. See *HAM*, 1:636 ff., and also the discussion of James O'Kelly and the Republican Methodists on pages 46–50 above.

12. Paine, *M'Kendree*, 1:397–404.

13. For narrative of the conference, see Bangs, *History*, 3:100–57; *HAM*, 1:642 ff.; Tigert, *History*, chapter 20; Buckley, *History*, chapters 41 and 42; and Drinkhouse, *Reform*, vol. 2, chapter 1.

14. Tigert, *History*, 339. The committee, appointed by George were (proponents) Ezekiel Cooper, John Emory, and Nathan Bangs, and (opponents) S. G. Roszel, Joshua Wells, and William Capers.

15. Paine, *M'Kendree*, 1:420–21.

16. Ibid., 1:419.

17. For a vivid and passionate first hand account of the proceedings, see the paper drafted by Ezekiel Cooper but published only later by his biographer, Geo. A. Phoebus, *Beams of Light on Early Methodism in America* (New York: Phillips & Hunt; Cincinnati: Cranston & Stowe, 1887), 298–308. A comparable perspective but on the other side of the debate is that of Stephen Roszel's found in Paine, *M'Kendree*, 1:408–14.

18. Among his arguments, McKendree advanced a point revelatory of the episcopacy's view of the growing regional character of annual conferences. He suggested that an effective general superintendency, supported by an appointive presiding eldership, protected "our itinerant plan of preaching the gospel" which "by removing preachers from District to District, and from Conference to Conference, (which no Annual Conference nor Presiding Elder can do,) perpetuate and extend missionary labors for the benefit of increasing thousands, who look unto us as teachers sent of God." Paine, *M'Kendree*, 1:444–58.

Bangs (*History*, 2:341–42) also listed that as among the arguments against the change, a telling one against the analogy of the British conference which stationed preachers with a committee:

> As to our British brethren, they had no other visible head than their conference. But we have, and therefore can act more efficiently through this medium, than we could do by a stationing committee. It was still further contended, and with great force of argument that if this power were taken from the bishops, it would be extremely difficult to keep up an interchange of preachers from one annual conference to another, a difficulty not felt in England, where they were all united in one conference, in which all their business was transacted.

19. For the text of two of these quite varying interpretations of the Constitution, namely those of Philadelphia and South Carolina, see Tigert, *History*, 370–71. Tigert viewed the division as sectional and anticipatory of the later rending of the church, a division at this point "on the nature of our ecclesiastical government, and particularly on the powers which the Delegated General Conference was entitled to exercise under the constitution. . . ."

20. *HAM*, 1:646–52.

21. "Remarks and Observations Addressed to Travelling Preachers," *Wesleyan Repository*, II (August 1822). Initially printed in December 1820 and circulated among travelling preachers. Reprinted by Nicholas Snethen in *Snethen on Lay Representation* (Baltimore: John J. Harrod, 1835), 37–58; 37. He continued: "The doctrines embraced by this writer teach him, that grace does not always act irresistibly;—that the spirit of infallibility, is not given to church rulers;—the passions of men in official stations do not become docile and inoffensive, in proportion, as legal

checks and restrains are removed; and that there is infinite danger in trusting unlimited power in the hands of any man, or sets of men."

22. "On Church Freedom," *Wesleyan Repository*, I (Dec. 20, 1821), in Snethen, *Lay Representation*, 75. "There is no, nor can there be, a form of religious government devised, that may not become tyrannical by deranging the balance of power; and this we conceive to be the reason why the scriptures are so silent upon the forms and modes of church government, and also why so little has been gained by changing its modes and names, in order to bring it more near to the scripture plan." (78)

23. Snethen, *Lay Representation*, 58. "We have," he indicated earlier in the essay (47), "no objection to a Methodist Episcopal Church, but to a patriarchal power in succession, in its bishops. Let us have bishops, and if all parties are agreed, a succession of them; but let all their power and authority be strictly legal, and let them be subject to legal restraints."

24. Emory, *Discipline*, 191–202. Lee (*Short History*, 255, 359, 362) had calculated the number and proportions of local preachers to traveling: in 1799 there were 850 local to 269 traveling, in 1809 1610 local to 589 traveling. McKendree gave the same proportions for 1812: 2,000 to 700. Mudge (*New England*, 239–40) noted:

> The lay or local preachers and exhorters have formed, from the beginning, a very important factor in the work. The great extent of the early circuits would of itself imply this. . . . We have no way of ascertaining accurately the number of these early local preachers, for the statistics of the Minutes do not recognize them till 1837, when the number in the whole church is given as 4,954 as against 2,933 in the itinerant ranks. Only eighty-five are reported at that time from the New England Conference, or about half the number of those traveling. In 1850 the local preachers of this Conference were eighty as compared with 113 traveling, and in the whole church 5,420 as compared with 3,777. In 1870 there were 10,340 local, and 8,830 traveling. In 1890 the numbers were practically equal, 14,072 local and 14,792 traveling. At present there are 14,743 local and 19,421 traveling.

25. See *Minutes MC* for the years 1773–1813 or Minutes for any subsequent year.

26. See Lee, *Short History*, 354, or the year-end tally for any prior year. Bangs took a similar 'body' count; see *History*, 3:183, for the 1820 accounting.

27. *JGC/MEC 1796–1836*, 148–52 (1816). That concern made the conference no more receptive to petitions by local preachers for representation; see ibid., 166–69 (1816).

28. In discussing the traveling preachers who located, Mudge (*New England*, 241) spoke of a contemporary of Snethen, his own kinsman Enoch Mudge, who after traveling with Lee and supervising Maine for six months in 1796, located at Orrington in 1799, "where he had married two years before":

> He remained there eighteen years. He became at once the teacher of the winter school (for a long time the only one in the place),

he was the local pastor, whoever might be the circuit preacher, he administered the sacraments, solemnized marriages, and conducted funerals throughout the surrounding country, and was emphatically *the* man of the whole region, sent repeatedly to the Legislature at Boston, and looked up to as one of the fathers of the town, although still young, so that his name became a household word there for a generation following.

29. Emory, *Discipline*, 193–96:

1. There shall be held annually, in each presiding elder's district, a district conference, of which all the local preachers in the district, who shall have been licensed two years, shall be members; and of which the presiding elder of the district for the time being shall be president; or, in case of his absence, the conference shall have authority to elect a president pro tem. . . .

2. The said district conference shall have authority to license proper persons to preach, and renew their license; to recommend suitable candidates to the annual conference for deacon's or elder's orders, in the local connection, for admission on trial in the travelling connection; and to try, suspend, expel, or acquit any local preacher. . . .

3. The district conference shall take cognizance of all the local preachers in the district, and shall inquire into the gifts, labours, and usefulness of each preacher by name.

30. "Letters from a Local Preacher to a Travelling Preacher," *Wesleyan Repository*, III (June 1823), in Snethen, *Lay Representation*, 184–93; 186. One complaint was that annual conferences pass on the character of the local preachers. "These travelling preachers cannot be called to account— a local preacher can have no redress. No matter what is said to injure him, he may neither hear nor reply." Snethen, *Wesleyan Repository*, III (Sept. 1823), in Snethen, *Lay Representation*, 216.

31. "Letters to a Member of the General Conference," *Wesleyan Repository*, III (Nov. 1823), in Snethen, *Lay Representation*, 233–34.

32. See discussion above in chapter 3, parts A and B.

33. In his insightful treatment of the reform movement and the founding of the Methodist Protestant Church, Douglas R. Chandler (*HAM*, 1:649) makes this suggestion: "On Monday morning, May 24 (Did anyone remember Aldersgate Day?), the measure was called up."

34. Bangs, *History*, 2:344. Of an earlier stage in the debate he observed, "Perhaps a greater amount of talent was never brought to bear on any question ever brought before the General Conference, than was elicited from both sides of the house in the discussion of this resolution" (2:334). Bangs also provided a convenient summation of the position of advocates and opponents of an elective presiding eldership (2:338–44).

35. *JGC/MEC 1796–1836*, 278–79 (1828).

36. The United Brethren, we should note, did include local preachers, a point of controversy between them and the Evangelical Alliance. Snethen invoked that precedent in *Mutual Rights*, II (1825): "We know that lay-representation is practicable in other churches; and the United

brethren have proved it to be practicable for the members to elect delegates from among their travelling and local preachers to their General Conference without destroying their itinerancy." He also noted similar patterns among Protestant Episcopal, Lutheran and German Reformed churches. Snethen, *Lay Representation*, 306.

37. "Matters worthy of the serious reflection of Travelling Preachers," *Mutual Rights*, II (April 1826), in Snethen, *Lay Representation*, 316–20; 317. Snethen looked back on 1808 as a missed opportunity to advance justice (317):

> Never were a set of men more free from foreign and adventitious influence; never did a body of men act under a consciousness of more plenary powers. Mr. Wesley's authority had been twice superceded— his name had been erased from the minutes— the council plan had been rejected—the notes on the discipline had been set at nought— and Dr. Coke was no longer in place; and yet, in 1808, in the city of Baltimore, a constitution, [as they have seen fit to call it,] was gotten up by American travelling preachers, to place themselves as nearly as possible in the condition of the hundred English preachers under the deed of declaration.

38. For discussion of the complex intertwinings of these two ideological constellations see J. G. A. Pocock, ed., *Three British Revolutions: 1641, 1688, 1776* (Princeton: Princeton University Press, 1980) and particularly the essay by John A. Murrin, "The Great Inversion," 368–453.

39. Bangs, *History*, 2:342–43. He continued, "while others contended, with more truth than either, it is believed, that each body and officer was accountable for its and his own conduct, and the latter to the tribunal from which he received his authority, and held the right to call him to an account for his acts and deeds."

40. Drinkhouse, *Reform*, 2:62–63; *HAM*, 1:650–51.

41. Often considered a continuation of the *Wesleyan Repository and Religious Intelligencer*.

42. *Mutual Rights* (August, 1824), 3.

43. *Journal of the Baltimore Conference* (April 18, 1827), 202, as cited in *HAM*, 1:653.

44. Alexander McCaine, *The History and Mystery of Methodist Episcopacy* (Baltimore, 1827), 74. The subtitle was "Or, A Glance at 'The Institutions of the Church, as We Received them from our Fathers.'" The quotation came from a letter sent prior to publication to Bishop McKendree setting forth the case against episcopacy in a series of questions and demands for documentation.

45. John Emory, *A Defense of "Our Fathers," and of the Original Organization of the Methodist Episcopal Church, Against the Rev. Alexander McCaine, and Others* (New York: N. Bangs and J. Emory, for the Methodist Episcopal Church, 1827); Thomas E. Bond, "An Appeal to the Methodists, in Opposition to the Changes Proposed in Their Church Government" (1827), in Bond, *The Economy of Methodism Illustrated and Defended* (New York: Lane & Scott, 1852), 9–56.

46. McCaine, *History and Mystery*, v.

47. Their opponents continued to see the reformers' proposals as capitulation. Bond, for instance rejected the analogy between church and the United States: "the two governments are totally dissimilar in their *origin*, in their *authority*, and in the *design* of their institution." See his "An Appeal to the Methodists," in *The Economy of Methodism*, 26. The Methodist Episcopal Church, he argued (27-28), "originated with the ministry." Its membership is voluntary:

> The rights which a Methodist, whether local preacher or layman, possesses, as such are purely conventional. They are not natural, but acquired rights. . . . The Church is a voluntary association, entered into for religious purposes; whoever enters into its communion is entitled to all the privileges and immunities which the articles of association hold out to him, and to no more.
> We should note that Bond, though rejecting a political image of the church, has taken over one no less current in the civil realm, namely that of a voluntary association. It was not the case that the reformers capitulated to civil analogy whereas the constitutionalists did not. Both did. They employed different analogies.

48. McCaine, *History and Mystery*, 9. McCaine appended to his volume (73–76) letters to Bishop McKendree and to preachers still living who had been at the 1784 Christmas Conference— Freeborn Garrettson, Lemuel Green, Thomas Ware, Nelson Reed, William Watters and Edward Dromgoole—demanding documentation of the Wesleyan counsel and directive for episcopal government.

49. Emory, *A Defence of "Our Fathers,"* 148. Emory went on to suggest that the ashes should be taken up and scattered or returned to Virginia. A footnote probed the actual relation between McCaine's volume and the Union Society.

50. Bond, "An Appeal to the Methodists," in *The Economy of Methodism*, 20.

51. The appeal to national itinerancy in earlier debates about the election of presiding elders was noted only in passing. See above, chapter 9, note 18.

52. Bond, "An Appeal to the Methodists," in *The Economy of Methodism*, 45.

53. Ibid., 48; this also gives a good description of a national itineracy.

54. Ibid., 37–38.

55. Bond (ibid., 49) noted as an argument against McCaine's proposal that the local preacher conferences, authorized in 1820, have not met or have dissolved "finding it impossible to induce the local brethren to attend, on account of the expense and loss of time which was involved in the duty."

56. Ibid., 39–40.

57. Cited by Drinkhouse, *Reform*, 2:128. See also "A Narrative and Defence of The Proceedings of the Methodist Episcopal Church in Baltimore City Station, Against Certain Local Preachers and Lay Members of Said Church," in Bond, *The Economy of Methodism*, 57–136.

58. Attenders were listed by Drinkhouse, *Reform*, 2:137–39.

59. Bangs reproduced the committee report on the Reformers' memorial and the resolutions on trials in *History*, 3:413–30.

60. *JGC/MEC 1796-1836*, 346 (1828). See Tigert, *History*, 400–403, for analysis and interpretation. Tigert noted that voting by annual conference, a feature of a prior version of the amendment as of practice, invoked American constitutional practice, a mistaken analogy:

> The truth is that the several Annual Conferences bear no such relation to the Connection as the several states bear to the general government of the Union. The number and extent of the Annual Conferences is a mere accident, mutable at the will of any General Conference. The Church was not formed by their amalgamation; but they were hewn out of the territory and the ministry of the Church. The one unbroken traveling Connection; the undivided body of itinerant preachers—this, and this only, was the original or primary constituency which gave existence to the Delegated General Conference, and prescribed the Constitution which defines its powers.

61. See Drinkhouse, *Reform*, 2:211–12, for a summary of the seventeen articles.

62. On the leadership provided by and centrality of Baltimore, see Baker, *Methodists*, 165.

63. For the text see Drinkhouse, *Reform*, 2:257–67.

64. It bore the name *The Mutual Rights and Methodist Protestant* from 1831 to 1834 and then continued as *The Methodist Protestant*.

65. Bangs (*History* 3:435) observed that "The offices of bishop and presiding elder were abolished."

66. See Drinkhouse, *Reform*, 2:287, 293, 296, 298, 315, 343, 349, 371–72. Compare Nathan Bangs, *The Present State, Prospects, and Responsibilities of the Methodist Episcopal Church: With an Appendix of Ecclesiastical Statistics* (New York: Lane and Scott, 1850).

67. See *HAM*, 1:617–35.

68. *JGC/MEC 1796–1836*, 338 (1828); Bangs, *History*, 3:389–90, reproduced the text of the enabling resolution and discussed the division, its rationale, and its results. See also Tigert, *History*, 405–9.

Notes to Chapter 10

1. *Constitution and Discipline of the Methodist Protestant Church* (Baltimore: Published for the Book Committee of the Methodist Protestant Church, 1830), 21. This had been the posture of the MEC from 1808 until 1820, when rescinded by General Conference at the prompting of the bishops and in the face of continued anti-slavery activity in northern and western conferences. For the MEC's 'Missouri Compromise', see Mathews, *Slavery*, 46–52; for the successive legislation on slavery see the Appendix in Mathews, 293–303, or Emory, *Discipline*, 17, 20, 372–79.

2. *Constitution and Discipline of the Methodist Protestant Church*, Articles VII and XII, 21–22 and 29. See also Drinkhouse, *Reform*, 2:261, 265.

3. See Mathews, *Slavery*, and for the north, A. Gregory Schneider, *The Way of the Cross Leads Home: The Domestication of American Methodism*

(Bloomington and Indianapolis: Indiana University Press, 1993). For transformations in evangelicalism as a whole, see Leonard I. Sweet, ed., *The Evangelical Tradition in America* (Macon, GA: Mercer University Press, 1984).

4. On Methodist relation to society see Richard M. Cameron, *Methodism and Society in Historical Perspective*, vol. 1 of *Methodism and Society*, undertaken by the Board of Social and Economic Relations and the Boston University School of Theology (New York: Abingdon Press, 1961).

5. See James Penn Pilkington and Walter N. Vernon, *The Methodist Publishing House*, 2 vols. (Nashville: Abingdon Press, 1968–1988), vol. 1, chapter 5.

6. The church continued to cling to the notion that the ministry was deployed nationally, as we have seen in the controversy over reform. A further illustration of that occurred in 1840, when General Conference voted down a memorial from New England to add to the Discipline a stipulation that "A bishop shall have no authority to transfer a member of one Conference to another Conference, in opposition to the wishes of said member, or in opposition to the wishes of a majority of the members of the Conference to which it is proposed to transfer said member." *JGC/MEC*, 1840, 56.

7. See *Minutes of the Annual Conferences of the Methodist Episcopal Church . . . 1773–1828* (New York: T. Mason and G. Lane, 1840), 419–48 (1824). Up until that point the structure was simply by question: "1. Who are admitted on trial? 2. Who remain on trial?" etc. The exception that the church made to the new organization was with the memoirs and beginning in 1825 placed them together with an asterisk at that question in each annual conference minutes carrying the notation, "See at the end of Minutes for this year." Ibid., 449, 451, 453, 457, 460, 463, 465. That honored the more national efforts of the deceased, some of whom would have served more than one conference, a pattern that would decrease year by year.

8. In 1816, the addresses of Asbury and McKendree were referred to a committee "whose duty it shall be to report to the conference the different subjects in them proper to be committed to district committees." That body reported out recommendations establishing six committees—episcopacy, book concerns, ways and means, review and revision, safety and temporal economy. Two committees, episcopacy and review and revision, were "of nine members, one from each annual conference." *JGC/MEC 1796–1836*, 126, 128–29 (1816).

The pattern of structuring the more important committees on a conference basis continued. The 1820 committees on episcopacy, boundaries, itinerancy, local preachers had twelve members (so as to represent each conference?), whereas other committees were smaller—e. g., rules, book concern, missions, education, "churches, parsonages, &c.," affairs of people of colour, revival, and unfinished business, Canada. Ibid., 246 (1820).

More explicitly in 1828, General Conference acted to make critical committees representative:

On motion of D. Ostrander, seconded by J. B. Finley, it was voted that a committee shall be appointed on the episcopacy, consisting of one member from each annual conference, to be selected by the delegates of the conferences respectively.

J. B. Finley moved, seconded by A. Hemphill, that in the appointment of the Committee on Itinerancy, the delegates from each annual conference be permitted to appoint one from their own number.

Moved by Laban Clark, and seconded by J. B. Finley and D. Ostrander, that a committee be appointed on the division and boundaries of the annual conferences, consisting of one member from each delegation, to be selected by the delegates in their separate capacity.

JGC/MEC 1796–1836, 304 (1828). In 1832, a series of motions established committees on episcopacy, itinerancy and boundaries as "committee to be appointed of one member from each annual conference." Ibid., 364 (1832). The year 1836 saw a series of motions establishing committees on episcopacy, itinerancy, boundaries, book concern, education and missions—the first four of which governed by the following: "that the said committee consist of one member from each annual conference, to be selected by the delegates from each conference." Ibid., 428 (1836).

9. *JGC/MEC*, 1840, 11–14. A committee on slavery had been established at the prior General Conference.

10. Tigert (*History*, 398) argued that "in this troublous period of 1820–1828 the work of division was really accomplished. The line, like a thread of scarlet, ran clearly and discernibly through the General Conference. It ran, openly and undisguisedly, through the Annual Conferences. It ran with decent concealment, but no less certainly and fatally, through the College of Bishops, and was intensified, if not rendered indelible, by their sectional administration."

11. The former is vigorously represented by Tigert, *History*, and Holland N. McTyeire, *A History of Methodism* (Nashville: Publishing House of the Methodist Episcopal Church, South, 1904). The latter is represented in various MEC histories, but especially in the 'external' perspectives of Mathews, *Slavery*, and Smith, *In His Image, But . . .* See Mathews, 250n, for an especially telling rebuttal to the constitutional readings.

12. Mudge, *New England*, 278 ff.

13. Shipley W. Willson, et al., *An Appeal on the Subject of Slavery Addressed to the Members of the New England and New Hampshire Conferences. . . .* (Boston: D. H. Ela, 1835), 3–23. See also Mathews, *Slavery*, 122–28.

14. The *Zion's Herald . . . Extra* follows the May 13, 1835 issue in the APS II microfilm series (reel 1574). Both D. D. Whedon, professor, and Wilbur Fisk, president of Wesleyan University, figured prominently in criticism of the Appeal and the anti-slavery advocates.

15. Mathews, *Slavery*, 133; Mudge, *New England*, 281.

16. Mathews, *Slavery*, 139–47.

17. Bangs, *History*, 4:259–60. He reproduced the entire address, 4:250–64. The admonition continued (261): "To be subject to the powers that be is a duty enjoined no less by Christianity, than it is a dictate of

common prudence, necessary to be observed for the preservation of good order, and the support and perpetuation of those civil and religious institutions which we so highly and justly value as freeman, as Christians, and as Methodists."

18. Cited by Mathews, *Slavery*, 138.

19. Mathews, *Slavery*, 148–57; Mudge, *New England*, 283–86.

20. On the evolution of Southern evangelicalism and its 'conscience' see, Donald G. Mathews, *Religion in the Old South* (Chicago: University of Chicago Press, 1977), 136–84.

21. *Southern Christian Advocate*, I (June 21, 1837), 1. He announced his intention to serve the "ten' thousand Methodist families and a much greater number attached to the Methodists, who have no weekly paper published among them." Then followed the statement cited.

22. Reported in *Southern Christian Advocate* (Jan. 5, 1838), 114; cited by Mathews, *Slavery*, 181.

23. See Homer L. Calkin's chapter in Baker, *Methodists*, 192–228.

24. *JGC/MEC*, 1840, 134–37. Bangs (*History*, 4:336–71) reproduced the entire episcopal address.

25. The United Brethren and Evangelical Association saw some abolitionist activity, but as predominantly northern bodies, escaped some of the intensity of the struggle and did not suffer rupture. See Behney/Eller, *History*, 123–25, 165–67, 198–99.

26. For a thorough assessment of the impact of the church splits on the nation, see C. C. Goen, *Broken Churches, Broken Nations: Denominational Schisms and the Coming of the Civil War* (Macon: Mercer University Press, 1985).

27. Mathews (*Slavery*, 192 ff.) divides the church, circa 1840, into three parties— abolitionists pressing for recommitment to the church's antislavery tradition, southerners threatening secession if such were done and conservatives attempting to hold the church together. Contemporaries also recognized three parties. For instance, in 1844 a southerner spoke of "three parties: the ultraists of the north, the anti-slavery men, and *what they call* the pro-slavery men. These anti-slavery men had assumed to be conservatives. . . ." See West, *Debates*, 16.

28. *JGC/MEC*, 1840, 133–39; Bangs, *History*, 4:349–50. The 1840 General Conference concurred in the bishops' judgment.

29. Bangs, *History*, 4:420. The emphasis is in Bangs, who reproduces the address (4:415–22).

30. In a retrospective one actor in these events argued, that even "The General Conference is an assembly of Christian pastors, not of legislators; not authorised to make laws, but to make 'such rules and regulations' as the state of the Church and the world may require, as necessary to carry into effect the laws already given by the only Lawgiver." Elliott, *Secession*, 229.

31. *Western Christian Advocate*, 7:46, cited by Elliott, *Secession*, 224– 25. Elliott reproduced articles from the several *Advocates*, General Conference and various reports, making it an invaluable resource. The first paragraph was an amendment; the remainder came from the committee's report, and were followed by specifics regarding New England's handling of the

cases of Orange Scott and La Roy Sunderland. Both amendment and this part of the report were tabled.

32. Bangs, *History*, vol. 4, appearing as an appendix beginning at what would be p. 463 and freshly numbered, 1–44. See 463/1 for a key to symbols. The fraternity included both living and dead, active and inactive. Those not living and active were marked as (l)ocated, (d)ied, (w)ithdrew or (e)xpelled. Lee might be considered to have begun the practice of naming the fraternity. Chapter 12 of Lee, *Short History* (316–40), was entitled "Containing a list of all the itinerant Methodist preachers, who have laboured in connection with the Methodist conference." However, precedent had been established by the publication of *Minutes of the Methodist Conferences Annually Held in America, from 1773 to 1794 Inclusive* (Philadelpha, 1795). The Preface indicated, "We are the more desirous to send this little publication into the world, because it contains in substance a brief history of the rise and progress of the travelling ministry, and the success of their labours through these United States. . . ."

Increasingly after Bangs the naming of the fraternity would be done annual conference by annual conference, though the church still struggled to find ways to symbolize the unity in the entire traveling fraternity. See, for instance, J. W. Hedges and A. E. Gibson, comps., *Crowned Victors: The Memoirs of Over Four Hundred Methodist Preachers, Including the First Two Hundred and Fifty Who Died on this Continent* (Baltimore: Methodist Episcopal Book Depository, 1878); and Matthew Simpson, ed., *Cyclopaedia of Methodism*, 5th ed. (Philadelphia: Louis H. Everts, 1883 [first published in 1876]).

Illustrative of annual conference efforts to name the fraternity was the "Alphabetical List of the Members of the New England Conference," New England *Minutes*, 1857, 33–35. Included were those in probationer, deacon, elder, supernumery, and superannuate relations. "The figures in the last column indicate whether it is the first or second year of appointment. Those in the first column, the time of their admission to Conference." By 1864, that conference had added to the Alphabetical List, a "Retrospective Register" covering the successive appointments of each minister and a list of "Deceased Members of the New England Conference," the latter in one page. So the entire New England fraternity, living and dead, was embraced. See New England *Minutes*, 1864, 45, 47–55, 56–58.

33. *JGC/MEC*, 1840, 139. Bangs, *History*, 4:350.

34. *JGC/MEC*, 1840, 60, 61, 87, 88, 109. The latter, known as the Few Resolution after its proposer Ignatius A. Few, read, "*Resolved*, That it is inexpedient and unjustifiable for any preacher among us to permit colored persons to give testimony against white persons, in any state where they are denied that privilege in trials at law." The proposal had a complicated fate at the Conference and even a more important symbolic one thereafter. See Tigert, *History*, 429–33; Mathews, *Slavery*, 201–04, 213–16. Mathews (213) says, "The Few resolution became the 'scarlet letter' that signified the shame of the Methodist Episcopal Church."

35. Baker, *Methodists*, 203 ff. The petition is reproduced by Norwood, *Sourcebook*, 252–53.

36. See Charles Reagan Wilson, *Baptized in Blood: The Religion of the Lost Cause, 1865–1920* (Athens: University of Georgia Press, 1980).

37. On these developments and their implications, see Mathews *Slavery*, 225–28. They declared their intention to be anti-slavery, but not radical.

38. Norwood, *Sourcebook*, 255–58. That was the first reason cited for their withdrawal. The second was "The government of the M.E. Church contains principles not laid down in the Scriptures, nor recognized in the usages of the primitive Church—principles which are subversive of the rights both of ministers and laymen." They had in mind the "power which our bishops claim and exercise, in the Annual Conferences (256)." On the initial stages of the movement, see *HAM*, 2:39–47.

39. "Pastoral Address" reproduced by Norwood, *Sourcebook*, 258–61:

> We may then congratulate ourselves, on the ground of having retained all that is essential to the identity, life, body and soul of Wesleyan Methodism, while we have separated ourselves from some of its objectionable features, which have been engrafted upon it in this country. . . .
>
> The cause of the bleeding slave, you will never forget; nor will you overlook the cause of Temperance, which has already done so much for the restoration of the degraded, and to make the wretched happy. In a word, we desire that every member of the Wesleyan Connection should not only be a zealous advocate of every branch of moral reform, but co-workers, even in the front rank, battling side by side with those who contend with the Lord's enemies.
>
> But above all, brethren, we exhort you to make holiness your motto. . . .

40. *Zion's Herald* (Dec. 7, 1842), 190, cited by Mathews, *Slavery*, 233.

41. See *HAM*, 2:33; Mathews, *Slavery*, 235–40.

42. L. L. Hamline answered that affirmatively: "This conference is the sun in our orderly and beautify system." West, *Debates*, 133.

43. Fulsome discussions of this conference can be found in *HAM*, 2:47–85; Mathews, *Slavery*, 246–82; Tigert, *History*, 435–59.

44. The limits placed on women and laity would be issues at later conferences.

45. *JGC/MEC*, 1844, 20. References to their presentation and reception abound; see 18–22, 25–27, 35–37, 39–41, 42–43, 44, 47–48, 54. They came from conferences and individual circuits. For examples, see Elliott, *Secession*, 971–73. Mathews (*Slavery*, 240) observes that "Almost every Northern annual conference petitioned the General Conference to take more decisive action against slavery."

46. *JGC/MEC*, 1844, 20–21. See also the following:

> [May 6] Genesee Conference.—G. Filmore presented the unanimous concurrence of this Conference with the resolutions of the New-York and New Jersey Conferences on temperance and slavery, and in reference to the trial of local preachers. Referred. (Ibid., 25)
>
> [May 18] F. Reed presented the resolutions of the New-York Conference on slavery and temperance; also the action of said Con-

ference on the Genessee resolution on slavery, and the New-Jersey resolution on the subject of local preachers; all of which were appropriately referred. (Ibid., 55)

Faced with the steady torrent of memorials, the Conference on its thirteenth day adopted the following:

> *Resolved*, That every member, when his Conference is called for memorials or Conference resolutions, shall present at once all such documents as he may have in his possession, or under his control; and that this Conference will receive no more petitions or memorials on general subjects after this week. (Ibid., 41)

47. *HAM*, 2:56–57; Baker, *Methodists*, 207.

48. West, *Debates*, 5. Capers "hoped to hear no more of a Committee on Slavery. It never did and never could do any Good. It had done much evil and always would do."

49. *JGC/MEC*, 1844, 13.

50. Ibid., 29. For narrative, see Baker, *Methodists*, 207–10; Mathews, *Slavery*, 251–54; *HAM*, 2:51–54. For text of arguments, see West, *Debates*, 18–52. In defending its handling of the Harding case, the Baltimore Conference cited five particulars against Harding, the fourth of which was:

> Because, by becoming a slaveholder, he rendered himself unavailable to us as a travelling preacher. . . . As a slaveholder, in the non-slaveholding portions of the conference, they would not hear him preach. He would have to be confined entirely to the slaveholding section. . . . It would have a direct tendency to locality, and would thus strike at the very root of our itinerant system. . . . He would have been to us a semi-local preacher. . . . Are there not tendencies enough already to locality in our system without increasing them? (West, *Debates*, 38)

51. In their opening address, the bishops had been insistent on this very point:

> [T]he superintendency . . . is *general, embracing the whole work in connectional order, and not diocesan, or sectional.* Consequently any division of the work into districts, or otherwise, so as to create a particular charge, with any other view, or in any order, than as a prudential measure to secure to all the Conferences the annual visits of the Superintendents, would be an innovation on the system.
>
> *[O]ur superintendency must be itinerant, and not local.* It was wisely provided in the system of Methodism, from its very foundation, that it should be the duty of the Superintendent "*to travel through the connection at large.*" (*JGC/MEC*, 1844, 156; italics in original)

52. For the Bishop's own statement of his situation see West, *Debates*, 148–50, or Elliott, *Secession*, 983–86. Particularly striking is Andrew's account of his reluctance to be nominated for the office and agreement only on the urging of a friend that his election would

> . . . tend to promote the peace of the Church, and . . . be especially important to the prosperity of Methodism at the south. . . . I was

never asked if I was a slaveholder—no man asked me what were my principles on the subject—no one dared to ask of me a pledge in this matter, or it would be been met as it deserved. Only one man, brother Winans, spoke to me on the subject: he said he could not vote for me because he believed I was nominated under the impression that I was not a slaveholder. I told him I had not sought the nomination, nor did I desire the office, and that my opinions on the propriety of making non-slaveholding a test of qualification for the office of bishop were entirely in unison with his own. (West, *Debates*, 148)

53. *The Life and Letters of Stephen Olin*, 2 vols. (New York: Harper & Brothers, 1853), 2:158. Olin would speak with some eloquence on behalf of Andrew, claiming that slaveholding was not under the Discipline, a "disqualification for the ministerial office," nor "constitutionally a forfeiture of a man's right, if he may be said to have one, to the office of a bishop" (168). The impact of this claim may have been undercut by Olin's admission that he had also owned slaves while in the south (168). See also West, *Debates*, 54–55. The report indicted that "He spoke under the most powerful emotion, and in a strain of tenderness that moved every member of the conference" (54).

54. *The Life and Letters of Stephen Olin*, 2:181.

55. George G. Smith, *The Life and Letters of James Osgood Andrew* (Nashville: Southern Methodist Publishing House, 1882), 342–43:

WHEREAS, Bishop Andrew has signified to the delegates of the Conferences in the slave-holding States a purpose to yield to the present distressing urgency of the brethren from the Northern States, and resign his office of Bishop, and whereas in a meeting of said delegates . . . it appears to us that his resignation would inflict an incurable wound on the whole South and inevitably lead to division in the Church, therefore we do unanimously concur in requesting the Bishop . . . not . . . to resign.

56. *JGC/MEC*, 1844, 64; West, *Debates*, 73, 82. Several matters intervened between the report and the motion, including a formal, written denial by Thomas E. Bond of the report, attributed to him, that "a plan has been formed by northern members of the conference, to force the south into secession. . . ." Others, including Nathan Bangs, indicated that they had heard such a report. See West, *Debates*, 74–75.

57. *JGC/MEC*, 1844, 65–66.

58. West, *Debates*, 150, or Elliott, *Secession*, 987. Later in the speech, Finley endeavored to put the constitutional and the moral issue on a plane, proclaiming:

There are two great principles to be determined in this resolution which have not been decided in the Methodist Episcopal Church. One is this: Has the General Conference a right, or has it the power, to remove from office one, or all of the bishops, if they, under any circumstances, become disqualified to carry out the great principles of our itinerant general superintendency? The second is: Will the Methodist Church admit the great evil of slavery into the itinerant general superintendency? (West, *Debates*, 150)

59. West, *Debates*, 128. Hamline insisted that "This conference, adjunct (but rarely) with the annual conferences, is supreme. Its supremacy is universal. It has legislative, judicial, and executive supremacy" (129). He continued:

> That the conference has executive authority is indisputable. For the bishop derives his authority from the conference. . . . Everything conveyed as a prerogative to bishops, presiding elders, preacher, &c., by statutory provision, and not by the constitution or in the restrictive rules, was in the General Conference. . . . Nor, sir, all that this conference can confer, it can withhold. And whatever it can confer and withhold, it can *resume* at will, unless a constitutional restriction forbids it.
>
> Here, Mr. President, let me say a word concerning our Church constitution. . . . It differs cardinally from most, or all civil constitutions. These generally proceed to demark the several departments of government— the legislative, judicial, and executive—and, by positive grant, assign each department its duties. Our constitution is different. It does not divide the powers of our government into legislative, judicial, and executive. It provides for a General Conference, and for an episcopacy, and general superintendency. It leaves all the powers of the three great departments of government, except what is essential to an episcopacy, &c., in this General Conference. (Ibid., 131)

60. Ibid., 134.

61. Ibid., 154–55.

62. Ibid., 168–69. John Price Durbin, then president of Dickinson College, responded directly to the conception of episcopacy presented by Winans and Soule:

> From whence is its power derived? Do we place it upon the ground of divine right? Surely not, sir. You do not plead any such doctrine. When, then is it derived? Solely, sir, from the suffrages of the General Conference. There, and there only, is the source of episcopal power in our Church. And the same power that conferred authority can remove it, if they see it necessary. (Ibid., 174)

Durbin then reviewed the history of the relation of conference and superintendency. See *Organization MECS*, 67–84, for Soule's remarks.

63. Samuel Dunwody of South Carolina objected to the resolution "for three grand reasons." "First, it was unscriptural; second, it was contrary to the rules and constitution of the Church; and, thirdly, it was mischievous in a very high degree" (West, *Debates*, 164).

64. James Finley showed one strand of fraternal principle in defending himself from southerners who termed him an abolitionist and abolitionists who thought him pro-slavery:

> I am a Methodist. I stand on the ground that my fathers in Methodism took, the great Wesley, Coke, Asbury, M'Kendree, and the venerable men of the old western conferences, the Youngs, Laken, Collins, Burk, Parker, Axley, Sale, and others, and from this

ground I will not move. I stand here as the representative of one of the largest annual conferences. My brethren have confided to my colleagues and myself the great principles of our Methodist confederacy and the interests of the Methodist Episcopal Church. Now, sir, if I would compromit these great principles, and return home to meet the people and preachers of my own conference—than whom I believe there are not a purer and more honourable or devoted set of ministers in the world—I would deserve to be branded with the name of Judas on my forehead. But sir, it shall never be said of James B. Finley, nor cast up to my children or grandchildren, Your ancestor was a traitor to the high trust confided to him by his brethren in the ministry and membership. (West, *Debates*, 151–52)

65. The resolution might not have differed much had (male) laity been present. One wonders how it might have unfolded and how the issues would have been named and framed had both women and African Americans participated.

66. *JGC/MEC*, 1844, 75. The letter extends to 76. Also in West, *Debates*, 184–85.

67. See James Porter, "General Conference of 1844," *Methodist Quarterly Review* 53 (April 1871), 234–50, 246.

68. *JGC/MEC*, 1844, 81: "BISHOP HEDDING said he wished to withdraw his name from the Address of the Bishops, presented yesterday. . . . he thought it would be a peace measure; but facts had come to his knowledge since, which led him to believe that such would not be the case." See also West, *Debates*, 188–89.

69. Tigert, *History*, 445.

70. *JGC/MEC*, 1844, 86:

Be it resolved by the delegates of all the Annual Conferences in General Conference assembled:

That we recommend to the Annual Conferences to suspend the constitutional restrictions which limit the powers of the General Conference so far, and so far only, as to allow of the following alterations in the government of the church, viz.:

That the Methodist Episcopal Church in these United States and territories, and the republic of Texas, shall constitute two General Conferences, to meet quadrennially, the one at some place, *south*, and the other *north* of the line which now divides between the states commonly designated as free states and those in which slavery exists.

2. That each of the two General Conferences thus constituted shall have full powers, under the limitations and restrictions which are now of force and binding on the General Conference, to make rules and regulations for the church, within their territorial limits respectively, and to elect Bishops for the same.

Four more enabling resolutions followed. (86–87) See also West, *Debates*, 192, or Elliott, *Secession*, 1008–9.

71. *JGC/MEC*, 1844, 109. Referred to the select committee of nine.

72. "The Protest of the Minority in the Case of Bishop Andrew." See West, *Debates*, 203–212; Elliott, *Secession*, 1017–29; or *Organization MECS*,

102–23. It began, "In behalf of thirteen annual conferences of the Methodist Episcopal Church, and portions of the ministry and membership of several other conferences. . . ."

73. West, *Debates*, 209:

> A bishop of the Methodist Episcopal Church is not a mere creature—is in no prominent sense an officer—of the General Conference. The General Conference, as such, cannot constitute a bishop. It is true the annual conferences select the bishops of the Church by the suffrage of their delegates, in General Conference assembled, but the General Conference, in its capacity of a representative body or any other in which it exists, does not possess the power of ordination, without which a bishop cannot be constituted. . . .
>
> In a sense by no means unimportant the General Conference is as much the creature of the episcopacy, as the bishops are the creatures of the General Conference. Constitutionally the bishops alone have the right to fix the time of holding the annual conferences, and should they refuse or neglect to do so, no annual conference could meet according to law, and, by consequence, no delegates could be chosen, and no General Conference could be chosen , or even exist. . . .
>
> The General Conference is in no sense the Church, not even representatively. It is merely the representative organ of the Church, with limited powers to do its business, in the discharge of a delegated trust.

74. *JGC/MEC*, 1844, 112. Conference took action passing the first item.

75. West, *Debates*, 229–37. It also reviewed and reiterated the larger debate to insist that the action in the case of Bishop Andrew followed the recurring and basic principle of itinerancy—the examination of character—a principle exercised in annual conference over traveling preachers and in general conference over bishops. It then rejected "episcopacy supremacy" as "at variance with the genius of Methodism," "the express language of the Discipline" and "the exposition of it by all our standard writers" (235). See also Elliott, *Secession*, 1030–41. In an abbreviated presentation of this, *Organization MECS*, 142–45, construed the Reply as a "reduction of episcopacy" with "a proportionate elevation of the powers of the General Conference, giving full control of the episcopal office to the extent of suspending or deposing without trial or other formality merely by the will of a majority of that body."

76. Peter Cartwright, who spoke immediately on the introduction of these resolutions, "thought the proposed arrangements would create war and strife in the border conferences" (West, *Debates*, 220).

77. West, *Debates*, 223–24.

78. On the propriety and legality of this gathering, see Tigert, *History*, 450–51.

79. *Organization MECS*, 147–52, or Elliott, *Secession*, 1045–48. It deferred discussion of the "equivocal suspension of Bishop Andrew" for later communications and stated the call in terms of slavery:

The opinions and purposes of the Church in the North on the subject of slavery, are in direct conflict with those of the South, and unless the South will submit to the dictation and interference of the North, greatly beyond what the existing law of the Church on slavery and abolition authorizes, there is no hope of any thing like union or harmony.

Notes to Chapter 11

1. Address "To the Ministers and Members of the Methodist Episcopal Church, in the Slaveholding States and Territories," *Organization MECS*, 150. This was, of course, the Southern construction of the division.

2. From resolutions by North Ohio Conference in August of 1844, cited in Elliott, *Secession*, 402. Michigan spoke of slavery causing a "deep affliction of our beloved Zion" (407). North Indiana pledged "to the best of our ability, to heal the wounds of Zion" (408). Compare on the southern side, the statement from Holston: "In common with our brethren all over our widely extended Zion, our hearts are exceedingly pained at the prospect of disunion. . . ." See "Report of the Committee on Separation," 1844 Holston Annual Conference, in *Organization MECS*, 179.

In their last address to the undivided church, the bishops had spoken of the glories of Zion. They claimed that "the work of the Lord steadily advanced; new and extensive fields of labour were constantly opening before us; the borders of our Zion were greatly enlarged." See "Address of the Bishops," *JGC/MEC*, 1844, 152.

3. "Report of the Committee on Division," 1844 Mississippi Annual Conference, in *Organization MECS*, 191. Similarly, the Committee on Episcopacy at the 1850 MECS General Conference in an encomium to Bishop Soule referred to him as "this strong pillar and bright light of our Zion." See *JGC/MECS 1846–1850*, 179 (1850).

4. See *Organization MECS*, 153–75, for its resolutions and the text of a long, closely argued "Address to the Members of the Methodist Episcopal Church within the bounds of the Kentucky Annual Conference." The resolutions insisted, as would the MECS thereafter, that a division "shall not be regarded as a secession," but "as a co-ordinate branch of the Methodist Episcopal Church in the United States of America, simply acting under a separate jurisdiction" (154).

The Address reviewed the history of Methodism and slavery. It termed the action in the case of Bishop Andrew as "a decree of ecclesiastical *outlawry*," and an exercise of "prerogative, now for the first time asserted":

To defend this position, then, became a prominent link in the strong chain of power forged by the dominant party in the last General Conference. To this end two processes are resorted to; the episcopal office is degraded, beyond all precedent of friend or foe, and the powers of the General Conference magnified in equal ratio. It is accordingly held that a Bishop is the mere creature and servant of the General Conference, and not the officer of the whole Church. . . . He is not appointed during life or good behavior, as has always been held by the whole Church and the whole world, but simply during the arbitrary pleasure of the General Conference. . . ." (163–64)

The Kentucky actions and those of other conferences are conveniently gathered also in Redford, *History MECS*, Appendix B, 594–628.

5. *HAM*, 2:99.

6. North Carolina *Minutes*, 2:15b (1844). Then subsequently "Ordered that Conference sit with closed doors during the examination of Character" (17b, 29b).

7. Soule's Address to the Convention, in *Organization MECS*, 246. Soule so reported for the conferences which he attended. The Holston Conference perhaps ran counter to form, in entering a corporate dissent from the stampede towards separation and in putting dissent from its action on record. It expressed pain "at the prospect of disunion" and proposed a mechanism for compromise. See typescript "Minutes of the Holston Annual Conference," Vol. 1: 1824–44 (Duke Divinity School Library), 115–19, especially 116 (1844). Compare *Organization MECS*, 179–81.) In response to the Holston gesture, a number of subsequent conferences took up its proposal but voted nonconcurrence. Among those were North Carolina, Tennessee, Mississippi, Georgia, Florida and Alabama (North Carolina *Minutes*, 2:17–24 [1844]; *Organization MECS*, 185, 193, 215, 216, 221). To the North Carolina committee which prepared its action had been referred the resolution of the Holston Conference and "all documents on the subject of the division." Such actions obliged conferences to act in self-consciously political fashion. The following year in responding affirmatively to the formation of the MECS, Holston recorded in the minutes the dissent of one George Ekin (typescript "Minutes of the Holston Annual Conference," Vol. 2: 1845–49 [Duke Divinity School Library], 126–27).

8. See, for instance, the Kentucky "Address to the Members of the Methodist Episcopal Church within the bounds of the Kentucky Annual Conference," *Organization MECS*, 156–75.

9. The easiest access to this warfare, albeit from a MEC perspective, is through Elliott, *Secession*. Himself editor of the *Western Christian Advocate*, Elliott collected clippings from these MEC (northern) papers and from their southern (MECS) counterparts, the *Southern Christian Advocate* (Charleston), the *Richmond Christian Advocate* and the *South-Western Christian Advocate* (Nashville). From what came to eight volumes and a total of 6,727 fourteen inch columns, he produced his *Secession*, which cites liberally from these papers, includes full statements of various conference actions and represents a companion to the southern *Organization MECS*. Reading the two together puts one into the fray.

10. Elliott, *Secession*, 402.

11. Ibid., 404.

12. Ibid., 405.

13. *Organization MECS*, 338.

14. Ibid., 262.

15. Ibid., 264–65. The language was that of the "Plan of Separation." Of importance here is simply the fact of its implementation and the

evocation of what would amount to warfare to establish a border between the MEC and the MECS.

16. Norwood, *Story*, 207–9; Baker, *Methodists*, 214–15; *HAM*, 2:127–28, 159–67.

17. Elliott, *Secession*, 585–90; 1083–85.

18. Ibid., 590–91, 1086–92.

19. Ibid., 591–93.

20. Charles Elliott, *South-Western Methodism: A History of the M.E. Church in the South-West, From 1844 to 1864*, edited and revised by Leroy M. Vernon (Cincinnati: Poe & Hitchcock, 1868).

21. *JGC/MEC*, 1848, 16, 21–22; Redford, *History MECS*, 533–34, 535–37, 537–38.

22. *JGC/MEC*, 1848, 80–85, 154–64.

23. *JGC/MECS 1846–1850*, 141 (1850).

24. In their address to the 1850 MECS General Conference (*JGC/MECS 1846–1850*, 130–43, 141), the Bishops recalled the appointment of Lovick Pierce as fraternal messenger and then affirmed:

> But your Messenger was rejected, and your offers of peace were met with contempt. Your Commissioners, charged with the management of the interests of the Southern Church in relation to the Book Concern and Chartered Fund, were treated with like discourtesy. Your claims were disposed of in a summary manner. The Plan of Separation was repudiated; the Southern claim to any portion of the Book Concern was denied; and the very men who, from sheer hatred to slavery, drove the South into separation, proved their sincerity and consistency by not only retaining all the slave-holding members already under their charge, but in making arrangements to gather as many more into the fold as practicable. The Plan of Separation was repudiated with the avowed purpose of invading Southern territory; and as an earnest of their intentions in this respect, a new Conference was organized, entirely within the limits of the Southern Church.

25. *HAM*, 2:339–60.

26. *JGC/MEC*, 1860, 260.

27. Philadelphia *Minutes*, 1861, 12.

28. An easy access to this political character, albeit only on the northern side, is through Rumsey Smithson's *Political Status of the Methodist Episcopal Church*, 2nd ed. (Canton, Ill.: H. S. Hill, 1868). Smithson excerpted the 'political' resolutions passed by MEC annual conferences from 1861 to 1866 (pp. 11–54). He argued that since the 1844 division, "the Methodist Episcopal Church, has maintained a non-secular character, while the M.E. Church (north) has boldly entered the arena of political agitation" (3).

29. Philadelphia *Minutes*, 1862, 7:

> The class of the second year was called up by the Bishop, and the usual Disciplinary questions asked and answered.
> By the direction of the Conference the following question was then proposed to the Class, and answered by each in the affirm-

ative:—

"Are you in favor of sustaining the Union, the Government and the Constitution of the United States against the present rebellion?"

30. William Warren Sweet, *The Methodist Episcopal Church and the Civil War* (Cincinnati: Methodist Book Concern Press, 1912); Donald G. Jones, *The Sectional Crisis and Northern Methodism: A Study in Piety, Political Ethics and Civil Religion* (Metuchen and London: Scarecrow Press, 1979); *HAM*, 2:206–56.

31. Sweet, *The Methodist Episcopal Church and the Civil War*, 98–99.

32. "The Palmyra Manifesto, June 1865," in Norwood, *Sourcebook*, 330–32. "Palmyra" was the community in which the gathering met.

33. See, for instance, Rumsey Smithson, *Political Status of The Methodist Episcopal Church*. 2nd ed., (Canton, Ill: H. S. Hill, 1868). Section III extracted 97 political platforms from 46 annual conferences covering the years 1861 to 1867, followed a given conference through that period, e.g. New England, and provided then a very handy summation of the political statements for that and other conferences. Smithson (12–14, 52–53) gathered 32 "teachings and principles" from these platforms, among them:

1. That the Church is the guardian of the nation.

2. That she has a right to discuss political issues.

3. That she has the right to dictate the duty and polity of the Government.

4. That it is the "duty and mission of the Church to secure and appropriate the whole country with all its resources to the spread of Christianity."

5. That she has a right to exhort and rebuke civil authority.

6. That the General Government is under obligations to the M.E. Church.

7. That it is to the interest of the Government that the M.E. Church be established throughout the South.

8. That the General Government be required to favor the M.E. Church.

9. That negroes be invested with all the privileges of citizenship—to be our legislators, judges, governors and presidents.

10. That there be perfect political, social and ecclesiastical equality of the races.

11. That the right of the negroes to all the privileges of citizenship is a *divine right*.

12. That a large portion of the white population of the country be disfranchised.

13. That the supremacy of negroes over white people in the South is to the interest of the Government.

. . . .

16. That the Federal Government have the support and co-operation of the M.E. Church in the prosecution of the war.

17. That God is a partisan in the war and that it is just and holy on the part of the North.

. . . .

32. That we rejoice in the triumph of our principles by means of fire and sword.

34. *Minutes of the Mississippi Annual Conference, MECS, 1865,* 25–29; cited in *HAM,* 2:269.

35. The line appeared in 1832 through 1844 but seems to have disappeared in the 1848 *Doctrines and Discipline of the Methodist Episcopal Church,* in some ways a fitting reminder of the political divisiveness of 1844.

36. This led the creation of the Wesleyan Methodist Connection when efforts to change the MEC proved futile.

37. *Zion's Herald,* VI (Jan. 14. 1835), 8. Scott proposed a remedy that was every bit as reflective of the changes in Methodism. He suggested that quarterly meetings be put on weekdays so as not to take ministers away from their own appointments on weekends and so that quarterly meetings would not interrupt congregational worship patterns: "Quarterly Meetings on week days are extra seasons of grace— they do not interfere with other appointments—we have our regular Sabbath privileges uninterrupted."

A respondent to Scott, J. G. Smith, objected strenuously to Scott's remedy and thought that week-day quarterly meetings were already killing the institution. He thought the decline of the quarterly meeting had to do with competition from another engine of local religiosity, the protracted meeting, with inattention to the love feast and with "the want of holiness among our preachers and people." *Zion's Herald,* VI (April 8, 1835).

Revival and spirituality had gone local. The quarterly meeting had lost its power to congregate and focus Methodist fervor. Both analysts saw the need for more spiritual intensity but could see no way to recover its former "conference" aspect.

38. *JGC/MEC,* 1844, 158.

39. Ibid., 157.

40. See David Sherman, *History of the Revisions of the Discipline of the Methodist Episcopal Church,* 3rd ed. (New York: Hunt & Eaton; Cincinnati: Cranston & Stowe, 1890), 158; P. A. Peterson, *History of the Revisions of the Discipline of the Methodist Episcopal Church, South,* (Nashville: Publishing House of the M. E. Church, South, 1889); Emory, *Discipline,* 140. With respect to quarterly conferences, Peterson (44) noted: "All the regulations on this subject existing prior to 1846, when this section was framed, were contained in those portions of the Discipline which related to Presiding Elders, preachers in charge, and local preachers."

41. Concerns about the health of the class meeting were voiced at various levels in the church. The North Carolina Conference took action in 1840 to bolster the institution: "*Resolved,* that the Preachers and Presiding Elders be required to report to the next Conference the number of class meetings they may have attended during the year." North Carolina *Minutes,* 2:41b (1840).

42. Wade Crawford Barclay and J. Tremayne Copplestone, *History of Methodist Missions*, 4 vols. (New York: Board of Missions/Board of Global Ministries, 1949–73), 1:257–79, 2:171–72.

43. "Address of the Bishops," *JGC/MEC*, 1844, 162–63. The bishops detailed the benefits thereof (163).

44. Sherman, *History of the Revisions of the Discipline*, 48.

45. *JGC/MECS*, 1846, in *Organization MECS*, 436–39.

46. *JGC/MEC*, 1864, 485–86.

47. Philadelphia *Minutes*, 1864, 47–48. A resolution of 1865 indicated that "Our colored people . . . have been generally organized into Circuits and Districts, in accordance with the recommendation of this Conference at its last session. . . ." Philadelphia *Minutes*, 1865, 53. On the division into two conferences see Philadelphia *Minutes*, 1860, 38; 1868, 51.

48. For a recent discussion that accents African American rather than white agency in this church's establishment, see Katharine L. Dvorak, *An African-American Exodus: The Segregation of the Southern Churches*, preface Jerald C. Brauer (Brooklyn: Carlson Publishing, Inc. 1991).

49. North Carolina *Minutes*, 2:20–24 (1844); *Organization MECS*, 201, 203, 220.

50. For treatment of this and the following see Baker, *Methodists*, 218–28.

51. Baltimore *Minutes*, 1861, 5, 18, 49. The "Protest of the Baltimore Annual Conference" of 1860 is found on 44-47 and the "Preamble and Resolutions" on 47–50.

52. Baltimore *Minutes*, 1862, 22–23. The action did provide for consideration of that withdrawal as null and void, if such members present themselves and cooperate at next conference.

Notes to Chapter 12

1. "Pastoral Address of the General Conference of 1846, to the Ministers and Members of the Methodist Episcopal Church, South," *Organization MECS*, 485–503. The sentence read:

> We greatly fear, that as the church has become enlarged, and its influence extended in the progress of years, we have been imperceptibly led to attach too much importance to mere matters of form and ecclesiastical arrangement, forgetting the ruling principle of the true Wesleyan school, that Methodism, without defection from the high principles of its origin, can never be brought into bondage to forms: that the piety of a church should never be confounded with its polity: that its religion, and the life and character of its ministers and members, cannot be separated: that without personal piety on the part of those composing it, the religion of a church is a lifeless corpse of mere form and order. (495)

2. *JGC/MEC*, 1840 (New York: G. Lane & C. B. Tippett, 1844); *JGC/MEC*, 1844 (New York: G. Lane & C. B. Tippett, 1844). The southern church published its first two journals together, *JGC/MECS 1846–1850*. In 1852, the MEC ordered "That the Book-agents at New-York be, and

they hereby are directed to publish the Journals of the General Conferences of the Methodist Episcopal Church, from 1800 to 1836 inclusive" (*JGC/MEC*, 1852, 62). For further discussion of annual conference minutes, see notes 6 and 13 below.

3. The young and small North Carolina Conference met Oct. 27, 1841, convening without the bishop. For structure, it elected a president and secretary and established the following:

— committee to provide for & superintend public preaching
— conference stewards
— committee on necessitous cases
— book committee
— committee on periodicals
— committee on academies
— committee on memoirs
— assistant secretary

The conference created other committees as it worked, including committees to advise on cases brought up from quarterly conferences. The conference received an interesting report advising against the propriety of creating a conference Bible society auxiliary to the American Bible Society on the grounds that the latter was "national and it might seem not in character to raise an auxiliary so entirely of one denomination" and that the action might lead to misunderstanding and frustrate cooperation with other denominations. North Carolina *Minutes*, 1:70b (1841).

4. Baltimore *Minutes*, 1853.

5. New England *Minutes*, 1845.

6. New England *Minutes*, 1845, 10. By 1848, the conference specified the Benevolent Operations collections only by month; see New England *Minutes*, 1848, 14.

7. New England *Minutes*, 1847, 15–16. Some stations made no report, some not for one or more causes.

8. As shown by the following chart from the New England *Minutes*, 1849, following p. 18, again missions (column 5) was the big item. The respective collections were:

	(1)	(2)	(3)	(4)	(5)	(6)	(7)
Boston, Bennett Street	5.26	9.25	—	34.46	70.00	—	—
Lynn Common	10.10	16.00	26.25	65.00	167.41	—	—

The next year the secretary replaced the fold-out chart with a five page table of statistics.

9. For their importance in one conference, see Mudge, *New England*, 324–56. And for the importance of conferences to one institution, see David B. Potts, *Wesleyan University, 1831–1910: Collegiate Enterprise in New England* (New Haven and London: Yale University Press, 1992).

10. North Carolina *Minutes*, 1:7b-13a (1838).

11. Baltimore *Minutes*, 1859.

12. See John D. Batsel & Lyda K. Batsel, *Union List of United Methodist Serials, 1773–1973* (Evanston: Commission on Archives and History of the

United Methodist Church, 1974). The Batsels identify apparent stray published versions as early as the 1820s (New York). Baltimore issued one in 1825; see Baker, *Methodists*, 512. But Baltimore began sustained publication of its minutes only in 1853. Philadelphia began at least as early as 1838; Providence and Maine on their separation from New England in 1841; New England itself apparently in 1845; New Jersey in 1844; Vermont in the year after its organization, 1847, Wisconsin for its third session, 1850. See for the MPs the *Minutes of the Twelfth Annual Conference of the Maryland District of the M. P. Church*, 1840.

13. See *Minutes NE*:

1838—A motion to publish the Minutes in pamphlet form was laid on the table (220).

1839—Voted, that the Secretary together with Revs. J. Horton and J. Porter be a committee whose duty it shall be to cause such parts of the journals of the Conference to be published as in their judgment shall subserve the interests within our bounds (238).

1841—It was also resolved that the Conference concur with the Providence Conference in the recommendation that the Conferences in New England should publish the Minutes in a volume together (273).

A Committee consisting of Dexter S. King and James Porter was appointed to publish the Minutes (274).

1843—Dexter S. King was requested to publish the Minutes and the preachers were requested to say how many copies they will take (299).

14. Virginia in 1868, South Carolina in 1870, and North Carolina in 1872.

15. New England *Minutes*, 1851, 3–15.

16. The latter section included also Bishop Janes's remarks spelling out reasons why he continued the four (rather than three) districts and presiding elders, apparently a recent innovation—essentially because of work-load and despite appeals to return to three.

17. Prompted by the increased attention and space devoted to such memories and memoirs, the Committee on the Book Concern of the 1844 General Conference recommended (among other things) "That the Editors of our periodicals be instructed to confine each obituary notice and memoir to the smallest practicable space . . . and that in general no obituary shall exceed two squares but an interesting memoir may be entered at the discretion of the Editor." *JGC/MEC*, 1844, 100.

18. On the Baltimore conference(s), see Baker, *Methodists*, passim.

19. Baltimore *Minutes*, 1857.

20. Baltimore *Minutes*, 1859. The Philadelphia Conference had begun such tabular remembering in 1856; see Philadelphia *Minutes*, 1856, 15–16, for the table "The Names of All the Travelling Preachers" with "the time each was admitted on trial":

1803	Henry White
1806	James Mitchell
1812	David Dailey
. . . .	
1856	[19 names]

The table was repeated in Philadelphia *Minutes*, 1857, 23–24, but without the name of White, but with a memoir for him.

21. See for instance the Philadelphia *Minutes*, 1861, which contain, in addition to the standard reporting tables, four of a historical sort: (1) "Bishops of the Methodist Episcopal Church Since its Organization in 1784" (37); (2) "Conference Retrospect," with columns headed "time, place, president, secretary, no. admitted on trial, no. of preachers appointed, deaths, locations, number of superannuated, members in society (white/col'd) and probationers (white/col'd)" (38–39); (3) "Conference Memorials," which listed names (by date when entered) and included also age, date of death, years of effective service (40–41); and (4) "Philadelphia Conference. Alphabetical Roll of Members," which featured the post office address but also listed time of entering travelling connection and date of appointment (apparently years in present appointment) (42–46).

22. *JGC/MEC*, 1848, 142–46, 148–49. In a comparable address to the Wesleyan Church in Canada, the General Conference was less effusive. It was this conference that pointedly refused "fraternal relations" with the MECS. Fittingly, the conference received a "Final Report—On the State of the Church" (154–64), which actually dealt with the Plan of Separation. See Redford, *History MECS*, 516–25, 530–33, 533 ff.

23. In 1840, "George Pickering was invited to preach a semi-centennial sermon the progress of religion in the Methodist Episcopal Church during the last fifty years" (*Minutes NE*, 2:154–55). The Ohio Conference requested a semi-centennial sermon from John Stewart; see Ohio *Minutes*, 1866. Two and four years later, Philadelphia acted similarly: "A resolution requesting J. P. Durbin, D.D., to preach a semi-centennial sermon at our next session, was adopted by a rising vote" (Philadelphia *Minutes*, 1868, 12). And in 1872, it passed a motion "requesting Dr. Castle to preach a semi-centennial sermon at the next Conference" (Ibid., 12, 47 (1872).

24. See Laban Clark, *A Semi-Centennial Sermon Delivered Before the New-York East Conference* (New York, 1851). For an early (1826) illustration of this genre see "Substance of the Semi-Centennial Sermon. . . ." by Rev. Freeborn Garrettson, in *American Methodist Pioneer*, 386–403. These became more common, if their publication is any indication, after the Civil War. A partial listing of such sermons and similar autobiographical statements, many of them semi-centennial in character, may be found in Kenneth E. Rowe, "The Background and Education of Methodist Ministers in the United States, 1790–1860 as Revealed in their Autobiographies" (B.A. Thesis, Drew University, 1959).

25. See James B. Finley, *Autobiography; or, Pioneer Life in the West*, ed. W. P. Strickland (Cincinnati: Methodist Book Concern, 1853) and *Sketches of Western Methodism: Biographical, Historical, and Miscellaneous*, ed. W. P. Strickland (Cincinnati: Methodist Book Concern, 1854).

26. *Autobiography of Peter Cartwright* (New York: Carlton & Porter, 1856); *Fifty Years as a Presiding Elder* (New York: Carlton and Lanahan, 1871); both were frequently reprinted.

27. Ohio *Minutes*, 1852, 3.

28. New England *Minutes*, 1853, 3.

29. Janes seems to have been intent upon making conferences as spiritual as he could. In one conference (at least), he strove for recovery of the quasi-eucharistic, love-feast pattern:

> We had an unusually pleasant session of the Cincinnati Conference. It was characterized by a high degree of spiritual interest. When I examined the candidates for admission into full connection, I requested several of the senior members of the Conference to give a relation of their ministerial experience—especially of their call and early ministry. We spent nearly two hours in these exercises and prayer. Sunday was a most gracious day. I preached at half past ten o'clock with considerable liberty and more unction than God has often granted me. Deep impressions were made. Bishop Simpson preached in the afternoon. God was with his servant and in his word. The evening meeting was a previous one. Several professed religion and joined the Church. Among those who joined during the Conference were a son and son-in-law of ex-Governor Trimble.

Henry B. Ridgaway, *The Life of Edmund S. Janes* (New York: Phillips & Hunt; Cincinnati: Walden & Stowe, 1882), 171–72.

30. See Ohio *Minutes*, 1858 and 1871, in which Janes presided and there was no sacrament. He also presided in 1861 and 1869 and did celebrate. Note for 1861: "The sacrament of the Lord's Supper was then administered. This service was interesting and profitable" (Ohio *Minutes*, 1861, 4).

For another illustration of Jane's eucharistic initiatives see the *Minutes of the Upper Iowa Annual Conference . . . 1856* (typescript of the organizing conference), 4.

31. "*Resolved*, That hereafter we set apart, from the commencement of the sessions of our Conference, a sufficient time for the celebration of the Lord's-supper; and that we, in future, make this our opening service." Ohio *Minutes*, 1875, 203.

32. New England *Minutes*:

> 1860—Bishop Janes, assisted by Rev. G. F. Cox, introduced the religious services, by reading the Scriptures, singing, and prayer, after which the holy sacrament was administered. (3)

> 1862—The religious services were opened with the reading of the Scriptures by the Rev. Bishop Janes, who presided at the Conference, and the singing of a hymn; after which Rev. Chas. Baker offered prayer.
>
> The Holy Sacrament was then administered to the members of the Conference, a large number of whom were present, and also to the members of the church who were in attendance. (3)

> 1863—Levi Scott, presiding . . . Scripture, hymn, communion. (3)

1866—"The Holy Sacrament" "several of the preachers assisting therein" (3).

The Philadelphia *Minutes*, 1861, 5, also recorded the opening with the sacrament, but do not again for at least a decade and had not previously.

33. New England *Minutes*, 1868, 8.

34. See "The Journals of the Illinois Annual Conference," in Sweet, *Methodists*, 263. In 1825, "Bishop McKendree opened the Conference by reading, singing, & prayer" (282), and in 1831, "Conference was opened by reading a portion of the Sacred Scriptures, Singing and prayer" (352).

See also *Minutes of the . . . Annual Conference of the Maryland District of the Methodist Protestant Church, 1840–62*. Typically, the Minutes did not initially indicate what constituted religious services; in 1844 the secretary noted "Scripture and prayer;" in 1846, he recorded "Scripture, singing and prayer." Beginning in 1863, specific hymns are noted and for five times in the next fifteen years # 557 is sung.

The pattern in the southern church was similar. The three-volume typescript "Minutes of the Holston Annual Conference" (Vol. 1: 1824–1844; Vol. 2: 1845–1849, and Vol. 3: 1851–1862 [Duke Divinity School Library]) described openings with "religious services, Scriptures, singing and prayer." The *Minutes of the . . . Virginia Annual Conference of the Methodist Episcopal Church, South*, 1868, indicated that Bp. William M. Wightman "opened with religious services." As late as 1879, the North Georgia Conference, MECS, observed the same formula, "Scripture, singing and prayer"; see The *Minutes of . . . North Georgia Annual Conference of the Methodist Episcopal Church, South*, 1879. Prior minutes that I examined did not indicate what was done. The following year, a specific hymn was indicated, #533. If that conference used the 1866 or 1880 new MECS hymnal, it did not then sing "And are we yet alive," which was #272.

35. See Russell E. Richey, "'And are we yet alive': A Study in Conference Self-Preoccupation," *Methodist History* 33 (July 1995), 249– 61, in regard to these several factors.

36. The tradition, though far from widespread, may well have preceded, indeed probably did precede, the codification of the hymn in hymnbooks in key places. One indication of that, the only that I have so far surfaced, comes in a retrospective from 1890, a "Semi-Centennial Address" by M. D'C. Crawford, D.D., in *Minutes of the New York Conference of the Methodist Episcopal Church, 1890*, 132:

> Let me introduce you to my first Annual Conference, when I was received on trial, in 1840. It met in Allen Street, in the city—my early religious hoome. I went to the church half an hour before the time, finding no one there but the sexton. Being well acquainted with him, however, I had a pleasant waiting. I cannot tell you how much interested I was in looking upon the members of the Conference as they came in one after another or in groups. I remember well the hymn sung, "An are we yet alive, and see each other's face?" The prayers that followed were also very impressive.

37. See *A Collection of Hymns for Public, Social, and Domestic Worship* (Charleston: John Early for the Methodist Episcopal Church, South, 1847).

38. *Minutes of the Eighth Session of the East Genesse Annual Conference of the M.E. Church*, 1855, 3.

39. This set a pattern; the sacrament seems to be thereafter a tradition. No hymn choices are indicated again until 1876. In that year, Western New York and East Genesee meet separately on October 4th and 5th, the former opening with # 266, the latter with # 700. Then they met as a re-united body and sang, "And are we yet alive."

40. *Register of the Baltimore Annual Conference of the Methodist Episcopal Church*, 1862, 22–23. These actions came in the adoption of the report of a Special Committee of Seven. See also discussion above on the lay actions contributed to the formation of the southern body.

41. *Minutes of the Sessions of the Baltimore Annual Conference of the Methodist Episcopal Church, Held at Harrisonburg . . . 1862, Churchville . . . 1863, Bridgewater . . . 1864, Salem . . . 1865, Rev. John S. Martin, Sec.* (Staunton: Stoneburner & Prufer, 1899).

42. Wesley, *Works*, 7: *A Collection of Hymns for the Use of the People Called Methodists*, ed. Franz Hildebrandt and Oliver A. Beckerlegge (Nashville: Abingdon Press, 1983), #466, p. 649.

43. See *Minutes MC*, 53 (1785), 58 (1786), and 64 (1787).

44. See the early Philadelphia *Minutes*, which in the years 1852 and earlier devoted to memoirs and statistics constitute a sizable proportion of the whole of the minutes.

45. Philadelphia *Minutes*, 1860, 9.

46. See the various tables of historical sort in the Philadelphia *Minutes*, 1861, 37–46. Included were listing of "Bishops of the Methodist Episcopal Church Since its Organization in 1784," a "Conference Retrospect" with columns headed—time, place, president, secretary, no. admitted on trial, no. of preachers appointed, deaths, locations, number of superannuated, members in society (white col'd) and probationers (white col'd), then *"Conference Memorials" with names (by date when entered), including age, date of death, years of effective service.* Then followed the "Philadelphia Conference. Alphabetical Roll of Members," with post office address, date of entering the travelling connection and date of appointment (apparently years in present appointment).

47. New England *Minutes*, 1865: "It was found, on examination, that since the organization of the New-England Conference, in 1796, sixty of its members have died" (8). [Then a followed a paragraph on the length of service of these men.]

The pattern was set. In 1866, the fifth day: "In the afternoon, a funeral service was held in behalf of the memory of Father Kilburn" (8).

In 1867, on the next to last day: "Nearly the whole of this session was occupied most profitably in listening to the memoirs of the *four* deceased members of the body. The services were impressive throughout" (11).

In 1868, on the sixth day: "In the afternoon a touching memorial service is held. Three members of our body have died during the interval of the last Conference, and the members pay an affecting tribute to their memory" (11).

48. Philadephia *Minutes*, 1867, 5, 8.

49. The passing of numbers of preachers or particularly important ones clearly stimulated the development of the pattern. In Philadelphia in 1870, "The Bishop was requested to appoint a committee of three to prepare a minute expressive of the sense of this Conference on the decease of Rev. John McClintock, D. D." The next day, "The hour of 9 o'clock A. M. on Monday, was fixed as the time for holding a Memorial Service in memory of our brethren who have deceased during the past year." On Saturday, the death of the son of W. H. Elliott was announced. And on Monday:

> At 9 o'clock the memorial service was held.
> The memoirs of the following deceased Ministers were read and adopted:. . . .
> The memorial minute on the death of Dr. McClintock, and the minute of condolence with W. H. Elliott, were also presented, read and adopted.
> Hymn 956 was sung; prayer was offered by Jos. Mason, and the third stanza of hymn 1053 was sung.
> The other statements were made and the resolutions adopted by all present.

See Philadelphia *Minutes*, 1870, 6, 8, 11.

50. Ohio *Minutes*, 1877, 3, 7, 13.

Notes to Chapter 13

1. For the flavor of such approbation see the sermon preached by Bishop Morris, before the 1864 General Conference, MEC. His topic was "the *Spirit of Methodism*," which he developed in a sequence of ten affirmations each begun "The Spirit of Methodism is . . ." (*JGC/MEC*, 1864, 281–91). The spirit of Methodism, he suggested, was:

— the spirit of truth;
— the spirit of revival;
— the spirit of enterprise;
— the spirit of sacrifice;
— the spirit of progress;
— the spirit of improvement;
— the spirit of loyalty to the civil government;
— the spirit of patriotism;
— the spirit of liberty;
— the spirit of liberality.

For a similar but fuller presentation see Abel Steven, *The Centenary of American Methodism: A Sketch of its History, Theology, Practical System, and Success. Prepared by Order of the Centenary Committee of the General Conference of the Methodist Episcopal Church* (New York: Carlton & Porter, 1865).

2. New England *Minutes*, 1864, 3.

3. New England *Minutes*, 1865, 3–10. The Abstract of Proceedings continued this year and indeed for the rest of the decade.

4. Such recollecting demanded the efforts of a specialist and New England had created one, a conference biographer or personal statistician and necrologist, William Bridge, a person who also held the position a long time, for twenty years. Mudge (*New England*, 168) noted that two years later "He and Secretary Manning, sent out, February 9, 1867, to all the preachers a circular asking them to fill in answers to twenty-seven questions, covering all the important points of their biography, for preservation in the archives and as contributions to the Conference annals."

5. New England *Minutes*, 1865, 47–51.

6. Mudge (*New England*, 98) noted,

> Up to the year 1828 all the Annual Conferences sat with closed doors, none being admitted except full members. This was convenient and almost necessary considering the extremely close and searching personal examination to which the members were subjected and the rigid scrutiny of all the candidates for admission or orders. But as the numbers grew larger and customs changed a little the rigidity of the rule was gradually relaxed.

That the practice remained in N.E. is indicated, Mudge noted, by a protest of 1839 against closed doors, but thereafter they were largely open. General Conference had resolved the prior year "That it is the sense of this General Conference that it is unnecessary for an Annual Conference to require its members who are elders to retire when their names are called in the examination of character." See *JGC/MEC*, 1864, 174, 361.

7. New England *Minutes*, 1871, 8–9. The following year (ibid., 1872, 5), the secretary affirmed in relation to the affirmation of character: "Then came the fiery ordeal, to which every member of the body must be annually subjected, for all the years of his ecclesiastical life in the Methodist communion."

8. The next year New England would achieve another efficiency by pre-constituting the Nominations Committee so that it could bring the nominations to conference instead of spending a day or so in making the nominations (New England *Minutes*, 1866, 4).

9. On the regional character of American society and American institutions, see Peter Dobkin Hall, *The Organization of American Culture, 1700–1900: Private Institutions, Elites, and the Origins of American Nationality* (New York: New York University Press, 1984), 240–42; and Thomas Bender, *Community and Social Change in America* (Baltimore and London: Johns Hopkins University Press, 1978), 108–20.

10. This conference heard a sermon on ministerial education.

11. Report of the Committee on Education appointed by the General Conference of 1860, *JGC/MEC*, 1864, 390, 391, 390–98.

12. New England *Minutes*, 1865, 3:

> An additional Committee was appointed on the reconstruction of the Methodist Church at the South. By this action the Conference has shown that it is still determined to march in the vanguard of the great army of liberty and pure religion.

It is now proposed to take such action as shall secure to us, as a church, not only the property which was wrongfully wrested from us by a mercenary court, but also to secure for Christ the whole southern land by the preaching of a free and full and pure salvation, with equal rights to all the people.

13. New England *Minutes*, 1865, 42–43. The report dealt especially with prejudice. It noted two dangers:

1. We must first shun the temptation of making the former church the centre around which we shall re-organize our own. That church has been so completely leagued with detestable sin, that its representative ministers and members are incapacitated for the work of social, civil, and religious regeneration . . .

2. We must avoid the danger of recognizing the distinction of color among the members of a common church and ministry.

It is on this rock that the church foundered. They began by erecting unscriptural barriers between the brothers and sisters of a common Redeemer; they ended by utterly despoiling these their brethren of every right, human and divine. . . .

14. Ibid., 1865, 45: "We deplore the organization of colored Conferences at the last session of the General Conference. . . ."

15. Ibid., 1865, 6.

16. Ibid., 1867, 39. In a similar report the following year, the conference again asserted "That these Conference lines ought to be changed, and to be conformed to those of the State so far as practicable. . . ." But the conference did recognize that churches and preachers then attached to other conferences might not wish to have their long-established fraternal bonds "rudely sundered" (ibid., 1868, 42– 43).

The Philadelphia Conference of 1868 adopted its "Report of the Committee on Boundaries": "That, after a careful consideration, we have concluded that a division of our Conference, by State lines, will be the most satisfactory and advantageous." It so recommended to General Conference (Philadelphia *Minutes*, 1868, 51).

17. In the 1860 General Conference, the Troy delegation registered a vehement dissent against its dismemberment. See "Minority Report on Boundaries," *JGC/MEC*, 1860, 448–54. They noted opposition within the affected St. Albans and Burlington Districts to their transfer from Troy to Vermont and an unanimous vote against it in Troy Conference as a whole. This proposed transfer originated with, and has been pressed by the Vermont Conference with a boldness and pertinacity worthy of a better cause (448). "We must in our arrangement of conferences be governed by circumstances and natural boundaries, and adaptation to our itinerant system, and not by state lines" (449). They appealed to history and geography—the ties that had bound these preachers and people together and the Green Mountains that had separated them the Vermont Conference.

18. New England *Minutes*, 1867, 9; Baltimore *Minutes*, 1873, 19– 22: The third day "of the session was up wholly, till evening, to the Re-union

Exercises of this and the Providence Conference, after twenty-seven years of separation."

19. Address of the Bishops, *JGC/MEC*, 1868, 359–70, 368–69. The Board of Bishops prefaced this assertion by saying:

> Heretofore, in fixing the boundaries of Annual Conferences, too little regard has been paid to the civil divisions of the country. Nor is this surprising, since in those instances in which the ecclesiastical organization preceded the civil it necessarily defined its limits by mountains, streams, or other topographical landmarks. This primitive mode of designation was naturally retained after its necessity ceased (368).

20. W. R. Goodwin, in "The Presiding Eldership," *Methodist Quarterly Review*, 57 (January 1875), 67–79 referred to conference efforts to expand the size of districts and keep down the number of presiding elders, a strategy motivated at least in part by pastors intent upon keeping the salary dollar closer to home.

21. Philadelphia *Minutes*, 1872, 16–22, 18. His colleague on the Harrisburg District, R. H. Pattison, reported: "During the year I have held 182 Quarterly Conferences, preached 145 times, and attended a love-feast nearly every Sabbath of the year, and traveled a little over 9,000 miles."

22. Baltimore *Minutes*, 1872, 14–15, 85–94.

23. *JGC/MECS*, 1866, 96, 99–100.

24. The 1868 General Conference made provision for a "Leaders' and Stewards' Meeting" a substitution for II, chap. ii, sec. 17, #8, pp. 96–97 of the 1864 Discipline (*The Doctrines and Discipline of the Methodist Episcopal Church, 1860*, 84–85), which had provided for a Leaders' Meeting. The Discipline had earlier read "Let none be received into the Church until they are recommended by a Leader with whom they have met at least six months on trial." The new legislation inserted instead "Let no one be received into the Church until such person has been at least six months on trial, and has been recommended by the Leaders' and Stewards' Meeting, or where no such meeting is held, by the Leader. . . ." The original report had used the phrase "Official Board" but J. McClintock had moved to amend and substitute "Leaders' and Stewards' Meeting." See *JGC/MEC*, 1868, 252–54, 539.

25. The same 1868 General Conference provided for the creation of "The Board of Education of the Methodist Episcopal Church," a body of twelve, six minister (two of them bishops) and six "laymen," with responsibility for the receipts of the Centenary Fund and for expenditure of the interest generated for persons training for missions or ministry and for theological schools and colleges. This was to be "a General Agency of the Church in behalf of ministerial and general education," with some responsibilities also for education in Sunday Schools, though that had its own organization, the Sunday School Union, with its own Board. This conference also reconstructed the Church Extension society. Ibid., 320–322.

26. Later renamed *The Sunday-School Teacher* and made a monthly. See Marianna C. Brown, *Sunday-School Movements in America* (New York, Chicago and Toronto: Fleming H. Revell, 1901), 78–79.

27. The 1852 General Conference (MEC) had passed a resolution giving "male superintendents of our Sunday schools . . . a seat in the Quarterly Conferences having supervision of their schools with the right to speak and vote on questions relating to Sunday schools, and on such questions only." *JGC/MEC*, 1852, 116.

28. Anne M. Boylan, in *Sunday School: The Formation of an American Institution, 1790–1880* (New Haven and London: Yale University Press, 1988), 92–93, indicates that the convention system showed Methodist organizational traditions to be

> . . . highly structured and enormously effective at mobilizing large numbers of people. The similarities between the Methodist system—congregationally based class meetings supplemented by local, regional, and national conferences—and the Sunday school conventions was not accident: the conventions had adapted the structure through the influence of their Methodist leaders. Likewise, it was Methodists like Vincent who championed the type of inter-denominational cooperation exemplified by the conventions, cooperation based on educational method and technique, not theology.

See also J. M. Freeman, "Growth of the Sunday-School Idea in the Methodist Episcopal Church," *Methodist Quarterly Review*, 53 (July 1871), 399–413; Robert W. Lynn and Elliott Wright, *The Big Little School: 200 Years of the Sunday School*, 2nd ed. (Birmingham: Religious Education Press; Nashville: Abingdon Press; 1980), 94–116.

29. *The Doctrines and Discipline of the Methodist Episcopal Church, 1832* had set forth as "VI. Support of Missions," the following:

> 1. It shall be the duty of each annual conference, where missions have been or are to be established, to appoint a standing committee, to be denominated the mission committee. . . . (179)

> 3. It is recommended that within the bounds of each annual conference there be established a conference missionary society, auxiliary to the Missionary Society of the Methodist Episcopal Church. (180)

30. Sweet, *The Methodist Episcopal Church and the Civil War*, 67, 68, referred to meetings in 1861 of the Boston Methodist Preachers' Meeting and to minutes of the same, a meeting held with some frequency, perhaps monthly.

31. This was already noted in Matthew Simpson, ed., *Cyclopaedia of Methodism*, 5th ed. (Philadelphia: Louis H. Everts, 1883), 162.

32. See Melvin E. Dieter, *The Holiness Revival of the Nineteenth Century* (Metuchen and London: Scarecrow Press, 1980), 103–55.

33. See Hilah F. Thomas, Rosemary Skinner Keller, and Louise L. Queen, eds., *Women in New Worlds*, 2 vols. (Nashville: Abingdon Press, 1981, 1982), especially Keller, "Creating a Sphere for Women," 1:246–60. Also see Ethel W. Born, *By My Spirit: The Story of Methodist Protestant Women in Mission 1879–1939* ([New York]: Women's Division, General Board of Global Ministries, UMC, 1990).

34. See Ruth Bordin, *Woman and Temperance: The Quest for Power and Liberty, 1873–1900* (Philadelphia: Temple University Press 1981) and *Frances Willard: A Biography* (Chapel Hill and London: University of North Carolina Press, 1986).

35. Philadelphia *Minutes*, 1870.

36. The secretary of the New England Conference spoke thus of the various anniversaries observed at conference (New England *Minutes*, 1873, 5): "[T]he grand feature of these incidentals of an annual Conference gathering, was reserved for sabbath evening, when the holy cause of missions drew an immense audience."

On the 2nd day of the 1879 conference (New England *Minutes*, 1879, 6), "The Woman's Foreign Missionary Society held a public meeting in the afternoon, and was fully attended. The principal address, an able effort, was by Mrs. Rev. S. L. Gracey. Brother W. R. Clark presided, and Mrs. Rev. D. Richards read the treasurer's report."

37. The 1864 General Conference (MEC) had, on recommendation of the committee on missions, approved the creation of mission annual conferences with all "the rights, powers, and privileges of other Annual Conferences, excepting that of sending delegates to the General Conference, and of drawing their annual dividends from the avails of the Book Concern and the Chartered Fund, and of voting on constitutional changes proposed in the Discipline" (*JGC/MEC*, 1864, 138, 384–85).

In its organization, the next General Conference, when confronted with a representative from the Mississippi Mission Conference, received a motion raising "the whole subject of representation of Mission Conferences in this body" and a substitute (defeated) recognizing organization of annual conferences in Delaware, Washington and the south and calling for their recognition with full powers. The initial motion was defeated and referred and the mission conference representatives listed separately (*JGC/MEC*, 1868, 23–24, 12).

38. Hilary T. Hudson, *The Methodist Armor: or A Popular Exposition of the Doctrines, Peculiar Usages, and Ecclesiastical Machinery of the Methodist Episcopal Church, South*, rev. and enl. (Nashville: Publishing House of the Methodist Episcopal Church, South, 1892), 146. See also *HAM*, 2:295–97.

39. See Bender, *Community and Social Change in America*, and Hall, *The Organization of American Culture, 1700–1900*.

Notes to Chapter 14

1. See *Discipline of the Methodist Episcopal Church*, 1872, 164, and the "Report of Committee on Benevolent Societies," *JGC/MEC*, 1872, 295–98. The report began: "The special Committee 'appointed to consider and report concerning the relations of our various benevolent societies to the authorities of the Church, and whether any action is necessary, and if so what, to place them under the full control of the General Conference,' has considered the subject stated. . . ." With respect to the Missionary Society incorporated by the New York Legislature, it noted "To place this corporation under the control of the General Conference, it will be proper to procure an act of the Legislature to amend the charter so as to provide

that the Board of Managers shall be elected by the General Conference" (297).

2. *JGC/MECS*, 1874, 445, 533.

3. For a discussion of the import of this change, see the "Report of the Board of Church Extension" after the change to the General Conference of 1876," by A. J. Kynett, *JGC/MEC*, 1876, 602–4. Kynett noted that previously:

> Although organized by order of the General Conference, the corporate body was, by the terms of its Constitution and Charter, a "Society" composed of such members and friends of the Church as might contribute to its funds the sum of one dollar per annum, or twenty dollars at one time. These had the legal right to elect its managers; but only such as could be present at the annual meetings in Philadelphia could share in the exercise of this right. It was, therefore, clearly beyond the reach of the Church government, and equally beyond the reach of all contributors to its funds, except only a portion of those who resided in the city of Philadelphia.

4. On the import of 1872 and these changes, see William McGuire King, "Denominational Modernization and Religious Identity: The Case of the Methodist Episcopal Church," in *POAM*, 343–55; also in *Methodist History*, 20 (Jan. 1982), 75–89.

5. Address of the Bishops," *JGC/MEC*, 1876, 393–405. See especially, 400–1:

> The connectional character of our Church we regard as of highest importance and greatest utility. . . .
>
> The Methodist Episcopal Church is not a confederacy of eighty-one Annual Conferences, nor a mere association of some nine thousand pastoral charges. It is a simple body, of which these pastors and Churches and Conferences are component parts, and all members one of another. . . .
>
> The connectional character of the Church is maintained largely by the law of affinity. The agreement in doctrines, the sameness of religious experience, and the similarity of usages which prevail throughout the connection, give us oneness of character, and assimilate us into one body. . . .
>
> The great agencies of the Church are bonds of union.
>
> [The bishops discussed Sunday schools as connectional but worried that children be taught "our doctrines" "our polity" and be "enlisted in the support of our institutions and benevolent agencies."]
>
> Our Missionary Society, with its numerous auxiliaries, is another of these bonds of connectional union. . . . [They used the metaphor of the heart to explain its role in the life of the church.]
>
> The Book Concern has also exerted a unifying power upon the Church. . . .
>
> The General Superintendency has always been, and still continues to be, a strong bond of unity. . . .

6. Italics added. The first major item of business was the report of a Committee on Plan of Organization, commissioned in 1876. It indicated:

We have found that all the General Conferences, from 1812 to 1876, have been accustomed to appoint Standing Committees, to consist of one from each Annual Conference. We find, also, that as the Annual Conferences increase in number, objections have arisen to these committees, both on account of their number and on account of their great size, now consisting of about ninety members each, instead of eight members each, as at first.

The committee recommended reserving the "every conference" provision for a select five committees; constituting seven others on benevolent and connectional objects, each consisting of three delegates from each of the twelve General Conference Districts; and putting only one from each District on another nine. The substitute was from Daniel Curry, then head of the Book Concern and editor of the *Methodist Quarterly Review*. See *JGC/MEC*, 1880, 41–2, 45.

7. The 1854 measure had been passed with a majority vote and was judged in 1870 to be of constitutional significance, therefore requiring both a two-thirds majority and concurrence of the annual conferences. The constitutional corrective action conveying such judicial review on the College of Bishops was achieved in 1874. See P. A. Peterson, *History of the Revisions of the Discipline of the Methodist Episcopal Church, South* (Nashville: Publishing House of the M. E. Church, South, 1889), 38, and Nolan B. Harmon, *The Organization of the Methodist Church*, 2nd rev. ed. (Nashville: Methodist Publishing House, 1962), 189–213.

8. *JGC/MEC*, 1876, 134.

9. *JGC/MEC*, 1884, 74. The MEC body did not have the power of judicial review that the southern bishops possessed, the ability to "arrest" or challenge legislation as unconstitutional.

10. *JGC/MECS*, 1866, 42.

11. Holland N. NcTyeire, *A Manual of the Discipline of The Methodist Episcopal Church, South, Including the Decisions of the College of Bishops* (Nashville: Southern Methodist Publishing House, 1870). For one of its updatings, see, for instance, under the same title the nineteenth edition: Originally prepared by Holland N. McTyeire; Revised and Enlarged by Collins Denny, 19th ed. (Nashville: Publishing House of the M.E. Church, South, 1931).

An older but different genre was the episcopal commentary on the Discipline. See Bishop Stephen M. Merrill's *A Digest of Methodist Law*, (Cincinnati: Cranston & Stowe; New York: Phillips & Hunt, 1885; rev. ed., Cincinnati: Jennings & Graham; New York: Eaton & Mains, 1904). Despite its title, this volume did not embrace episcopal rulings or judicial committee decisions but was really a commentary on the Discipline.

12. See, for instance, the third edition (New York and Cincinnati: Methodist Book Concern, 1918), which was "published under a resolution adopted unanimously by the General Conference of 1916" (xiii).

13. See *Reports of the Committee on Judiciary of the General Conference of the Methodist Episcopal Church with Rulings by the Board of Bishops* compiled under the authority of the General Conference by Arthur Benton Sanford (New York: Methodist Book Concern, 1924). In an "Introduction," Henry Wade Rogers, chair of Committee on Judiciary, 1908, 1912, 1916, 1920,

complained: "The Committee on Judiciary has heretofore been seriously embarrassed in the discharge of its duties by not having ready access to the reports of the action of the Judiciary Committees of former years and of the action of General Conference relating thereto" (v).

14. This is the title of the volume that documents the formal fraternity between the MEC and MECS: *Formal Fraternity, Proceedings of the General Conferences of the Methodist Episcopal Church and of the Methodist Episcopal Church, South, in 1872, 1874 and 1876, and of the Joint Commission of the Two Churches on Fraternal Relations, at Cape May, New Jersey, August 16–23, 1876* (New York: Nelson and Phillips, 1876).

15. The General Conference of 1872 had resolved "That in all matters connected with the election of lay delegates the word 'laymen' must be understood to include all the members of the Church who are not members of the Annual Conferences" (*JGC/MEC*, 1872, 442).

16. See "Report on Woman's Work in the Church," *JGC/MEC*, 1872, 391–93. The MECS established its Woman's Foreign Missionary Society in 1878, The Methodist Protestant Church (MP) the following year. The United Brethren in Christ formed its Women's Missionary Association in 1875, the Evangelical Association a Woman's Missionary Society in 1884.

17. Again see Dvorak, *An African-American Exodus*, for exploration of the black agency in this separation. On 1866, see 134–37.

18. For MEC permissive legislation see Report No. II of the Committee on the State of the Church, *JGC/MEC*, 1876, 329–31. After an agonizing disquisition on the "caste spirit," the committee proposed and conference acted:

> *Resolved*, 1. That where it is the general desire of the members of an Annual Conference that there should be no division of such Conference into two or more Conferences in the same territory . . . , it is the opinion of this General Conference that such division should not be made.
>
> *Resolved*, 2. That whenever it shall be requested by a majority of the white members, and also a majority of the colored members of any Annual Conference that it be divided, then it is the opinion of this General Conference that such division should be made, and in that case the Bishop presiding is hereby authorized to organize the new Conference or Conferences (331).

19. This latter question the General Conference of 1872 resolved in the negative, *JGC/MEC*, 1872, 253.

20. The committee, noting "that the growing catholicity of the age is ever enlarging our circle of fraternal correspondence and increasing the number of delegations bringing fraternal greetings; that there is reasonable expectation that we shall soon be exchanging periodical salutations with Lutherans, Baptists, Episcopalians, and all other members of the Church Catholic, as well as Methodists and Presbyterians . . . ," recommended "that Wednesday, May 10th, 1876 be the day ordered for the reception of fraternal delegations." *JGC/MEC*, 1872, 387–88.

21. On recommendation of the Committee on the State of the Church, the 1872 General Conference (MEC) adopted a resolution (*JGC/MEC*, 1872, 402–3) which concluded:

> To place ourselves in the truly fraternal relations toward our Southern brethren which the sentiments of our people demand, and to prepare the way for the opening of formal fraternity with them, be it hereby
> *Resolved*, That this General Conference will appoint a delegation, consisting of two ministers and one layman, to convey our fraternal greetings to the General Conference of the Methodist Episcopal Church, South, at its next ensuing session.

22. See "Early Efforts at Reunion," *HAM*, 2:660–706.

23. *JGC/MEC*, 1876, 274: "That, in order to remove all obstacles to formal fraternity between the two Churches, our Board of Bishops are directed to appoint a Commission authorized by the General Conference of the Methodist Episcopal Church, South, to adjust all existing difficulties."

24. Charles Spencer Smith, *A History of the African Methodist Episcopal Church* (Philadelphia: Book Concern of the A.M.E. Church, 1922), 371–72, 491; *HAM*, 2:672.

25. David H. Bradley, *A History of the A.M.E. Zion Church*, 2 vols. (Nashville: Parthenon Press, 1956, 1970), 2:314–18; William J. Walls, *The African Methodist Episcopal Zion Church* (Charlotte: A.M.E. Zion Publishing House, 1974), 460–64; John J. Moore, *History of the A.M.E. Zion Church in America* (York, Pa. Teachers Journal Office, 1884), 235–36; *HAM*, 2:675.

26. Walls, *The African Methodist Episcopal Zion Church*, 464–66; Bradley, *History of the A.M.E. Zion Church*, 2:319, 321, 332; Moore, *History of the A.M.E. Zion Church*, 262–63; *HAM*, 2:677.

27. *JGC/MEC*, 1868, 264, 199, 227, 238, 471–76.

28. See their Episcopal Address of 1872 in Moore, *History of the A.M.E. Zion Church*, 271–72; *HAM*, 2:678–79. See also the letter of Bishop Singleton T. Jones to the 1872 MEC General Conference, *JGC/MEC*, 1872, 534.

29. *JGC/MECS*, 1874, 560. That southern delegation included the aged Lovick Pierce, the fraternal representative not received in 1848 and able to convey his sentiments only by letter.

Fraternal gestures occurred on less official and juridical bases as well. Attesting something of the genuinely 'fraternal' aspects of fraternal relations was a camp meeting in the summer of 1874. See *Fraternal Camp-Meeting Sermons. Preached by Ministers of the various Branches of Methodism at the Round Lake Camp-Meeting, New York, 1874. With an Account of the Fraternal Meeting* (New York: Nelson & Phillips, 1875).

30. *Formal Fraternity*, 60–61, 67.

31. *Journal of the Proceedings of the Board of Commissioners of the Methodist Episcopal Church, South, 1876*, 112.

32. *HAM*, 2:667.

33. *Formal Fraternity*, 69–70.

34. *HAM*, 3:407–78; James H. Straughn, *Inside Methodist Union* (Nashville: Methodist Publishing House, 1958), 52–55.

35. *Proceedings of the Oecumenical Methodist Conference . . . 1881* (London: Wesleyan Conference Office, 1881). See *HAM*, 2:696–701.

36. See H. K. Carroll, et al., eds., *Proceedings, Sermons, Essays, and Addresses of the Centennial Methodist Conference . . . 1884* (New York: Phillips and Hunt, 1885), and W. H. DePuy, ed., *The Methodist Centennial Year-Book for 1884* (New York: Phillips & Hunt; Cincinnati: Walden & Stowe, 1883).

37. Carroll, *Proceedings, Sermons, Essays, and Addresses of the Centennial Methodist Conference . . . 1884*, "Historical Statement," ix–xi. Also not apparently included were the small delegations (two persons) of Methodist Protestants, Independent Methodists, Primitive Methodists, Canadian Methodists and the Bible Christian (one). For the delegations see 7–18.

38. *HAM*, 2:683–89.

39. In 1872 and 1876, General Conference (MEC) empowered its Committee on Boundaries to deal with the geographical, civil and size issues by providing for representation from every conference, elected respectively by each delegation and by stipulating that affected conferences would have prior notice. Sherman, *History of the Revisions of the Discipline*, 318–19.

40. At the 1880 MEC General Conference a resolution again called for "the election of a colored man to the episcopacy." The Committee on Episcopacy concurred, seeking the election "of one or more . . . General Superintendents . . . of the African descent." However, a minority report termed it "inexpedient" in view of "the state of our religious work among the colored people of the South," and also in view of "their white co-laborers." The proposal was postponed indefinitely by a 228 to 137 vote. 'Indefinitely' came in 1920. *JGC/MEC*, 1880, 199, 281–82.

41. See Elaine Magalis, *Conduct Becoming to a Woman* (Women's Division/Board of Global Ministries/The United Methodist Church, 1973?), and the following essays in Thomas, Keller, and Queen, *Women in New Worlds*: Virginia Shadron, "The Laity Rights Movement, 1906– 1918: Woman's Suffrage in the Methodist Episcopal Church, South," 1:261–75; William T. Noll, "Laity Rights and Leadership: Winning Them for Women in the Methodist Protestant Church, 1860–1900," 1:219–32; Donald K. Gorrell, "'A New Impulse': Progress in Lay Leadership and Service by Women of the United Brethren in Christ and the Evangelical Association, 1870–1910," 1:233–45; Rosemary Skinner Keller, "Creating a Sphere for Women: The Methodist Episcopal Church, 1869–1906," 1:246–60.

42. Kenneth E. Rowe, "The Ordination of Women: Round One; Anna Oliver and the General Conference of 1880," in *POAM*, 298–308.

43. Ibid., 302–4.

44. *HAM*, 3:56–58; Harmon, *Organization of the Methodist Church*, 121–23.

45. They noted that women had been elected, "regularly certified from Electoral Conferences, as lay delegates to this body" and indicated that they [the bishops] had not ruled on the legality of such action within the Electoral Conferences "neither does it appear that any one is authorized to decide questions of law in them." They continued: "If women were included in the original constitutional provision for lay delegates they are here by constitutional right. If they were not so included it is beyond the

power of this body to give them membership lawfully except by the formal amendment of the Constitution, which cannot be effected without the consent of the Annual Conferences." *JGC/MEC*, 1888, "Address of the Bishops," 33–63, 51.

46. The Report as adopted asserted that the Church in amending the Second Restrictive Rule "contemplated the admission of men only as lay representatives" and that therefore "under the Constitution and laws of the Church as they now are women are not eligible as lay delegates in the General Conference." *JGC/MEC*, 1888, 463.

47. When the report was considered, T. B. Neely proposed the submission to the annual conferences of an amendment of the second Restrictive Rule "by adding the words, 'and said delegates may be men or women'." *JGC/MEC*, 1888, 95; Buckley, *History*, 307–9.

48. Noll, "Laity Rights and Leadership: Winning Them for Women in the Methodist Protestant Church, 1860–1900," 219, 226–30.

49. Shadron, "The Laity Rights Movement, 1906–1918," 270–74.

50. Buckley, *History*, 314–26; Harmon, *Organization of the Methodist Church*, 114, 122.

51. Buckley, *History*, 315.

52. This proposal came from a lay-clergy commission established by the 1876 General Conference and empowered to consider the introduction of lay representation into annual conferences. It recommended one body with laity empowered to speak on all issues and to vote on all questions "except those affecting the conduct, character, and relations of traveling elders, and the election of ministerial delegates to the General Conference." The matter was reported out favorably by a Committee on Lay Representation but tabled 184 to 140. *JGC/MEC*, 1880, 92–93, 276, 310, 311.

53. In 1884, General Conference affirmed: "All candidates for our ministry are earnestly advised to attend, if possible, one or more of the literary and theological institutions of our Church before applying to an Annual Conference for admission on trial;" but, they continued "they shall not, on account of such attendance, be excused from examination on any part of the Conference courses of study." *JGC/MEC*, 1888, 248, 287, 355.

See my "Ministerial Education: The Early Methodist Episcopal Experience," in *Theological Education in the Evangelical Tradition*, ed. D. G. Hart and R. Albert Mohler, forthcoming; also Glenn T. Miller, *Piety and Intellect. The Aims and Purposes of Ante-Bellum Theological Education* (Atlanta: Scholars Press, 1990); L. Dale Patterson, "The Ministerial Mind of American Methodism: The Course of Study for the Ministry of the Methodist Episcopal Church, the Methodist Episcopal Church, South and the Methodist Protestant Church, 1876–1920," Ph.D. Dissertation, Drew University, 1984; Behney/Eller, *History*, 158–59, 192– 93; Gerald O. McCulloh, *Ministerial Education in the American Methodist Movement* (Nashville: United Methodist Board of Higher Education and Ministry, 1980), 11–15.

54. In a remarkably insightful statement in 1872, William F. Warren noted the following checks on the then three theological schools (Boston, Garrett, Drew):

1. Each is officially placed under the direct supervision of the bishops of the Methodist Episcopal Church.

2. No professor can be appointed to any chair in either of the three institutions without the concurrence of the bishops.

3. In at least two of them no professor can take his chair until, in the presence of the Board of Trust, he have signed a solemn declaration, to the effect that so long as he occupies the same he will teach nothing inconsistent with the doctrines and discipline of the Methodist Episcopal Church.

4. At the Annual Conference examination of character, every professor —save one who chances to be a layman—is each year liable to arrest if even a rumor of heterodoxy is abroad against him.

5. Each institution is inspected, and its pupils annually examined as to what they have been taught, by visitors delegated from adjacent annual conferences.

6. Each has ecclesiastical qualifications affecting the appointment of trustees.

7. Each is required to report to every General Conference.

William F. Warren, "Ministerial Education in Our Church," *Methodist Quarterly Review*, 54 (April 1872), 246–67, 260.

55. *JGC/MEC*, 1888, 354–56.

56. As late as 1931, the 19th edition of McTyeire's *Manual of the Discipline of The Methodist Episcopal Church, South* carried a section entitled "Of the Junior Preacher," 95–96.

57. Warren, in "Ministerial Education in Our Church," observed that "There is in this country one theological school of special interest. It is the largest in the world. Its last Freshman class numbered seven hundred and ninety-three. The entire number of students now in attendance is about three thousand" (246). Its "fundamental principles," he asserted were three: (1) "It is based upon the idea *that the professional instruction and training of the ministry ought to be in the hands of the Church*" (248; italics in the original). (2) "The system adopted by our fathers *proposed to train for the ministry no man whom God had not called to the ministry*" (249–50; italics in the original). It "demanded . . . provision for legitimate ecclesiastical control," "affirmed the essential freedom of the human soul, and jealously guarded responsible personal agency." It "demanded . . . that it restrict itself to legitimate subjects; that is, to those who have been called of God to the work of the ministry, and whose divine call has been accepted and ratified by the individual and the Church" (250). (3) "The system inaugurated by our fathers provided for a happy blending of the theoretical and practical in ministerial education" (250–51).

58. Warren, "Ministerial Education in Our Church," 253.

59. Warren, "Ministerial Education in Our Church," 257. The bishops came to the same conclusion but two decades later; see *JGC/MEC*, 1896, 50:

The conditions of admitting preachers to our Conferences are based on a state of things that existed many years ago, when circumstances were very different. Our whole system has been based on gifts, graces, and usefulness developed by a course of study pursued amid the difficulties of regular work by junior preachers under a senior. As a regular drill in practical work it could not be easily surpassed. But it is not now practicable to so relate junior and senior preachers, and the course of study is much better pursued in our colleges and theological seminaries. . . . We believe the time has fully come when the Church should recognize in the conditions to admission on trial to our Conferences the preparation gained in the theological schools. The Church has already advanced one step in this direction by ordaining as deacons those who have been local preachers, have been students for two years in one of our regular theological seminaries, and have completed the first two years of the Conference Course of Study. We now recommend that the Church take one more step in advance and enact that any student shall be credited on the Conference Course of Study with examination in any of the books of the first two years of the Conference Course which any theological school, whose professors are nominated and confirmed by the bishops, shall certify that he has satisfactorily passed.

60. See Philadephia *Minutes*, 1889, 29, for the motions of J. M. Hinson and T. B. Neely:

WHEREAS, There are sixty-two appointments out of the two hundred and forty-five on the Conference roll, that pay a salary of five hundred dollars or less, many of this class receiving aid from the Sustentation Fund, and being served by members of the Conference; therefore,

Resolved, That we deem it inexpedient to admit any on trial at this session of the Conference.

T. B. Neely proposed a substitute, which prevailed, "That we admit not more than four on trial in the Annual Conference." He then also moved that the Report of the Committee on General Qualifications be presented before taking action in any particular case. The motion prevailed. Eventually ten names were presented for the four spots.

61. The first resolution was adopted, as was a second that read:

Resolved, 2. That, in case any preacher shall be transferred from this Conference, we respectfully request the Bishop to transfer to this Conference our brother, William Rink, formerly associated with us, and now a member of the Central Pennsylvania Conference."

The third was tabled. Philadelphia *Minutes*, 1879, 6–7.

62. Philadelphia *Minutes*, 1882, 17. The motion was proposed by T. B. Neely, later to be elected to the episcopacy. An earlier resolution touched on a similar concern:

Resolved, That we respectfully request that no transfers be made to this Conference, except where they can be assigned to work of similar character to that which has been occupied by transfers from this Conference (10).

In 1885 the following resolution was offered by W. M. Ridgway:

> *Resolved*, That in view of the crowded condition of the Confer-
> ence, we respectfully protest against any and all transfers to this
> Conference, without a transfer of the same number of equal position
> from this body.

Later a stronger substitute was proposed:

> WHEREAS, The transfer of preachers into this Conference, as
> practiced for some years, is fruitful of embarrassment to the appoint-
> ing power, of hardship to the members of the Conference, and of
> disturbance of the harmony that should subsist between the ministry
> and the churches, therefore . . .

It then called for a system of equitable exchange and for some plan from
the Bishops. The substitute was tabled and the original resolution
adopted. Philadelphia *Minutes*, 1885, 11, 13, 18.

63. Philadelphia *Minutes*, 1881, 9:

> *Resolved*, That we respectfully request the Presiding Bishop to
> re-arrange the work of the Conference in four (4) districts, equalizing
> the size and financial ability as nearly as possible, and dividing the
> work in the city of Philadelphia as nearly equally among them as is
> practicable.

A subsequent motion substituting "five" for "four" was defeated 121 to 33
(by tabling).

64. Philadelphia *Minutes*, 1880, 18, 19:

> *Resolved*, That in the judgment of this Conference, it is highly
> improper for any preacher in charge to engage in any secular
> employment or occupation, whether professional, mercantile, offi-
> cial, or otherwise. . . .

The motion was tabled but a substitute from T. B. Neely accepted that
registered the judgment "that preachers should not allow secular matters
to interfere with the faithful discharge of their ministerial duties" and went
on to speak against multiplication of charges and creation of non-viable
appointments.

65. A motion from T. B. Neely was adopted in 1883 that affirmed:

> *Resolved*, That next year the Committee on Studies report, not
> only to the Conference, but also to the Committee on General
> Qualifications of Candidates for Admission on Trial, so that the latter
> committee may, in its report, take said examination into their con-
> sideration, and present to the Conference the names of the candi-
> dates in the order of general merit and fitness, so that the Conference
> may first vote upon and select the best.

Philadelphia *Minutes*, 1883, 23. See note #51 for similar action in 1889.

66. The Education Committee Report was amended by G. D. Carrow
so as to conclude: "We recommend all candidates for admission to our
traveling ministry to seek a classical and theological education as a qualification for the duties of the same." Philadelphia *Minutes*, 1889, 88–89, 41.

Notes to Chapter 15

1. This comes from the 1900 Episcopal Address in which the bishops devoted a section to the "State of the Church," and a sub-section thereof to "Spiritual Life," *JGC/MEC*, 1900, 59–60; The address is 48–79; section is 56–61. Incidentally, the bishops come down for growth rather than decay.

2. *JGC/MEC*, 1884, 337, 261, 280.

3. See the *Proceedings of the . . . Annual Meeting of the National Association of Local Preachers of the Methodist Episcopal Church*, a body which met from the late 1850s onward, in national and regional gatherings, and regularly voiced frustration with a church structure which no longer seemed to have place, responsibility for, oversight of and sympathy for the local preacher. In 1871, the national gathering passed a resolution to General Conference calling for organization of a district conference to include traveling and local preachers and to meet quarterly and the authorizing of it "to receive, license, try, and expel local preachers" and to make recommendations to annual conference for traveling connection. *Proceedings of the Fourteenth Annual Meeting of the National Association of Local Preachers of the Methodist Episcopal Church . . . October 21–24, 1871* (Pittsburgh, 1871?), 30.

4. *Proceedings of the Twenty-First Annual Meeting of the National Association of Local Preachers of the Methodist Episcopal Church . . . October 26–29, 1878* (Pittsburgh, 1878?), 7–8. He continued:

> 1. It is clear that many isolated local preachers are disheartened by isolation. . . .
>
> 2. Another class of local preachers are either useless or burdensome. They have lost their zeal, their standing in the community, their fitness to speak for the Church. Their licenses are annually renewed on the understanding that no work is desired or expected, or because the Quarterly Conference is composed of men who wish not to offend them. An organization of local preachers ought to give the annual review of all the members in each district into the hands of local men exclusively. It is the only safe way to weed out the ineffective (not superannuated) and the unworthy. . . . It is said that local preachers do not attend District Conferences. Why should they? We asked for a Local Preachers' Conference and were given a *place* in a very different body. A fair trial of us under organized responsibility ought to be made.

5. The Philadelphia Conference petitioned General Conference (Philadelphia *Minutes*, 1892, 38):

> WHEREAS, The provisions of the Discipline, with reference to District Conferences, have been found to be so exceedingly objectionable to many of our people, leading to the discontinuance of the District Conferences in nearly all the older and more influential Annual Conferences of the Church; and,
>
> WHEREAS, There is a manifest necessity for something in the nature of a responsible and somewhat authoritative body that shall be representative in its character and district in its bounds, as seen

by the large number of District Conventions held in the various parts
of our work, which Conventions fail largely because of their lack of
authority; therefore,

Resolved, That this Conference petition the General Conference
so to amend the Discipline as to provide for District Conferences,
without giving to them the functions now exercised by the Quarterly
Conference.

6. In an address on "District Conferences" at the 1878 meeting of
local preachers, C. C. Leigh recalled that the National Association had
initiated the proposal for District Conferences which would have oversight
over local preachers and their work; see *Proceedings of the Twenty-First
Annual Meeting of the National Association of Local Preachers of the Methodist
Episcopal Church . . . October 26–29, 1878*, 29–31:

> By the very general adoption of the station system each local
> preacher was fast becoming a fixture within the society to which he
> held his membership. The preacher in charge and the quarterly
> conference require his presence at every session of the Church. In
> this way he was fast losing sight of the wants of the great world outside
> of the walls of his own church building: this being the case, we feared
> our church was losing the aggressive work which has been her glory
> and her success . . .
>
> But the District Conferences are a very different affair from what
> the local preachers asked for. As now organized, the members com-
> posing it are all the travelling and local preachers, exhorters, stew-
> ards, and superintendents of Sabbath-Schools in the districts, with
> the presiding elder in the chair.
>
> By this arrangement the local preacher is outnumbered and his
> work is overshadowed by the reports of the elder, the travelling
> preacher, the stewards and superintendents of Sunday-schools, with
> their long catalogue of wants and labors, which are often of such
> general and frequently of such absorbing interest to the conference,
> that the special work of providing preaching in destitute places in
> the district is overlooked and not attended to.

7. Philadelphia *Minutes*, 1889, 54.

8. Typical was the report for the West District Superintendent who
in 1908 reported the year's highlights church-by-church (Philadelphia
Journal, 1908, 71):

> Coatesville—Conversions, 212; on probation, 113; from proba-
> tion, 50; membership, 901; gain 78. Paid on church improvements,
> $7,500. Total cost of addition to church, $28,500; present debt,
> $11,000. But for industrial depression would have been paid off.
> Church caring for the poor, distributed 674 pieces of clothing. Dorcas
> Society busy day and night. Pastor president of Citizens' United
> Charities. Benevolent collections excellent, considering the home
> conditions. Hundreds out of work. Great year.

9. Philadelphia *Minutes*, 1880, 26.

10. Philadelphia *Minutes*, 1881, 21. In 1883, the conference heard a
report on "The Sabbath" which expressed great concern about railroads

and camp meetings (Philadelphia *Minutes*, 1883, 49–51). In 1888, the resolutions adopted included one concerning conduct of camp meetings so as to respect Sabbath and avoid Sunday excursions and traffic (Philadelphia *Minutes*, 1888, 146–47). And again in 1899, the conference by resolution empowered an investigation into camp meetings to determine whether their activities appropriately respected the sabbath (Philadelphia *Minutes*, 1899, 29–30).

11. See, for instance, the petitions to General Conference complaining of camp meetings on the Sabbath which "induce our people to neglect or forsake the ordinary home Church services on the Sabbath" (*JGC/MEC*, 1880, 181, 212).

In their 1888 address, the bishops identified the following as "Moral Questions" to which the church need pay attention: observation of the sabbath, temperance, polygamy, divorce and various other forms of unrighteousness (*JGC/MEC*, 1888, "Address of the Bishops," 33–63). In 1896, they devoted long discussions to "The Church and Social Problems" and "The Church and Public Morals," into the latter of which they put temperance, marriage and divorce, amusements and sabbath desecration (*JGC/MEC*, 1896, 69–72, 72–75).

Conferences routinely passed resolutions endorsing the efforts of The American Sabbath Union or complaining of instances of sabbath desecration (*JGC/MEC*, 1892, 459). The Philadelphia Conference, for instance, expressed concern over Sabbath observance and passed a motion rejoicing when Pennsylvania's House of Representatives negated the Sunday Newspaper Bill, "an agency which is of great evil in secularizing the Sabbath" (Philadelphia *Minutes*, 1893, 16). In another session it again passed a resolution opposing legislation that would repeal the sabbath law (Philadelphia *Journal*, 1899, 22–23). And 1901 showed a variety of concerns for sabbath observance. One of its own and later bishop, T. B. Neely addressed the conference as "Secretary of the Sunday School Union" and was listed as special appointment in Northwest District; conference passed a resolution calling for Sunday closing of the Pan-American Exposition to be held at Buffalo; and then endorsed a number of resolutions on Sabbath and Temperance from a standing committee on Temperance and Sabbath (Philadelphia *Journal*, 1901, 20, 46, 23, 141–43).

The concern continued well into the 20th century. In 1914, Philadelphia's Permanent Committee on the Sabbath resolved: "The observance of the Sabbath is at the very base of our American civilization. The perpetuity of the Church, the purity of the home, and the security of the Government are dependent upon its preservation. . . ." It went on to identify two forces to preserve the Sabbath—civil law and "the proper observance of the day by Christian people," reported activity under both rubrics, and commended conference and national agencies for their work (Philadelphia *Journal*, 1914, 167). In 1919, Philadelphia endorsed a long resolution on Sabbath Observance protesting pending legalization of moving pictures and entertainments on Lord's Day, heard Bishop Berry speak on the issue, and passed other temperance and sabbath resolutions (Philadelphia *Journal*, 1919, 469). And in some self-criticism, the conference in 1920 expressed its disapproval "use of the moving pictures in our

Sunday evening service as urged by the Centenary Conservation Committee" (Philadelphia *Journal*, 1920, 692; compare "The Church and Moral Reforms" on amusements, sabbath, divorce, Mormonism, and temperance, in *JGC/MEC*, 1916, 191–96).

12. Philadelphia *Minutes*, 1886.

13. The District Superintendent for the South District, Frank R. Lynch, began his 1908 report (Philadelphia *Journal*, 1908, 65):

> The South District, in the city of Philadelphia, sociologically and religiously considered, presents problems as intricate, difficulties as trying and situations as hard to meet as any in American Methodism. In this territory we have probably, 70,000 Italians, 90,000 Jews and 80,000 people of color. The tides of foreign population have arisen above the river banks, covered the marshlands and threaten one day to submerge the entire south-western wards of our city. Gradually they have swept back the people from whom we draw our reinforcements, leaving behind those who are bound to their homes by business or family ties. These have taken up the burden of supporting large and expensive churches and of holding up the banner of our Methodism in the midst of a strange people. I have watched the unequal strife for years now, and I utter it as my profound conviction that Methodism never had a more heroic following, a more deserving army of Christian soldiers than are those who support the interests of our church in the locality herein named.

14. "City Missionary and Church Extension Society. Report of the Corresponding Secretary," Philadelphia *Journal*, 1908, 113–14. The entire report is 110–18. The District Superintendent was more terse: "At St. Paul's the pastor has established schools for cooking, sewing, music, and I know not what else, and continues his penny concerts to the delight of thousands of young Jews, Italians, and Americans who throng to hear them" (67). Note the statement cited from him in the previous note.

15. *JGC/MEC*, 1896, 48–49:

> From observation and trustworthy information the question is pressed upon us whether the time has not come for considering the possibility and expediency of substituting our Quarterly Conferences by Local Conferences, to meet semiannually, in which the presiding elder can be more generally present than is possible in quarterly meetings. . . . Much of the business of the Quarterly Conference has already been transferred to the Official Boards and the District Conferences, and its composition has undergone such changes that it is no longer fitted for the most important duties with which it is charged. With its mixed membership, consisting of men and women, old and young, it is unbecoming that it should act as a court for the trial of accused local preachers, and it is equally unsuitable for acting as an appellate court for hearing all classes of appeals of private members. . . .

They went on to register similar complaints about the District Conferences, as bodies that had not proved "as serviceable as was expected" (49).

16. Constitutional Amendment to change "Quarterly" to "Local" amending Division III, Chapter, I, Article II, para. 35, in *JGC/MEC*, 1920, 1457, 424–25: "A Local Conference shall be organized in each Pastoral Charge, and be composed of such persons and have such powers as the General Conference may direct." In the floor action and debate, the original language of the legislation which had spoken of "Church conference" was amended to "Local Conference."

17. *JGC/MEC*, 1908, 493, 439.

18. Ibid., 519–20, 432–33.

19. Philadelphia *Journal*, 1908, 65.

20. Philadelphia *Journal*, 1910, 54.

21. Philadelphia *Journal*, 1911, "Reports of District Superintendents," 105–11. The D. S. was Frank P. Parkin.

22. Nolan B. Harmon, *The Organization of the Methodist Church*, 2nd rev. ed. (Nashville: The Methodist Publishing House, 1962), 157–63.

23. "The Episcopal Address," *JGC/MEC*, 1928, 148–208, 152.

24. The MECS had, really from 1870, treated "Church Conferences."

25. The Council of Bishops of The United Methodist Church, *Vital Congregations—Faithful Disciples: Vision for the Church*, Foundation Document (Nashville: The General Board of Discipleship, 1990).

26. Philadelphia *Minutes*, 1891, 15. Motions of prior years suggested that the process still had some bite; see Philadelphia *Minutes*, 1888, 28:

> WHEREAS, Our Book of Discipline, paragraph 79, question 20, provides for the annual examination of character of each preacher, and whereas, charges and inquiries are sometimes made in an open session of the Conference, which are exceedingly hurtful to the church and damaging to the accused, who may be innocent of any offence; therefore,
>
> *Resolved*, That we respectfully petition the General Conference to so amend paragraph 79 that it shall require each Annual Conference to sit with closed doors for such part of its first day's session as may be necessary to refer all cases involving character to such committees as the Discipline or the Conference may require.

27. Ibid., 23.

28. Philadelphia *Journal*, 1900, 20, 22, 23.

29. Philadelphia *Minutes*, 1879, 10. This was the formula for all the districts and routine thereafter. For the presiding elder, the minute had more programmatic than fiscal force: "The Presiding Elder of the South Philadelphia District, W. J. Paxson, was called, his character passed, and he presented and read a report of the state of the work on his district" (10). The language for 1900 was the same: "The names of the effective elders on the Northwest District were called, their characters passed and they reported their missionary collections" (Philadelphia *Journal*, 1900, 20).

30. This amended the Discipline for presiding elders and pastors (10 of para 190 and 27 of para 193) by adding the language cited. When the item came up "J. M. Buckley moved to strike out that part of the report which relates to the preacher making report of his collections on the floor

of the Conference" then moved to table his own amendment. "Report XVIII of the Committee on Revisals," *JGC/MEC*, 1900, 431, 299–300.

31. Philadelphia *Journal*, 1905, 20.

32. Philadelphia *Journal*, 1906, 20.

33. This blanket commentary, without calling the individual names, did not become routine that year; see Philadelphia *Journal*, 1907, 23, 26:

> Bishop Goodsell called the list of effective elders of the West District, and asked of each, "Have you done your work according to the plan of the Discipline?" The answer in each case, either in person or by the Presiding Elder for him, was, "yes" or "in part."

34. Philadelphia *Journal*, 1911, 71:

> QUESTION FOURTEEN.—Question Fourteen: "Was the character of each preacher examined?" was taken up.
> The names of the five District Superintendents . . . were called, their characters passed and they presented and read a report of the work on their respective districts. The Bishop asked of each of the District Superintendents: "Have the provisions of the discipline in the Quarterly Conferences been carried out, touching the benevolences?" The answer in each case was in the affirmative.
> The names of the effective elders of the Conference, except as already noted, were called, their characters passed, and they reported the benevolent collections.

This was but one item in a very busy morning and was not the process by which charges were levied. Charges had already been levied against a member or two.

35. Philadelphia *Journal*, 1920, 674; cf. 1921, 49.

36. See the "Report of the Board of Education of the Methodist Episcopal Church," *JGC/MEC*, 1896, especially 727–37.

37. *JGC/MEC*, 1896, 402, 225. The Committee on Education, in making their recommendation, observed: "At present the young man who desires to master a thorough academic, collegiate, and theological course finds that at the end of the ten years required for such mastery he will have done nothing which the Conference examiners have authority to recognize" (402).

38. Philadelphia *Journal*, 1898, 22–23, 44:

> *Resolved*, That a certificate from any of the regular Theological Schools of the Methodist Episcopal Church, or from any of the schools recognized as colleges by the University Senate of the Methodist Episcopal Church, that a candidate has passed a satisfactory examination in any of the studies prescribed in the Discipline be accepted in place of the examination in those studies. Certificates will not be accepted in place of syllabi, essays, sermons, exegeses, nor in place of examination on Discipline and Doctrine.

This resolution was defeated, 107 to 117. The following year, conference leader and later bishop, A. G. Kynett, proposed but saw defeated, 89 to 129, the following (Philadelphia *Journal*, 1899, 23):

Resolved, That the Board of Examiners of the Philadelphia Conference be and they are hereby authorized and instructed to accept certificates instead of examinations as provided for in the permissive action of the General Conference of 1896 in the "Course of Study for Ministers," the application of the rule in each individual case and the details of the plan of procedure being with the Board of Examiners. . . .

39. Philadelphia *Journal*, 1903, 15.

40. *JGC/MEC*, 1896, 296–97.

41. Philadelphia *Journal*, 1897, 174–76; Philadelphia *Journal*, 1898, 173–80.

42. Philadelphia *Journal*, 1898, 173:

For the 'books to be read' the examiners will require a syllabus of each book, and will expect said syllabus not only to give an analysis of the work, but also to show that the book has been mastered by the candidate. The syllabus must be more than a table of contents. It should be a fair outline of the book.

43. Ibid., 173:

The sheets of the written work such as sermons, essays, exegeses, and syllabi should be fastened together so as to hold them in place and yet to allow an easy handling by the reader. It is requested that the paper be the large letter size so as to secure uniformity in form. The writing should be on only one side of the leaf.

44. *JGC/MEC*, 1920, 1162–63.

45. Ibid., 1357–64, 1362.

46. "Report of the Commission on Courses of Study," *JGC/MEC*, 1924, 1612–24.

47. See, for instance, actions taken in the Philadelphia Conference, beginning in 1917 Philadelphia *Journal*, 1917, 61):

CONFERENCE COURSE OF STUDY.—S. M. Verson presented the following resolutions, which, on motion of J. Watchorn, were unanimously adopted:

WHEREAS, The Course of Study for the ministers of the Methodist Episcopal Church adopted and published in the Discipline of 1916 has awakened considerable dissatisfaction; therefore

Resolved, First, that we earnestly recommend a careful reconsideration and reconstruction of the Course of Study so as to bring it in harmony with Methodist history, doctrine and literature.

Resolved, Second, that the Secretary of this Conference is hereby instructed to send a copy of this paper to the spring meeting of the Bishops of the Methodist Episcopal Church.

The following year, the conference passed another set of resolutions on the Course of Study (Philadelphia *Journal*, 1918, 261–62) expressing appreciation to Board of Bishops for changes made, hoping for further change as Bishops intimate, then going on to resolve,

First, That we most earnestly insist upon such a revision of the Conference Course of Study for ministers as will bring it into harmony with the well-known standards of Methodist doctrine, and that will do justice to our Methodist history and institutions.

Second, That we positively object to the retention in the present Course of Study of the books that have proven themselves opposed to Methodist doctrine, subversive of gospel truth as we understand it, destructive of the evangelistic spirit, and promotive of controversy and dissension in the church.

48. Philadelphia *Journal*, 1901, 4–13.

49. Note, for instance, this Philadelphia action (Philadelphia *Journal*, 1911, 86):

RESOLUTION ON MINIMUM SALARY OF $800.—On Motion of J. Watchorn, the following was adopted:

Resolved, That a committee of fifteen, including the five District Superintendents, five ministers, one from each district, and five laymen, one from each district, be appointed to prepare an equitable plan to raise the minimum salary of all effective members of the Conference and members on trial to $800, and to report the same at the next Annual Conference.

50. See, for instance, the attention to group life insurance by the Philadelphia Annual Conference in 1924 (Philadelphia *Journal*, 1925, 837–40), and similarly the following year (ibid., 1926, 44) and in 1930 (ibid., 1930, 295).

51. The 1928 Philadelphia Conference passed a resolution for General Conference asking that any changes in the pension system "assure adequate and full protection to all the approved claims of the present members of the Conference, and that no plan be approved that proposes apportionments above the present rate, or the raising of additional funds, without the consideration and consent of the Annual Conference" (Philadelphia *Journal*, 1928, 762). The same conference urged a commission "to study the matter of pastors' salaries, so that a minimum salary of living support shall be given to every member of each Annual Conference" (774).

52. "The Episcopal Address," *JGC/MEC*, 1912, 160–233, 178–79: "'Salary,' on the other hand," they insisted, "implies a stated stipend proposed as compensation for services to be rendered, fixed before the service begins and as a condition to its beginning at all."

53. Ibid, 180–82: "Thus is pulpit service commercialized, and thus in time every prominent preacher is practically appraised, and not always by the gospel standard of success. His 'rank' or appoint availability in cabinet is determined—himself, alas! too often consenting— by lay valuation in dollars and prospects." The bishops then put the following questions:

1. Can the Itinerancy continue unless equitably applied to all who owe it allegiance?

2. Can the appointing power hold the confidence of preachers and Churches unless absolutely impartial in its administration?

If any one answers that it is for the bishops to regulate this entire matter, than we respectfully ask a third question:

3. Will the General Conference and the Church uphold the bishops in refusing to consummate any arrangement involving a preliminary "call" or understanding in violation of the common rights and common interests of all the preachers and all the Churches? If not, then the time has fully come for a legal modification of the Itinerant system, and a *new order* which shall be of universal application.

54. *JGC/MEC*, 1912, 591.

Notes to Chapter 16

1. See *A Record of All Agreements Concerning Fraternity and Federation Between the Methodist Episcopal Church and the Methodist Episcopal Church, South* (Nashville: Publishing House of the Methodist Episcopal Church, South, 1914); Thomas B. Neely, *American Methodism: Its Divisions and Unification* (New York: Fleming H. Revell Company, 1915); *A Working Conference on the Union of American Methodism, Northwestern University* (NY: Methodist Book Concern, 1916); Paul N. Garber, *The Methodists are One People* (Nashville: Cokesbury Press, 1939); John M. Moore, *The Long Road to Methodist Union* (Nashville: The Methodist Publishing House, 1948); James H. Straughn, *Inside Methodist Union* (Nashville: The Methodist Publishing House, 1958); Frederick E. Maser, "The Story of Unification, 1874–1939," *HAM*, 3:407–78; Walter G. Muelder, *Methodism and Society in the Twentieth Century* (New York and Nashville: Abingdon Press, 1961), 251–71; Nolan B. Harmon, *The Organization of the Methodist Church*, 2nd rev. ed. (Nashville: Methodist Publishing House, 1962), 167–82; Robert Watson Sledge, *Hands on the Ark: The Struggle for Change in the Methodist Episcopal Church, South, 1914–1939* (Lake Junaluska, NC: Commission on Archives and History, UMC, 1975), 90–123; Grant S. Shockley, ed., *Heritage and Hope: The African-American Presence in United Methodism* (Nashville: Abingdon Press, 1991); William B. McClain, *Black People in the Methodist Church* (Cambridge: Schenkman Publishing Co., 1984); James S. Thomas, *Methodism's Racial Dilemma: The Story of the Central Jurisdiction* (Nashville: Abingdon Press, 1992).

2. *Unification*, 1:274. The language is that of A. J. Lamar, one of the southern commissioners in the Joint Commission on Unification of The Methodist Episcopal Church, South and The Methodist Episcopal Church.

3. By 1916, the MECS had a made the creation of a supreme court-like judicial body a third concern. In the initial meeting of the 1916–20 round of discussions, Bishop Warren Candler stated the understandings of powers and duties conferred upon the southern commissioners (*Unification*, 1:46):

The Commission does feel bound, however, by certain essential and specific basal principles from which we do not feel free to depart. . . . The first of these principles is that we consider ourselves bound, with reference to the powers of the General Conference and Quadrennial Conferences, that no one of these Conferences shall be authorized to pass upon and determine the constitutionality of its own acts. In the second place, we feel bound, as to the Jurisdictional

Conferences, that they shall have their autonomy, legislating upon matters involved in their own jurisdictions. And in the third place, that the colored membership of the Methodist Episcopal Church, and of such Colored Churches as may elect to enter into the reorganization of American Methodism, are to be deal with in such manner as shall make full recognition of race consciousness and at the same time offer them the most fraternal cooperation and brotherly assistance.

4. This plan also provided, as would subsequent proposals, for fuller lay representation in annual conferences, a concession to the Methodist Protestants and to advocates of lay rights within the MEC and MECS. See *A Record of All Agreements Concerning Fraternity and Federation Between the Methodist Episcopal Church and the Methodist Episcopal Church, South, and the Declaration in Favor of Unification Made by the General Conference of the Methodist Episcopal Church, South* (Nashville: Publishing House of the Methodist Episcopal Church, South, 1914), 38–39, 43–44. *HAM*, 3:415–23. This Joint Commission and round of discussions had been stimulated by a conference of MP and MEC laity in Baltimore and out of that lay conference by a spirited address to the MEC General Conference of 1908 by the MP college president, Thomas H. Lewis of Western Maryland.

5. *Unification*, 1:42–43; *JGC/MECS*, 1914, 263–64.

6. *JGC/MEC*, 1916, 710–15, 711, 712.

7. Mid-point in the discussions, A. J. Lamar made that clear (*Unification*, 2:24):

We all know and we have known from the beginning that the crux of the situation is that Status of the Colored Membership in the Methodist Episcopal Church. We can arrange everything else, and yet when we come to that, if we can't arrange that, if we come to a deadlock on that, it renders null and void everything that we have done before.

Towards the end of the discussions, he affirmed (ibid., 3:368):

A great many things are not vital. But three things are vital. One is the relation of the colored membership of the Methodist Church in the reorganized Church. A second is the organization, the powers and rights, of the Regional Conferences. The third is your Judicial Council. Those are the three big things we have got to consider.

8. *Unification*, 1:131, 133, 134–35, 137–38.

9. One of the few other moral witnesses against racism and a racial division of the church came from an unnamed southern woman whose long letter of protest and call for a vision "of the truth of God's word to teach us the right relation to our fellow man" was read by R. E. Blackwell. The members of the commission were, incidentally, all male. *Unification*, 2:228–31.

10. Bishop Hoss had responded to MEC objection to the CME-like solution (*Unification*, 1:144):

If you are going to magnify the impropriety of drawing the color line, you must take it out of your Discipline; you must abolish the colored Conferences. What more wrong is there in a colored General Conference than in a colored Annual Conference? Show me a single white Church that has a colored pastor in your denomination or a single colored Church that has a white pastor in your denomination.

I. G. Penn, an African American, replied (ibid., 148):

The concession in the matter of the negro and his status cannot come from the Methodist Episcopal Church. These people are members of the Church like anybody else. . . . The white people have not drawn the color line in the Methodist Episcopal Church without our consent. . . . I have even written certain pages of the Discipline myself which drew the color line. . . . The colored people have colored Annual Conferences because they preferred such. All that there is in the colored line in the Church is with their consent. . . . The colored people are ready to be a jurisdiction of the united Church, with their own bishops and representation in the General Conference.

11. One early version of the jurisdictional plan, proposed as "preferred" by the Committee on the Status of the Negro in the Reorganized Church put Africans and African Americans in one "Associate Regional Conference," parallel to four others, missionary in their character, embracing Latin-America, Europe, Eastern Asia and Southern Asia. A minority report held out for an "Associate General Conference" for black members, with all the episcopal, conference, judicial and board structure of the white church and tied to the latter only a Constitutional Council. See *Unification*, 2:100–3.

A perfected version of this scheme, worked out by a Joint Committee of Eight, retained its African American and African definition and provided for an overture to the CME to join. Ibid., 2:438–40.

12. *Unification*, 2:173–75. In the same session, the southern editor and commissioner, A. J. Lamar (ibid, 24) had affirmed:

We all know and we have known from the beginning that the crux of the situation is that Status of the Colored Membership in the Methodist Episcopal Church. We can arrange everything else, and yet when we come to that, if we can't arrange that, if we come to a deadlock on that, it renders null and void everything that we have done before.

H. H. White, in a prepared statement, insisted:

The South and our grand division of the Methodist Church believe: That the color line must be drawn firmly and unflinchingly, in State, Church, and society, without any deviation whatever; and no matter what the virtues, abilities, or accomplishments of individuals may be, there must be absolute separation of social relations. . . .

He concluded "That the Southern Church will not be willing to go into any arrangement by virtue of which the colored delegates sit either in a

General Conference or Supreme Court, and take part in their delibera-
tions, on any basis whatever. . . ." (ibid., 136, 138–39)

13. For a summation thereof, see *HAM*, 3:423–34.

14. "Report Submitted by the Ad Interim Committee, Richmond, VA.,
November 7, 1919," *Unification*, 3:561–67.

15. Some saw and bemoaned the effect of these plans on both conference and episcopacy (*Unification*, 3:41):

> Bishop R. J. Cooke: "We were sent here to unify the Church, not
> to divide it; but with these Regional Conferences with such regional
> powers we are dividing the Church again. We may deny it, and keep
> on denying it; but you do not do away with the thing. Where is your
> episcopacy? Were we sent here to destroy the itinerant general
> superintendency?"
>
> E. C. Reeves: "That is what we are doing."
>
> Bishop Cooke: "Of course, and we know it, no matter what we
> say to the contrary. You know very well you have not got itinerant
> general superintendency in regional superintendency as localized in
> your regions. We all know that. And we were not sent here to do that."

16. "Report," *Unification*, 3:565–67.

17. *JGC/MEC*, 1920, 181–82.

18. Ibid., 701–4.

19. Sledge, *Hands on the Ark*, 90–123.

20. *Journal of the Special Session of the General Conference of the Methodist
Episcopal Church, South*, 1924, 20, 22, 52–54.

21. Ibid., 114–117. The entire Minority Report is pp. 96–120.

22. Sledge, *Hands on the Ark*, 104–7.

23. *JGC/MECS*, 1926, 161–63. It did constitute a Committee of Research and Investigation and order it "to make a careful and scientific
study of the whole question in its historic, economic, social, legal, and
other respects, and report their findings in detail to our next General
Conference in 1930."

24. See *JGC/MEC*, 1928. Delegates at that MEC general conference
had throughout concerned themselves with the 'color' of Methodism.
They had debated the powers and prerogatives of the central conferences,
many of them in Africa and Asia; elected bishops for such conferences,
including E. Stanley Jones; brought to the podium by resolution and
heard a speech from Dr. I. Garland Penn, senior member of the General
Conference and one of the two African American representatives on the
Joint Commission of 1916–20; been presided over by the other black
representative, Bishop Robert E. Jones; paid tribute to Bishop William A.
Quayle as friend to "the Negro race" and effective mediator during the
East St. Louis race riot (257); recognized Mrs. M. A. Camphor, delegate
from Delaware and widow of African Missionary Bishop Camphor; passed
a resolution calling for equal educational opportunity in the South (259–
60); recognized the service of Joseph C. Hartzell "to the African race both
in the United States and in Africa" (262); passed a motion against U.S.
policy restricting "immigration and the rights of citizenship on grounds

of race and color" (271); passed a resolution on behalf of Melville Cox and the centenary of Liberian missions (276); and recognized Mary McLeod Bethune, especially for her presidency of The National Federated Clubs of Colored Women (296).

25. Moore, *Long Road to Methodist Union*, 183.

26. After the College of Bishops, MECS, declared the plan's adoption, Bishop John M. Moore, President of the College, submitted a written request for a declaratory opinion about the adoption and its legality to the southern Judicial Council, a maneuver calculated to stave off a future legal challenge to unification. See Moore, *Long Road to Methodist Union*, 200–207.

27. Shockley, *Heritage and Hope*, 115; *HAM*, 3:456–57.

28. See *Doctrines and Discipline of The Methodist Church, 1940*, 350–51, for stipulations for staffing of the Board of Education and elsewhere for other boards.

29. Judge Nathan Newby (Pacific), *The Daily Christian Advocate*, (1939), 181. Speaking for the committee, Paul Quillian again raised the specter of the great mass of General Conference acting mob-like in selection and of the ephemeral character of general conferences and contrasted that with the informed and careful selection possible in board election. He affirmed: "If you are a member of a general board at the present ask yourself this question: Would you desire to serve during the coming four years with your administrative officers chosen carefully by your General Board or chosen by the General Conference who did not understand your particular problems?" (183–84).

30. *The Daily Christian Advocate*, (1939), 179, 181, 182. He added two other points:

> (3) [W]e masses do elect the President of the United States . . . we ought to be able to pick out a man big enough to run a Methodist board. . . . [T]he Methodist Church, if it moves from election in its General Conference back to election in its board, is going in exactly the opposite direction from that in which political life in America is going.
>
> (4) [Y]ou will open the door to the influence of smaller values upon the creating of these great offices.

31. *HAM*, 3:482–83.

32. Shockley, *Heritage and Hope*, 117–72. This really is the motif of *Methodism's Racial Dilemma* by Bishop Thomas.

33. Shockley, *Heritage and Hope*, 131–37; *To a Higher Glory: The Growth and Development of Black Women Organized for Mission in The Methodist Church, 1940–1968*, (Cincinnati: Women's Division, Board of Global Ministries, UMC, 1978).

34. Major J. Jones, "The Central Jurisdiction: Passive Resistance," in Shockley, *Heritage and Hope*, 189–207; Thomas, *Methodism's Racial Dilemma*, 84–147.

Notes to Chapter 17

1. *The Daily Christian Advocate* (1939), 454–58; *Journal of the Uniting Conference of The Methodist Church*, 1939, 509.

2. That the issue is not more remarked is perhaps an indicator of how very 'congregational' Methodism has become. The laity are short-term members of annual conference. They are long-term members of the local church that has sent them and longer term typically in that church than the pastor who accompanies them to conference. They have by virtue of their representation of that local covenanted community a very legitimate long-term stake in the annual conference. Nevertheless, as individuals they are often short-term in the larger body. By focussing on their legitimate, long-term congregational representative role we tend to obscure their insecurity in this marriage. We observe it primarily in providing for training sessions for annual conference, a tactical not theological treatment of the matter.

3. The Baltimore Conference had been split in 1857 into Baltimore and East Baltimore in consequence of having grown to 363 traveling preachers, the largest conference in Methodism, too large. Hence the division but only one of many that Baltimore had experienced over the years.

4. For these figures I have used the first roll call vote rather than the opening call of the roll.

5. The MEC had made Disciplinary provision for united sessions of the annual and lay conferences and allocated financial, budgetary and campaign decisions to such gatherings where the laity also participated.

6. *Official Minutes . . . Indiana Annual Conference . . . Methodist Protestant Church . . .* 1937, 12; . . . 1938, 13; . . . 1939, 14; *Official Minutes . . . Ohio Annual Conference of the Methodist Protestant Church . . .* 1937, 8; . . . 1938, 22.

7. The pattern in the Virginia (MECS) conference was

1936	251 ministers	115 laity
1937	275	115
1938	247	94
1939	269	127

The Virginia Conference Annual . . . the Methodist Episcopal Church, South . . . 1936, 31; . . . 1937, 28; . . . 1938, 21; . . . 1939, 23; *The Virginia Conference Annual . . . of the Methodist Church . . .* 1939, 39–41; . . . 1940, 32.

8. The 1939 MEC 1939 conference had included laity (in anticipation of unification) and the numbers had been 170 clergy, 33 supply, 41 laity. *Official Record and Year Book of the West Virginia Annual Conference of the Methodist Episcopal Church . . .* 1938, 17; . . . 1939, 31; *Journal . . . of the West Virginia Conference of the Methodist Protestant Church . . .* 1936, 9–12; *Journal of the . . . Western Virginia Conference . . . Methodist Episcopal Church, South . . .* 1938, 25–26; *Official Record and Year Book of the West Virginia Annual Conference of the Methodist Church . . .* 1939, 368–69; . . . 1940, 15.

9. The actual number of effective ministers for 1940 for West Virginia was 369 and the number of pastoral charges 470, 357 of which were

filled by episcopal appointment. *Minutes of the Annual Conferences of the Methodist (Episcopal) Church, Spring Conferences*, 1940, 259.

10. The East German, Eastern Swedish and Porto Rico conferences were even smaller, each having about twenty effective ministers.

11. Harmon, *Organization of the Methodist Church*, 137.

12. For a charting of conference mergers, see *The Encyclopedia of World Methodism*, ed. Nolan B. Harmon, 2 vols. (Nashville: United Methodist Publishing House, 1974): Albea Godbold, "Table of Methodist Conferences (U.S.A.)," 1:2656–2675; John H. Ness, Jr., "Table of E. U. B. Conferences," 1:2676–85.

13. *General Minutes of the Annual Conferences of the United Methodist Church*, 1970, 36–57. The comparable figures for total ministerial membership and pastoral charges were Baltimore 770/541, Eastern Pennsylvania (Philadelphia) 624/467, West Virginia 617/598, Virginia 1,040/768, Texas 718/527, Southern California-Arizona 934/495, East Ohio 908/689, Iowa 905/575, West Ohio 1,402/1,014, Western North Carolina 961/687 and Florida 953/585.

14. Now an autonomous Methodist Church in affiliated relationship with the United Methodist Church.

15. Shockley, *Heritage and Hope*, 209–10, 225–28.

16. Homer Noley, *First White Frost: Native Americans and United Methodism* (Nashville: Abingdon Press, 1991), 225–30.

17. Justo L. González, ed., *Each in Our Own Tongue: A History of Hispanic United Methodism* (Nashville: Abingdon Press, 1991), 60–61, 155–59.

18. Artemio R. Guillermo, ed., *Churches Aflame: Asian Americans and United Methodism* (Nashville: Abingdon Press, 1991), 135–53.

19. The term and the recognition of these as a prevalent late 20th century denomination pattern are Robert Wuthnow's. See *The Restructuring of American Religion* (Princeton: Princeton University Press, 1988); *The Struggle for America's Soul* (Grand Rapids: Eerdmans, 1989); *Christianity in the Twenty-first Century* (New York: Oxford University Press, 1993). See also my essay in Robert Bruce Mullin and Russell E. Richey, eds., *Reimagining Denominationalism* (New York: Oxford University Press, 1994).

20. *The Book of Discipline of The United Methodist Church*, 1968, 195–98.

21. *The Book of Discipline of The United Methodist Church*, 1976, 320–22. The youth membership was further particularized "not less than 13 percent between the ages of eighteen and thirty, not less than 7 percent age seventeen or under at the time of election."

22. Paul A. Mickey and Robert L. Wilson, *What New Creation? The Agony of Church Restructure* (Nashville: Abingdon Press, 1977), 24–25.

23. Symbolic was the "Historical Statement" that American Episcopal Methodism had placed first in its *Discipline* as self-identification and self-description, that had been altered by denominations that gave themselves distinct institutional expression, that had been recast on the unifications of 1939 and 1968, and that in 1976 was again altered to make a several page declaration concerning "Black People and Their United Methodist Heritage." *The Book of Discipline of The United Methodist Church*, 1976, 14–16. For exploration of the significance of these historical statements see Russell E. Richey, "History in the Discipline," in Thomas A.

Langford, ed., *Doctrine and Theology in The United Methodist Church* (Nashville: Kingswood Books, 1991), 190–202, and in *Quarterly Review* 9 (Winter 1989), 3–20.

24. See Albert C. Outler, "Introduction to the Report of the 1968–72 Theological Study Commission," in Langford, *Doctrine and Theology*, 20–25, and in *Daily Christian Advocate* (UMC), 1972, 218–22. Outler (21) observed:

> Somewhere in The United Methodist Church there is somebody urging every kind of theology still alive and not a few that are dead, but your commission came to realize that this apparent bedlam is, at least in part, the perversion of an older, profounder principle of positive importance, that is to say, of doctrinal pluralism, doctrinal diversity-in Christological-unity. Far from being a license to doctrinal recklessness of indifferentism, the Wesleyan principle of pluralism holds in dynamic balance both the biblical focus of all Christian doctrine and also the responsible freedom that all Christians must have in their theological reflections and public teaching.

25. See *The Book of Discipline of The United Methodist Church*, 1972, 68–82, especially 69–70, 75–78, and Langford, *Doctrine and Theology*, passim. On the quadrilateral see Ted Campbell's essay, "The 'Wesleyan Quadrilateral': The Story of a Modern Methodist Myth," in Langford, *Doctrine and Theology*, 154–61.

26. See his essay, "In Search of Continuity and Consensus: The Road to the 1988 Doctrinal Statement," in Langford, *Doctrine and Theology*, 93–108.

27. Richard P. Heitzenrater, "A Critical Analysis of the Ministry Studies Since 1948," in *POAM*, 431–47, and as *Occasional Paper*, 76 (Sept. 1988), United Methodist General Board of Higher Education and Ministry.

Notes to Chapter 18

1. (Nashville: The United Methodist Publishing House, 1989). It is too early to determine whether *The United Methodist Book of Worship* (Nashville: The United Methodist Publishing House, 1992) or the founding of Africa University will be similar triumphs.

2. These statements are not intended to assert, as my earlier discussion ought to make clear, that either Wesley or American Methodists adequately lived up to such gracious ideals.

Index

301